A Holy Baptism of Fire and Blood

A Holy Baptism of Fire and Blood

The Bible and the American Civil War

JAMES P. BYRD

OXFORD
UNIVERSITY PRESS

OXFORD
UNIVERSITY PRESS

Oxford University Press is a department of the University of Oxford. It furthers
the University's objective of excellence in research, scholarship, and education
by publishing worldwide. Oxford is a registered trade mark of Oxford University
Press in the UK and certain other countries.

Published in the United States of America by Oxford University Press
198 Madison Avenue, New York, NY 10016, United States of America.

© Oxford University Press 2021

Library of Congress Cataloging-in-Publication Data
Names: Byrd, James P., 1965– author.
Title: A holy baptism of fire and blood : the Bible and the
American Civil War / James P. Byrd.
Description: New York, NY : Oxford University Press, [2021] |
Includes bibliographical references and index.
Identifiers: LCCN 2020028349 (print) | LCCN 2020028350 (ebook) |
ISBN 9780190902797 (hardback) | ISBN 9780190902810 (epub)
Subjects: LCSH: Bible—Study and teaching—United States—History—
19th century. | Bible and politics—United States—History—19th century. |
War—Religious aspects—Christianity—History—19th century. |
Religion and politics—United States. | United States—History—Civil War,
1861–1865—Religious aspects—Christianity. | United States—
Religion—19th century. | United States—Religious life and customs.
Classification: LCC E635 .B98 2020 (print) | LCC E635 (ebook) |
DDC 277.3/081—dc23
LC record available at https://lccn.loc.gov/2020028349
LC ebook record available at https://lccn.loc.gov/2020028350

DOI: 10.1093/oso/9780190902797.001.0001

3 5 7 9 8 6 4 2

Printed by Sheridan Books, Inc., United States of America

In memory
Linda Byrd Earley

Contents

Acknowledgments

I am grateful for the advice of friends and colleagues who helped me to write this book. Lincoln Mullen's expertise in digital humanities, particularly his use of machine learning to identify biblical verses in text files, allowed me to draw from extensive databases of biblical citations. Mullen also read the entire manuscript and offered many helpful suggestions. I am also grateful to Douglas Sweeney, who read the proposal and offered valuable insights, and to Chris Benda, who gave me a helpful assessment of an early chapter. Special thanks go to the research assistants who helped me to retrieve primary sources, convert them to electronic format, and organize biblical citations into various databases. Jennifer Axsom Adler, Alex Ayris, Noah Frens, and Alan Murphy were graduate students in religious history at Vanderbilt when they worked on this project. Their work made this a much better book than it would have been otherwise. Rachel G. McKane, a graduate student in sociology, was incredibly helpful with her expertise in R programming. Early in the project, Jacob Berexa assisted in developing the bibliography of primary sources. In the late stages of the work, Glenda Mernaugh reviewed the full manuscript and made useful suggestions. The peer reviewers for Oxford University Press offered valuable recommendations on the proposal and the final manuscript. My thanks go to the editors at Oxford University Press who did an outstanding job on this book. It was a delight to work with Theo Calderara, Editor-in-Chief of Humanities, who made excellent suggestions at every point in the process. I also want to thank Suganya Elango, the production editor who brought this book to its conclusion. I greatly appreciate the support and friendship of my faculty and administrative colleagues at Vanderbilt. Most of all, I am thankful for my family, especially my wife, Karen Byrd, and our daughters, Olivia and Caroline.

James P. Byrd
September 2020

Introduction

In his Second Inaugural Address, delivered years into a war that had torn the nation apart, Abraham Lincoln remarked that both North and South "read the same Bible and pray to the same God, and each invokes His aid against the other."[1] The speech was brimming with biblical quotations—"more like a sermon than a state paper," according to Frederick Douglass.[2]

But Lincoln's famous speech was only the most prominent example of biblically infused wartime rhetoric. The Bible saturated the Civil War. Preachers, politicians, and people everywhere reached for the Bible because it was a text for the times. It evoked sacred history and sacrifice. It presented a drama of salvation and damnation, of providence and judgment.

It was also a book of war. In the Old Testament, God's people of Israel battled Canaanites, Philistines, and others.[3] Sometimes they even fought among themselves—Israel erupted into a civil war between northern and southern kingdoms after King Solomon's death. The New Testament also highlighted war, but in different ways. The Gospels and epistles represented the Christian life as spiritual warfare, and the book of Revelation offered a tale of cosmic war.

Much of this was common knowledge during the Civil War; from Massachusetts to Mississippi and beyond, the Bible was the nation's most-read and most-respected book.[4] B. H. Nadal, a Methodist pastor in Washington, DC, and a southerner who sided with the North, found the Bible wherever he looked: "So thoroughly does the Bible pervade the country, that no house is respectable without it, every room in the chief hotels contains it; it is found in every steamboat cabin; its teachings are sought to be illustrated and enforced by largely more than half the literature of the country."[5]

By the time of the Civil War, Christianity was prospering in the United States. Protestants dominated, with more churches, more members, and more money than other religious groups. In 1860, about fifty thousand Protestant churches were spread across the nation, compared with seventy-seven synagogues or temples and approximately twenty-five hundred Catholic churches.[6] There were an estimated 450,000 enslaved Christians by the beginning of the war, most of them Baptist or Methodist.[7] Americans seemed more involved in churches than in national politics. "Nearly four times as many attended church every Sunday in 1860 as voted in that year's critical presidential election," wrote Drew Gilpin Faust.[8]

This religious nation shaped a religious military. "Civil War armies were, arguably, the most religious in American history," James McPherson has written.[9] Americans cited the Bible in addressing many wartime issues, including slavery, secession, patriotism, federal versus state authority, white supremacy, and violence. In scripture, both Union and Confederate soldiers found inspiration for dying and killing on a scale never before seen in American history: the war's approximately 750,000 fatalities are far more than the nation suffered in any other conflict.[10]

"War is hell," as many have said, including General William Tecumseh Sherman. Americans who endured the Civil War agreed. "War is the highest exhibition of hatred on the largest scale," said a Virginia minister in 1861.[11] Hell though it was, war often served divine purposes, many Americans believed. Wars could be both terrible and righteous. Americans fought the Civil War with Bibles in hand, with both sides calling the war just and sacred. This is a book about how Americans enlisted the Bible in the nation's most bloody and arguably most biblically infused war.[12]

"The Bible Is a Wonderfully Simple Book"

Although Protestantism dominated the religious landscape during the Civil War, the Bible's appeal extended beyond Protestantism, beyond Catholicism and Judaism, beyond any religious tradition. Even Americans who claimed no religious affiliation could find political value in the scriptures. Americans sometimes "detheologized" the Bible, believing that it held political insights regardless of whether it was the inspired Word of God.[13]

When searching for biblical guidance on the war and other issues, especially slavery, Americans often looked to ministers as the leading experts on scripture, but not always. Some found insightful biblical commentary in poetry, as in the writings of abolitionist and lecturer Frances E. W. Harper, including her "Bible Defense of Slavery."[14] Few speakers rivaled the fame of abolitionist Frederick Douglass, who fine-tuned the prophetic witness of scripture and, as historian David Blight wrote, "mastered the oratorical art of the jeremiad, the rhetorical device made famous in America by the

Puritans." The jeremiad—named for the Old Testament prophet Jeremiah—confronted people with their sins, warned that God would punish them unless they repented, and promised that repentance would lead to redemption. In the hands of Douglass and countless others, the jeremiad flourished during the Civil War, in Union and Confederate variations.[15]

The Bible's status was growing as the Civil War approached. After the Revolution, Americans gained more trust in their ability to govern themselves and to think for themselves. As they trusted themselves more, Americans depended on other authorities less, including their traditional superiors in social class, politics, and religion—except for the Bible, that is. As other traditional authorities lost credibility, the Bible gained religious and cultural authority.[16]

Diverse as they were, many Americans united around their respect for the Bible. Americans typically had a common-sense view of biblical interpretation, and they took the Bible at face value, without thinking of it as a collection of texts from an ancient world far removed from the nineteenth-century United States. Many Americans agreed with Methodist author and evangelist Phoebe Palmer's statement from 1865: "The Bible is a wonderfully simple book; and, if you had taken the naked word of God as . . . your counsel, instead of taking the opinions of men in regard to that *Word*, you might have been a more enlightened, simple, happy and useful Christian."[17]

Not everything in scripture had to be read literally—some texts were poetic, some contained metaphors and symbols. But the dominant mode of reading the Bible at the time suggested that if a text described a historical event, that event occurred. Although modern biblical criticism, much of it originating in Germany, had made inroads into the United States, most Americans didn't know about it. When Americans argued over the Bible—as when they defended or attacked slavery—they usually collected as many quotations as they could to support their points. Yet that way of reading scripture only went so far, as many Americans came to see during the Civil War. Too often, biblical debates over slavery and the war had no clear winner.[18]

Americans cited the Bible in various ways. Sometimes a text from scripture was a rhetorical allusion, used to support a viewpoint but with little or no elaboration on the scripture, its context, or its full meaning. At other times, biblical passages received extensive focus. Most often Americans looked for analogies between biblical wars and the Civil War. It seemed to them that biblical heroes, villains, and battles leapt off the page, strikingly relevant to the heroes, villains, and battles of the Civil War.[19] Americans also called on biblical precepts—including the Old Testament command "Thou shalt not kill" and Jesus's commands to love one's enemies and to turn the other cheek—and argued for their relevance to the war.[20]

Americans' use of scripture wasn't always simple. In his book on Lincoln, historian Joseph R. Fornieri identified several ways Lincoln cited scripture, including *theologically* (discussing God and providence), *civil theologically* ("as a transcendent rule and measure to judge public life"), and *evocatively* ("for stylistic purposes and rhetorical emphasis"). While Americans may have read the same Bible, they appealed to it in many ways. Whether examined closely, alluded to briefly, or cited in an offhand, poetic, or even sarcastic way, the Bible appeared almost everywhere during the Civil War.[21]

"The Bible Is Eminently a Patriotic Book"

No matter where or how they cited it, many Americans believed the Bible had a unique connection to the United States. They often said God worked through providence, guiding history—and guiding the nation—but they disagreed on how providence worked, and differing views of providence shaped differing opinions on the Bible.[22]

Because many Americans believed that God controlled the war, they pondered the roles of human agency and free will. In 1862, Bishop Charles Pettit McIlvaine of the Northern Episcopal church wrote of "the great rebellion," saying, "There are two aspects in which we must contemplate it"—how it came "*by the agency of man*, and as it comes *from the Providence of God.*" He advised people to remember that "God's Providence has no interference with man's responsibility."[23] Charles Hodge, professor at Princeton Theological Seminary, offered an explanation of providence when the nation seemed to need it most—after Lincoln's assassination. Hodge said that God "governs free agents with certainty, but without destroying their liberty"— a point often made but often misunderstood during the Civil War. "Every great event," wrote Hodge, "is to be viewed in two different aspects: first, as the effect of natural causes; and, secondly, as a design and result of God's providence."[24]

Both human agency and divine providence brought about the Civil War, and many believed that Americans needed to see it that way. This was a delicate balance, in victory and defeat. Ministers instructed soldiers to trust in God, not in their own effort in combat—but not too much. They needed to drill and fight zealously, and not depend only on God, because God helped soldiers who helped themselves.

Scripture demanded patriotism, Americans vowed. "The Bible is eminently a patriotic book," preached William Barrows to a regiment of Massachusetts volunteers in 1863. The Bible, Barrows told these troops, promoted "the love of country" and opposed "treason and rebellion." The Bible, Americans believed, supported personal virtue, political liberty, and republican government—a lesson drawn from the American Revolution.[25]

Sometimes patriotism went too far. "God cannot afford to do without America," said Methodist bishop Matthew Simpson.[26] Idolatry—worship of the nation—was a real danger, many believed, and they used scripture to draw the line between patriotism and blasphemy. "One cause of our present adversity is found in the *national idolatry* to which we have been addicted," said a Baptist minister in Philadelphia. As northerners waved American flags like never before, he cautioned, "We have been disposed to love our country with an undue affection." People thought of the Union as "some deity worthy of our homage. We have thought that there was such magic in that word 'Union,' that no assault made upon it could be successful."[27]

Lincoln had fabricated an idol out of the nation and forced the people to worship it, southerners claimed. Lincoln was "the American Nebuchadnezzar," the Babylonian king discussed in the book of Daniel, who ransacked Jerusalem, forced God's people into exile, and commanded them to worship a golden image.[28] In turn, many northerners charged the South with crafting its own golden image out of slavery.

These ideas relate to "civil religion," which, in George Rable's brilliantly concise definition, was "a set of beliefs about the relationship between God and the nation that emphasized national virtue, national purpose, and national destiny." Religious views of the nation varied and shifted over time, but in general most Americans believed in some version of civil religion. The Civil War strengthened this belief for most Americans on both sides of the fighting, and Americans used the Bible to shape their views of national destiny—and national idolatry.[29]

"A Holy Baptism of Fire and Blood"

In addition to the massive death tolls in the Civil War, *the way* Americans died still shocks us. During "Pickett's charge" at Gettysburg, about fourteen thousand Confederate soldiers advanced against heavy fire—a virtual suicide mission. James McPherson has asked: "What made these men do it?" Compared with soldiers in other wars, many soldiers in the Civil War were more willing to sacrifice themselves in battle. Several factors accounted for this courage, and religion was one of the major ones, with some soldiers calling the war "a crusade."[30]

Martyrdom and blood sacrifice surrounded the Civil War. The pages of the Bible were filled with martyrs, and martyrdom was a major theme shared by the Old and New Testaments. "The Bible gives a significance to the shedding of blood, such as no human history ever did or ever will," said a Congregationalist in Minnesota. "The shedding of blood in war, terrible and awful as it is, is sometimes not only justifiable, but absolutely demanded by the Almighty."[31] "Our cause is sacred," said a North Carolina minister, responding to the Battle of Shiloh in 1862. "How can we doubt it, when we know it has been consecrated by a holy baptism of fire and blood." The war "has been rendered glorious by the martyr-like devotion of [Confederates] who have offered their lives as a sacrifice on the altar of their country's freedom."[32]

Preachers were not alone in this martyrdom obsession. Southerner Lucy Rebecca Buck wrote in her diary about visiting soldiers' graves in 1862: "There under my very feet they rested so still, so silent, those men who had for the love of country and freedom risked their lives and lost them in battling the usurper of their sacred rights." So many of these soldiers did not die in glorious battles; they succumbed to disease, languishing "in agony upon friendless couches." But these men "died no less martyrs to their cause."[33]

Biblical views of sacrifice resonated so strongly because of the unprecedented death toll of the war, which, as Drew Gilpin Faust wrote, was "approximately equal to the total American fatalities in the Revolution, the War of 1812, the Mexican War, the Spanish-American War, World War I, World War II, and the Korean War combined." Further, "The Civil War's rate of death, its incidence in comparison with the size of the American population, was six times that of World War II." The toll was worse on the South, as "Confederate men died at a rate three times that of their Yankee counterparts; one in five white Southern men of military age did not survive the Civil War."[34]

The body counts skyrocketed partially because military technology had improved. Smoothbore muskets with a range of one hundred yards were being replaced by rifles, accurate to three hundred yards. By late 1864 some Union soldiers had breech-loading rifles, which could be loaded more quickly and thus fire more rounds. Cannons killed thousands of soldiers in the war. Still, in comparison with more recent wars, few Civil War deaths were impersonally inflicted—that is, killed from long distance. Faust argues that "physical distance between enemies facilitates emotional distance from destructive acts." In the Civil War, much of the killing was up close and personal.[35]

Many Americans who lost family members had nothing to bury—their loved ones' remains lay unidentified, often in mass graves near battlefields. This was particularly traumatizing to Americans in the nineteenth century, when many believed in a bodily resurrection and insisted on a proper burial. Many Americans didn't think it strange, for instance, that Abraham Lincoln reportedly had his son Willie's coffin exhumed on two occasions; it comforted Lincoln to see his son's body. Such comfort was impossible for thousands of Americans who lost loved ones in the war, and many turned to the Bible to deal with the death they encountered. All this death had cheapened human life, many believed, and they revered the Bible's teachings on the sacredness of the body and life in this world, not just in the hereafter.[36]

"Harder Courage"

Dying for God and homeland was honorable, respected on earth and rewarded in heaven. But what about killing? In 1862, Orestes Brownson ruminated on the horrific bloodshed that gripped the nation. "It is real blood, not red paint that flows, and real life-warm blood must still flow, and flow in torrents." Shedding this blood was terrible but necessary, he wrote. "We must have not only the courage to be killed, but we must have . . . the harder courage to kill,—not simply to bear, but to do harm, to strike the enemy in his tenderest part our quickest and heaviest blows."[37] As Drew Gilpin Faust wrote, motivating soldiers to kill was more difficult than inspiring them to die for the cause. It "required the more significant departure from soldiers' understandings of themselves as human beings and . . . as Christians."[38]

The Bible made it hard for many Americans to kill. The Ten Commandments declared, "Thou shalt not kill," even though the Old Testament itself was suffused with war and killing. The New Testament, by contrast, seemed to forbid killing. Many Americans—including some Protestants, Catholics, and especially Mennonites and Quakers—believed Jesus rejected war, indeed any kind of violence.[39] Jesus refused to fight to defend himself, choosing instead to die on a cross, and in his Sermon on the Mount he commanded his followers to turn the other cheek, not to strike back when attacked. These words dampened wartime zeal—and not just for those in traditionally pacifist denominations. Many agreed with an officer from Indiana: "Read all Christ's teaching, and then tell me whether *one engaged in maiming and butchering men . . . can be saved* under the Gospel."[40]

This explained why a Jewish woman from Richmond reportedly claimed she was glad to be "born of a nation, and religion that did not enjoin forgiveness on its enemies, that enjoyed the blessed privilege of praying for an eye for an eye" (Exodus 21:24). She told her Christian friends that "till the war was over they should all join the Jewish Church, let forgiveness and peace and good will alone and put their trust in the sword of the Lord and Gideon" (Judges 7:20).[41] Throughout the war, Americans often turned to scripture to inspire the "harder courage to kill," and this involved convincing Americans that the Bible didn't forbid war.

"History Ever Repeats"

"Even the simplest records of the word of God" were "many-sided, and full of light," said a minister in 1865.[42] As Americans pored over every detail of the Bible, searching for God's will, they often found uncanny similarities between biblical events and current events. "We have had parallels given us from all history,—from the old history of the Bible," said a minister in 1863. These parallels were "very eloquent and convincing, showing how History ever repeats" itself.[43]

Wars held special meaning in God's providence, many Americans believed. Wars signaled turning points in the history of nations, and people seemed more attentive to God's providence in wartime.[44] Americans often agreed with Southern Methodist John Caldwell's statement that God "is in every war, in every campaign, in every battle, in every great political and social change, and directs every movement for the accomplishment of his own grand purposes. If war results in the subjugation of a people, or the annihilation of an institution of society, we must accept such result as Heaven's decree."[45]

In theory, then, belief in providence should bring comfort in wartime—all events rested securely in God's hands. In reality, however, faith in providence could falter. In an unpublished letter from 1862, a woman from Georgia wrote to her husband that she would "try to believe that providence has called you to the field for some special work, and I pray I may be spared to see some of the fruits of your labors."[46]

Both Yankees and Confederates looked for evidence that God was on their side. Defeats didn't mean God had abandoned a nation; they meant God had punished the nation, perhaps in order to redeem it. In an unpublished letter from 1862, Chaplain Richard Johnson of South Carolina wrote, "It is folly to suppose that a war which has assumed such gigantic proportions can be ended without a great deal of blood-shed." The reason? "God is chastening us, but he has not forsaken us. If we endure not chastisement whereof all are partakers, then are we not sons but bastards."[47] Consequently, God punished those whom God loved, and the Bible is replete with evidence for this in the Old Testament, which Americans turned to for comfort in hard times.

"An Admirable Political Sermon Very Warlike in Its Tone"

War, Jill Lepore writes, involves "wounds and words"—violence and interpretation, words to justify killing, to cope with loss, and to make sense of victory and defeat. In the Civil War, these words of war often came from scripture, and people often encountered them in preaching. Sermons filled the Civil War—spoken and printed, both separately and in thousands of newspapers. In his history of religion in the Civil War, George Rable states, "Sermons are vitally important, often revealing, and occasionally even stimulating sources for understanding how Americans interpreted the war through a religious lens."[48]

Americans were used to wartime preaching. They frequently labeled the Civil War as a second American Revolution, and ministers followed rituals of wartime preaching that figured so prominently in the Revolution. Americans heard sermons on special days of prayer and fasting, when people were called on to repent and to ask for God's help during times of defeat and trial, and on days of thanksgiving, when they were called to thank God for victories. These rituals, which had flourished in Puritan New England and in Revolutionary America, expanded during the Civil War. Southerners embraced these rituals—in fact, "The Confederacy would employ the public fast *more* frequently than the North," Harry S. Stout concluded. "In all, Abraham Lincoln would proclaim three national fasts throughout the war while, in the same period, Jefferson Davis would proclaim ten," not counting the many "state and local fasts" held in the South, in addition to "fasts in the army." Lincoln proclaimed more thanksgiving days (four) than Davis (two) as, over time, the progress of the war gave the North more to be thankful for.[49]

Ministers called people to pray and fast for both spiritual and military reasons. As in the Revolutionary War, Christians in the Civil War saw a clear connection between spiritual warfare, a fight between good and evil in the soul, and military struggle. Prayer, then, could have strategic power, and ministers found biblical texts to prove this point. In an unprinted manuscript sermon from 1862, an Episcopal bishop in Tennessee wrote, "We know not how often prayer spreads an adamantine armor around those, near & dear to our hearts, who like the men of Zebulun & Naphtali jeopard their lives, for country's sake, in the high places of the battle-field" (Judges 5:18).[50]

Evangelical Protestantism dominated in the South before and during the Civil War, and the sermon was central to evangelical worship. New England Puritans may have introduced the jeremiad to colonial America, but southern preachers tried to perfect it.[51] Sermons echoed throughout the Civil War, as they had throughout the Revolutionary War, but Civil War sermons had even more exposure, as they frequently appeared in thousands of newspapers. When Americans saw or heard the Bible applied to the war, it was often in sermons.

Not all sermons were profound, however. Americans, especially those who loved scripture, could be harsh critics of bad sermons. "Does it not seem that the ministry is overstocked with fools?" asked Sarah Morgan of Louisiana in 1862. As she wrote of a bad preacher in her diary, "The most beautiful passages of the bible, those I cry over alone, appear absurd from his lips."[52]

Americans were just as ready to praise a good preacher. A year earlier Emma Holmes, a South Carolinian in her twenties, applauded a preacher who showed "an exact parallel between the separation of the Israelites from the Jewish Nation under Rehoboam's oppressive rule and our secession." In December of that year she glowed over "a most beautiful & appropriate sermon," noting that "the text [was] the most appropriate that could have been chosen: Job's reply to his wife, 'We have received good from the Lord & shall we not receive evil also.'" It was a fitting text, since "Many of the congregation had lost their homes & almost everything." Understandably, "There were but few dry eyes when he finished." Again, in February 1862, she reported on "an admirable political sermon very warlike in its tone."[53]

If Emma Holmes liked a sermon "very warlike in its tone," she was not alone. As had been the case during the American Revolution, Civil War preachers strove to meet military needs, often enlisting the Bible to inspire soldiers to join up and fight.[54]

Many of these "warlike" sermons focused on the New Testament, which was the trend of the times. As Eran Shalev has argued, "By the second half of the nineteenth century the Old Testament's influence on the American political imagination had dramatically diminished." Americans had turned to the New Testament, in part because of revivalism and in part because many Americans used the New Testament to address slavery. In wartime, however, Americans often turned back to the Old Testament, with its stories of God's people at war, led by heroes like David and Joshua. "The Old Testament, in our current notions and sympathies, has been almost outlawed from human affairs," said A. L. Stone of Boston in 1862. "We have turned its leaves for its curious and quaint old histories, but felt as though we were living under a new dispensation." The war had changed that, however. As he said, "Now the days have come upon us, for which these strong-chorded elder Scriptures have been waiting. Their representations of God, as the Rewarder of the evil doer, the Avenger of the wronged . . . suit the day and the hour of the intense present."[55]

Americans continued to hold on to the image of the United States as "God's new Israel" in every arena in which people discussed politics—newspapers, sermons, letters, and diaries. This view had a long history. Beginning in Europe and extending through colonial America, some political thinkers looked to the Old Testament for models of republican government. Historians have shown how traditions of "Hebraic Republicanism" shaped "an American national and political culture from the Revolution to the Civil War."[56] What happened during the Civil War, when God's new Israel ruptured? Which side—the Union or the Confederacy—could claim to be God's chosen nation in 1861? This was no mere academic question for many Americans.

"The tragic irony of the Civil War," wrote James McPherson, "is that both sides professed to fight for the heritage of liberty bequeathed to them by the Founding Fathers. North and South alike in 1861 wrapped themselves in the mantle of 1776."[57] This reverence for the Revolution was almost universal. An African Methodist Episcopal publication called on the memory of African Americans who fought in the Revolution: "Colored Americans! From the blood-consecrated soil of Lexington, and the heroic heights of Bunker Hill . . . the martial spirit of your brave progenitors, calls upon you now to do your duty to the 'stars and the stripes.'" From the other side,

Confederates showed their loyalty to the Revolution by fighting against the nation the Revolution created. In an unprinted manuscript sermon preached from New Orleans in November 1861, Methodist minister Linus Parker said, "The principles of the first revolution are involved in this effort of the South to shake off the oppressive shackles of northern domination & Tyranny."[58]

Americans admired the patriots of the Revolution, and among those patriots were preachers. During the Civil War, ministers read and even imitated sermons preached during the Revolution. After the fall of Fort Sumter, a Philadelphia minister titled his sermon after a patriotic sermon from 1775 and held up a Bible used during the American Revolution. Like many, this minister proclaimed (in all caps) that cowardice was unbiblical: "The last OF ALL PLACES IN THE UNIVERSE, BEHIND WHICH FOR COWARDICE TO SKULK OR FIND REFUGE, IS THE HOLY BIBLE."[59] Americans in the Civil War had the Revolution on their minds, not only as they fought the war but also as they preached and read the Bible.

"The Negro Is Not Your Equal, Unless the Bible Be Untrue"

The debate over the Bible's view of slavery had raged for decades before the Civil War, and it picked up greater intensity—with higher stakes—during the war. As noted earlier, Americans typically assumed a democratic view of biblical interpretation—they claimed that individuals had the right to read the Bible for themselves, with no interference from any tradition or higher authority than the conscience. What happened, then, when Americans disagreed on what the Bible said about slavery? There was no authority in place to mediate the dispute; only war could settle the issue.[60]

For antislavery Americans, one of slavery's greatest offenses was that it denied enslaved people the right to read, which meant it kept them from reading the Bible. Access to the Bible was a sacred right, and securing that access was a Christian responsibility. To block the Bible was to block salvation.

Slavery was one issue; race was another. Regardless of white Americans' views of slavery, most of them believed their race to be superior to all others. Some of the most egregious uses of the Bible surfaced in racist biblical satire. In 1864, so-called "Peace Democrats" or "copperheads"—northerners who opposed Lincoln and the war—published a *Lincoln Catechism*, calling him "Abraham Africanus the First." Included therein were Lincoln's "Ten

Commandments," such as "Thou shalt have no other God but the Negro" and "Thou shalt steal—everything that belongeth to a slaveholder."[61]

Many white Americans, even in the North, agreed with several South Carolinians who declared, "The negro is not your equal, unless the Bible be untrue."[62] These racist assumptions went unchallenged by most Americans, even though supporters of these views struggled to find biblical evidence for them. Evidence or not, many Americans' views of the Bible were replete with racist views, which whites were often oblivious to, despite efforts of many African Americans to strip scripture of its racist veneer.

"If the Bible Can't Prevent War, How Is It to Stop a Bullet?"

The Bible had an important *physical* presence in the Civil War. As Mark Noll wrote, the Bible was "America's most comprehensively present 'thing' from first European contact through the American War of Independence."[63] That was true also during the Civil War era. If Americans owned any books, the Bible was probably one of them. "If we did not have a Bible," said Lizzie Ozburn in Georgia, "what would we do—tis more comfort to me than anything else now."[64] A copy of the Bible could offer solace in times of trial; it could also be essential battle gear. "Gallant sons of a gallant State," preached a Methodist minister to South Carolina troops, "away to the battle field, with the Bible in your arms and its precepts in your hearts."[65]

Americans did try to send soldiers into battle with the scriptures in their arms. Bible distribution was an enormous task, with chaplains and Bible societies handing out complete Bibles and New Testaments to soldiers. Printing presses, powered by steam, churned out thousands of Bibles for mass distribution. The American Bible Society had been in existence for forty-five years when the Civil War began, and with the war came the challenge of reaching the troops with the scriptures—a challenge the society accepted, reportedly handing out more than three million copies of the Bible or New Testament during the war.[66]

Bible distribution faltered in the South, and southerners often received Bibles from the American Bible Society. The Confederacy inaugurated its own Bible society in 1862, which tried, but failed, to meet the demand. The war made it difficult for the ABS to get Bibles to the South, in part because of logistical problems and in part because many southerners did not want Yankee Bibles.[67]

The Authorized Version of the Bible—the "King James" translation, so named because England's King James I authorized it in 1611—was by far the most used version of scripture in the United States. The King James Bible dominated because Protestants dominated. The King James, in the view of most Protestants, was the only Bible.

Not so for Catholics and Jews. Catholics preferred the Douay-Reims, a translation from the Latin Vulgate, and, shortly before the Civil War, many Jews praised a new translation by Rabbi Isaac Leeser of Pennsylvania. Finally, Jews could put aside the Bible of "a deceased king of England [King James] who certainly was no prophet," wrote Leeser. This statement offended Protestants, who distrusted Catholics and Jews even more because they rejected the King James Bible.[68]

The King James Bible exerted a tremendous influence on language and literature in the United States. This was the case with soldiers in the Civil War, as well as with President Lincoln, whose speeches were often strewn with language that resembled phrasings from the King James Bible.

Many soldiers treasured their copies of the scriptures; others ignored them or spat tobacco into their pages. A colonel from Pennsylvania bragged, "I know but one text of the scriptures, 'Cain murdered Abel'; go and do likewise." Regardless, when offered Bibles or testaments, soldiers rarely turned them down.[69]

Soldiers often claimed that the Bible could save them in the heat of battle. In any war, control could seem to be an illusion—it seems like nothing ever happened as planned. Many soldiers trusted in God's providential control; others entrusted their lives to the whims of chance or fate, and they grasped at any opportunity for comfort in the chaos. In some wars, soldiers relied on charms, including rabbits' feet and locks of hair, for good luck. But this was not so prevalent in the Civil War. In his study of soldiers' motivations, James McPherson found "no evidence of Civil War soldiers carrying rabbits' feet or anything else that they might have considered a talisman. But many of them did carry pocket Bibles or New Testaments, and numerous are the Civil War stories of a Bible in a breast pocket stopping a bullet."[70]

Even those who were not religious sometimes kept a Bible around for protection. A soldier from the Third New York Independent Battery reported "cases when card players, on going into battle, would throw away their cards and place their testament in their breast pocket over the heart."[71] Scripture was both sword and shield, sometimes literally.

The Bible didn't always work its bulletproof magic, however. Mary Chesnut noted a soldier was "found with a bullet through his heart and a Bible in his pocket, marked: 'From the Bible Society to the defender of his country.'" She observed, "If the Bible can't prevent war, how is it to stop a bullet?"[72]

The Data: Confederate and Union Bibles

Both North and South "read the same Bible," Lincoln said. But the Bible is a large collection of books. Which biblical texts did Americans turn to most often in the Civil War? In pursuing this question, I have examined thousands of biblical citations in over two thousand sources, including sermons, diaries, letters, and newspapers.[73] Consequently this book reveals more information than ever before about the Bible's ubiquitous presence in the American Civil War.

The book's appendix lists rankings of the most-cited biblical texts in the Civil War era, including separate rankings of the most popular scriptures in the Union and the Confederacy. These rankings indicate the contrasting approaches northerners and southerners took to the Bible. Although there was no single "northern" view of the Bible any more than there was one unified "southern" view, certain biblical texts rose to the forefront during the war. Overall, the most cited texts of the "Union Bible" were used to defend Lincoln and the nation against rebellion, which often involved insisting that the United States was God's chosen nation. Among the critical passages was Romans 13, which Union interpreters used to condemn rebellion by citing Paul's threat of damnation against radicals who attacked their God-given rulers. How could anyone rebel against the government if to do so was to rebel against God?

Yet the Confederates had a strong retort: didn't the patriots of 1776 revolt against their "higher powers"? Revolt was not out of the question for Americans, and Romans 13 had been popular in the American Revolution, used by loyalists and patriots alike. Arguments for and against "rebellion"— or "revolution"—were just part of the appeal of Romans 13. Americans also quoted it to call for justified violence, citing Paul's endorsement of the civil ruler as God's "revenger to execute wrath upon him that doeth evil." Typical was a letter to Lincoln, printed in a Methodist newspaper after Bull Run, telling the president that Paul gave him permission to be God's "revenger," and pledging devotion to Lincoln "in the holy bonds of patriotism."[74]

Much of the Union Bible attacked slavery, evidenced by many texts examined in this book, but what about racism? Most white Americans—North and South—assumed the white race was superior to all others. Arguments over this issue often turned on a statement Paul made, insisting that God made all people "of one blood" (Acts 17:26). This scripture condemned slavery—and perhaps racism—many interpreters claimed, but slaveholders had their own take on this text, arguing that it was about providence, not slavery, and certainly not racial equality.

If the Union Bible attacked slavery and defended the nation—and its violence—with God's blessing, the Confederate Bible defended slavery and blessed the rebellion. Most of all, however, southerners cited scripture to make sense of the war's horrific losses. Although the war punished both sides, it devastated the Confederacy, wracking the South with more death and destruction than the North experienced. Confederates coped by citing many scriptures, and one of the most popular, "The Lord of hosts is with us; the God of Jacob is our refuge" (Psalms 46:7; cf. 46:1), was a text of comfort, reassuring them that God was with the South. "Now is the time for every Southern man to stretch every nerve, for every soldier 'to do or die,'" said a North Carolina newspaper in 1862. Trust in "God who will fight our battles for us," and "we will not fear, for the Lord of hosts is with us; the God of Jacob is our refuge."[75]

God and scripture were a refuge for Confederates as they turned to providential hope even amid devastation and defeat. They looked to Job, who knew much about loss, to ponder how "the Lord gave, and the Lord hath taken away; blessed be the name of the Lord," and to visualize a place where "the wicked cease from troubling; and there the weary be at rest" (Job 1:21, 3:17). Typical of this thinking is a newspaper article from Staunton, Virginia, paying tribute to "brother Elliott," a soldier slain in July 1863, who was "a noble and brave defender of [the Confederacy's] rights and liberties." Yet "The Providence of God . . . doeth all things right," and "The Lord gave and the Lord hath taken away, blessed be the name of the Lord."[76] The war reminded everyone that life was fragile, and death was always close at hand. The "King of Terrors" eventually seized everyone: "His shafts are levelled equally against [the] rich & [the] poor, the great & [the] small," wrote a chaplain with the Eleventh North Carolina Regiment in an unprinted sermon manuscript.[77]

In pursuing these Union and Confederate Bibles, I focus most intently on the texts that were most cited during the Civil War. But I also examine unique interpretations of texts, even some texts that were not cited as often as others.

I've tried to set interpretations in conversation with each other, attempting to capture the depth and breadth of the way the Bible was read and used in the Civil War.

In attempting to do this, I recognize that Americans didn't read scripture in isolation; they read it to deal with the war, which means the context is as important as the texts. Although many Americans claimed to follow the "the Bible alone," everyone read scripture in a place and time, and those conditions influenced how people interpreted the Bible. Although Americans often thought of the Bible as their highest authority in life, they also dealt with other authorities in their lives—governments, laws, churches, parents, spouses, ministers, presidents, and (for many) slaveholders, just to name a few. To say some person, or text, has authority only makes sense when we think of the relationship between that authority and other authorities. The key, as Seth Perry writes, is to examine "the Bible's *authoritative use* by individuals in their relations with others, not from the assumption that the inert book itself possessed authority." In the Civil War, Americans rarely focused on "the Bible alone." Instead, they enlisted the Bible to lend divine sanction to other authorities, including political authorities (such as the Union and the Confederacy) and authoritative ideas (such as patriotism and various views on race).[78]

The Bible, therefore, was not just text; it was text in action—spoken in sermons, read in devotions, printed in newspapers, and more. From battle to battle, Americans employed the Bible to shape enduring views of religious violence, politics, race, patriotism, the nation, and other issues.

In this history of the Bible and the American Civil War, I've proceeded chronologically, narrating how Americans experienced scripture as they experienced the war. Each chapter covers a period in the war, focusing on how people used the Bible to address various concerns during that time, though occasionally I backtrack or move forward to discuss a theme or to compare interpretations of a scripture text across time. This narrative cannot include every detail of the war, but I discuss the events, ideas, and people necessary for readers to understand the major biblical texts and themes addressed as the war raged on for four devastating years.

1

"His Terrible Swift Sword"

The Civil War resulted from a division that had existed since the nation's founding. As Abraham Lincoln said in his Second Inaugural Address, "Slaves constituted a peculiar and powerful interest. All knew that this interest was somehow the cause of the war."[1] This division pitted those who believed slavery to be a biblical institution—and compatible with the ideals of the nation—against those who believed slavery violated both scripture and the nation's founding ideals. This conflict was present at the time a prominent slaveholder wrote:

> We hold these truths to be self-evident: That all men are created equal; that they are endowed by their Creator with certain unalienable rights; that among these are life, liberty, and the pursuit of happiness.[2]

With these famous lines, Thomas Jefferson brought God into the Declaration of Independence, and proclaimed the Creator to be on the side of equality and "unalienable rights." Jefferson did not quote scripture here, but many Americans did from that time on as they discussed, debated, and killed to defend or to attack slavery. As they did so, the Bible—as it was during the American Revolution—became a book of war. For some, the Bible ignited a fierce war of words over slavery; for others, the Bible called God's people to shed blood to eradicate slavery from the land. These debates and revolts—often inspired by scripture—set the stage for the unprecedented bloodshed of the Civil War.

The Liberator

There was a big difference between a war of words and a real war that shed blood, but, as everyone knew, one could lead to the other. When he launched his war of words against slavery, William Lloyd Garrison, one of the nation's most famous abolitionists, wanted nothing to do with a bloody war. A devoted pacifist, his weapons would be the pen and press, chiefly his newspaper, *The Liberator*, which ran from 1831 until the end of the Civil War.

In his attacks on slavery, Garrison had reservations about enlisting the Bible. He realized that some biblical passages seemed to support slavery, at least as many Americans read them. Yet Garrison didn't reject the Bible completely. As Frederick Douglass said, "The Bible was [Garrison's] text book—held sacred, as the word of the Eternal Father." Historians have called Garrison's abolitionism a movement of "Bible politics." But, as Douglass said, Garrison believed the central premise of the Bible was Jesus's call to justice and pacifism, "complete submission to insults and injuries—literal obedience to the injunction, if smitten on one side to turn the other also."[3]

Because Garrison valued Jesus and the Gospels, with their message of pacifism, love, and justice, it frustrated him to see other scriptures misused to justify violence. One key example was Romans 13. Garrison especially despised verse 4, which called the civil ruler "the minister of God, a revenger to execute wrath upon him that doeth evil." As a pacifist, Garrison loathed interpretations of this verse that endorsed violence in God's name. "In almost every attempt made to justify the punishment of enemies, or uphold human government based upon brute force," Garrison said, "the 13th chapter of Romans is regarded as a frowning Gibraltar, inaccessible by sea and land, filled with troops and all warlike instruments, and able to vanquish every assailing foe."[4]

Romans 13 contradicted the peaceful teachings of most of the New Testament, Garrison believed. And that explained why people quoted Romans 13 so often—it was one of the few New Testament texts that enabled the civil ruler to inflict violence in God's name. Romans 13 thus was a popular scripture, but that was a good reason to doubt its truth; in the context of the New Testament as a whole, Romans 13 was an outlier.[5]

This example illustrates Garrison's frustration with the Bible. The "divine authority of the Bible" was a question "of grave importance," Garrison admitted, but it was also a question with too many answers. It seemed that everyone had a different opinion on the Bible.[6] His main problem was with the all-or-nothing view of scripture—its readers must accept the truth of all of it, or they "are 'infidels,' who will justly deserve to be 'cast into the lake of fire and brimstone.'" When it came to scripture, often "investigation is made a criminal act." Many Christians insisted that biblical writers were "only machines, operated upon by a divine power, to communicate to the world, in an infallible manner, the contents of the book: so that it is free from all error."

That was "a monstrous absurdity," Garrison stated. In fact, "To say that every thing contained within the lids of the Bible is divinely inspired" was "a bold fiction," he wrote.[7]

Equally wrong were those who rejected all of scripture, looking on the Bible with "bitterness and contempt of spirit." Some said "the Bible is like a fiddle; you can play any tune on it you please." But, then, "The fault must be in the player, rather than in the instrument. Shall the instrument therefore be broken in pieces?" In all, the Bible "embodies an amount of excellence so great as to make it, in my estimation, THE BOOK OF BOOKS."[8]

Although Garrison called the Bible the book of books, he sounded radical to a lot of Americans who only wanted to hear that the Bible was fully true and fully understandable to anyone with common sense. Garrison's skeptical view of scripture played into the hands of proslavery advocates, who attacked abolitionists as "infidels" who hated the Bible because it supported slavery.[9]

"You and Your Country Are Gone!!!!!!"

Many black abolitionists hailed from evangelical traditions, especially Baptist and Methodist churches—denominations most popular with African Americans who became Christians. Consider the case of Richard Allen, first bishop of the African Methodist Episcopal Church. Although there were a variety of denominations in America, "The Methodists were the first people that brought glad tidings to the colored people," Allen wrote. Methodists and other evangelicals rode the wave of the Second Great Awakening, which focused on a heartfelt experience of the Holy Spirit, not doctrine or theological concepts. Most Methodist and Baptist preachers had little if any formal education, so their message was accessible to most whites and blacks in the United States. As Allen wrote, "I feel thankful that ever I heard a Methodist preach. We are beholden to the Methodists, under God, for the light of the Gospel we enjoy; for all other denominations preached so high-flown that we were not able to comprehend their doctrine."[10]

Early Methodists followed their founder, John Wesley, in opposing slavery. But this commitment faded as the movement grew, especially in the South. To be a true Methodist, Richard Allen realized, involved protest and sacrifice. After he and other black worshippers were accosted while praying—literally pulled up while they were on their knees because they were sitting in an area reserved for whites—they left the white-controlled St. George's Methodist

Episcopal Church in Philadelphia. Allen, then, led in founding the African Methodist Episcopal Church, recognizing that African Americans would be second-class citizens, at best, in white churches.[11]

Allen had no greater admirer than David Walker, a fellow member of the African Methodist Episcopal Church. It annoyed Walker that so few whites knew about Bishop Allen, but he understood why—American history was dominated by whites who often ignored African Americans. Walker looked to the future, "when the Lord shall raise up coloured historians in succeeding generations, to present the crimes of this nation." Those historians would obey "the Holy Ghost," who "will make them do justice to the name of Bishop Allen," who would then "stand on the pages of history among the greatest divines who have lived since the apostolic age."[12]

White Americans assumed their race was superior, Walker knew, and this assumption dominated their view of history as well as their view of scripture. But Walker challenged white supremacy and proved to be one of the most prophetic writers in the United States. Born in Wilmington, North Carolina, Walker's mother was free and his father was enslaved. Walker's hatred of slavery drove him to the Northeast, where he settled in Boston in 1827 and opened a clothing store. In 1829, Walker ignited controversy from north to south with his *Appeal . . . to the Coloured Citizens of the World, but in Particular, and Very Expressly, to Those of the United States of America.*[13]

It was inevitable that Walker's attack on slavery would alarm the South. His warning was not merely of a war of words, but rather a bloody war aimed at eradicating slavery in America. Enslaved people, he argued, should revolt against their masters.

Walker used the Bible to make his case. Like other opponents of slavery, he looked to the book of Exodus, with its description of Egyptian slavery. But unlike others, who condemned the Egyptians as an evil people for enslaving the Israelites, Walker said American slavery was even worse than Egyptian slavery. Unlike American slaveholders, Egyptians were not racists, Walker said. "The Egyptians . . . were Africans or coloured people, such as we are—some of them yellow and others dark—a mixture of Ethiopians and the natives of Egypt—about the same as you see the coloured people of the United States at the present day." Moreover, the pharaoh put Joseph, an Israelite, in power, making him a ruler in Egypt (Genesis 41:40–44). That would never happen to a black person in the United States, Walker noted. "Show me a coloured President, a Governor, a Legislator, a Senator, a Mayor, or an Attorney at the Bar. . . . show me a man of colour, who holds the low office of a Constable, or one who sits in a Juror Box, even on a case of one of his wretched brethren, throughout this great Republic!!"[14]

Pharaoh even gave Joseph an Egyptian wife (Genesis 41:45), Walker noted. How different was this acceptance of intermarriage from the United States, where states passed laws making it illegal for whites to marry blacks? Even if it were legal for whites and blacks to marry, Walker did not recommend it due to racism. "I would not give *a pinch of snuff* to be married to any white person I ever saw in all the days of my life," said Walker. Any black man who married a white woman would "be a double slave to her, just because she is *white*." Walker made this observation "to show how much lower we are held, and how much more cruel we are treated by the Americans, than were the children of Jacob, by the Egyptians."[15]

The Egyptians never called their enslaved people inhuman. By comparison, white Americans—even such "enlightened" founders as Thomas Jefferson—claimed the superiority of whites to blacks, Walker said, and he quoted liberally from Jefferson's *Notes on the State of Virginia* to prove it. Did not American whites claim that their enslaved people descended "originally from the tribes of Monkeys or Orang-Outangs?" Indeed, "The whites have always been an unjust, jealous, unmerciful, avaricious and blood-thirsty set of beings, always seeking after power and authority."[16]

"Have not the Americans the Bible in their hands?" Walker asked. "Do they believe it? Surely they do not. See how they treat us in open violation of the Bible!!" By enslaving human beings, white Americans violated Christ's golden rule: "All things whatsoever ye would that men should do unto you, do ye even so unto them." Even so, "An American minister, with the Bible in his hand, holds us and our children in the most abject slavery and wretchedness. Now I ask them, would they like for us to hold them and their children in abject slavery and wretchedness?"[17]

Scripture knew nothing of racism, Walker wrote. "How can the preachers and people of America believe the Bible? Does it teach them any distinction on account of a man's colour?" No—scripture opposed racism and slavery, which was a major reason why southern states passed laws forbidding enslaved people to read.[18] A literate population of enslaved people could read scripture and challenge slavery with biblical knowledge. "For colored people to acquire learning in this country, makes tyrants quake and tremble on their sandy foundation" because "they know that their infernal deeds of cruelty will be made known to the world." "I cannot but think upon Christian Americans!!!—What Kind of people can they be?"[19]

The God of the Bible would violently attack injustice, Walker warned. "I tell you Americans! that unless you speedily alter your course, *you* and your *Country are gone!!!!!!* For God Almighty will tear up the very face of the earth!!!" Walker turned to the book of Revelation: "Will not that very remarkable passage of Scripture be fulfilled on Christian Americans? Hear it Americans!! 'He that is unjust, let him be unjust still:—and he which is filthy, let him be filthy still: and he that is righteous, let him be righteous still: and he that is holy, let him be holy still' " (Revelation 22:11). These were the words of Jesus, warning that his judgment was coming, where good and evil would receive their rewards.[20]

American whites should be afraid, Walker threatened: "The whites want slaves, and want us for their slaves, but some of them will curse the day they ever saw us. As true as the sun ever shone in its meridian splendor, my colour will root some of them out of the very face of the earth." Walker knew well how white America would hear these words. "This language, perhaps is too harsh for the American's delicate ears," Walker said. "But Oh Americans! Americans!! I warn you in the name of the Lord, (whether you will hear, or forbear,) to repent and reform, or you are ruined!!!" Again he said, "O Americans! Americans!! I call God—I call angels—I call men, to witness, that your DESTRUCTION *is at hand*, and will be speedily consummated unless you REPENT."[21] Walker continued, "The Americans do their very best to keep my Brethren from receiving and reading my 'Appeal' for fear they will find in it an extract which I made from their Declaration of Independence, which says, 'we hold these truths to be self-evident, that all men are created equal.' " If enslaved blacks could read his book—along with the Bible and the Declaration of Independence—they would see clearly the nation's hypocrisy, Walker proclaimed.[22]

These were some of the most radical and courageous words written against slavery in the nineteenth century. Walker died in August 1830, the year after he published the *Appeal*. His death was sudden and suspicious. Some whites had put a price on his head, but there was no clear evidence of murder.[23]

"O, America, Foul and Indelible Is Thy Stain!"

David Walker influenced his colleague Maria Stewart, who became one of the nation's first African American women to speak and publish on politics. Stewart was also a colleague of Garrison and published in *The Liberator*. The

Bible shaped Stewart's thought as it did Walker's, although she did not endorse violence. "Away with tyranny and oppression!" Stewart proclaimed to African American Baptists in Boston. "Far be it from me to recommend to you either to kill, burn, or destroy. But I would strongly recommend to you to . . . show forth your powers of mind."[24]

In 1831, Stewart published *Religion and the Pure Principles of Morality*, arguing that God created blacks in God's image, the same as whites. She called on the founding of the nation, which rested on the belief that God "hath made all men free and equal." She was willing to die in defense of this belief, and she believed God would "protect me from the rage and malice of mine enemies," or God would "take me to himself, as He did the most noble, fearless, and undaunted David Walker."[25]

Some of her biblical language had an apocalyptic tone. In the book of Revelation, Christ is portrayed as the wrathful Lamb of God who waged war against Satan and his nations. Christ fought to rescue the martyrs who had suffered persecution and death for Christ's sake. One vision showed a "great whore," who sat on "a scarlet coloured beast, full of names of blasphemy." This woman symbolized all the empires and kings who had murdered Christians—so the woman was "drunken with the blood of the saints, and with the blood of the martyrs of Jesus" (Revelation 17:6). Maria Stewart echoed this scene in condemning the United States for slavery. "O, America, foul and indelible is thy stain! Dark and dismal is the cloud that hangs over thee for thy cruel wrongs . . . to the fallen sons of Africa. The blood of her murdered ones cries to heaven for vengeance against thee." America had "almost become drunken with the blood of [Africa's] slain; thou hast enriched thyself through her toils."[26]

Stewart then shifted to a vision of the day of judgment, when powerful men who had persecuted Christians would hide in the mountains from Christ and would say to "the mountains and rocks, fall on us, and hide us from the . . . wrath of the Lamb" (Revelation 6:16). Stewart believed this passage would be fulfilled in America: "O, ye great and mighty men of America, ye rich and powerful ones, many of you will call for the rocks and mountains to fall upon you, and to hide you from the wrath of the lamb." Meanwhile, many "sable-skinned Africans you now despise, will shine in the kingdom of heaven as the stars, forever and ever."[27]

Although neither Walker nor Stewart took it that far, biblical attacks on slavery did incite actual violence, as Americans witnessed in Nat Turner's slave revolt, the most violent in American history. Beginning on August 21,

1831, Turner led other enslaved men in killing over fifty whites in a series of attacks in Southampton County, Virginia. After Turner's capture, Thomas R. Gray, a white attorney, interviewed him and published *The Confessions of Nat Turner*, which, according to historian Patrick Breen, "may be the most important work on slavery written and published in the slaveholding South."[28] Although scholars debate how faithful Gray's narrative was to what Turner actually said, the *Confession* remains the best evidence we have on Turner's motivations.

Turner had planned his attack for July 4—it would be his Independence Day—but logistical problems forced a delay.[29] Still, we cannot miss his plan to connect his "revolution" with that of 1776, nor can we miss his connection with the Bible. Turner found inspiration in a vision that encompassed biblical scenes from the Gospels and the book of Revelation: "On the 12th of May, 1828, I heard a loud noise in the heavens, and the Spirit instantly appeared to me and said the Serpent was loosened, and Christ had laid down the yoke he had borne for the sins of men, and that I should take it on and fight against the Serpent, for the time was fast approaching when the first should be last and the last should be first" (cf. Matthew 19:30; Revelation 20).[30]

Turner compared his fight against slavery to Christ's fight against Satan (called "the Serpent" in Revelation 20). In this battle, those enslaved would win—they were "the last" who would "be first." Turner's *Confession* served notice on America that enslaved people would enlist the Bible to inspire violence against slavery.[31]

"Reflect on the Appalling Character of a Civil War"

These and other attacks on slavery provoked intense proslavery defenses. John C. Calhoun, senator from South Carolina, said abolitionism "strikes directly and fatally, not only at our prosperity, but our existence, as a people." Decades earlier, many southern whites, including Thomas Jefferson and George Washington, had looked on slavery as a necessary but corrupt system that needed to die. Since neither Washington, nor Jefferson, nor their colleagues knew how to end slavery and keep southern states in the Union, they kept slavery alive, hoping someday Americans would find a way to outlaw it. This was a mistake, Calhoun believed, because slavery should never die—it was a moral institution. "The relation now existing in the slaveholding states between the two [races] is, instead of an evil, a good—a positive good,"

Calhoun wrote. Slavery is "the most solid and durable foundation on which to rear free and stable political institutions."[32]

When the founders had envisioned a future nation that could live without slavery, they didn't know cotton production would become the South's biggest moneymaker after the cotton gin streamlined production. By the beginning of the Civil War, the South was by far the world's leading producer of cotton. "No power on earth dares to make war upon" cotton, said South Carolina senator James Henry Hammond, because "Cotton is king." As Methodist minister Andrew Lipscomb of Georgia said in 1860, "Every bale of cotton is five hundred pounds of diplomatic influence." Or, as Methodist minister B. H. Nadal put it, "A Yankee . . . invented the cotton gin, which turned black men into masses of gold."[33] As this empire of cotton expanded in the South, the northern economy moved away from agriculture, developing its economy through industry, aided by expanded transportation with steamships, canals, and expanded railroads. These shifts set up social and economic differences between North and South that fed into the debates over slavery.

The national division over slavery intensified and finally ruptured the major Protestant denominations. Presbyterians had separated twice—in 1837 and 1857—generating divisions that, while not exclusively centered on slavery, still viewed it as an important factor. Slavery figured centrally in Methodist and Baptists divisions. The Methodist Episcopal Church split into northern and southern factions in 1844; one year later the Baptists did the same. The Methodists argued over whether bishops could be slaveholders, while the Baptists had similar disagreements over missionaries.[34] Almost immediately, Americans sensed the dire consequences of these dissolutions. If Christians, led by ministers, could not solve the slavery crisis, what chance did politicians have?

The crisis showed that compromise was not a strength of many evangelicals during this period. Decades of revivalist sermons had taught them that the world was caught in an ultimate struggle between God and Satan, heaven and hell, and this way of thinking influenced their political views. For them, political issues—including slavery—involved questions of good versus evil, with little room for negotiation.[35]

Biblical debates over slavery were nothing new, but they were never more intense, nor more politically crucial, than during these years.[36] In 1845, the same year that Baptists in the South separated from Northern Baptists to form the Southern Baptist Convention, Reverend Richard Fuller of South

Carolina published a letter defending slavery in the *Christian Reflector*, igniting a debate with his Northern Baptist friend, Francis Wayland of Brown University. Later that year they published their letters in a book, *Domestic Slavery Considered as a Scriptural Institution*, which gave Americans a point-by-point debate on the Bible's view of slavery, with Fuller and Wayland rehearsing many of the arguments that later appeared during the Civil War.

Fuller cited the Bible's references to slavery, both instructions on caring for slaves and narratives of slavery, with no direct condemnation of slavery in either the Old or the New Testament. How, then, could slavery be a great evil if the Bible did not condemn it? Wayland responded that slavery violated the basic moral principles of scripture, including the golden rule and Paul's teaching that all people were created "of one blood" and thus share the same nature (Acts 17:26). Besides, slavery violated the Declaration of Independence's statement that "all men are created equal" with "inalienable rights." Although Fuller supported slavery, he despised many of the horrific practices that marred southern slavery and gave the institution a bad reputation. Although Wayland opposed slavery, he attacked abolitionists for their pacifism and radical views of scripture.[37]

This was no mere academic debate. Fuller and Wayland called the crisis over slavery *the* issue that divided the nation and threatened to provoke war. "Compared with slavery," Fuller wrote, "all other topics which now shake and inflame men's passions in these United States, are really trifling." Fuller worried that Christian arguments over slavery would spell doom for the nation. "Reflect on the appalling character of a civil war; and if you love the country, or the slave, do not sever the bands which unite the Baptist churches," he wrote.[38]

In 1846, the year after Fuller and Wayland watched their Baptist denomination split over slavery, the United States declared war on Mexico—a war that lasted almost two years before Mexico surrendered vast territories to the United States, including all of Texas north of the Rio Grande and present-day New Mexico and California. Would these territories be open to slavery? There would be no peaceful answer to this question, and some questioned if this new land was more curse than blessing. Ralph Waldo Emerson made an ominous comment: "The United States will conquer Mexico, but it will be as the man who swallows the arsenic, which brings him down in turn. Mexico will poison us."[39]

The poison began to take effect within months. Some northerners sided with Pennsylvania representative David Wilmot's proviso, which excluded slavery from the new territories. In turn, most southerners sided with Calhoun, who said that citizens moving to the new lands had every right to bring their property with them, even if this property included enslaved people. Others sought a compromise between these two views, and this eventually won out as the Compromise of 1850.

On the antislavery side, this compromise added California to the Union as a free state, an important move because now the nation would have more free states (sixteen) than slave states (fifteen). On the proslavery side, the compromise included a revised Fugitive Slave Act, which strengthened a similar act from 1793. Unless they had official papers proving their freedom, African Americans accused as fugitives had few rights—not the right to testify in court to defend themselves, not the right to a jury trial, not the right to give evidence they had been raped or beaten. Anyone who helped fugitives—through the Underground Railroad or otherwise—was branded a criminal. African Americans who had never been enslaved feared they would be captured by a lying slaveholder who claimed they were his property.

The Fugitive Slave Act became law on September 18, 1850. Now the devil could "rent out hell and move to the United States," wrote Baptist minister and former slave William P. Newman in a letter to Frederick Douglass.[40]

Uncle Tom's Cabin

The Fugitive Slave Act, as Andrew Delbanco wrote, "lit the fuse that led to civil war," because it exposed the hypocrisy of a slaveholding nation that claimed to stand for liberty. Many whites in the North had remained oblivious to slavery's horrors until confronted with fugitives from slavery who fled to northern states. These "fugitive slaves exposed the contradiction between the myth that slavery was a benign institution and the reality that a nation putatively based on the principle of human equality was actually a prison house in which millions of Americans had no rights at all." Conflict over what to do with fugitives "was the war before the war."[41]

The Fugitive Slave Act inspired Harriet Beecher Stowe to write *Uncle Tom's Cabin; or, Life Among the Lowly*, which, as James McPherson wrote, was "the most influential indictment of slavery of all time." Stowe's novel displayed the horrors of slavery, especially focusing on how slavery ripped families apart, selling children away from parents who would never see them again. These sentiments affected northerners who were suddenly confronted with what it would be like if someone bought their children, spouses, or parents and took them away.[42]

Stowe published *Uncle Tom's Cabin* in serial form in a newspaper over a nine-month period, starting in 1850. The novel appeared as a book in two volumes on March 20, 1852. Because the initial printing of 5,000 copies sold so well, the publisher printed another 50,000 copies by May. After one year in print, Americans had purchased about 310,000 copies—triple the current sales record for novels. Sales were even higher in England, where readers snapped up one million copies within the novel's first year in print.[43]

Abraham Lincoln probably never called Stowe "the little woman who wrote the book that made this great war," as was often reported.[44] But the novel helped to spark the war—not only did it confront northerners with slavery's evils, but it also outraged the South, incentivizing southerners to defend slavery against Stowe's portrayal.

Many Americans who read *Uncle Tom's Cabin* believed that slavery offended God's "higher law" of justice, regardless of what the Constitution or other human laws said about slavery. As Frederick Douglass wrote, "The touching, but too truthful tale of *Uncle Tom's Cabin* . . . rekindled the slumbering embers of anti-slavery zeal into an active flame." Stowe's novel aroused the emotions of many "who before cared nothing for the bleeding slave."[45]

Stowe gave God credit for inspiring her to write the novel, which may partially explain why she filled it with scripture.[46] In a digital archive, "*Uncle Tom's Cabin* & American Culture," Professor Stephen Railton of the University of Virginia revealed nearly "100 quotations from or direct allusions to the King James version of the Bible" in the novel. Stowe's characters argued over the Bible's use to justify slavery and showed how biblical texts could be used to support almost any agenda, including slavery. Even so, Stowe wanted to demonstrate that the Bible, when read properly, condemned slavery. A significant theme in the novel, which Uncle Tom quoted to his master, Augustine St. Clare, was that God had hidden truths "from the wise and prudent, and hast revealed them unto babes" (Luke 10:21). Although Tom could barely read the Bible, he understood biblical truths better than his educated master.[47]

Uncle Tom's Cabin struck a powerful blow against slavery, but it also revealed Stowe's anti-Catholicism. Even so, Stowe was not so fiercely anti-Catholic as her father, Lyman Beecher, who published a popular anti-Catholic sermon, *A Plea for the West*, in which he called Catholicism "the most skillful, powerful, dreadful system of corruption to those who wield it and of debasement and slavery to those who live under it, which ever spread darkness and desolation over the earth."[48]

The novel also revealed Stowe's racism. She depicted African Americans as more religious than whites, but intellectually inferior.[49] Over time people used the term "Uncle Tom" to criticize blacks who cowardly served white agendas. Yet some argue that the Uncle Tom character in the novel was neither a traitor nor a coward. Tom stood up to his evil master Simon Legree and helped other enslaved people escape, even though it cost him his life. Uncle Tom was the hero of the novel, a Christ figure who sacrificed himself for his people. As Tom faced his last days, he read the Passion story from the Gospels and "a vision rose before him of One crowned with thorns"—presumably Jesus—who said to Tom, "He that overcometh shall sit down with me on my throne, even as I also overcame, and set down with my Father on his throne."[50]

Not only did *Uncle Tom's Cabin* draw many texts and themes from the Bible, but the novel also stimulated Bible sales, and some saw it "as a new Bible, with its ideal expression of religion for the era," David Reynolds observed.[51] As Stowe watched the churches divide, she wrote *Uncle Tom's Cabin* in part to show that the Bible really did condemn slavery. "By showing in virtually every scene of Uncle Tom's Cabin that the Bible was antislavery," wrote Reynolds, Stowe challenged proslavery Christians, but she also called out abolitionists who had given up on the Bible as a weapon against slavery. To make this point, Stowe praised Garrison's *The Liberator*, but feared "that it will take from poor Uncle Tom his Bible and give him nothing in its place."[52]

"What to the Slave Is the Fourth of July?"

By the time *Uncle Tom's Cabin* had seized Americans' attention, nearly everyone knew who Frederick Douglass was. He became not only "the most photographed American of the nineteenth century," according to David Blight, but also rivaled Mark Twain as "the most widely traveled American public figure of his century." People flocked to hear him speak; he was a "wonder of the American world."[53]

When Americans heard Douglass speak, often they heard the Bible. Douglass spoke in "King James cadences," according to Blight; he "loved the language of the King James Bible," and he read his times within a biblical worldview, giving special attention to the prophets of the Old Testament.[54]

These prophets warned kings of the consequences of their sins. Evil would reap destruction on God's nation, prophets cautioned, and God's people would feel God's wrath.[55] These prophetic messages translated well into Douglass's world. As he saw it, Americans would suffer destruction. Douglass's employment of the Old Testament prophets shaped his thought so much that two biographies of Douglass published in 2018 included the word "prophet" in their titles: Blight's *Frederick Douglass: Prophet of Freedom* and D. H. Dilbeck's *Frederick Douglass: America's Prophet.*[56]

Like David Walker, Maria Stewart, and others, Douglass turned his prophetic attacks on American Christianity. "Christianity" in the United States had opposite meanings, Douglass wrote. It could refer to the corrupt, "slaveholding religion of this land," or in contrast, it could mean "the Christianity of Christ."[57] Slaveholding Christianity violated the Bible above all. "In America, Bibles and slaveholders go hand in hand. The church and the slave prison stand together, and while you hear the chanting of psalms in one, you hear the clanking of chains in the other."[58]

In one of his most famous speeches, Douglass cited scripture to attack corrupt patriotism. It was an Independence Day speech—delivered on July 5, 1852—entitled "What to the Slave Is the Fourth of July?"[59] This was, according to Blight, "the rhetorical masterpiece of American abolitionism."[60]

This masterpiece questioned how Americans remembered their history: "We have to do with the past only as we can make it useful to the present and to the future," Douglass said.[61] People often distorted history; they celebrated the past to justify "some folly or wickedness" in the present. The Fourth of July was a prime example—Americans celebrated the founders but rejected their principles.[62] "The signers of the Declaration of Independence were brave men," Douglass said, "patriots and heroes," filled with courage and virtue. What made them great? They wanted peace but "preferred revolution to peaceful submission to bondage."[63] Douglass put aside his concern with the founders' slaveholding—an issue he did engage, and we will discuss it later. On this day Douglass had another point to make: the founders mustered the courage to risk their lives in a fight for freedom.

Douglass questioned why he was invited to deliver a Fourth of July speech. "What have I, or those I represent, to do with your national independence?" The nation's founding "principles of political freedom and of natural justice" had no relevance to blacks. "This Fourth of July is yours, not mine." The entire event seemed like a sham. "Do you mean, citizens, to mock me by asking me to speak today?"[64]

Douglass employed biblical references, specifically Psalm 137, which told of the Israelites' experience while living in captivity in Babylon, the empire that had destroyed Jerusalem and forced God's people into exile. As they wept, the Babylonians mocked them, asking the captives to entertain them by singing a song about their destroyed homeland: "They that wasted us required of us mirth, saying, Sing us one of the songs of Zion." This was a cruel request, and the Israelites responded, "How shall we sing the Lord's song in a strange land? If I forget thee, O Jerusalem, let my right hand forget her cunning. If I do not remember thee, let my tongue cleave to the roof of my mouth" (Psalms 137:1–6).

Douglass therein compared enslaved people to the Jews captured in Babylon. "Fellow-citizens," Douglass said, "above your national, tumultuous joy, I hear the mournful wail of millions! Whose chains, heavy and grievous yesterday, are, today, rendered more intolerable by the jubilee shouts that reach them." Like the psalmist, Douglass said, "If I do forget, if I do not faithfully remember those bleeding children of sorrow this day, 'may my right hand forget her cunning, and may my tongue cleave to the roof of my mouth!' " The Fourth of July put the hypocrisy of the nation on display— "This nation never looked blacker to me than on this 4th of July!"[65] Douglass vented his outrage, "in the name of liberty which is fettered, in the name of the constitution and the Bible which are disregarded and trampled upon."[66]

Not only was slavery the nation's "great sin and shame," but everyone knew it. Douglass dismissed any claim that slavery was moral: "There is not a man beneath the canopy of heaven that does not know that slavery is wrong for him." Did he really have "to argue that it is wrong to make men brutes, to rob them of their liberty, to work them without wages . . . to beat them with sticks, to flay their flesh with the lash . . . to sunder their families . . . ?" And did he really have to argue that God opposed slavery? If slavery is "inhuman," it "cannot be divine!" America did not need good arguments; it needed "scorching irony," he proclaimed. If he could only speak to the nation, he would "pour out a fiery stream of biting ridicule, blasting reproach, withering sarcasm, and stern rebuke." Americans deserved judgment—"not the gentle shower, but thunder."[67]

The Bible was not the nation's book; it was the nation's judgment. Douglass held up "the language of Isaiah," who spoke of God's attack on the people for valuing religion over justice: "Bring no more vain oblations; incense is an abomination unto me; the new moons and sabbaths, the calling of assemblies, I cannot away with; it is iniquity, even the solemn meeting. Your new moons and your appointed feasts my soul hateth: they are a trouble unto me; I am weary to bear them. And when ye spread forth your hands, I will hide mine eyes from you: yea, when ye make many prayers, I will not hear: YOUR HANDS ARE FULL OF BLOOD" (Isaiah 1:13–15). The tragedy of the American churches was in ministers' distortions of scripture—they insisted "that we ought to obey man's law before the law of God." This was nothing more than "blasphemy."[68]

As his argument unfolded fiercely against his white audience, Douglass quoted from what became one of the most-cited Bible verses in the Civil War: God "hath made of one blood all nations of men for to dwell on all the face of the earth" (Acts 17:26), a verse that had been cited against slavery since before the Revolution. All races were of the same human family, related and commanded to love each other. And Douglass did what many others would do later—he connected this verse with the Declaration of Independence, especially the claim that "all men are created equal; and are endowed by their Creator with certain inalienable rights," including "life, liberty and the pursuit of happiness." Here the Bible and the Declaration of Independence spoke a united voice that rejected slavery outright, and still Americans and their churches embraced human bondage. "The existence of slavery in this country brands your republicanism as a sham, your humanity as a base pretense, and your Christianity as a lie."[69]

Anyone questioning whether American republicanism was a sham needed look no further than in the Dred Scott case, Douglass believed. Dred Scott, a man who had been enslaved, sued for his freedom on the grounds that he had lived for almost five years in the North, spending time in a free state (Illinois) and in other free territories. After it spent years in lower courts, the Supreme Court ruled on the case in March 1857. Chief Justice Roger B. Taney, with a seven-to-two majority, declared that Scott's race made him ineligible for citizenship, and, therefore, ineligible to file a federal lawsuit. Slaveholders had the right to their enslaved property, no matter which territory or state they were in. The United States was a nation ruled by whites, for whites. As Taney ruled, black people "had for more than a century before [1776] been regarded as beings of an inferior order, and altogether unfit to associate with the white race, either in social or political relations; and so far inferior that they had no rights which the white man was bound to respect; and that the negro might justly and lawfully be reduced to slavery for his benefit." To opponents of slavery, the Dred Scott decision made it clearer than ever that the political power of slavery had a stranglehold on the nation.[70]

In his response to the Dred Scott decision, Frederick Douglass recognized that opponents of slavery seemed overmatched, so he called on the story of David and Goliath: "David, you know, looked small and insignificant when going to meet Goliath, but looked larger when he had slain his foe" (cf. 1 Samuel 17).[71] Douglass appealed to the doctrine of a "higher law." "The Supreme Court of the United States is not the only power in this world," he asserted, because "the Supreme Court of the Almighty is greater." Mighty as he is, "Judge Taney . . . cannot perform impossibilities." Taney "cannot reverse the decision of the Most High," and Taney cannot make "evil good, and good, evil." In a shocking move, Douglass endorsed violent opposition to slavery, quoting from his poem "The Tyrant's Jubilee," including the lines

> The flames are extinguished, but the embers remain.
> One terrible blast may produce an ignition,
> Which shall wrap the whole South in wild conflagration"[72]

"John Brown's Body"

A "terrible blast" would "produce an ignition" sooner than many expected. Douglass's reputation attracted the attention of John Brown, a white abolitionist who declared war on slavery, and not only a war of words. Nearly two years before the Civil War, Brown led a band of whites and formerly enslaved people in a raid on the federal arsenal at Harpers Ferry, Virginia. Their goal was to seize weapons and lead a guerrilla war on slavery. Brown tried to enlist Douglass, but he declined, telling Brown the attack had little chance of success.

Brown also tried to enlist Harriet Tubman, the well-known abolitionist and leader in the Underground Railroad. Tubman, who escaped from slavery in 1849, seemed fearless in the face of dangerous plans with little chance of success. She had traveled from North to South and back again numerous times, defying all hazards to bring enslaved people to freedom. Tubman's heroics had earned her a biblical title—Moses—and that was more than enough to impress John Brown. In April 1858, Brown wrote of Tubman, "He is the most of a man, naturally, that I ever met with." Note Brown's use of the masculine pronoun to refer to Tubman. Brown meant it as a compliment, a reference to her courage, as others did when they called Tubman "Moses."[73]

As it turned out, Frederick Douglass was right—Brown's plan failed. He and his accomplices captured Harpers Ferry, but only briefly, and then Robert E. Lee and his marines defeated them. Brown and his men were captured, tried, convicted, and executed. This was not Brown's first assault on slavery. When the Kansas-Nebraska Act of 1854 turned the Kansas territory into a battleground between proslavery and antislavery forces, Brown did his part to create a "Bleeding Kansas." In May 1856, Brown led a nighttime attack on five proslavery men, seizing them from their homes and murdering them with broadswords.

Although Douglass refused to join Brown's band of fighters at Harpers Ferry, he admired Brown's assault against slavery, and he appreciated Brown's use of the Bible. The admiration was mutual. "Brown trusted Douglass's knowledge of Scripture as he poured forth passages from the Old and New Testaments," wrote David Blight. "To a degree Brown and Douglass shared a biblical grounding." We have seen how much Douglass admired the biblical prophets; in Brown, he found a man who seemed to be a fighting prophet, ready to bring down hellfire and brimstone on slaveholders.[74]

Brown cited scripture to justify his actions, but not only scripture. His biblical arguments carried with them ideas about liberty learned from the American Revolution. As Frederick Douglass said, Brown believed "the Declaration of Independence to be true, and the Bible to be a guide to human conduct, and acting upon the doctrines of both, he threw himself against the serried ranks of American oppression, and translated into heroic deeds the love of liberty and hatred of tyrants."[75] As Brown explained his position, "I believe in the Golden Rule . . . and the Declaration of Independence. I think that both mean the same thing; and it is better that a whole generation should fall off the face of the earth—men, women, and children—by a violent death than that one jot of either should fail in this country."[76]

The Bible and the Declaration of Independence—a vital combination for Brown—was most clearly revealed in his "Declaration of Liberty by the Representatives of the Slave Population of the United States of America." Not only did Brown add large sections of the Declaration of Independence in his "Declaration," but he also wrote his document on foolscap, glued it to a white cloth, and rolled it up so that it resembled a biblical scroll. After Brown's capture, soldiers found this scroll, along with maps of his planned revolutionary war on slavery, complete with X marks on southern areas where there were more blacks than whites.[77]

Brown's "Declaration," like the Declaration of Independence, announced revolution and war. "We will Obtain these rights or Die in the Struggle to obtain them." This was a war in defense "of the Great Principles set forth in Our Declaration of Independence." Like that war, Brown's war was a battle against tyranny, "with a firm reliance on the protection of Devine Providence," with all of his band mutually pledging "Our Lives, and Our Sacred Honor."[78]

After the trial, after the court had pronounced the guilty verdict, Brown called on the Bible. "This Court acknowledges, too, as I suppose, the validity of the law of God. I see a book kissed, which I suppose to be the Bible, or at least the New Testament, which teaches me that all things whatsoever I would that men should do to me, I should do even so to them." He also cited Acts 10:34: "God is no respecter of persons," and on that principle Jesus worked "in behalf of His despised poor," even though it meant death for him. If justice called him to "mingle my blood" with enslaved people, "I say let it be done."[79]

While in prison awaiting execution, Brown studied his Bible—the King James version, of course, with a leather cover. He marked several favorite texts, including "The LORD said, I have surely seen the affliction of my people which are in Egypt, and have heard their cry by reason of their taskmasters . . . and I am come down to deliver them out of the land of the Egyptians" (Exodus 3:7–8). Also, "Rob not the poor. . . . For the LORD will plead their cause, and spoil the soul of those that spoiled them" (Proverbs 22:22–23). Brown used these and other scriptures in preparing statements; he wanted to set the historical record straight and to defend his attacks on slavery.[80]

As James McPherson wrote, John Brown had "the glint of a Biblical warrior in his eye"—he resembled the biblical judge Samson, "who slew his enemies with the jawbone of an ass," although "Brown favored more up-to-date weapons" to punish God's enemies.[81] Brown admired both Samson's viciousness and his self-sacrifice. Captured and blinded by Philistines, Samson pushed down the pillars of a Philistine temple, collapsing it and killing himself and countless Philistines, which the author of Judges celebrated by writing, "So the dead which [Samson] slew at his death were more than they which he slew in his life" (Judges 16:30). Brown pondered Samson's actions in his final days, hoping that, like Samson's, his death could "be of vastly more value than my life is." Frederick Douglass liked the comparison: "Like Samson, [Brown] has laid his hands upon the pillars of this great national temple of cruelty and blood, and when he falls, that temple will speedily crumble to its final doom, burying its denizens in its ruins."[82]

Similarly, Brown closed a letter from prison with his famous words, "I, John Brown, am now quite *certain* that the crimes of this *guilty land* will never be purged away but with *blood*. I had, as I now think vainly, flattered myself that without very much bloodshed it might be done."[83] He called on biblical themes of violence and martyrdom, themes that would echo throughout the Civil War. Brown's execution drew a crowd of well over a thousand soldiers, including John Wilkes Booth.[84]

How should we remember John Brown? Was he a hero, fighting for freedom and justice? Or was he a terrorist, comparable to Timothy McVeigh, the Oklahoma City bomber who claimed Brown as his inspiration?

At the time of his execution, some in the North regarded Brown as a martyr for abolition. This was the view held by Harriet Beecher Stowe's brother, Henry Ward Beecher, "the Billy Graham of his era," according to Mark Noll.[85] As Brown awaited execution, Beecher said, "Let Virginia make him a martyr." Brown's hanging would transform "Brown's failure with a heroic success."[86] Henry David Thoreau agreed: "Some eighteen hundred years ago Christ was crucified; this morning, perchance, Captain Brown was hung." Christ's crucifixion and Brown's execution were "the two ends of a chain," and Brown transformed from "Old Brown" to "an angel of light." Brown "was a superior man" and was "the most American of us all," according to Thoreau. "To Northern abolitionists," Jill Lepore wrote, Brown's "death marked the beginning of a second American Revolution." Henry Wadsworth Longfellow wrote that "the second of December, 1859," would "be a great day in our history; the date of a new Revolution, — quite as much needed as the old one."[87]

This celebration of Brown continued long after the Civil War ended. In a biography of Brown published in 1909, W. E. B. Du Bois argued that "the memory of John Brown stands to-day as a mighty warning to this country." Brown saw slavery's evil and threat to the nation, and he knew that the longer the nation allowed its injustice to thrive the more disastrous its effects would become. Du Bois called Brown "the man who of all Americans has perhaps come nearest to touching the real souls of black folk."[88]

In 2009, a favorable view of Brown appeared in the *New York Times*. Historian David S. Reynolds appealed to President Obama and to the governor of Virginia to pardon Brown. Brown was "freedom's martyr," wrote Reynolds—a brave freedom fighter who had been "despised by history." "Justice would be served," therefore, "if President Obama and Governor

Kaine found a way to pardon" Brown, liberating him "from the loony bin of history."[89] Princeton historian Sean Wilentz disagreed and argued that Brown was "a violent charismatic anti-slavery terrorist and traitor, capable of cruelty to his family as well as to his foes."[90] Extreme viewpoints on Brown were nothing new; they emerged the moment the nation heard about his attack at Harpers Ferry.

John Brown may have become most renowned for the song "John Brown's Body." Although originally inspired by another John Brown, this martial hymn became associated with the radical of Harpers Ferry, especially when Union soldiers sang it. The song contained the lines "John Brown's body lies a-mouldering in the grave" and "his soul is marching on." Several versions also included "He's gone to be a soldier in the army of the Lord" and "They will hang Jeff Davis to a tree!"[91]

Versions of the song multiplied throughout the Civil War, with several calling on biblical themes. In 1861, Congregationalist minister William W. Patton penned a version with the famous lines:

"John Brown was John the Baptist of the Christ we are to see
Christ who of the bondsman shall the Liberator be
And soon throughout the sunny South the slaves shall all be free,
For his soul is marching on!"[92]

William Lloyd Garrison published his own version for the Fourth of July 1862, adding the biblical line: "the Lord our God" led the Union in "the Red Sea of his justice" and "our cause is marching on."[93]

The song inspired the "Battle Hymn of the Republic," written by Julia Ward Howe the morning after she sang "John Brown's Body" with Union soldiers near Washington. A few weeks later she published "The Battle Hymn" in the *Atlantic Monthly*. In this version, Howe replaced John Brown with the angry God whom Brown worshiped—a God who "loosed the fateful lightnings of His terrible swift sword." Christ appeared in the song as, like Brown, a model for those sacrificing their lives to free the enslaved people: "As he died to make men holy, let us die to make men free."[94]

The "Battle Hymn"—as the title indicates—is a militant hymn. It celebrates the coming of a God who will fight slavery, and it reflects the spirit of John Brown and the Bible. "Mine eyes have seen the glory of the coming of the Lord" echoed the prophet Isaiah's "Mine eyes have seen the King, the Lord of hosts" (Isaiah 6:5). The God who "is trampling out the vintage where the grapes of wrath are stored" recalled a vision from the book of Revelation, in which condemned souls who "worship the beast" and allow the mark of the beast will "drink of the wine of the wrath of God" and "be tormented with fire and brimstone" (Revelation 14:9–10).

This vision of an angry God's judgment describes "the great winepress of the wrath of God" and blood ushering "out of the winepress"—enough blood to cover the earth, rising as high as "the horse bridles" (Revelation 14:19–20). This and other visions in Revelation speak of a militant God who punishes sinners without mercy. Howe probably drew her reference to God's "terrible swift sword" from Revelation 19, where Jesus charged into battle on a white horse, with "a sharp sword" that he would use to "smite the nations" (Revelation 19, especially verses 11–15). This was an apocalyptic hymn featuring a warrior God who would lead a rampage against evil and charge toward a millennial kingdom. With such stirring biblical images, Howe's "Battle Hymn" became "the leading anthem of the Union cause during the Civil War."[95]

In the decades before the Civil War, therefore, the Bible supplied Americans with evidence—on both sides—for the fight over slavery. Just as the Bible became a powerful yet indecisive authority on slavery, it also became more important as a book of judgment on a nation for profiting from human bondage. African Americans—including Frederick Douglass, Maria Stewart, David Walker, Nat Turner, and many more—drew on a full range of scriptures, from Old Testament prophets to the Gospels and the apocalyptic visions of Revelation and other scriptures. In all these biblical arguments, Americans reaffirmed their belief in the Bible as a book of war—just as it had been in the American Revolution. If the Civil War was—as many believed—a Second American Revolution, these new revolutionaries on both sides returned to the Bible that they believed had served so authoritatively in the first.

2

"The Stone Which the Builders Rejected"

"The Christian has a motive for patriotism far stronger and holier than those of all other men," said Robert L. Dabney of Virginia on November 1, 1860—five days before the election of Abraham Lincoln. Dabney, a Presbyterian minister and professor of theology, would later serve as a Confederate chaplain and chief of staff of Confederate general Thomas J. "Stonewall" Jackson. But on this day, he wanted to avoid the secession and war that loomed as the presidential election approached.

In his sermon in the College Church at Hampden Sydney, Virginia, Dabney revisited Israel's greatest ruler, David—"a patriotic king," a godly leader who tried to secure peace for the "Hebrew Commonwealth." Although skilled at war, David yearned for peace because no one hated bloodshed like a great warrior. In war, "Death holds his cruel carnival," Dabney said, so southerners should "weep tears of blood at the wretched and wicked thought" of war between North and South. "Christians of America—Brothers—Shall all this be?" Think of the legacy of the nation, and of the churches. Future Americans would judge them, asking how did the churches "permit our mother-country to be slain?" The churches had a responsibility to work for peace, and if they failed, "Shame on the boasted Christianity of America, and of the nineteenth century!"[1]

Was the United States headed for disaster? If so, what role did religion play in the nation's downfall? Americans pondered these questions as the drama unfolded in the secession crisis after Lincoln's election. The nation they cherished—the pride of the founders—faced its most critical struggle for survival. The crisis—and religion's place in it—pushed many Americans to the Bible. Now more than ever Americans glimpsed the roles scripture would play when secession led to war.

"A House Divided Against Itself Cannot Stand"

When the nation elected Abraham Lincoln, few imagined that 150 years later Americans would hail him as one of the greatest presidents in US history. What were people to think of this backwoods Republican? When Lincoln's train stopped off in Cincinnati on its way to the White House, Rabbi Isaac Mayer Wise, leader of Reform Judaism and one of the most influential religious leaders in the nation, quoted scripture to criticize the crowds that gathered around the new president. "The Philistines from all corners of the land congregate around their Dagon and worship him," Wise said. To him, Lincoln looked "like a country squire for the first time in the city," a man who "will look queer in the white house, with his primitive manner."[2]

The election was hardly a landslide—under 40 percent of Americans voted for Lincoln. Most votes were divided among three other candidates: southern Democrat John C. Breckenridge, northern Democrat Stephen A. Douglas, and Tennessean John Bell, the candidate from the newly formed Constitutional Union Party. Combined, these three candidates received almost one million more votes than Lincoln.

For southerners, Lincoln's election proved their alarming loss of influence in the nation. He had been elected, despite winning zero electoral votes from the South—not surprising, as he was the candidate from the Republican Party, widely known for its opposition to slavery. The North now dominated politics in the United States, ominous news for the South, because southerners were used to a federal government that protected slavery.[3] Of the thirty-four Supreme Court justices from Washington's presidency on, nineteen had been slaveholders. Those days were over, southerners feared, once a Republican moved into the White House.[4]

Lincoln tried to calm these fears. Although he despised slavery, he tried to reassure people from the South and the border states that he wasn't a radical abolitionist. He opposed slavery's expansion, but he promised not to interfere with slavery where it existed. But most southern whites didn't believe Lincoln, especially when they heard contradictory messages from the North.

Take, for instance, northerners who hailed Lincoln as the second coming of John Brown. "This glorious victory assures the speedy abolition of slavery," proclaimed Methodist minister and abolitionist Gilbert Haven in his sermon *The Cause and Consequence of the Election of Abraham Lincoln*. Brown's attack on slavery was a "heroic deed," said Haven, and Brown died as bravely as any Christian martyr ever had.[5] Lincoln would attack slavery as fiercely as

Brown had, but the president would do it legally—and effectively. This idea horrified southerners and many northerners as well—likely even Lincoln, who tried to distance himself from Brown. Although John Brown possessed "great courage [and] rare unselfishness," he also suffered from insanity, Lincoln said. But the image stuck. In the minds of southerners, Lincoln would use his power to make Brown's abolitionist dreams a reality.[6]

Southerners couldn't forget that a couple of years earlier Lincoln had caused a stir by quoting a Bible verse: "A house divided against itself cannot stand" (cf. Matthew 12:25). Jesus had been referring to the kingdom of God versus the kingdom of Satan, and Lincoln was referring to proslavery versus antislavery Americans. The nation could not live with this conflict; it was extreme, perhaps even as radical as the contrast between God and Satan. As Lincoln said, "This government cannot endure, permanently half *slave* and half *free*." Eventually, slavery would either be extinct or established. The United States could not disagree on slavery and remain *united* states.[7]

These and other statements left no doubt in the South: Lincoln hated slavery. Even so, it wasn't clear how he could have outlawed slavery even if he had wanted to. As a North Carolina newspaper put it, Lincoln was "powerless to do harm to the South if he desired, inasmuch as he has neither judicial nor legislative power to aid him."[8] Over time, however, a president who opposed slavery could outlaw it. Any territories or new states would be free, and eventually free states would outnumber slave states and control the nation.[9] For many in the South, therefore, Lincoln's election spelled the end of the United States as they knew it. The South had to either secede or submit to northern domination.

"Slavery a Divine Trust"

In late November 1860, Benjamin Morgan Palmer, a well-known Presbyterian minister, delivered a message that would reverberate throughout the South. From his pulpit in the First Presbyterian Church in New Orleans, Palmer proclaimed that God had entrusted the South "to conserve and to perpetuate the institution of domestic slavery." Because the South took this responsibility seriously, the nation was on "the brink of revolution." The issue, then, was not only political, but was "a question of morals and religion."[10]

And commerce, of course, had to be considered. Palmer paraphrased a statement from the prophet Obadiah: "All the men of our Confederacy, the men that were at peace with us, have eaten our bread at the very time they have deceived and laid a wound under us" (cf. Obadiah 1:7). This was a verse about betrayal, and it expressed the situation between the North and the South, Palmer said. The North had deceived the South while enjoying the fruits of southern labors. Regardless of what northerners thought of slavery, they profited from it. Slave labor delivered cotton to the North, where northerners produced cloth and then sold it.[11]

Slavery held moral and spiritual value for white southerners. "In this great struggle," Palmer preached, "we defend the cause of God and religion. The abolition spirit is undeniably atheistic." Although abolitionism cloaked itself as a defender of "human rights," its purpose was to divide and to weaken the nation.

With the election of Lincoln, Palmer said that "now, at last" abolitionism "has seated its high priest upon the throne, clad in the black garments of discord and schism." Republicans had devised a party of perjury that threatened the South—comparable to the serpent in the Garden of Eden. The abolitionist "serpent" tempted southerners to abandon slavery. "No: we have seen the trail of the serpent five and twenty years in our Eden; twined now in the branches of the forbidden tree, we feel the pangs of death already begun as its hot breath is upon our cheek, hissing out the original falsehood, 'ye shall not surely die'" (Genesis 3:4). But the South *would* surely die without slavery, and many northerners knew it.[12]

Accusations flew from the North, accusing the South of betraying the nation's sacred founders. But southerners were not rejecting the nation the founders created, Palmer argued, because Lincoln's election had already destroyed it. What should the South do? Palmer drew a bold conclusion: "I throw off the yoke of" Lincoln's government just as the Revolutionary patriots threw off "the yoke of King George III." Palmer's sermon had a large audience. Reportedly two thousand people heard him preach it from his impressive Gothic pulpit, and some ninety thousand copies circulated with several northern and southern newspapers reprinting it.[13]

"What Portion Have We in David?"

Not all southerners were ready to secede, even in the lower South. Georgia congressman Alexander Stephens urged southerners to remain loyal to the Union. In a speech before the Georgia legislature on November 14,

1860, Stephens said that secession violated the Constitution, and the South would be wrong to do so. That same month at St. John's Episcopal Church in Savannah, Georgia, Reverend George Clark preached a fast day sermon from Isaiah: "They shall look unto the earth, and behold trouble in darkness" (Isaiah 8:22). Southerners who thought lightly of secession needed to think again, Clark warned, while describing the nation's obliteration in graphic terms: "I see, springing up from the battered dust of the fair and beautiful Statue of Liberty . . . a hundred headed monster, waving his black flags, and brandishing his blood red weapons."[14]

From the Bible, Americans learned that civil wars were the worst wars, and that even God's chosen nations could self-destruct. The classic case was the divided kingdoms of Israel and Judah (1 Kings 12). David had been the greatest king in Israel's history, but his dynasty crumbled after his death. David's son, Solomon, was a flawed ruler, despite his wealth and wisdom, and Solomon's son, Rehoboam, was even worse. The trouble began on his disastrous coronation day. Rehoboam's advisers counseled him to be good to the people so that they would serve him well. But Rehoboam rejected this advice, blustering that he would be harsher than his father, vowing that his "little finger shall be thicker than my father's loins." Whereas Solomon worked the people hard, Rehoboam would work them harder. "My father hath chastised you with whips, but I will chastise you with scorpions," he warned.

In response, the people rebelled—they wanted nothing to do with David's dynasty: "What portion have we in David?" they asked. Rehoboam's harsh policies had backfired; the rebellion divided his kingdom, with Jeroboam ruling the northern tribes.

What was the result of this rebellion? Did the rebels prosper? No, said John Cotton Smith, an Episcopal minister in New York. Neither kingdom won in this upheaval. Instead, foreign kingdoms invaded and overtook them both. Their civil war resulted only in exile and captivity. "This melancholy history of the rending asunder and the subsequent ruin of a mighty kingdom, has a solemn warning for the people of this land," preached Smith. A civil war would prove tragic for both sides.[15]

Not surprisingly, the South read a different message in this biblical civil war: if the North didn't want a rebellion, then it should stop acting like Rehoboam. As a minister in Charleston, South Carolina, put it, Republicans were modern Rehoboams, saying to the South, "Stand aside, we are holier than you. You are not our equals; you must be content to accept a subordinate position in our [government]." As to your enslaved people, you will hold them "at our option; and when our time shall arrive, you must submit to the loss of your institutions, and acquiesce in our determination for you." Like the people of Israel, then, secessionists were saying to the modern Rehoboams of the Union, "What portion have we in David?"[16]

Even faced with an American Rehoboam as president, the crisis did not have to lead to war, argued many southerners, including ministers who scoured the scriptures to find examples of peaceful separations. They often quoted the story of Abram and Lot, who dealt with the strife between them by agreeing to separate peacefully, each to his own land. Abram said to Lot, "Is not the whole land before thee? separate thyself, I pray thee, from me: if thou wilt take the left hand, then I will go to the right; or if thou depart to the right hand, then I will go to the left" (Genesis 13:9). From a southern perspective, this was a biblical solution to the dispute between northern and southern states. Why didn't the North do as Abram and let the South go without forcing a greedy war?[17]

Regardless of what happened, southerners had to decide where their ultimate loyalty would lie. Another popular scripture in the South after Lincoln's election was Ruth 1:16, which southerners cited to compare their devotion to the South to Ruth's devotion to Naomi. As a contributor to the *Daily Nashville Patriot* wrote in the December 5, 1860, edition, "If the North shall prove to be irremediably drunk with the excess of her recent triumph," then I shall feel like saying to the people of the South, "Whither thou goest I will go, and where thou lodgest I will lodge; thy people shall be my people, and thy God my God."[18]

"Render unto Caesar the Things That Are Caesar's"

Secession provoked a crisis in American patriotism in part because Americans had grown up admiring the courageous patriots of the Revolutionary War. A ruptured nation meant the sacred founders' dream would die; the nation built on liberty would collapse. To avoid this catastrophe, warnings against secession poured from northern pulpits. On January 4, William Adams, cofounder of New York's Union Theological Seminary, preached restraint in his sermon *The Duty of Christian Patriots*. At stake was the nation's legacy of liberty. "What will the nations say if our experiment of self-government should thus early prove a failure? How should we be ashamed to confess before the world our weakness and imbecility, if the bond of our Confederated States should prove a rope of sand, instead of a chain of gold."[19]

The New Testament taught patience in politics, and Americans should follow that direction, Adams said. Jesus and his disciples struggled under a tyrannical Roman Empire. What, then, did Jesus and his disciples do about it? Did they rebel? "Never. The very opposite"—Jesus said, "Render unto Caesar the things that are Caesar's." They hated Roman tyranny, but they knew it would have been futile to fight Rome at the height of its power.[20]

The same was true of slavery—Jesus and Paul knew the time was not right to fight it. The lesson was that "men may be impatient, fret and goad themselves and others into madness, but God has his own time and method, and we do well sometimes to think of the slow yet certain processes of his Spirit and Providence." Both North and South should heed this lesson, said Adams, embracing "patriotism, a true love for country, a sentiment" that "Christianity cherishes." So, "partisanship" should give way to "patriotism," and "sectionalism must give place to an intense love for the whole nationality."[21]

Outgoing president James Buchanan also tried to extinguish the fires of disunion. In his Fourth Annual Message to Congress on December 3, 1860, he combined an argument against secession with an attack on abolitionists who, he believed, had stirred up the trouble. If slavery was a problem, southerners would have to solve it, and they should do so without northern interference. What was needed, Buchanan insisted, was compromise, mainly from Republicans.[22]

Many shared Buchanan's opinion that agitation over slavery was the problem. On December 9, six days after Buchanan's address, Presbyterian Henry Van Dyke preached a controversial sermon, *The Character and Influence of Abolitionism!* in the First Presbyterian Church, Brooklyn, New York. Abolitionism, Van Dyke proclaimed, was "evil and only evil, root and branch, flower and leaf and fruit," a poisonous tree that grew "from and is nourished by an utter rejection of the Scriptures."

Van Dyke argued from both Old and New Testament scriptures, trying to prove that slavery was biblical. He didn't think that slavery would continue for all time, but slavery was "an important and necessary process in [the Africans'] transition from heathenism to Christianity—a wheel in the great machinery of Providence, by which the final redemption is to be accomplished." In contrast, abolitionism was a "stumbling block in the way of the Gospel" in the South. Abolitionism "does not try slavery by the Bible";

instead, "It tries the Bible by the principles of freedom," insisting that "the word of God must be made to support certain human opinions."[23]

Another important biblical issue seized the attention of southern Presbyterian minister Joseph R. Wilson, whose son, Woodrow, would later become the twenty-eighth president of the United States. No one doubted that scripture contained teaching about slavery—enslaved people were present in both testaments, from the patriarchs to Paul. But did slavery in the Bible have anything to do with slavery in the American South? No, said some of slavery's attackers—the slavery of the Bible was an ancient institution, different from American slavery, and so the biblical permissions of slavery no longer applied. If that were true, Joseph Wilson wrote, biblical endorsements of slavery were nothing more than "a dead letter."

But it was not true, Wilson insisted. The Bible was ancient but not dated—its teachings were eternally relevant. "The Bible was intended for all times in all ages, and not for one period and a single country." If the Bible endorsed slavery in the ancient world, that endorsement also applied to the modern world. Slavery was just one of many "inequalities in society," such as relations between parents and children, Wilson believed. Slavery was biblical because of what the scripture said and what it did not say. The Bible contained directions for holding enslaved people, and no biblical text clearly forbade slavery. So, slavery was "directly sanctioned by both the utterance and silence of Scripture."[24]

Others added their voices to this chorus. According to Rabbi Bernard Illowry of Baltimore's Lloyd Street Synagogue, the real biblical issue was not slavery; it was northern interference with southern property. He used Moses an example, arguing that Moses opposed slavery, but he refused to ban slavery. Moses allowed Israelites to buy and sell enslaved captives from other lands. The same was true with Abraham, who received enslaved people as presents from an Egyptian pharaoh. In Rabbi Illowry's view, the nation was heading for disaster because of antislavery zealots who claimed to be more philanthropic than Moses and Abraham. These abolitionists "are not what they pretend to be, the agents of Religion and Philanthropy." The nation had only one chance for salvation: cling to "no other guide than the book of G-d and the virtues which it teaches," which include respect for the slaveholding rights of other states and nations.[25]

Abolitionists had as bad a reputation with some Jews as they did with southern Christians—due mainly to abolitionists who had expressed anti-Semitic views. Theodore Parker, known for his hatred of slavery, called Jews "lecherous" and even diabolical. Jews "did sometimes kill a Christian baby at the Passover," he said. Moreover, perhaps the most famous abolitionist, William Lloyd Garrison, called New York judge Mordecai Manual Noah a "miscreant Jew" and "a Shylock," even "the enemy of Christ and liberty" who descended from "the monsters who nailed Jesus to the cross."[26]

"The Negro Is Not Your Equal, Unless the Bible Be Untrue"

Most white southerners were not slaveholders. By the beginning of the Civil War, 75 percent of white families did not own slaves, and only 3 percent of households included as many as twenty enslaved persons. Would the majority of non-slaveholding whites support secession? Would they go to war to defend slavery? These questions concerned those who supported secession, especially slaveholders. They knew that some northerners, including Lincoln, believed that non-slaveholding southerners would remain loyal to the Union in the current crisis.[27]

This would be a disaster, secessionists believed, and they looked for ways to convince *all* southern whites to support slavery and secession. A critical book was *The Interest in Slavery of the Southern Non-Slaveholder*, published in 1860 by James D. B. De Bow. Slavery, De Bow argued, rested "upon the sure testimony of God's Holy Book," and it protected the interests of all white southerners. Non-slaveholders, he argued, were better off in the South than in the North, where they would have to compete for jobs in crowded sweatshops and dirty factories. More importantly, the southern non-slaveholder enjoyed "the status of the white man, and is not regarded as an inferior or a dependant."[28]

Whites had a responsibility to uphold their supremacy over blacks, De Bow argued. To support this view, he cited the argument against slavery that came from the biblical teaching of the jubilee year, an event occurring every fifty years, when God required Israelites to release enslaved people (Leviticus 25). De Bow and others pointed out that the jubilee referred only to Israelite slaves of the Israelite people, not "slaves of foreign birth. There was no year of jubilee provided for them."[29] According to this argument, Africans could be enslaved because they were foreign and racially inferior to whites.

To persuade non-slaveholding southerners to back secession, therefore, slaveholders appealed to white supremacy. Republicans, they argued, elevated African Americans to the status of whites. If Lincoln and the

Republicans had their way, a Georgia man said, "in TEN years or less our CHILDREN will be the *slaves* of negroes."[30]

Southern ministers added their voices to the white supremacist argument. Within two weeks of Lincoln's election, James C. Furman, a Baptist minister and president of Furman University, joined three colleagues to publish a "Letter to the Citizens of the Greenville District," which attempted to recruit South Carolinians to the secessionist cause. The letter attacked "the Gospel of Northern fanaticism," namely the view "that every man is born free and equal." This idea "contradicts common sense, contradicts all history, contradicts the Bible." If this idea were to win out, as Lincoln and the Republicans planned, "Abolition preachers will be at hand to consummate the marriage of your daughters to black husbands!" Southern women would face this reality "if their fathers and their brothers have not the spirit to break loose from a government whose elected Chief Magistrate aims to establish such a state of things."[31]

The Bible supported white supremacy, Furman and his colleagues believed, asserting that "the negro is not your equal, unless the Bible be untrue." One needed to look no further than the Ten Commandments to find support for slavery: "Thou shalt not covet thy neighbor's . . . *man servant*, nor his *maid servant*'" (Exodus 20:17). There was also plenty of support for slavery in the New Testament. To cite one example, the Furman letter called on Paul's letter to Philemon, noting that Paul sent the slave Onesimus home to his owner, Philemon. Abolitionists—not Paul—would have helped Onesimus to escape, because Paul supported the rights of slaveowners. According to the Furman letter, then, abolitionist "tirades against slaveholders" were "an outrage on the authority of God's word."[32]

Although Furman and his coauthors said that "the negro is not your equal, unless the Bible be untrue," they cited no biblical justification for this claim. The texts they discussed pertained to slavery only, not race. They assumed that any biblical reference that endorsed slavery also endorsed black inferiority, because only blacks were suited to slavery. This was nothing new. Long before the Civil War whites who used the Bible to support slavery assumed that all slavery was black slavery. They rarely considered that if the Bible endorsed slavery, why not enslave whites?[33]

A few whites made this point before the Civil War. In 1849, James M. Pendleton of Kentucky had heard enough of the ridiculous claims that slavery was a benevolent institution where enslaved people were virtuous and happy. If it were true that "slavery promotes the holiness and happiness of slaves," he said, then slaveholders should enslave whites as well. Why should whites miss out on the "holiness and happiness" of human bondage?[34]

In 1851, John G. Fee, another Kentucky minister, called out this racist assumption about biblical slavery. The apostles, he said, knew nothing about black slavery. For them, "SLAVERY WAS WHITE SLAVERY." In the New Testament era, "The large portion of those enslaved were *as white, and many of them whiter than their masters.*" This was slavery in the Roman Empire, and "The Romans had no slave trade to the western coast of Africa." It followed, therefore, that if "the apostles sanctioned slavery, they sanctioned white slavery."[35]

Why enslave only blacks? Because, many whites believed, blacks were intellectually inferior to whites. This was poor logic, Fee said. Even if one could prove whites were intellectually superior to blacks, that wouldn't justify enslaving blacks. Superior intelligence did not give one the right to enslave those less intelligent. If it did, "The most intellectual man that exists may have a right to enslave every other man—white and black," Fee wrote. Also, intellectual capacity aside, physical difference—including darker skin—did not justify enslavement. If that were the case, the fairest-skinned person in the world would have the right to enslave everyone else. So, "Black skin, and all the features of the negro, do not of themselves constitute a reason why a man should be enslaved."[36]

Another man from Kentucky—Abraham Lincoln—made a similar argument when debating Stephen Douglas in 1858: "In Kentucky, perhaps, in many of the Slave States certainly, you are trying to establish the rightfulness of Slavery by reference to the Bible," Lincoln said. "You are trying to show that slavery existed in the Bible times by Divine ordinance." Yet Stephen Douglas had not mentioned this biblical argument. Why? Because "Douglas knows that whenever you establish that Slavery was right by the Bible, it will occur that that Slavery was the Slavery of the white man—of men without reference to color."[37] Few whites appreciated Lincoln's point.

During the secession crisis, therefore, James C. Furman and other secessionists in South Carolina could assert with confidence—but without biblical evidence—"The negro is not your equal, unless the Bible be untrue."[38] It was time to take a stand against Republican radicalism, Furman and his colleagues believed. "What shall the State do?" they asked rhetorically. "Shall she remain in a Union thus attended with danger and dishonor, 'to be girt about by a belt of fire,' or driven to die like a poisoned rat in its hole? Or shall she assume her unquestionable Independence, ready to enter, when other Southern States shall be prepared for it, into a new confederacy with them?"[39]

Furman and his coauthors were preaching to the choir, at least in their home state. Less than one month later, on December 20, 1860, South Carolina became the first state to secede from the Union. After the convention in South Carolina voted unanimously for secession, other states in the lower South followed suit: Mississippi (January 9, 1861), Florida (January 10), Alabama (January 11), Georgia (January 19), Louisiana (January 26), and Texas (February 1). Several of these votes were close, with contentious debates and much opposition to secession. However, that did not stop many southerners from exaggerating, claiming that the votes were nearly unanimous. As a Louisiana senator put it, the move for secession was "a revolution . . . of the most intense character," and it could "no more be" extinguished "than a prairie fire by a gardener's watering pot."[40]

Many in the Upper South wanted to throw water on that fire. After all, folks in Virginia, Tennessee, and North Carolina were closer to the North, and were in the direct line of fire if war started. The Lower South had lost its mind, according to Reverend B. F. Brooke, a Methodist minister in Virginia. He preached to the YMCA on February 3. The next day the seven states that had seceded would meet to form the Confederate States of America, and just over a week later his home state would hold a convention to decide about secession. The timing was right for Brooke's sermon. Although he was in the minority, he begged Virginians to stay out of the Confederacy.

Brooke saw in these days "tidings of Civil war! Which may drench this land of WASHINGTON in brothers' blood from Atlantic waves to Pacific shores!" He cautioned Virginians to avoid the disease emanating from South Carolina, a state that was "like the Red Dragon in the Apocalypse, curling his tail" around the other states, dragging "them down to the tail-end of a Confederacy, of which she hopes to be the head" (cf. Revelation 12:3–4; Ezekiel 29:3–4). He supported the Union because of the nation's "religious mission and destiny." This nation had a role to play in redeeming the world. "American, protestant Christianity was the lever by which Providence was to lift the world to its predicted spiritual grandeur." This nation "was discovered for Christ, and this Union built for the spread of his kingdom."[41]

"The Stone Which the Builders Rejected Is Become the Head Stone"

The Confederate States of America elected Jefferson Davis president on February 9, 1861. Davis, former secretary of war and senator from Mississippi, won fame for his heroic service in the Mexican War. Alexander Hamilton Stephens of Georgia accepted the vice presidency of the Confederacy. Stephens, nicknamed "Little Ellick" because he weighed not much more than one hundred pounds, had served in the House of Representatives, was a friend of Abraham Lincoln's, and had urged southerners to move cautiously before breaking up the nation. Stephens wanted to protect slavery, but he also wanted secession to be a last resort.[42]

Once the secessionist die was cast, Stephens delivered the most memorable speech of the new Confederacy: the so-called cornerstone speech. Stephens did not cite a specific verse from scripture, but he referred to a statement that appears in several forms in the Bible, including, "The stone which the builders rejected is become the head of the corner" (cf. Mark 12:10).[43] This image referred to a great reversal—that which was rejected became the most important of all. In the New Testament, this statement referred to Jesus, who suffered ridicule and crucifixion, but rose from the dead to become the resurrected Lord. In Stephens's speech, slavery was the stone that the builders rejected, and it had become the "cornerstone" of the Confederacy.

As Stephens proclaimed this, the audience applauded, because many white southerners agreed that race-based slavery was the "cornerstone" of the South's economy and society. But who were the "builders" who had rejected this "cornerstone"? None other than the founders—Benjamin Franklin, George Washington, and especially Thomas Jefferson. Although southerners had tried to claim the founders for their side, pointing out that most of them owned slaves, Alexander Stephens gave up the argument. The founders had failed, he admitted, because they believed "that the enslavement of the African was in violation of the laws of nature; that it was wrong in principle, socially, morally and politically." The founders believed slavery was evil, and they hoped "that, somehow or other," through "Providence, the institution would be evanescent and pass away." On this point, the founders "were fundamentally wrong." They erroneously assumed racial equality. The Confederacy "is founded upon exactly the opposite idea"—the "cornerstone" of the Confederacy was "the great truth that the Negro is not equal to the white man; that slavery, subordination to the superior race, is his natural and moral condition," Stephens said.[44]

Stephens's cornerstone speech made an impression on the South. It was one of the most widely distributed speeches after secession. But its statement about the founders provoked controversy.[45] Were they really believers in racial equality? Many southerners scoffed at the suggestion, but Stephens had struck a nerve. Southerners wondered about the Declaration of Independence, with its statement that "all men are created equal." Did not this statement undermine slavery?

Yes, claimed Abraham Lincoln. In a speech delivered at Independence Hall in February 1861, Lincoln said, "I have never had a feeling politically that did not spring from the sentiments embodied in the Declaration of Independence." For Lincoln, the Declaration promised "liberty, not alone to the people of this country, but hope to the world for all future time." As Lincoln said, "the sentiment embodied in that Declaration of Independence" was that "the weights should be lifted from the shoulders of all men, and that all should have an equal chance." If that principle died, so did the nation, in Lincoln's view. "I would rather be assassinated on this spot than to surrender" this principle expressed in the Declaration.[46]

Statements such as this turned Stephens and some other southerners against the Declaration of Independence. As a Presbyterian from Charleston, South Carolina, said, "the Declaration is Godless." Even though it mentioned the "Creator," it quickly "banished" God to preach human equality, which was "an atheistic, revolutionary and anarchic principle."[47]

Despite the Declaration of Independence, many southerners refused to believe that the founders opposed slavery and white supremacy. Several of the founders owned enslaved people, after all. And even if the Declaration seemed to promote equity, the founders corrected this error in the Constitution. William L. Harris, a commissioner from Mississippi, told the House of Representatives in Georgia that "our fathers made this a government for the white man, rejecting the negro, as an ignorant, inferior, barbarian race, incapable of self-government, and not, therefore, entitled to be associated with the white man upon terms of civil, political, or socially equality." In his appeal for Georgia to follow Mississippi in voting for secession, Harris said citizens of his state would rather die "than see them subjected to the degradation of civil, political and social equality with the negro race."[48]

Jefferson Davis agreed. In his farewell speech to the Senate on January 21, Davis said, "The sacred Declaration of Independence has been invoked to maintain the position of the equality of the races." This was wrong. The Declaration of Independence included "no reference to the slave." The statement "All men are created free and equal" only referred to men who could vote. The purpose was to deny that anyone had the "divine right to rule," referring to the inherited privileges of monarchs like King George III. To apply the Declaration of Independence to slavery was to take it out of context and to distort its purpose. Thankfully, the founders reaffirmed their beliefs about slavery more clearly in the Constitution, saying enslaved people did not merit "equality with white men—not even upon that of paupers and convicts." Instead, the Constitution "discriminated against" enslaved people, valuing them at "three fifths" of a white person.[49]

By the time of Lincoln's inauguration on March 4, 1861, Jefferson Davis had served for almost a month as provisional president of the Confederate States. Seven states of the Lower South had joined the Confederacy, but eight states in the Upper South—in addition to the border states—remained in the Union. Lincoln wanted to keep it that way, so he used his first inaugural address to reject the idea of secession. It was, according to Jill Lepore, "the most eloquent inaugural address in American history."[50]

"The Union of these States is perpetual," Lincoln said. Against Confederate claims that the Union was always secondary to state sovereignty and could be terminated at any time the states desired, Lincoln said that "no government proper, ever had a provision in its organic law for its own termination." One of the Constitution's major objectives was "to form a more perfect Union," which it could not be "if destruction of the Union, by one, or by a part only, of the States, be lawfully possible." No "state, upon its own mere motion, can lawfully get out of the Union." And any violent attacks on the United States by a state "are insurrectionary or revolutionary." "Plainly," he said, "the central idea of secession, is the essence of anarchy." Secession rejected the majority, which "is the only true sovereign of a free people." In Lincoln's view, the Union had formed the states, not vice versa.

Lincoln closed his address with a theological reflection on patience and providence. Both North and South stood confident in their own positions, but God would decide the matter in time. "If the Almighty Ruler of Nations, with his eternal truth and justice, be on your side of the North, or on yours of the South, that truth and that justice will surely prevail by the judgment of this great tribunal of the American people." The fact that he, a Republican president, took office should not compel southerners to secede. Neither his presidency, nor any "administration, by any extreme of wickedness or folly, can very seriously injure the government in the short space of four years," he said. "My countrymen, one and all, think calmly and well upon this whole subject. Nothing valuable can be lost by taking time." The United States had much going for it even in this crisis. "Intelligence, patriotism, Christianity, and a firm reliance on Him who has never yet forsaken this favored land, are still competent to adjust in the best way all our present difficulty." Secession showed a lack of faith in God's commitment to "his favored land."[51]

Above all, secession provoked questions of authority. Under what authority did the southern states secede from the Union? Under what authority could the national government wage war to force the Confederate States back into the Union? When debating these questions, northerners and southerners disagreed on how to speak coherently from their authoritative texts—the Declaration of Independence, the Constitution, and the Bible. Although some Americans cautioned restraint and reflection, often even they sensed that it was too late—war was looming, and with it would come battles over the Bible that would parallel the battles that ravished the nation.

3

"The Red Sea of War"

War may be hell, but even hell had advantages. Although detractors cautioned that a civil war would devastate the country, many northerners praised war's benefits. Six months after the war began, *Harper's Weekly* ran an article, "War as a Schoolmaster," that lambasted opponents who had droned on with platitudes "about the evils of war." Northerners had heard enough of that. "Too little attention" focused on "the benefits of war." Namely, "Peace enervates and corrupts society; war strengthens and purifies." In peacetime, people worshiped luxury and money. "If this evil can be cured, it must be done by raising up some rival influence to that of sheer dollars. This a war will do." War "appeals to our noblest and purest impulses—courage, honor, patriotism, self-devotion, self-denial." War counteracted the acquisitive spirit of the marketplace that corrupted the nation. "The merchant's aim is profit, the soldier's, glory. The merchant's means are cunning and calculation, the soldier's, daring and chivalry." War was good because it "will consolidate us as a nation." Peace and prosperity sapped a nation of its vigor. "Half a century of undisputed peace and the pursuit of gain have rusted [Americans'] hearts."[1]

War, then, made people better, and it made nations better. This same enthusiasm for the war filled the nation six months earlier. As news spread about the crisis at Fort Sumter, many in the North responded with righteous fury. They picked up their weapons and their Bibles to make a case for a war. Leading the way was Henry Ward Beecher, who proclaimed one of many views on the Exodus in the war. Other northern clergy—including Catholics—joined him in arousing zeal for the war, helping Abraham Lincoln to recruit volunteers for his army.

"We Never Were Alive Till Now"

Just as secession had begun in South Carolina, so did the war. The nation focused on Charleston's picturesque harbor, which had two forts, Moultrie and Sumter. As the secession crisis intensified, these forts stood in a precarious position. While they belonged to the federal government, Confederates believed the forts were rightfully theirs, and they had no intention of allowing Lincoln to seize them.

In the spotlight was Major Robert Anderson, a career military man who hated war and a former slaveowner who loved the Union. An 1825 graduate of West Point, he served in the Mexican War, where he distinguished himself as an impressive leader.[2] Anderson had commanded Fort Moultrie since November 1860, when President Buchanan put him in this difficult position and did little to support him. As he assessed the situation, Anderson knew that his best chance of holding off Confederate attacks was to move his men from Fort Moultrie to Fort Sumter. Not only was Moultrie a relic, it was too close to the mainland, which left it vulnerable to attack. Not only was Sumter more strategically located, but it was also a new fort—technically not quite completed—and it had forty-foot walls that offered greater protection. Anderson waited until Christmas and then, under the cover of nightfall, he and his men rowed across the harbor to Fort Sumter. The next day, Charlestonians looked across the water and saw the US flag flying over Sumter. They may have been too far away to hear the band playing "Hail Columbia," and soldiers cheering their flag in the face of Confederate authority.[3]

With news of Anderson's daring feat spreading quickly, the North had its first hero—and a Christian hero at that. "I put my trust in God," Anderson said, "and I firmly believe that God put it into my heart to do what I did." It was God, Anderson continued, who directed "every act that was performed in that harbor from the 21st of November, when I took command."[4]

Although the North hailed Anderson's heroism, Charleston residents seethed. Confederate troops took over Fort Moultrie and aimed their guns at Sumter. Finally, President Buchanan came to Anderson's aid. On January 9, the *Star of the West*, a ship filled with provisions and two hundred men, entered Charleston Harbor. Even though this was not a military vessel, Charlestonians would have none of it. Guns blazed from the Charleston battery, pushing the *Star of the West* away from Sumter.

Anderson's situation was desperate. He refused to return fire, not wanting the blame for starting a civil war. Instead he asked for help. With less than two months of supplies left, he sent a dispatch to Buchanan on February 28. That dispatch, and the problems it described, soon became Abraham Lincoln's.[5]

President Lincoln received Anderson's message on the morning of his first day in office. This was an ominous beginning for his presidency, and it would not improve. Four years later Ralph Waldo Emerson wrote of "the whirlwind of war" that greeted Lincoln when he arrived at the White House. "Here was place for no holiday magistrate, no fair-weathered sailor; the new pilot was hurried to the helm in a tornado." Lincoln was unprepared to be a wartime president, especially when compared with his chief adversary, Jefferson Davis, a graduate of West Point who served admirably in the Mexican War. Right away, then, the crisis tested Lincoln's resolve. Would he make good his promise to "hold, occupy and possess" all federal property, including Fort Sumter?[6]

Lincoln agonized over this decision. The stress almost overwhelmed him; his head ached and he lost countless hours of sleep. Later, when he thought of this period, he said, "of all the trials I have had since I came here, none begin to compare with those I had between the inauguration and the fall of Fort Sumpter [sic]. They were so great that could I have anticipated them, I would not have believed it possible to survive them."[7]

With Anderson and his garrison outnumbered in Fort Sumter, Lincoln faced a dilemma with several scenarios. In early April, Lincoln decided. Refusing to launch a full-scale assault on Charleston Harbor, and thus take the blame for starting the war, Lincoln approved a peaceful mission to bring supplies to Sumter. Warships would accompany the supply tugs but would stand idle unless the Confederates fired first. If the war started, the blame would fall on the Confederate States, Lincoln surmised. If that happened, it would unite and enrage the North, and would likely alienate many southerners. Yet if southerners held their fire and let the supplies reach Sumter, the North would maintain control over this important fort in the center of the Confederacy. This approach was genius. Either way, Lincoln figured, he won, and Jefferson Davis lost.[8]

The South fired first. Knowing that a fleet of ships was on its way to relieve Sumter, Charleston commander P. G. T. Beauregard had orders to capture the fort as soon as possible. Led by Beauregard, Confederates launched their attack before dawn on April 12. Meanwhile, Lincoln's fleet of ships, led by Gustavus V. Fox, encountered bad weather that prevented them from aiding Sumter in the battle. By the time Anderson surrendered thirty-three hours later, Sumter was ablaze, having endured four thousand hits while returning about one thousand rounds in the fort's defense. On the afternoon of April 13, Beauregard telegrammed Jefferson Davis: "Quarters in Sumter all burned down. White flag up. Have sent a boat to receive surrender." Davis replied: "If occasion offers, tender my friendly remembrance to Major Anderson."[9]

Nothing inspired patriotism like war. Many northerners who had expressed reluctance for war now relished it. "It seems as if we never were alive till now; never had a country till now," said a man from New York. Lincoln did not want war, but if war had to come, all the better that the South started it and that he had the North behind him. "They attacked Sumter," Lincoln said. "It fell and thus did more service than it otherwise would."[10]

"The Red Sea of War"

Christianity was a religion of peace—virtually all ministers and church members, North and South, seemed to agree on that conviction. But few of them were pacifists. Among Quakers and other religious groups that were traditionally pacifist, the loss of Sumter meant that they had to wrestle with their convictions, and often with their neighbors, who challenged them to join the fight. Just over a week after Sumter fell, Ann Stevens, a Quaker from East Montpelier, Vermont, prayed for peace. Even with the war fever raging, she held out hope that God would "have mercy and turn the thunderbolt from this land."[11]

Such hopes for peace were mere fantasies, in the view of Henry Ward Beecher. For him, the Bible favored war in these times, and he made no apologies for it. In fact, the term "Beecher's Bibles" came to be known as a common reference for rifles, since Beecher famously remarked that "the Sharp's rifle was a truly *moral* agency, and . . . there was more moral power in one of those instruments, so far as the slaveholders of Kansas were con-cerned, than in a hundred Bibles."[12] Not surprisingly, then, as the drama unfolded in Charleston Harbor, Beecher called the North to war. And he did so in perhaps the most cited northern sermon after Sumter—a sermon that drew the nation's attention to the book of Exodus.[13]

Americans knew the story—the people of Israel were in Egypt, suffering under slavery. Moses arose as God's freedom fighter, the man called to lead the people out of bondage.[14] Called by God, Moses said to Pharaoh: "Let my people go!" When Pharaoh refused, God sent plagues, including frogs, disease, locusts, hail, lice, water that turned to blood, and darkness. Only the last and most terrible plague—the curse of death on Egypt's first-born children—persuaded Pharaoh to let the people go (Exodus 7–12).

Just as quickly, however, Pharaoh wanted his enslaved workforce back. He pursued the Israelites to the edge of the Red Sea. As the they watched the advancing Egyptian armies, terror gripped them. Surely, they would be slaughtered! Was it because "there were no more graves in Egypt" that Moses doomed them to death in the wilderness? Given the choice between death and slavery, the Israelites preferred slavery. This was not surprising, Beecher said. It was "just what slavery makes everybody to be." Slavery robbed people of their natural desire for liberty.[15]

But Americans needed to inspire that desire for liberty if they were to defeat slavery. The cost would be high—only war and bloodshed could pay it. For most people, war was fine if someone else was doing the fighting. And that "someone else" in scripture was often God. It was tempting to call on God to fight the battles. This option attracted many in the North, even those opposed to slavery. Perhaps, in time, God would find a way to defeat slavery without war. Faith in providence, it seemed, often was no faith at all but only cowardly avoidance.

Even Moses fell for this temptation, telling the Israelites to "stand still" and that God would "fight for you." But Moses was wrong, Beecher said, so God corrected him, saying, "Speak unto the children of Israel, that they go forward." That is, demand that the Israelites do something for themselves. Beecher put it this way—God's people were "to dare something for their liberty. No standing still, but going forward!"

The Israelites did "go forward," and in a most dramatic fashion. "Lift up thy rod," God told Moses, "and stretch out thine hand over these, and divide it." Moses did as God commanded, and the Red Sea divided, allowing the Israelites to walk through the sea on a path of dry land, with the waters standing as a wall on either side of them. When the Egyptians tried to pursue them, the walls of water collapsed, drowning them.[16]

God wouldn't defeat the Egyptians alone, but rather commanded the Israelites to join the fight. That was the message the North needed to hear in Sumter's wake. Victory meant sacrifice. God said, "Go forward! Venture everything! Endure everything! Yield the precious truths never!" God required courage.[17] "Right before us lies the Red Sea of war. It is red indeed. There is blood in it. We have come to the very edge of it, and the Word of God to us to-day is, 'Speak unto this people that they go forward!' "[18]

It didn't surprise Beecher that southern states seceded—the South had never been patriotic, he said. "There has been a spirit of patriotism in the North; but never . . . in the South. I never heard a man from the South speak of himself as an American. Men from the South always speak of themselves as Southerners." Southerners were "hot, narrow, and boastful"—they would take the American eagle, "strike out his eyes," and "pluck off his wings."[19]

Wars needed heroes. In fact, war created heroes, in scripture as well as in the United States. If God decided "to wrap this nation in war," God would call the people "to the heroism of doing and daring, and bearing and suffering, for the things which we believe to be vital to the salvation of this people."[20]

"Sometimes Gunpowder Smells Good"

Where would Lincoln find these heroes? His army was in no shape to wage war. He could call on over 15,000 men enlisted in the army and over 1,000 officers. But those numbers were deceptive, as over 30 percent of these officers were southerners, most of whom likely would join the Confederacy if the war started. To make matters worse, the army was scattered across the nation—many were in the West, far from where Lincoln needed them.[21]

Additionally, there was the tricky issue of calling the army to service. According to the Constitution, Congress, not the president, had the authority to call armies into action.[22] But Congress was not in session and could not be quickly reconvened. Lincoln ultimately exercised the Militia Act, dating back to Washington's presidency, which gave the president authority to call up state militias for federal service for ninety days.[23]

Southerners fumed. "President Lincoln does not pause," a Charleston editorialist wrote. "He boldly calls for seventy five thousand men of the militia of the Northern states, to conquer and subdue seven sovereign States who have left the late Union." Paraphrasing Jesus's statement that "all they that take the sword shall perish with the sword," this editorialist said of Lincoln: "Seeking the sword, in spite of all moral or constitutional restraints and obligations, he may perish by the sword."[24]

Despite such protests, the Militia Act probably did grant Lincoln the right to call for the state militia. But it did not give him the authority do what he did on May 3—call for additional state volunteers (some 43,034 men), and add 22,714 soldiers to the army and 18,000 to the navy. Lincoln had also overstepped his constitutional boundaries on April 19, when he ordered a blockade on southern ports. Congress later voted to legalize Lincoln's actions.[25]

When Lincoln later recalled his technically unconstitutional actions during the crisis, he said, "Was it possible to lose the nation, and yet preserve the constitution? By general law life *and* limb must be protected; yet often a limb must be amputated to save a life; but a life is never wisely given to save a limb. I felt that measures, otherwise unconstitutional, might become lawful, by becoming indispensable to the preservation of the constitution, through the preservation of the nation."[26]

Lincoln would show the Confederacy that he meant business. A strong exercise of military force could intimidate the Confederates into abandoning the rebellion. Most southerners, Lincoln believed, remained loyal to the Union in their hearts (except in South Carolina). He was wrong. When Lincoln called for state militias to defend the Union, states in the Upper South refused. These states had refrained from seceding, but that did not mean that they were willing to fight their neighbors. They had remained neutral, but now Lincoln forced their hand, and they joined the Confederacy. "Tennessee will not furnish a single man for . . . coercion," the governor of Tennessee said, "but fifty thousand if necessary for the defense of our rights and those of our Southern brothers." Similar responses came from other states.[27] On May 15, a North Carolinian expressed the thoughts of many: "I think the South is committing suicide, but my lot is cast with the South and being unable to manage the ship, I intend to face the breakers manfully and go down with my companions."[28] North Carolina seceded five days later.

States in the Upper South continued to join the secession. On June 8, Tennessee seceded, despite objections from the strongly anti-secessionist east Tennessee, bringing the total number of states in the Confederacy to eleven.[29] Following Virginia's secession, the capital of the Confederate government moved from Montgomery, Alabama, to Richmond, Virginia. As historian Allen Guelzo wrote, "Lincoln could now look out of the White House windows and see the new Confederate flag waving naughtily from housetops across the Potomac in Alexandria."[30]

Lincoln's call for state volunteers infuriated the South and inspired the North.[31] One Vermont minister was thrilled by his state's response to Lincoln's call. "The people of the loyal States are all moved by the same mighty spirit of patriotism," he preached. As in the Bible, the time had come to follow the advice of Joab, David's military commander, and "be of good courage, and let us play the men for our people, and for the cities of our God" (2 Samuel 10:12). This verse could fit into nearly any wartime situation; it was masculine and powerful—like David, Joab, and all other true warriors. With these words, God commanded northern men to "be of good courage"—that is, be real men, and defend "the cities of our God."[32] Evidently many northerners were ready to follow Joab's call—in all, Lincoln asked for seventy-five thousand men and eventually received approximately ninety thousand.[33]

Even as they pushed toward war, Americans began to see what it meant for God's people to kill each other. Put aside the question of whether the United States was a Christian nation—many Americans thought it was. What would happen to the faith, then, when that Christian nation erupted in violence? Christians in the North would fight Christians in the South who worshiped and believed in much the same ways. Baptists would fight Baptists; Methodists would fight Methodists, and Presbyterians would fight Presbyterians—a difficult reality for many Christians to face.

The situation was different for religious groups outside of the Protestant mainstream. Anti-Catholicism flooded the Protestant-dominated United States, and this was nothing new. Fear and hatred of Catholicism had developed from the Reformation and intensified during the American Revolution as colonial Protestants viewed Catholicism as an anti-biblical and anti-republican religion. As Mark Noll states, "From earliest days, and deep into American history, positive commitment to Scripture remained extreme because of extreme Protestant depictions of Catholicism as an anti-biblical religion." This anti-Catholic fervor reached new heights in antebellum America, due in part to revivals called the "Second Great Awakening," but the main contributing factor was the rapid increase in Catholic immigration, especially from Ireland but also from Germany. By the beginning of the war, approximately one out of ten Americans was Catholic, with as many as 3.1 million Catholics in the nation. For many Protestants, the pope was the "anti-Christ" and Catholic Church was "the whore of Babylon," a reference from the book of Revelation (chapter 17). Some northern Protestants were as anti-Catholic as they were antislavery, because they saw both as anti-republican, anti-biblical, and anti-American.[34]

Leading up to the Civil War, most Catholics—unlike most Protestants—avoided the crisis and tried to say no more than they had to on political issues. At the Ninth Provincial Council of Baltimore in 1858, bishops cautioned priests against speaking out on politics. During the war, most Catholics followed the views of their regions or remained silent. The situation was particularly dicey in the North, where Catholics were divided over the war. Many northern Catholics supported the Democratic Party and often opposed Lincoln, the war, and abolitionism. Other Catholics supported the war. An estimated 145,000 Irish Catholics fought for the Union, and many of them saw military service as an opportunity to prove their loyalty to the United States. On April 21, Father Creedon of Auburn, New York, urged the men of his congregation to answer President Lincoln's call to support the Union. "This is the first country the Irishman ever had that he could call his own country. The flag of the Stars and Stripes is the only flag he can fight under and defend as his own flag." Now, as civil war approached, "Let every Irishman show that he is worthy to be part of this great and glorious nation." There could be no compromise in such dire times. In Father Creedon's view, "There are two classes whom I most despise—cowards and traitors; and those who can enlist, and do not, are either one or the other."[35]

Other Catholics agreed, and believed that military service would earn the respect of all Americans. Orestes Brownson, one of the few leading Catholics who voted for Lincoln, attacked secession, saying, "The American citizen who seeks to overthrow the American government is not only a traitor, but . . . a dis-humanized monster not fit to live or to inhabit any part of this globe: he has no suitable place this side of hell."[36]

This kind of zeal for war inspired many northerners after Sumter. "Sometimes gunpowder smells good," wrote Ralph Waldo Emerson in April 1861.[37] Some of the North's leading library figures shared Emerson's excitement. "I've often longed to see a war," wrote *Little Women* author Louisa May Alcott, "and now I have my wish. I long to be a man, but as I can't fight, I will content myself with working for those who can."[38] Nathaniel Hawthorne agreed, writing in May 1861: "The war, strange to say, has had a beneficial effect upon my spirits." He continued, "It was delightful to share in the heroic sentiment of the time, and to feel that I had a country." Hawthorne only regretted that "I am too old to shoulder a musket myself."[39]

4

"This Second War I Consider Equally as Holy as the First"

Americans rarely saw flags until 1861. Few people put up flags outside their homes, and churches did not normally fly them. With the onset of the war, however, flags appeared everywhere in the North—in churches, homes, businesses, and elsewhere. The flag northerners flew honored the nation of the beloved founders—a flag descended from the flag of the American Revolution—and as northerners honored the flag, they compared their war with the Revolutionary War. "This second war I consider equally as holy as the first," said a soldier from Wisconsin. The Revolution was the war "by which we gained those liberties and privileges" that the South threatened. So now they had to fight a civil war—which "is a calamity to any country"—to save the nation from "this monstrous rebellion."[1]

Not to be outdone, southerners insisted that they, not the northern aggressors, were carrying on the revolutionary legacy. "The present is by far the most important and glorious struggle through which the nation has ever passed," said Benjamin Morgan Palmer in 1861. "The parallel which has been drawn between it and the contest of the Revolution, has not been seen in its full significance," he said.[2] Many southerners cited this parallel—they were the revolutionaries, the heirs of the patriots of 1776, now fighting a new tyrannical nation—the United States was the new British tyranny, and Abraham Lincoln was the new George III.

Which side was more faithful to the American Revolution? Americans debated this question throughout the war, and never more fervently than at the war's beginning. As each side claimed to be most faithful to the patriots of 1776, they employed the Bible to support their arguments and to recruit soldiers for the fight.

Along with all the flag-waving and patriotic rhetoric, two biblical texts rose to prominence, especially in the North: Paul's command to obey civil rulers in Romans 13 and the tragic rebellion of Absalom, David's son. Discussions of these biblical texts continued throughout the war, but they were never more important than in the early days of the conflict. Through these biblical passages and others, ministers seized their militant calling during this time, publicizing their responsibility to proclaim the sacred character of a "second American Revolution" that would be as holy as the first.

"He Beareth Not the Sword in Vain"

Rebellions weren't always evil—most Americans agreed on that point. The patriots of the American Revolution were rebels against Britain, and they would likely have suffered execution if the Revolution had failed. "It is difficult, sometimes, to mark the line between an unrighteous rebellion and a righteous revolution," said William Barrows of Reading, Massachusetts, to a company of Massachusetts volunteers. Furthermore, he noted that often "the unsuccessful revolutionist is called a traitor, and the successful one a patriot."[3]

As Americans considered the merits of the southern "revolution," they often looked to the Bible, and one of the most important scriptures they found was Romans 13:

> Let every soul be subject unto the higher powers. For there is no power but of God: the powers that be are ordained of God. Whosoever therefore resisteth the power, resisteth the ordinance of God: and they that resist shall receive to themselves damnation. For rulers are not a terror to good works, but to the evil. Wilt thou then not be afraid of the power? do that which is good, and thou shalt have praise of the same: For he is the minister of God to thee for good. But if thou do that which is evil, be afraid; for he beareth not the sword in vain: for he is the minister of God, a revenger to execute wrath upon him that doeth evil. (Romans 13:1–4)

After the fall of Sumter, Unionists had to walk a fine line. From one perspective, Paul's strong enforcement of political authority helped their cause. The Lincoln-led United States represented God, and the southern rebels had sinned by rebelling. And yet Unionists had to deal with the legacy of the Revolution. The heroic patriots of 1776 rebelled against the king, yet surely they had not violated Paul's commands. (It is little wonder that Romans 13 was a much-debated text during the American Revolution.)[4] Only one conclusion was possible—Paul had set the bar for revolution high, but he had not ruled it out. What, then, distinguished the godly revolution of 1776 from the evil rebellion of 1861?

One minister who took on this question after Sumter's fall was Samuel Spear, a Presbyterian pastor in Brooklyn, New York. The Confederate rebellion, he argued, violated Paul's command that Christians obey the government. To emphasize just how strong Paul's defense of political authorities was, Spear pointed out that Paul lived under Emperor Nero, a persecutor of Christians and "one of the most barbarous and cruel monarchs that ever disgraced the civil power." Yet Paul demanded obedience to the political ruler, *even* if that ruler was the infamous Nero. If Paul demanded that Christians obey Nero's government, what would he say to the Confederates as they rebelled against the United States? No matter what they thought of Lincoln, he was better than Nero.[5]

According to this scripture, therefore, the southern rebellion was not only treasonous, it was sinful. Speaking of the Confederates, this preacher said: "I confess myself utterly unable to see how they can ignore the claims of the Apostle's precept."[6]

If Paul would condemn the rebellion of 1861, why would he have approved the revolution of 1776? First, Spear said revolution was a last resort in 1776— it "was no hasty act" fueled by "misguided passion." The colonists rebelled— and created the new nation, not out of ambition, but out of necessity, to protect their rights. In contrast, the creation of the Confederacy was a hotheaded overreaction to proper government—no rights were violated, Spear argued.[7]

Second, Spear argued, a revolution could not be justified unless it had the support of the majority. The patriots of 1776 were right to rebel because they represented an oppressed majority of colonists, while the southerners of 1861 had no right to rebel because they were in the minority of Americans. If a disgruntled minority in any land could rebel against the government that the majority supported, where would it end?[8]

Rebellion against a republican nation was always evil, Spear said, because republics governed by popular rule, not through some tyrant or "hereditary sovereign clinging to his throne," as was the case when the patriots rebelled against Britain. In the United States of the nineteenth century, the people were in charge. Rebellion against a republic was rebellion against the citizens themselves, which was indefensible.[9]

If some Americans worried too much about close relations between church and state, Paul had no such qualms, Spear said. "In [Paul's] view, civil society, with Government for its agent, is clothed with a divine prerogative." Confederate rebels, by rejecting the nation, followed Satan when he rebelled against God's heavenly throne. "This fallen angel is the first secessionist." Fighting Confederates was the right thing to do—as right as "hanging pirates."[10]

Not surprisingly, southerners rejected these Yankee views of Paul and rebellion. A southerner who discussed Romans 13 was William W. Lord, rector of Christ Episcopal Church in Vicksburg. Later in the war, he became well known as chaplain for the First Mississippi Brigade, and he led services during the Siege of Vicksburg. In 1861, Lord addressed Paul's claim that civil government was "ordained by God." By this Paul only meant that God supported *the idea* of civil government, not that God supported all rulers and empires. Not every government, and not every ruler, deserved obedience. Paul would not have required southerners to obey a ruler, like Lincoln, who waged war on them.[11]

But what about northerners' claims that Paul had supported Emperor Nero and the Roman Empire, even though they persecuted Christians? Didn't this prove that Paul would have rejected the Confederate rebellion? Lord agreed on what the text said: Romans 13—along with Jesus's command to "render unto Caesar the things which are Caesar's"—commanded obedience to government, even the Roman Empire, which persecuted Christians "with fire and sword." Rome, like all governments, had the right to power *if* it was "just and impartial" in executing its authority. Christians were to support any government—even the Roman Empire—"so long as it stands at the head of the people, and makes war *for* them and not *upon* them."[12]

But Rome persecuted Christians—was that not the same as making war on them? Not according to Lord. In his view, Rome's persecution of Christians was based on a mistake—they thought Christians were criminals, "guilty of the most shocking violations of nature." But Christians were not criminals. Thus, Paul and Peter told Christians to prove the Romans wrong by being "both good citizens and good soldiers," and thereby "put to silence the ignorance of foolish men" by their "exact obedience to the government and the law."[13]

Lord's trump card was the American Revolution. "I trust in God, who so wonderfully appeared for the cause of our fathers, which to-day is ours." In the Revolution, as in 1861, there was a "stern necessity of resisting authority" when it was unjust. In the Civil War, "The world is governed by God's high providence, and not by fate or chance or wicked and tyrannical men, who build their greatness on the ruin of their country, and seek to cement it with the blood of their countrymen." Paul's words in Romans 13 did not condemn rebellion when it was justified, either in 1776 or in 1861.[14]

"[The] Flag Carries American Ideas, American History and American Feelings"

As flags waved throughout the North, preachers quoted scripture and stirred memories of the Revolution to inspire the people to war. In 1861, Henry Ward Beecher found a biblical reference to honor the Stars and Stripes: "Thou hast given a banner to them that fear thee, that it may be displayed because of the truth" (Psalms 60:4). In ancient Israel, God gave his holy nation a banner to fight under. Likewise, Beecher insisted, "Our flag means, then, all that our fathers meant in the Revolutionary War; it means all that the Declaration of Independence meant." The founders, Beecher said, feared God, so God gave them the flag, which "they have handed it down to us. And I thank God that it is still in the hands of men that fear him and love righteousness."[15]

The Confederacy had adopted its own flag, and Beecher was happy to hear it. At least the Confederates would leave the Stars and Stripes untainted. "God be blessed," Beecher proclaimed, that the Confederates "took another flag to do the Devil's work, and left our flag to do the work of God!"[16]

For many, the Union was a sacred cause. John Cotton Smith, an Episcopal rector in New York, said people shouldn't forget "the moral and religious destiny of the nation." It was thanks to the Bible's prevalence that the nation's "religious and political principles were to so great an extent derived from God's word."[17] God had a plan for the Union, a plan revealed in scripture. "Some peculiar destiny is set before this nation, and . . . it is closely connected in the providence of God with the preservation of the union," Smith said.[18]

For any nation, a civil war would be tragic, but for the United States, a civil war could threaten God's purposes in the world. That was the view expressed by Bible scholar Albert Barnes, pastor of the First Presbyterian Church of Philadelphia. After the fall of Sumter, Barnes preached on "The Love of Country." "It would be wrong not to love" this nation, Barnes said, "for it seems to have been reserved as the last best earthly gift of Heaven to man; a place where man may make a new and fresh experiment to be happy, and great, and free." Given the greatness of the Union, any civil war that would threaten it would be catastrophic. "No words can describe the evils which must result from the overthrow of such a government." A war that defeated the Union would threaten "the great cause of liberty in the world."[19]

This kind of patriotic rhetoric, linking the cause of the war with the cause of God, surged after Sumter's defeat, but northern African Americans qualified their patriotism with skepticism. An editorial in the *Christian Recorder*, an African Methodist Episcopal weekly and one of the nation's most influential African American publications, stated the issue in the title: "The Star-Spangled Banner, and the Duty of Colored Americans to That Flag," making the case that the American Revolution was not exclusively a white revolution. "Eighty-six years ago, when the thunder of the Revolution first pealed in the heavens . . . where were the men of color? Right by their country's side, to make their breasts a rampart, and to pour forth their blood, a free-will offering for the nation's good." What, then, was their duty now that Sumter had fallen? Should African Americans join the fight for the Union? The answer was no—at least not yet. "To offer ourselves for military service now, is to abandon self-respect, and invite insult" because "now, in 1861, not only our citizenship, but even our common humanity is denied."

And yet African Americans did have a patriotic duty and a religious duty to pray. Through prayer, "The humblest slave, as well as the most cultivated man of color, can do something to bring the nation out of its dilemma, and defend, maintain, and perpetuate the eternal principles of liberty, justice, and equity." In prayer, African Americans could address God, who does not recognize humanity and human rights "in the color of the skin" nor "by the texture of the hair." "Though disfranchised in the North, and enslaved in the South, you can now wield a power more terrible than the rifle, the revolver, or the howitzer—it is the effectual fervent prayer of a righteous man." The author continued:

> Colored Americans! From the blood-consecrated soil of Lexington, and the heroic heights of Bunker Hill—from the battle-fields of Red Bank and New Orleans, the martial spirit of your brave progenitors, calls upon you now to do your duty to the "stars and the stripes," even as they did theirs. Not, however, by the use of deadly weapons, but by mightier—the omnipotent power of prayer.

It was not that fighting was ever out of the question for African Americans. To the contrary, this newspaper implored its readers: "If the nation, in its bloody conflict with armed treason, should be so pressed as to have its heart harmonized towards you, and then call upon you for martial aid, you may fly swifter than eagles, stronger than lions, to sustain the national flag." Until that time, these African Americans declared their devotion to God and to the legacy of the American Revolution.[20]

"Absalom the Usurper"

As Lincoln called for additional troops to support the war effort, northern ministers stepped up to inspire Americans to enlist—a duty they again connected with the patriots of the Revolution. Sermons often included references to Washington and other founding heroes, and books about Revolutionary-era ministers, including Revolutionary-era sermons, were published in the 1860s, with titles such as *Patriot Preachers of the American Revolution*, *The Chaplains and Clergy of the Revolution*, and *The Pulpit of the American Revolution: Or, The Political Sermons of the Period of 1776*. One of these authors, J. T. Headley, hoped patriotic ministers in Revolutionary America would inspire the nation. "The Revolution would have been less sacred," Headley wrote, "if [ministers'] blood had not mingled in the costly sacrifice that was laid on the altar of freedom."[21]

Even if ministers had been heroes during the Revolutionary War, that was not enough incentive to recruit enough chaplains for the Civil War. According to Edwin M. Stanton, the secretary of war, the Union had 437 chaplains serving 676 regiments in 1862. Many agreed with the assessment of an Iowa soldier: "We have no chaplain now and never one that amounted to much. A good, working Chaplain would be of immense service to this regiment and I do not see why some one does not apply for the place." Even so, chaplains were not a high priority for the government. Upon the outbreak of the conflict, the War Department planned for one chaplain for each regiment, required that chaplains be ordained in "some Christian denomination," but gave few details otherwise. Chaplains would receive pay on the level of a cavalry captain ($1,747 per year), but they would have no rank, nor would they receive uniforms. Chaplains were no higher a priority in the Confederate government. In an unprinted letter from 1862, Morgan Callaway, a Methodist from Georgia, wrote to his wife, "I was appointed Chaplain. I will have to buy a uniform which will cost me very high. I will also have to purchase a horse."[22]

This was the case, even though many believed that ministers had the unique responsibility of arousing wartime zeal, just as they believed that the Bible of the Civil War reflected the legacy of the American Revolution's Bible. In that nostalgia for the Spirit of '76, Presbyterian George Duffield, Jr. of Philadelphia titled his sermon of April 1861 after a patriotic sermon from 1775: *Courage in a Good Cause; or, The Lawful and Courageous Use of the Sword.* If Duffield hoped to call up the revolutionary spirit from this sermon, he also caught that spirit himself, declaring that he "this day offered my services to the Governor of Pennsylvania as Chaplain of one of the Philadelphia regiments."[23]

For dramatic effect, Duffield held up a Bible from the American Revolution. "This very copy [of the Bible] that I now hold in my hand, is one of the rare edition published by authority of the old Continental Congress in 1781." He knew this Bible was authentic—Duffield's great-grandfather had been a chaplain to the Continental Congress. This Bible had supported a war to found the nation, and it would support a war to rescue the nation "now that it is in such imminent peril."[24]

Sacred as the American Revolution was, there was also something mystical about this Civil War. It seemed to evoke the scriptures. Throughout the war, Americans marveled at how closely the Civil War resembled biblical wars. One key comparison was the story of David's son, Absalom. It told of a family dispute that caused a political revolution and, finally, a ruptured nation. The only rebellion evil enough to compare to that of the Confederacy was, as George Duffield wrote, "the rebellion of the proud, luxurious, lascivious, unprincipled, murderous Absalom, against his noble, unsuspecting, too affectionate, and overindulgent father, David."[25]

Almost everyone knew the story. David was Israel's greatest king—literally a "man after God's own heart"—and Absalom was his handsome and ambitious son. Through a series of intriguing events, which included Absalom's murder of his brother for raping their sister, Absalom turned against David and plotted to overthrow him. Over time, Absalom "stole the hearts of the men of Israel" by convincing them that he understood their needs better than David. Finally, Absalom forced his father from his throne. Defeated and humbled, David fled Jerusalem. Absalom's reign did not last long, however, as David and his army regrouped and defeated Absalom's men. In the aftermath, Absalom died an inglorious death. As he rode his mule under an oak tree, his long hair caught in the branches and trapped him. He was hanging there until Joab, David's military commander, stabbed him in the heart. Absalom got what he deserved, some said, although his death devastated David (2 Samuel 13–20). This was a critical part of the Absalom story—David's agony at the loss of his son—and many could relate to it in the Civil War. Regardless of Absalom's crimes, he was David's flesh and blood, and David mourned his terrible yet necessary death.

Absalom's narrative functioned on several levels in the Civil War. It revealed the fallout from an unjust revolt, and the force needed to defeat it. But the victors couldn't celebrate their triumph—it was too tragic. "There can be no glory in this war, however it may result, and whatever brilliant deeds may be done," preached Baptist minister Daniel Eddy of Boston. "There was glory at Lexington and Bunker Hill," he continued, "but there can be none in this cruel, civil war. Our great nation at its close will weep as David did over Absalom. There will be no monuments erected to its heroes," and "no American will ever wish to read its record." "We shall pray to have it forgotten," Eddy said. The reason? "It is a fratricidal war; brother is butchering brother," and "it is our own blood that is flowing."[26]

Eddy was wrong and right, of course—wrong because there would be many books written on the Civil War, many monuments erected. But he was right about the tragic nature of the conflict. Although blood would be shed—brothers' blood, and the blood of sons against fathers—this war was worth the sacrifice. "The existence of this Union to mankind, is worth all the blood we have to shed, all the treasures we have to spend."[27]

"The rebellion of Absalom was," as Duffield preached, just "as uncalled for and outrageous as the bombardment of Fort Sumter on the part of South Carolina." The rebellions of both Absalom and Jefferson Davis hurled outrageous "personal indignities and abuse" on the nation's true leaders, David and Lincoln. But perhaps the most crucial parallel was that both rebellions seemed to be successful, as was often the case with rebellions "at the beginning." Duffield concluded that the loss of Fort Sumter did not spell doom for the Union. A strong start did not portend a victorious end, as the Absalom story proved. "The last we see of Absalom, the traitor and the usurper, he is hanging in an oak, with three arrows" piercing "his ungrateful and rebellious heart." "So perish all traitors," Duffield proclaimed to a chorus of "Amens" from the congregation, "and for the good of the country, and the honor of humanity, and the glory of God, the sooner they perish the better!"[28]

But they would not perish without a fight. So, "as in the days of David," when "it was the duty of all Israel to unite" against "Absalom the usurper," so in the aftermath of Sumter it was "now the duty of our whole nation, the duty of every State, every city, every town, every family, and person" to fight the Confederate traitors. Absalom had been reborn in Jefferson Davis, and his Confederate minions planned to hoist "the reptile flag" over the US Capitol. Never! Duffield would rather see the Capitol "reduced to a heap of ruins, and not one stone remain upon another!"[29]

"It Is God's Hand, that Presses the Cup of Blood to Our Lips"

The American Revolution had modeled heroism for Americans; it had also modeled patriotic preaching, and ministers followed the lead to inspire people for war. To refuse war, Duffield proclaimed, makes a man "less a Christian than he might have been, less a lover of his country." Cowardice, he insisted, was unpatriotic, unmanly—and unbiblical. "THE LAST OF ALL PLACES IN THE UNIVERSE, BEHIND WHICH FOR COWARDICE TO SKULK OR FIND REFUGE, IS THE HOLY BIBLE," Duffield proclaimed, using all caps for emphasis.[30]

Duffield called on militant scriptures from the Old Testament, including the prophet Jeremiah's command, "Cursed is he that keepeth back his sword from blood" (Jeremiah 48:10); David's assertion, "Blessed be the Lord, my strength, which teacheth my hands to war and my fingers to fight" (Psalms 144:1), and Deborah's curse of the people of "Meroz" for refusing to wage war against God's enemies (Judges 5:23). These scriptures had a legacy of military service in the Revolutionary War, and preachers would extend that legacy in the Civil War.[31]

Given his militant sermon and call for patriotism, it makes sense that Duffield wrote the popular hymn "Stand Up, Stand Up for Jesus," which implored worshipers to

> Stand up, stand up for Jesus, Ye soldiers of the cross;
> Lift high His royal banner, It must not suffer loss.
> From victory unto victory, His army shall He lead,
> Till every foe is vanquished, And Christ is Lord indeed.[32]

When they sang this hymn over the years, most Christians spiritualized it—Christ's army was the spiritual power of the church, and the war was against sin, not an actual army on the battlefield. Yet the Civil War forged an alliance between spiritual and military warfare—just the Revolutionary War had. In both wars, preachers called on a militant Christ for inspiration in military as well as spiritual struggles.[33]

By associating wartime service with spiritual duty, ministers endorsed the brutal work of war, giving it a divine mandate that hopefully would make it bearable for young men as they marched off to battle. Nearly two weeks after Sumter's fall, a Congregationalist from Massachusetts said that "the lesson of the hour is war," and "war is a horrid game." Never truly glorious, war was "mere wholesale butchery," and "a battle-field is the shambles of human flesh." And yet this was a war with God's blessing. "It is God's hand, that presses the cup of blood to our lips. If it be his will we will drain it to the lowest dregs."[34]

Not only *could* Christians fight in this war, but they *should* fight, because Christian soldiers were the best fighters. "The hand of the Lord is in" the war, proclaimed a Congregationalist minister from Milwaukee, Wisconsin, in his sermon on April 28—"It is the Lord of hosts who is mustering our armies." Lincoln's armies needed Christians above all. "Let us fight like Christians," this preacher proclaimed. "There are no such warriors as" men who "enter the battle-field fresh from communion with God. There is something fearfully sublime in the thought of a Christian hero, arming himself, not for spiritual, but physical victories."[35]

Many have called the Civil War a "second American Revolution," and for good reason—both northerners and southerners saw it that way. Both sides claimed to be following those heroic patriots of the nation's founding, and both sides used the Bible to make those claims. Many preachers knew how critical the Bible was in the Revolution, and they enlisted that legacy in this new fight. As it did in the Revolution, war provided Christians with opportunities to prove their spiritual and physical courage and masculinity.

War created heroes; war also created heroic saints. Ministers believed they could be heroes, too. Not only could they preach patriotic sermons, inspiring troops for battle, but they could recruit volunteers by assuring them of the spiritual importance of military service. Preachers, then, could play a role as important as any general on the battlefield. Lincoln's call for state militias and volunteers enlisted ministers in a sacred duty—a duty they relished because it placed them alongside patriotic preachers from the American Revolution. Along with all the flag-waving, therefore, pulpits unleashed a flurry of sermons after Sumter's fall. As they did, they shaped a self-understanding as militant preachers for a righteous cause. If the Civil War was a holy war, it became so through the efforts of ministers who unleashed a scriptural arsenal into the crisis.

5

"A Covenant of Death"

After the battle of Fort Sumter, southerners turned to the Bible to inspire their own religious zeal for war, much as northerners did, but with key differences. While northerners attacked rebellion, finding biblical ammunition in Paul's teachings in Romans 13, the tragic revolt of Absalom, and other texts, southerners proclaimed biblical condemnations of idolatry, accusing the North of carving an idol out of the Union. Lincoln was an "American Nebuchadnezzar," they argued, a tyrant who wanted to cast the South into his fiery furnace. Northern patriotism looked nothing like the courageous devotion of the founders; it was idolatry masquerading as patriotism, a self-righteous worship of the nation that betrayed God and mocked Christianity. The Confederacy, then, would fight a just war, not an idolatrous war, and southerners knew God had approved it, in part because of the miraculous (and bloodless) victory at Fort Sumter.

From the beginning of the war, therefore, the North and the South sharpened their biblical exegesis for battle, both asserting their faithfulness to scripture and their claims to be God's people. But these were not the only American views on the war. Looking on from Utah, the Latter-day Saints declared their own biblical assessment of the war, accusing both North and South of blaspheming God and perverting scripture. Led by Brigham Young, these Saints saw themselves as God's *true* New Israel and interpreted the war as divine judgment on the United States.

"It Is a War of Purification"

Unlike preachers in the North, who reflected on the battle of Fort Sumter from a safe distance, Charleston ministers lived through it. Reverend J. H. Elliott had a firsthand view of the battle. He recalled that the bombardment began on Friday as the people gathered in St. Michael's Church. As the congregation prayed, they heard "the measured tramp of soldiers marching to their several posts—the rush and clamor of the thronging people." It was an eerie experience as "the deep thunder of the distant guns, and even the fearful hurtling of their iron storm, mingled with our devotions." Not surprisingly, they had a hard time focusing on worship: "With throbbing hearts we watched each vivid flash that poured its thunders on Sumter's dark and silent walls, and traced the flight of the bursting shell as it specked the heavens with its little cloud of smoke."[1]

The Yankee fleet was offshore, they knew, preparing to reinforce Sumter, and ready "to crimson our sand with the best blood of our people." Charleston residents watched as the fleet approached—"huge ships, laden with troops," looking "like great clouds out of the sea, charged with ruin and with death." But God had other plans. Providentially, these ships arrived just in time "to witness our triumph—to behold their flag, which had been dishonored into an emblem of injustice and treachery, struck from its high perch and hurled into the dust."

All this was evidence of God's defense of the South—God's "mighty arm" had fought for the Confederacy in "this great Revolution." Only those who were "profane and stupid" would fail to see it. And only the "profane and stupid" could miss the miraculous result of the battle—no one died. It was a "bloodless victory," but they could not count on similar miraculous outcomes in future battles.[2]

The victory at Sumter was a sign of God's favor, but some dreaded the war, while others were happy to see it arrive. When the roar of cannons woke Emma Holmes on April 12, 1861, she was glad to hear it. The war had finally begun, ending months of worry, speculation, and indecision. Later that day, she wrote that almost "every body seems calm & grave" in Charleston. Most folks seemed "so impressed with the justice of our cause that they place entire confidence in the God of battles."[3] It was no wonder that the Confederate motto was *Deo Vindice*—"Defended by God."[4] Another Charlestonian, Mary Chesnut, wrote on April 13, "How gay we were last night." The women she talked to had no doubts that God favored the South. "'God is on our side,' they cry." When Chesnut asked why they were so confident, they replied, "Of course He hates the Yankees."[5]

Like these women, Ada Bacot, another South Carolinian, was ready for war—perhaps too ready for a woman, some thought. "I wonder some times if people think it strange I should be so warm a secessionist," she wrote in her diary three months before the cannon boomed in Charleston Harbor. "But why should they," she asked. "Has not every woman a right to express her opinions upon such subjects, in private if not in public." In private and in public, she beamed with pride that her home state led the way in secession. "My love for S. Carolina is that of an affectionate daughter for a mother, the purest love in the world. I would feel as much mortified if S.C. should disgrace her self as I would if my mother should." It frustrated Bacot that she could not fight the Yankees. "I know I am not able to do anything for [South Carolina's] defense being a woman, still that does not prevent my being interested."[6]

The battle of Fort Sumter, with its lack of casualties, seemed to support widespread confidence that the war would be a brief and nearly bloodless affair. "A lady's thimble will hold all the blood that will be shed" in a war with the North, some southerners had said. Likewise, according to James McPherson, former senator James Chesnut—Mary Chesnut's husband—"offered to drink all the blood shed as a consequence of secession."[7]

Others thought that the war's bloodshed would serve divine purposes, testing but ultimately vindicating the South. "I rejoice in this war," said Virginia's governor, Henry A. Wise. "It is a war of purification. You want war, fire, blood to purify you; and the Lord of Hosts has demanded that you should walk through fire and blood."[8] Speaking alongside Governor Wise, former president Tyler reportedly said that the South had embarked upon a "holy effort for the maintenance of liberty and independence," and if the Confederates performed their "duty as Christians and patriots, the same benign Providence which favored the cause of our forefathers in the Revolution of 1776, would again crown our efforts with similar success."[9]

"Worship the Deity Represented by the Stars and Stripes"

For every American who was glad to see the war arrive, there was another who found it hard to be optimistic, especially those who saw their families ripped apart. Virginia was the childhood home to two brothers, John and James Welsh. Before the war, James moved north while John stayed in Virginia. In 1861, James wrote his brother, referring to "Jeff Davis and his crew of pirates" who were breaking up the nation. John responded that he could not believe that "I have a brother who would advocate sending men here to butcher his own friends and relations. . . . I have always opposed secession but I shall vote for it today because I don't intend to submit to black Republican rule." James replied in turn that he could not believe his own brother would dare to "raise a hand to tear down the glorious Stars and Stripes, a flag that we have been taught from our cradle to look on with pride . . . I would strike down my own brother if he dare to raise a hand to destroy that flag." That was their last correspondence.[10]

Tough choices—forcing people to decide between state loyalty and national allegiance—yielded historic consequences. Perhaps the decision with the most repercussions was Robert E. Lee's. For him, the crisis came after April 17 when the convention in his home state of Virginia voted to join the Confederacy (it became official on May 23). Both the Union and the Confederacy coveted Lee's services—and for good reason. His military pedigree was second to none. His father had served admirably in the Revolutionary War, and Lee had followed with an even more notable military career—graduating near the top of his class at West Point, serving impressively in the Mexican War, and achieving the rank of colonel in March 1861.[11]

Lee disliked slavery and loved the Union. In January 1861, he reflected on a biography of George Washington he had been reading: "How his spirit would be grieved could he see the wreck of his mighty labors!" He continued, "I can anticipate no greater calamity for the country than a dissolution of the Union." For him, "Secession is nothing but revolution," and the founders wouldn't have "exhausted so much labor, wisdom and forbearance" in framing the Constitution "if it was intended to be broken by every member of the Confederacy at will." The nation was, Lee wrote, "between a state of anarchy and civil war. May God avert both of these evils from us!" Lee's Christian faith led him to pray for peace, but his assessment of the crisis moved him to prepare for war.[12]

When the war came, Lee knew he would fight, but on which side? On April 18, he received word from General Winfield Scott, offering him command of the US Army. But he also heard that Virginia, his home state, had seceded. Two days later, Lee wrote to Scott, "To no one, General, have I been as much indebted as to yourself for uniform kindness and consideration, and it has always been my ardent desire to meet your approbation." For Lee, however, state loyalty trumped national loyalty. He resigned from the army, saying, "Save in the defense of my native State, I never desire again to draw my sword."[13]

This kind of loyalty to home above all appeared in many sources. In discussing the quandaries of slavery and the war, Mary Chesnut agreed with a quotation that she attributed to frontiersman David Crockett: "My country, may she be right—but my country, right or wrong."[14]

Likewise, David Camden DeLeon, a Jewish man from South Carolina who had served heroically in the Mexican War, sided with the Confederacy. He served as acting surgeon general—the first for the Confederacy. His decision, like that of Robert E. Lee, was a difficult one. "I have loved my country. I have fought under its flag and every star and stripe is dear to me," he wrote to his brother. And yet he knew he had to side with the South. "When a Southern Confederacy is acknowledged or inaugurated, then I shall take my stand"—which he did a month after writing this.[15]

These decisions made sense to many southerners who could not see how motivated northerners would be to fight for the Union. Southerners, on the other hand, thought they had more clear incentives—they fought to protect their homes (including slavery). John Jones of the Confederate War Department put it this way: "Our men *must* prevail in combat, or lose their property, country, freedom, everything. . . . On the other hand the enemy, in yielding the contest, may retire into their own country, and possess everything they enjoyed before the war began."[16]

Unlike southerners, northerners weren't fighting for their homeland; they were fighting for the "Union," which had deep meaning for many Americans, so deep in fact that southerners often called northern patriotism an idolatrous worship of the Union.

Even some northern ministers shared this concern. "One cause of our present adversity is found in the *national idolatry* to which we had been addicted," said Baptist minister William Brantly in Philadelphia. "We have been disposed to love our country with an undue affection." People thought of the Union as "some deity worthy of our homage. We have thought that there was such magic in that word 'Union,' that no assault made upon it could be successful." In Brantly's view, a visitor from Japan would probably think that Americans "worship a deity represented by the stars and stripes." Could it be that God was using the crisis to punish Americans for worshiping the Union? Now, it seemed, God had set North against South so that the nation would see that ultimate allegiance belongs to the Lord. The Bible was full of such warnings. Ancient Egypt worshiped itself, so God sent plagues to defile the sacred land and its revered Nile River. Now "Our Union, which we have loved, perhaps too inordinately, is now in danger of dismemberment, and of destruction."[17]

"The American Nebuchadnezzar"

In southern eyes, the chief idolater was Abraham Lincoln, the diabolical president who had fabricated an idol out of the nation and forced the people to worship it. After the battle at Fort Sumter, a prominent southern minister dubbed Lincoln "the American Nebuchadnezzar" in reference to one of the Bible's most idolatrous kings.[18]

Nebuchadnezzar, a Babylonian ruler discussed in the book of Daniel, had led the Babylonians when they attacked Jerusalem, destroyed the Temple, and forced God's people into exile. When he commanded the people to worship a golden image, three devout Jews—Shadrach, Meshach, and Abednego—refused to obey. Furious at their insolence, Nebuchadnezzar tried to burn them alive. He threw them into a fiery furnace, but they miraculously survived with not a hair on their heads singed.[19]

Nebuchadnezzar's golden statue had been born again in Lincoln's presidency, said Presbyterian minister Thomas Smyth of Charleston. As Nebuchadnezzar commanded worship of his golden image, Lincoln demanded "the pulpit, the Bible, the church" and even "democracy" all "bow the knee to" his despotic "golden image." In this state worship, "The star-spangled banner takes the place of the cross." The nation demanded that all Americans revere "the Lincoln dictatorship," obeying it or risking "damnation."[20] From his New Orleans pulpit, Benjamin Morgan Palmer preached a similar message: "We have sinned against God in the idolatry of our History, and in the boastful spirit it has naturally begotten." Palmer also referred to the story of Nebuchadnezzar as "a lesson for all time," and especially their time. "Woe to the nation that with pride of heart lifts itself against God!"[21]

Lincoln, southerners claimed, had shoved them into the fiery furnace of the Civil War. Because the South had asserted its independence, Lincoln and his troops would seek vengeance—"the sleeping lion is now rampant, and has sprung upon her," preached Smyth. "His eyes glare perdition. His claws are in her sides. His appetite for blood is now whetted. His horrid teeth stare frightfully from his opened jaws, and we are in the death struggle for liberty."[22] Lincoln was an "unscrupulous and audacious tyrant" who "sanctions acts of military dictatorship which transcend the power of any monarch upon earth."[23]

Hatred of Lincoln was almost unlimited in the South, as southerners insulted nearly everything about him, from his speeches and ideas to the way he dressed himself and his physical appearance. "They say Lincoln is frightfully uncouth and ugly—with the keenest sense of coarse humor," said Mary Chesnut in a typical southern insult.[24]

This harsh language fit the mood of the time, expressing the anger southerners felt, but it also expressed the urgency of the crime. National idolatry insulted God and doomed the United States, they believed. The dream of the nation, of the heroic founders, was over, at least in the North. Perhaps even that was poetic justice because American idolatry, some southerners claimed, began with the founders. For all their merits, the founders made a mistake in leaving God out of the Constitution. How could greats like Washington, Jefferson, and Franklin have made such an error? Southern ministers did not know for sure, but some, like Benjamin Palmer, suspected that a "free-thinking and infidel spirit" infected the founders, leading them astray.[25] On this topic, a Presbyterian minister from Alabama retold a famous anecdote: when someone asked Alexander Hamilton why they left God out of the Constitution, he replied, "We entire forgot it!" This story reinforced the Confederates' belief that "the Constitution of the United States is a Godless instrument."[26]

Tragically, as Episcopal bishop Stephen Elliott of Georgia said, the Union had substituted "a gospel of the stars and stripes for the gospel of Jesus Christ."[27] The founders had left God out of the Constitution, so "It is not surprising," Benjamin Palmer preached, that God, "who proclaims his jealousy of his own glory, should let fall the blow which has shattered" the United States.[28] As a North Carolina minister put it, "The Union and the American Flag should no longer be possessed with charms for any Southerner, but all should hold them as objects of disgust, because they are polluted by Northern fanaticism, mingled with cruel wrongs."[29] Southerners commented on this radical shift from one flag to another. Sarah Morgan of Louisiana said of the US flag, "much as I once loved that flag, I *hate* it now!"[30]

"The Conduct of Cain on an Enlarged Scale"

The Confederate constitution would right the wrongs of the founders, southerners hoped, by restoring God to the center of government. Its preamble called on "the favor and guidance of Almighty God" to "ordain and establish this Constitution for the Confederate States of America." The Confederate constitution was, as Benjamin Palmer said, "the return of the prodigal to the bosom of his father."[31]

Although Confederates had placed God at the heart of their constitution, many southerners believed the Confederate States of America would collapse if they failed to live up to God's expectations. Jefferson Davis proclaimed the first Confederate fast day on June 13, 1861. Fast days called on the people to go without food and to pray for the nation during a time of crisis. The Confederacy would set itself apart in its commitment to religious liberty, ministers promised. Church and state remained distinct, but interrelated. "We do not believe in the union of church and state. We grant to every man the right to worship according to the dictates of his conscience," said a Virginia pastor. "But we do believe in the union of religion and government. The freest government on earth must be most rigid in its adherence to principles—for liberty is not license—and consists not in doing what we please, but in doing what is right. Without justice, without rectitude, and without obedience to the law of God, we can have no true liberty."[32] A minister from Alabama agreed: "While the kingdom of this world, and the kingdom of Christ are, and should be, separate and distinct, yet the principles of the latter should be the very foundation upon which this Commonwealth should plant itself.—Her breath should be inhaled from the pure atmosphere of the Bible."[33]

The Confederacy would be a biblical nation, and yet it would honor the separation of church and state. Many saw no contradiction in this plan. The bottom line was, as a North Carolina pastor said, "This nation is neither Pagan nor Mohamedan—we are a christian people."[34]

Only a biblical nation could be a just nation, ministers insisted. Scripture shaped a virtuous people, and only virtue could produce justice, no matter what form of government the nation had. As a Methodist from Columbia, South Carolina, said, "Any form of government will be good" if its leaders and people have wisdom and virtue. The opposite is also true: "With weak and wicked rulers, and weak and wicked people, no form of government can secure national prosperity." He continued, "Good morals may make good governments, but good governments will never make good morals." The nation required "a national religion, founded upon the gospel of the Lord Jesus Christ."[35]

The Confederate States' morality would set them apart from the immoral Union. For southerners, the corruption of the United States took several forms—greed, hypocrisy, and even murder at the highest levels of government. The war itself, many believed, was no more than murder on a national scale. Southern ministers were nearly unanimous on this point, and they often used the Old Testament to defend it. A Lutheran minister in North Carolina called on the biblical story of the first murder—when Cain killed his brother, Abel—arguing that this war was the Cain and Abel story in national scope: "No sane man would make war upon his own family, and he who does so, is a madman, and fit only for bedlam. And yet, such is the nature of the present war, declared by Mr. Lincoln, against the South." Lincoln's mother-in-law supported the South, this pastor said, and Lincoln's brother-in-law fought for the Confederacy. This was the divided situation of many American families. "And after the fury of battle is over," many would see "brother, son or father weltering in his own blood." This war, started by Lincoln, was "the conduct of Cain on an enlarged scale," so God would mark the United States as he did Cain. Lincoln was motivated by "ambition and vain glory, and if this country is to be drenched with the blood of human beings, slain in civil war, their blood will be required at his hands and the hands of his party."[36]

The Cain and Abel story resonated with Americans in a war that literally pitted brother against brother. In the Bible, this was the first murder—perhaps symbolically because many people believed that violence between brothers was the worst kind of bloodshed.

"We Have Crossed Swords with the Northern Confederacy over the Bible"

As we have seen, southern ministers rounded up numerous biblical images to condemn the Union after Sumter's fall. It was a diabolical war in the spirit of Cain, a war that pitted brother against brother, a war fueled by idolatry disguised as patriotism. But perhaps most offensive was the way northern ministers used God to defend their attack on the South and, more importantly, on Christianity itself. "The North is frantic with rage," preached a North Carolina pastor, and "the church must bleed at every pore, as this unholy war progresses."[37]

That was the key term—Lincoln had launched an "unholy war," but worse, northern ministers helped him execute his barbaric attacks. A minister from Mobile, Alabama, agreed, finding it particularly troubling that much of the northern rage against the South came from Henry Ward Beecher and other abolitionist preachers who "have shown their hostility to us in their prayers," using "prayer as a vehicle through which to breathe out threatenings and slaughter against us."[38] The North had infused this war with religious meaning. The result was, as Charleston minister Thomas Smyth said, the North saw "good in evil, and evil in good," and saw "a holy and sacred war" in what was really "a diabolical and unnatural invasion of sovereign States."[39]

Lincoln and his Union hordes had launched an unjust war, an invasion, hell-bent on conquest, but the South would fight a defensive war, which was the only kind of war that God endorsed. According to just war theory, only defensive wars were justifiable, not wars of conquest for treasure or blood. This was the message Stephen Elliott preached to the Pulaski Guards in Savannah, Georgia, just before they left to join other Confederate troops from Virginia. He drew his scripture text from God's advice on war to Moses and his people:

> If ye go to war in your land against the enemy that oppresseth you, then ye shall blow an alarm with the trumpets; and ye shall be remembered before the Lord your God, and ye shall be saved from your enemies. (Numbers 10:9)

The people were only to fight "against the enemy that oppresseth you," defensive wars against oppressors—like Yankees invading the South. When fighting this kind of war, God instructed the people to blow one of the silver trumpets he had instructed Moses to craft, and this would inspire the people for the fight. "In this way," Elliott preached, "war [was] consecrated by religion, and the heart of courage was lighted anew from the altar of God." The war should be reasoned, just, and godly, and not the bloodthirsty war the North was intent on waging on the South. As much as they would like to do so, southerners could not wage a hateful war of vengeance without violating the biblical command: "Vengeance belongeth to me—I will repay, saith the Lord" (cf. Romans 12:19; Deuteronomy 32:35). Elliott's advice to Confederate soldiers, then, was to "strike no more blows than are necessary for victory," grant any "cry for mercy," and "let the flag under which you fight be stained with no unnecessary blood."[40]

This would be difficult, Elliott admitted, but Confederate troops must not stoop to the Yankees' level in the war. "All war has a tendency to excite the passions, to infuriate the temper, and to harden the heart, but especially a war such as this." He admitted that it would be "difficult to observe the limits of Christian warfare in a conflict" waged by "burglars and cut-throats," and he cautioned that "it will require an almost divine moderation to stay the arm of vengeance."[41]

A war of vengeance would be easy, because rage consumed many southerners. Congregations often demanded sermons that called for revenge against northern aggression, but their ministers did not always oblige them. "Perhaps I do not speak strongly enough to satisfy your tastes," proclaimed a Baptist minister in Charleston, South Carolina. "Perhaps you would have me recite, in words hot with burning indignation, the alleged outrages and barbarities of the invader, and kindle your souls to a fury against him." His congregation desired preaching that "would stir your spirits like the blast of a trumpet, until, transported with martial ardor, you should pant for the strife and thirst for blood." But he refused to preach that kind of sermon—"You do not need this sort of address to stimulate your patriotic devotion and excite you to defend and maintain your rights." Not only that, but this kind of bloodthirsty sermon was not "appropriate to the pulpit."[42]

Just as southern preachers warned Confederate troops against fighting hateful wars inspired by vengeance, they also implored them to fight for God's purposes, equipped with divine assistance on the battlefield. "We have a sacred duty to perform," preached H. N. Pierce in Mobile, Alabama. Confederates must "meet manfully the evil of war." The fighting men of the Confederacy were "the sacred ministers of eternal justice and right"; they would impress the world with their heroism. The Confederate soldier who devoted himself to God "is invincible." He would "stand as firm in danger as did the old Christian martyrs when threatened with the wild beasts of the amphitheater, the torturing rack, or the fiery stake."[43]

Confederate soldiers could be "invincible" only if they devoted themselves to the crucial alliance between God and the Confederate armies. The key to victory in war was in this relationship, a covenant modeled in the Old Testament, a connection between God and his people in which the people fought alongside God. If asked, "Who gave the victory in war?" all would respond that God did. But God did not work alone. God fought for those who fought for themselves. Dramatic battles filled the Old Testament, and the most glorious ones pivoted on this divine–human alliance. To make this point, J. C. Mitchell, a minister in Mobile, Alabama, called on the confrontation between Israel and the Amalekites, which was "very pertinent to our present purposes."[44]

In this battle, Joshua and his men fought the Amalekites while Moses stood on a nearby hilltop, holding the rod of the Lord in his hand. If Moses held up his arm, Israel had the upper hand in battle. When Moses tired and lowered his arm, the battle favored the Amalekites. When Moses was too weary to hold his arm up at all, Aaron and Hur raised it for him. "Here then we have that hallowed combination of agencies," Mitchell wrote, "which ought never to be separated—the dependence upon heaven, with the use of appointed means. The rod in the hand of Moses, and the sword in that of Joshua." The *rod* in Moses's hand represented the appeal to God in prayer, relying on him for deliverance, while the *sword* in Joshua's hand represented military strength.[45]

In war, then, God's people could no more forget prayer than they could forget their guns—but one was useless without the other.[46] Ministers in the Revolutionary War made the same point, as did northern ministers in the Civil War. All declared the need for both prayer and guns—spiritual warfare and military warfare. As James Otey, an Episcopal bishop in Tennessee, wrote in an unpublished sermon manuscript on this same biblical battle: "That the affairs of men should thus depend on earthly influences, & Heavenly—on temporal things & eternal, is the ordinance of God." Otey chose this text "because of the completeness both of the material & spiritual elements employed in the action." He continued, "Without the wonder-working rod & the supplications of Moses, the skill of Joshua & the bravery of his forces would have been vain: while without that skill & bravery, no victory would have been achieved."[47]

To be worthy of God's deliverance, the South needed to remain true to the Bible in fighting the war. "We have crossed swords with the Northern Confederacy over the Bible," preached Charlestonian Thomas Smyth.[48] Who would claim victory in this biblical warfare? In his Second Inaugural Address almost four years later, Lincoln would state famously that both North and South "read the same Bible and pray to the same God, and each invokes His aid against the other."[49] This was ironic and tragic, often seen as a failure of religion, and perhaps it was. But Lincoln was not alone in recognizing this tragedy, even from the beginning of the war. From Charleston, Smyth reflected that North and South had worshipped "at the same altar, invoked fire from heaven on each other, and appealed to the God of battles, to whom belongeth vengeance, to avenge us against our adversaries." Both sides had confidence in their own righteousness. Americans, both North and South, looked to God "to consecrate the war as holy and sacred." Yet Smyth blamed Lincoln and northern preachers for turning this into an unholy war. "What a spectacle to God, to angels, and to the world! What lamentation in heaven! What a jubilee in hell!"[50]

How would God judge between the Union and the Confederacy? That was the mysterious and agonizing question that only battles could answer. Being on God's side was one thing; victory was another. Even if God saw the South as more righteous than the North, that did not guarantee the South would win the war. In May 1861, an Episcopal bishop in Wilmington, North Carolina, preached that one would have to be hallucinating to doubt that the South's cause was righteous. Righteous did not mean victorious, however. He hoped that God would give victory to the Confederacy, but he cautioned that God "may not, however, for He does not always see fit to make right visibly triumphant."[51]

In Mobile, Alabama, Reverend H. N. Pierce said, "Let us not place too much dependence in the mere fact that our cause is a just and good one." Scripture showed that, even with a person who is "in the right, yet God might permit him to be overthrown in the combat, as a punishment for other sins yet unrepented of."[52] So southern preachers, including J. R. Kendrick of Charleston, warned southerners to resist "any confident and dogmatic interpretation of Providence." Even if it seemed that God favored them, one "cannot read the purposes of Jehovah." Both sides believed God was on their side. "In such a strange case, where two Christian peoples are solemnly appealing to heaven to witness the rectitude of their motives and the justice of their cause, God must and *will* judge betwixt them."[53]

"Your Agreement with Hell Shall Not Stand"

Perhaps God would indeed "judge betwixt" the Union and the Confederacy, or perhaps God would punish both. Perhaps both North and South were wrong about the Bible—and perhaps that was why they were on the verge of destruction. So said the Mormons.

This upstart religious community had a controversial history beginning in 1830, when Joseph Smith, their prophet and founder, published the Book of Mormon, a new scripture that enraged Americans who saw it as a rival to the Bible. This new prophet and his new scripture revived ancient practices, including polygamy, that alarmed Americans. After an angry horde murdered Smith in an Illinois jail, the Mormons, led by Brigham Young, moved to the Utah territory, where they constructed an autonomous and nearly theocratic government. Even from the distant West, Mormons provoked controversy and drew fire from President Buchanan, who launched a military campaign—the so-called Mormon War—against them in 1857–58. This "war" shed little blood, but it triggered hostility between Mormons and the US government that endured for decades.[54]

When the secession crisis followed on the heels of this "Mormon War," Mormons saw the nation's troubles as divine judgment on the United States for persecuting God's chosen people. "I feel perfectly satisfied with the events that are transpiring," wrote Elder John Taylor on April 28, 1861.

Taylor, a native of England and former Methodist, would later succeed Brigham Young as president of the church. More importantly, Taylor had been in the Illinois jail with Joseph Smith when a mob stormed in and murdered the Mormon prophet and his brother, Hyrum. Taylor had tried to fend off the attackers, but he and his walking stick were no match for men armed with rifles. The mob shot Taylor four times—twice in his left leg, his hand, and his hip. A bullet that probably would have killed him ricocheted off a watch he kept in his breast pocket.

From a Mormon perspective the United States was less a nation of freedom than an empire of persecution, bent on annihilating God's chosen people. Most Americans would celebrate the destruction of the Mormons, Taylor wrote to readers in England in 1861. "How was it when Joseph Smith was killed? There was a general rejoicing through the length and breadth of the whole land." And in the "Mormon War," if the US "army sent against us had swept us off from this stage of action, there would have been loud hosannahs" ringing from Americans and their churches.[55]

But God had not allowed that to happen. The secession crisis intervened—it diverted "their attention from us," and the United States backed off "open hostilities against us." This was good news for Mormons. Taylor introduced these thoughts with a warning from the prophet Isaiah: "your covenant with death shall be disannulled, and your agreement with hell shall not stand; when the overflowing scourge shall pass through, then ye shall be trodden down by it" (Isaiah 28:18). The United States had signed a "covenant with death," plotting the annihilation of the Latter-day Saints. The nation had "unblushingly used . . . force and strength to bring about the destruction of God's people." But, as the prophet Isaiah said, this "agreement with hell shall not stand." Instead, Taylor claimed, Americans were "bent upon their own destruction." They were "full of enmity, hatred, war, and bloodshed." Soon, however, perhaps in this coming civil war, Americans "will be arrayed against each other, and" their "destruction will be terrible." "We would a great deal prefer to have them use their armies upon themselves than upon us." He continued, "I do not fret myself much about North or South, or any other nation."[56]

This Mormon elder recognized one of the war's ironies: "Both the North and the South are praying fervently to the same God, that they may have power to destroy their enemies." The problem, as Elder Taylor saw it, was that both North and South had been led astray by corrupt faiths. Americans "are all very religious; good Baptists, good Methodists, good Quakers, good Catholics, good Episcopalians; in fact, they think that they are all good, pious souls." These American Christians loved to pray to "the God of battles to give them success" in war. And yet "Who is this God of battles? Why, the Devil, the prince and power of the air"—the Devil "is the god they risk their cause with, and it is for him to handle them as he sees fit."[57]

One of America's main problems was a biblical problem, a problem of revelation. Unlike most American Christians, including Protestants and Catholics, Mormons believed that God's revelation did not stop with the New Testament. It continued, written in the Book of Mormon and other scriptures, and God still revealed new teachings through his Mormon prophet on earth. Because most American Christians believed only in the Bible and rejected the Book of Mormon and God's continuing revelation through his prophets, they misunderstood scripture and their place in God's plan.

Would Americans have been on the verge of civil war if they were Mormon? Certainly not, Taylor believed, because they would have been following God's continual guidance. As it was, however, Americans "have no inspiration, no revelation from God, no Prophet's voice to point out the path of safety," so "they are led captive by the Devil, and are in a great measure controlled by him."[58]

Mormon President Brigham Young agreed. The week before the fall of Sumter, he proclaimed that "the wicked and the ungodly are preparing for their own utter overthrow, and the nation in which we live is doing so as fast as the wheels of time can roll, and ere long sudden destruction will come upon them." A republican movement could survive only if it stood "upon the eternal rock of truth and virtue," Young asserted. This nation had failed on both counts. The government had turned against the truth and persecuted God's saints. "Our present president," which was Buchanan at the time, "is like a rope of sand, or like a rope made of water. He is as weak as water."[59]

When Elder Taylor quoted Isaiah's line about a "covenant with death," he had in mind the nation's plot to wipe out the Mormons. This plan would fail, he said, but it would set in motion another deal with death, an alliance with the Devil that could bring the self-destruction of the nation. His prediction almost came true. Covenant with the Devil or not, there would be death in unprecedented measure.

These two chapters have shown how, after the battle of Fort Sumter, northerners and southerners vied over the Bible, each side accusing the other of violating scripture in fighting the wrong kind of war. This was tricky business for both sides. Religious wars could be the most dangerous of wars—that was a common opinion of their time (and ours). Holy wars knew no boundaries; they could spiral out of control into bloodbaths fueled by vengeance, even targeting civilian lives—unlike limited wars, fought against the military only, and for justifiable reasons. But that did not mean God should have no part in war—far from it. God stood on the side of justice and commanded his people to fight just wars. And yet that was the difficulty, as the line between just and holy war could be indistinguishable. Both sides defended their version of the war, calling it sacred, while outsiders like the Mormons tried to call down God's biblical vengeance on both North and South.

6

"Trust in Providence and Keep Your Powder Dry"

In the spring and early summer of 1861, soldiers boarded trains as bands played and people cheered. In June, South Carolinian Mary Chesnut wrote, "The war is making us all tenderly sentimental. No casualties yet, no real mourning, nobody hurt. So it is all parade, fife, and fine feathers."[1] Both sides of a divided nation united in their zeal for war. "War fever" ran rampant throughout the nation, with both northerners and southerners eager for the fight.[2]

Both sides finally got what they wanted in July at the First Battle of Bull Run—here was a real battle, giving both sides the chance to face off against the enemy. Here also was the first major providential test of the war, the first indication of which side God would take once the fighting started. For many southerners, the battle confirmed their reading of God's will; for many northerners, Bull Run stirred disillusionment and a call for the nation to re-dedicate itself to God. The battle also provoked revaluations of several key biblical texts, especially passages from Exodus in the South and Romans 13 in the North, with both sides trying to tease out the relationship between the Bible and Bull Run.

"A Cruel, Crazy, Mad, Hopeless Panic"

Americans wanted war, but few knew what it would look like. In the North, Lincoln's generals disagreed over whether to pursue an aggressive strategy or to take a defensive approach. No general in the United States knew more about war strategy than Lieutenant General Winfield Scott. That was the good news for Lincoln and the Union. The bad news was that Scott was seventy-five years old, in poor health, and tended to doze off in meetings.[3]

Even if Scott had been young and ready to fight, he did not want to fight with the volunteers Lincoln had available, largely because of the bad experiences he had with volunteers in the Mexican War. These men lacked character, Scott said. "Our militia & volunteers, if a tenth of what is said be true, have committed atrocities—horrors—in Mexico, sufficient to make Heaven weep, & every American, of Christian morals *blush* for his country," Scott wrote in 1847.[4]

General Scott had good reason to worry—not only about the quality of the volunteers, but about the nation's preparations for war. "The United States has usually prepared for its wars after getting into them," James McPherson wrote. And "Never was this more true than in the Civil War."[5] The army was too small to wage a war over such a large territory, and one in four of Lincoln's officers would take their leadership skills to the Confederacy. Even if the army wanted to invade the South, troops would have trouble finding their way because good maps of southern territory were hard to come by. The situation was so bad that General Halleck had to resort to maps he had found in a bookshop in Missouri.[6]

The South had an even steeper hill to climb in preparation for war. While southerners possessed a wealth of military leadership, they lacked the resources of the North. The Union far outpaced the Confederacy in industry, producing 90 percent or more of the nation's guns, cloth, boots, and pig iron. Additionally, the North had far more mileage in railroads, roads, and canals than the South. Confederate soldiers suffered constant shortages in basic clothing, tents, and horses. As the war progressed, soldiers in the Confederate army would make do with clothing peeled off the bodies of dead Yankees.[7]

That was the reality that existed with respect to the war. But Americans didn't want reality in 1861. They yearned for the glamor of the war they envisioned in their minds, which explained why many disliked Scott's conservative "Anaconda Plan." Like the snake from which the plan drew its name, Scott wanted to surround the South and squeeze it into submission. The navy would set up a blockade all along the southern coastline. The army would establish a cordon along the northern borderline of the Confederate states, and the Union would seal the western border by sending an expedition down the Mississippi River. It was a conservative strategy aimed at giving the South time to come to its senses. But Scott's patience was out of sync with the times. Too many northerners thirsted for war.[8]

Lincoln was among those who wanted to strike quickly against the enemy. Seeing that his plan had little support, Scott relented and put Irvin McDowell in command of thirty-five thousand volunteers who prepared to invade

Virginia.[9] On July 16, McDowell led his army south from Washington, preparing to attack the Confederates at the railroad junction at Manassas. The Confederates in that area had solid leaders: Pierre G. T. Beauregard—Fort Sumter's "hero"—was in command, supported by Joseph E. Johnston and his soldiers from the Shenandoah Valley. Beauregard and his twenty thousand men moved close to Manassas Junction, positioned near the Bull Run, a small stream.[10]

At first, the battle seemed to be going well for McDowell. His troops pushed the Confederates back near Henry House Hill, where Judith Henry was killed because she refused to leave. The Union troops appeared to be on the verge of success, and many Confederates retreated. McDowell, it seemed, had won the first major land battle of the war.

Spectators, including congressmen and newspaper reporters, had traveled down to watch the expected onslaught, and they buzzed with excitement when they heard news of McDowell's victory.[11] Yet they would be disappointed. Despite the promising beginning, the Union lost—badly. As the battle turned into a rout, Union troops dropped their guns and fled, creating quite a scene. The sight of all the panicked and fleeing soldiers disgusted the spectators. One congressman said that "it seemed as if the very devil of panic and cowardice seized" officers and soldiers alike. As the soldiers and officers ran past, "We called them cowards, . . . put out our heavy revolvers, and threatened to shoot them, but all in vain; a cruel, crazy, mad, hopeless panic possessed them."[12]

Southerners called it the battle of Manassas; northerners called it the battle of Bull Run. Confederates lost 400 men in battle and an additional 225 who later died of their injuries. The Union lost 625 men, and the Confederates took an additional 1,200 Union soldiers as prisoners of war.[13]

In the South, the victory at Manassas fueled overconfidence. As James McPherson noted, southerners forgot "the Biblical injunction that pride goeth before a fall" (Proverbs 16:18). Other biblical warnings would follow—some heeded, others ignored. As they read scripture, northerners and southerners pondered the relationship between the Bible and Bull Run.[14]

"The Glory of God, the Defense of the South"

After the battle, Thomas "Stonewall" Jackson, fresh off the heroics that earned his reputation as a great warrior, turned his thoughts to another hero of the conflict—God. He wrote to his wife, "Yesterday we fought a great battle and gained a great victory, for which all the glory is due to God *alone*."[15]

Jackson thought it remarkable that many hours of fighting had resulted in only one injury—a bullet had grazed the middle finger of his left hand. Had it been just a fraction to the left, he would have lost the finger. But God protected him, just as God protected his horse, which suffered wounds but survived. "The battle was the hardest that I have ever been in," wrote Jackson. Furthermore, "God made my brigade more instrumental than any other in repulsing the main attack"—which explained how he earned his famous nickname, "Stonewall." As he acknowledged, however, God was the true stone wall in the attack. Three times in the letter he said God had won the battle. It was with reluctance that he even mentioned his role in the victory, cautioning his wife that "this is for your information only—say nothing about it. Let others speak praise, not myself."[16]

What explained Jackson's comments? Faith in providence? Modesty? Perhaps both? Nevertheless, he expressed a continual refrain here: God, the warrior, gained the victory. This battle was "the greatest battle of modern times," and the South won one of modern history's greatest victories, according to a chaplain of the Seventh Regiment of Louisiana Volunteers.[17]

Many believed that the meaning of this battle had been foretold in scripture. Newspapers reminded everyone that "Manassas" had a biblical parallel. In the Old Testament, "Manasseh" meant "making to forget." A key verse was Genesis 41:51: "And Joseph called the name of the firstborn Manasseh: For God, said he, hath made me forget all my toil, and all my father's house."[18]

Most Americans knew Joseph's story. The son of Rachel and Jacob, Joseph was his father's favorite, which aroused his older brothers' jealousy. They debated killing him but instead decided to sell him into Egyptian slavery. Yet Joseph survived and thrived, rising to power in Egypt. Later, when Joseph had a son, he named him "Manasseh" because he wanted "to forget" all that his brothers put him through.

An article in the *Memphis Daily Appeal* compared "Manasseh"—Joseph's son—with the battle of Manassas, "the first or first born of our battles and victories." This was a work of God, "remarkable" in its wonder. Here, the Yankees were like Joseph's evil brothers who had persecuted their youngest brother. In contrast, Joseph represented the South. In this battle at Manassas, God made the South "forget all our toil, and all our father's house, or the unkindness of our brethren of the old political household, who are the cause of all our trouble."[19]

If the Joseph story revealed the biblical meaning of "Manassas," the Exodus story gained even more attention after the battle. The Exodus, a Louisiana chaplain said, was "strikingly analogous" to the battle of Manassas.[20] Why? Wasn't the Exodus a narrative of liberation from slavery? If so, it supported the North, not the South. As antislavery clergy in the North argued, the Exodus was the story of a God who liberates people from slavery and oppression—freeing them from all kinds of pharaohs, including the plantation pharaohs of the South.

It was not that simple, however. Granted, God's people in the Exodus story suffered in slavery, which God condemned by liberating them from their Egyptian masters. But did the "slavery" of the Exodus truly parallel the slavery of the American South? Or was "slavery" a metaphor for another kind of bondage?

Consider a key example. In the American Revolution, patriots saw their victory as an Exodus from the tyrannical hands of the British pharaoh, King George III. As many patriots interpreted the Exodus, the slavery of the Israelites was a metaphor for tyranny, like the tyranny they suffered in the 1770s.

It was both ironic and tragic that Revolutionary-era patriots could wail about their "slavery" at the hands of Britain while they themselves enslaved Africans and later established a nation based on liberty. Many British observers attacked American patriots for this hypocrisy. As British Methodist John Fletcher put it, the so-called American patriots were "hypocritical friends of liberty, who buy, and sell, and whip their fellow men as if they were brutes; and absurdly complain that *they* are enslaved, when it is they themselves, who deal in the liberties and bodies of men."[21]

As enslaved people listened to patriots' complaints about their "slavery," they also overheard the Exodus story. It did not take long before men and women in slavery embraced the Exodus as a biblical parallel to their lives, and they yearned for God's liberation from American pharaohs. "There is no part of the Bible with which [enslaved people] are so familiar as the story of the deliverance of Israel," said a Union Army chaplain. "Moses is their *ideal* of all that is high, and noble, and perfect, in man. I think they have been accustomed to regard Christ not so much in the light of a *spiritual* Deliverer, as that of a second Moses who would eventually lead *them* out of their prison-house of bondage."[22]

After Manassas, southern whites tried to reconceptualize the Exodus story: it was not about victory *over* slavery, it was a victory *for* slavery.

Confederates believed they, not enslaved people, paralleled the enslaved Israelites of Egypt. And they were the ones God liberated at Manassas, freeing them to keep slavery alive. In this view, the Exodus was about secession, not slavery. The children of Israel in the Exodus were like the Confederates— both wanted to secede from oppressive governments.[23]

This analogy between the Egyptian pharaoh and the tyrannical Union remained a popular belief in the South. The Union, claimed Episcopal bishop Stephen Elliott of Savannah, embodied the spirit of a Yankee pharaoh. "In the very language of Pharaoh," newspapers throughout the North proclaimed, "'We will pursue, we will overtake, we will divide the spoil; our hands shall destroy them'" (Exodus 15:9). The northern churches, too, acted like a modern pharaoh in desecrating their communion tables and "their altars with the star-spangled banners."[24]

A key example of this came in a sermon entitled *The Glory of God, the Defense of the South*, preached in Yorkville, South Carolina, by Methodist minister John T. Wightman. It was one week after the battle of Manassas, and Wightman proclaimed, "Let Pharaoh descend with chariots of Egypt, the guiding pillar will become darkness and terror to our foes, but a pathway of glory to Israel," making it clear that Union troops were the modern-day chariots of Pharaoh. They could do their worst, but the Confederacy would prevail, because "God is here. Bayonets do not legislate for us, nor standing armies crush with the weight of cannon the uprising of disloyal masses." In the Old Testament, God guided the people of Israel in a pillar of cloud and a pillar of fire. Likewise, in the South "the pillar of fire is police and pilot." War came, but the South lay under God's protection, "teeming with millions of happy slaves," sleeping "in unbroken tranquility amid the shout of cannon and the tread of advancing legions."[25]

"Happy slaves?" This was typical of slavery's defenders—they painted an idealistic picture of the enslaved life, with benevolent masters and carefree people in bondage. This was self-serving rhetoric, but many slaveholders sincerely believed that, in enslaving people, they were serving them.[26] Even the Exodus story could be shaped to fit this agenda. Confederates turned the Exodus from a story about liberation from slavery into a celebration of slavery.

Exodus was not alone, as Wightman found support in other scriptures as well, including a text from the Song of Solomon, which he used to support the argument that black skin destined people to slavery:

I am black, but comely. . . . Look not upon me, because I am black. . . . my mother's children were angry with me; they made me the keeper of the vineyards; but mine own vineyard have I not kept. (Song of Solomon 1:5–6)

This was biblical evidence of slavery's role in "the triumphs of the Church," said Wightman. Taking a common view of the Song of Solomon, he interpreted it not as erotic poetry between two lovers, but as a symbolic revelation of God's love for his people, represented as his "spouse." In this scenario, "The daughter of Africa is the 'beloved' of the Spouse"—that is, Africans had a major role in supporting Christianity and God's mission in the world. They fulfilled God's plan by working in their masters' fields—as this text put it, they kept "vineyards" that did not belong to them. Their productive work empowered the South to construct a prosperous society built on scripture and agriculture, according to God's will. To those who scoffed at the notion that enslaved people had such a major role to play in God's plan, Wightman responded that God often chose "the weak things of the world to confound the mighty."[27]

The victory of Manassas did that—it confounded the mighty; a smaller southern force had triumphed, and southern preachers made this point repeatedly. A Presbyterian from Alabama preached on the story of David and Goliath, focusing on young David's daring words to Goliath just before he killed and beheaded the Philistine giant: "The Lord saveth not with sword and spear: for the battle is the Lord's, and he will give you into our hands" (1 Samuel 17:47). The Yankees were the modern Philistines, waging "a war of conquest and subjugation." Just as the Philistines relied on "their champion Goliath . . . so has the North" depended on "the military genius and prowess of Gen. Scott, their great leader." The parallels were endless, and the result was the same: God delivered the victory to his people who appeared to be weaker, though they prevailed, stronger in morality and spirit.[28]

A week after the battle, William Butler, rector at St. John's Church in Richmond, Virginia paraphrased a psalm: "The stout-hearted are spoiled . . . and all the men whose hands were mighty have found nothing" (cf. Psalms 76:5). This victory was the "triumph of the moral over the physical" and "a voice of thunder from the throne of God," proclaiming "assurance to the true patriot's heart—thy enemies are God's enemies, and thy cause is His cause." For Butler, the Manassas victory could be explained only by divine deliverance. "We say, and say truly, that God was on that battle-field, and decided its result," but "not by a miracle, but by the faithful use of every means—moral, intellectual and physical—which God had provided for and bestowed upon us," Butler preached.[29]

Likewise, for Wightman, this victory was God's deliverance, as it was the first major strike in a war that would do so much good for the church that it was comparable in scope to the Protestant Reformation. It was tragic that southern blood was shed, but "No work of God, no reformation can be accomplished without resistance, revolution, and blood." Moses proved this in his revolution against Egypt, but the same was true for George Washington and his brave patriots. They proved that "oppressive tyranny only could be revolutionized by the blood of martyrs." The greatest example was, of course, Jesus—"Even he who won our liberty on the cross died in the achievement." It was naive to think the Union would abandon their tyrannous treatment of the South without bloodshed.[30]

Terrible as it was, bloodshed was an acceptable sacrifice to protect slavery, in Wightman's view. "The eminence of the South is the result of her domestic slavery," he said. Slavery was "the feature which gives character to [southern] history, and which marshals the mighty events now at work for her defense and perpetuity." In defending slavery, southerners were also defending the scriptures. Southern "government is built on the Bible," Wightman claimed.[31]

"Courage of the True Patriot and Christian Warrior"

The clergy often had an awkward relationship with war. They preached patriotism but did not want their people to call them warmongers.[32] Likewise, militant religion worried Americans in the nineteenth century, and the Crusades were the prime example. "Mohammad taught the Arabs, that he who died for the Koran was a martyr, who went straight to the bliss of paradise," preached Thomas Smyth in a reflection on war after Manassas. The Catholic Church instilled in their crusaders much the same idea—fighting for God would free them from time in purgatory. These were "superstitious dreams," in Smyth's view, and they inspired nightmares of slaughter in holy wars.[33]

Was the Civil War yet another holy war? Confederates claimed to be fighting for God's cause. Were they launching another bloody crusade? Not according to Smyth. Religiously inspired warfare was not always wrong. Religious violence had to be judged by the religion that inspired the violence. As many southern Protestants saw it, the problem with the Crusades was that both Islam and Catholicism were errant faiths. In contrast, southern Protestants were neither superstitious Catholics nor misguided Muslims. They were Christians who read scripture correctly. They proved yet again that "the truest instances of martial heroism have ever been found among enlightened Christians." Their models were Oliver Cromwell's soldiers in the English Civil War, godly men "who passed from the prayer-meeting to the field of battle, with their Bibles girt under their armour."[34]

War, Smyth acknowledged, brought out the best and worst in humanity. War was always hell, but war often brought God and people together unlike any other events in history. "War is the sternest exercise of man's highest prerogatives and powers, and the field of battle the theatre of earth's most magnificent array, and of man's most splendid and heroic achievements," Smyth preached. War often began with lust and greed, and brought out "the monstrous passions of malice, hatred, and . . . blood-thirsty revenge." But war "also develops the loftiest virtues which can adorn humanity," including "honor, patriotism, fortitude, courage," and the final "victory over death and the grave."[35]

It was no wonder, then, that the Bible was full of war. God was a warrior, and "Faith is the parent and nurse of courage, confidence and heroism." Throughout history, "Religious faith has in all ages sustained heroic valour" and "animates the soul to a dauntless intrepidity and daring chivalry."[36]

Southern Christians often warned of a "sneering atheism" that infected some soldiers who believed that men, not God, controlled the outcome of battles. According to this cynical view, "Divine Providence is on the side of the strongest battalion."[37] If this "sneering atheism" filled the Confederacy, the cause was lost. The southern cause needed courageous soldiers, but Confederates needed to have the right kind of courage, the courage shown in scripture. Far more common was a false courage, fueled by "evil passions," including "lust, avarice, revenge." So preached Presbyterian minister George Armstrong to his congregation in Norfolk, Virginia, soon after Manassas. This was the courage of "the midnight robber, the assassin, the pirate," evildoers who feared nothing although they really had much to fear. This courage was often "cruel" and "desperate," but never reliable.[38] True courage stood stronger and longer, with a fearless calm based on love "of justice, love of country, love of kindred, love of truth, love of God." This was "the courage of the true patriot and Christian warrior," always "ready 'to do or die.'" This was the courage that won the day at Manassas, Armstrong believed.[39]

After Manassas, southern ministers expressed again one of the most critical concerns of the war—the need to give credit where it was due for the victory. Both Armstrong in Virginia and Smyth in South Carolina quoted Exodus 15:3, "The Lord is a man of war," asserting that the God of the Exodus (and Manassas) was a militant God. God won the victory, of course, but God did not win it alone. Victory, they insisted, resulted from aligned forces of divine providence and martial courage. As Smyth put it, "This victory has a two-fold aspect; one, as it is human, and the result of human agency; and another, as it is divine, and is the effect of Divine wisdom and power." "Soldiers were necessary—true soldiers—with arm to strike and soul to dare," Smyth asserted. The South needed soldiers who echoed Patrick Henry's famous words in the American Revolution: "Onward—for God and freedom! Give us liberty, or give us death!"[40]

To fight alongside this warrior God, the people needed to reflect God's military might. In military warfare, as in spiritual warfare, faith was essential but, to paraphrase the apostle James, faith without works was dead (James 2:17). The authentic Christian prayed "as if every thing depended upon God, and works as if every thing depended upon his own exertions—his own skill, and diligence, and fortitude." The case was similar in military warfare, where the best advice was "Trust in Providence, and keep your powder dry."[41]

"Fear of the Lord Is the Beginning of Wisdom"

While the South celebrated, the North mourned. Many northerners could relate to Horace Greeley of the *New York Tribune*, who wrote to Lincoln on July 29: "On every brow sits sullen, scorching, black despair." Greeley even suggested that Lincoln give up the fight. "If it is best for the country and for mankind that we make peace with the rebels, and on their own terms, do not shrink even from that." If the rebels "cannot be beaten,—if our recent disaster is fatal,—do not fear to sacrifice yourself to your country." Greeley further quoted Jesus: "Whoso would lose his life for my sake shall save it" (cf. Matthew 16:25).[42]

One week earlier, Catholic archbishop John Hughes saw a providential purpose in the defeat—perhaps it was God's way of telling Lincoln to send more troops to the battlefield. As he wrote to Secretary of State Seward, the defeat at Bull Run "may be providential, and I think that it is, and its benefits should be to make the federal government more alert in meeting the difficulties without regard to cost of men or money." Many northerners took the approach of Archbishop Hughes, looking for ways to see a providential victory in the defeat at Bull Run.[43]

The Bible is full of losers. In biblical wars, God's people lost about as often as they won. In the Old Testament, when the people were obedient, God usually blessed them with victory. When the people disobeyed, God often punished them by allowing their enemies to defeat them. But sometimes bad wars happened to good people—God's nations obeyed God, but still lost. When the world did not seem to make sense, people looked for answers in the wisdom literature of the Old Testament, specifically the books of Proverbs, Ecclesiastes, and Job.

President Lincoln led the way. His proclamation of a "day of Fasting, Humiliation, and Prayer" (to be observed on September 26) quoted Proverbs 9:10, "The fear of the Lord is the beginning of wisdom." Frequent reprintings of this proclamation made this verse the most cited scripture text in newspapers in the weeks after Bull Run.[44] "Fear" was the key word in this verse; it captured the somber, reverent, even anxious approach Lincoln thought the North should have in appealing for God's help. Americans, he said, should look to themselves, "confess and deplore their sins," humbling themselves, submitting to God's "chastisements"—including the chastisement at Bull Run.[45]

At Bull Run, the North felt the vengeance of God. God could even destroy the United States, said Boston Unitarian John F. W. Ware. God may want the South to succeed so that everyone would see what a nation of slavery looked like. The South would be a lesson in evil for all the world to behold, "in all its horror and iniquity," before it would "fall once and for ever."[46]

Perhaps the Union lost because it resisted emancipation. Frederick Douglass said, "To fight against slaveholders, without fighting against slavery, is but a half-hearted business, and paralyzes the hands engaged in it." As Douglass insisted, "War for the destruction of liberty must be met with war for the destruction of slavery."[47] Here Douglass hinted at an important argument: if northern whites would not oppose slavery for moral reasons, they should oppose slavery for military reasons. The southern cause would crumble without slave labor. "Arrest that hoe in the hands of the negro, and you smite the rebellion in the very seat of its life," said Douglass.[48]

Some northerners agreed, even within the Union army. In May, General Benjamin Butler had refused to return three enslaved men who had fled from their master and sought refuge with him at Fortress Monroe, Virginia. Their owner, a Confederate officer, demanded that Butler return his property—the Fugitive Slave Law dictated that Butler give them back. Butler's response was ingenious: these Confederates could not appeal to the Fugitive Slave Law because it was a law of the United States, which Confederates claimed had no authority over them. These men, Butler argued, were no longer enslaved— they were "contraband of war," workers for the Union army.[49]

Lincoln tried to walk a fine line on this issue. He hated slavery, and he wanted to punish the South and to deplete their power by seizing enslaved people as "contrabands." Yet he needed to do so without making the war primarily a war against slavery, which likely would enrage many in the border states who fought with the Union, but not for emancipation. Even so, Lincoln agreed with what Butler had done, and he agreed with the policy. From that point on, thousands of "contrabands" escaped slavery to seek refuge with the Union army.[50]

"Make Their State a Bible-State and Their Church a Bible-Church"

Not all northerners blamed slavery for the defeat at Bull Run. Slavery, some people thought, was a symptom of the real problem: the North had removed God from the nation's government.

In perhaps the most popular sermon after Bull Run, Yale-educated pastor Horace Bushnell of Connecticut traced the roots of this war to America's founding. Great as they were, the founders failed by shaping a government "without moral or religious ideas." The United States was "merely [a] manmade compact," and that weakness became America's downfall.

On this issue—perhaps only this issue—the North could take lessons from the Confederacy, Bushnell said. Repulsed by the secularism of the North, the Confederates founded their government on Christian principles because the founders had failed to do so. The Union faced its worst crisis ever because it had removed God from its center.[51]

It had not always been that way, Bushnell argued. The American Revolution had two religious ideas, one rooted in Puritan New England, which saw God as the head of government, and the other influenced by Thomas Jefferson, a southerner, who thought government should be "atheistic," a "mere human composition." These two contrasting political views—the Puritan and the Jeffersonian—formed the United States. And from the beginning these two views had "been struggling in the womb" of the nation like the biblical twins Jacob and Esau, battling it out from the nation's founding to the present.[52]

Unfortunately, Jefferson's view won—with disastrous consequences. As Bushnell saw it, the tragedy of American politics was that the nation tried "to maintain a government without moral ideas," a godless government that demanded loyalty to mere "human compacts."[53]

America's politicians "are not atheists," but they may as well have been. They ignored Paul's command in Romans 13: "Let every soul be subject unto the higher powers. For there is no power but of God: the powers that be are ordained of God" (Romans 13:1). They disregarded scripture's teaching that God "dominates in all history, building all societies into forms of order and law." When people formed governments and framed constitutions, they really came from God, who "has prepared them, and stamped them with his own providential sovereignty."[54] This mattered because in wartime, a nation had to be worth dying for—it could not command loyalty "to our mere compacts and man-made sovereignties," Bushnell said. Without divine sanction, the nation no longer commanded "reverence to its honor, care for its safety, integrity in maintaining it" and "willingness to make sacrifices for it."[55]

Thomas H. Stockton, Methodist minister and chaplain for the US House of Representatives, also cited Romans 13 after Bull Run, as did several newspapers. A prominent minister in Washington, DC, Stockton was a friend of Abraham Lincoln who would later offer a moving prayer at Gettysburg just before Lincoln delivered his famous address. After Bull Run, Stockton repeated Paul's command: "Let every soul be subject unto the higher powers. For there is no power but of God: the powers that be are ordained of God" (Romans 13:1). Preaching to Congress, Stockton said the nation's leaders not only missed Paul's political teachings, they missed almost all of scripture. They had downgraded the role of the Bible in American government, with tragic results.

In both church and state, Stockton told Congress, the Bible was "a visible representative of Divine sovereignty among" the people.[56] God commanded the Puritans "to found the State and [to] found the Church, on the Bible; to make their State a Bible-State and their Church a Bible-Church." The Puritans had emigrated because British and European empires had marginalized the Bible, holding it "under the foot of the State, and under the thumb of the Church." With the Puritans, therefore, God lifted the Bible to its proper place—at the head of government. Indeed, American freedom was primarily the freedom to obey scripture, as God "made His people free on purpose that they might thus honor His book."[57] Again, as Paul wrote, everyone was to "be subject to the higher powers"—but only *because* these powers came from God. The men in Congress needed to know that their authority came solely from God, as Paul stated.

In the aftermath of Bull Run, Stockton told Congress, "The *first* sovereignty in our land is the sovereignty of the Bible—representing the sovereignty of God." Second in importance was "the sovereignty of the people," followed in order by "the sovereignty of the State" and "the sovereignty of the Church."[58]

Tragically, the US Constitution had replaced the Bible as the ultimate authority for many Americans. Misinformed Americans had made the Constitution "the supreme law of the land," when in reality the Constitution was secondary to the authority of the people and, above all, "the Bible, and the God of the Bible." Again, overzealous advocates of the Constitution should heed Paul's command: "There is no power but of God: the powers that be are ordained of God" (Romans 13:1).[59]

Was this the design of the founders? That was the key question. As we have seen, both southerners and northerners, such as Bushnell, blamed the founders for setting up a godless national government. But Stockton disagreed: "When they had ordained and established the Constitution of the United States, they regarded and confessed themselves as completely subject to the Bible and the Bible's God," he said. The Constitution's "principles and promises are alike derived from the Bible." And the Constitution "has no value except as the Bible sanctions it."[60]

The war had called the nation back to the Bible, Stockton told Congress. Scripture informed the state which wars it could declare, and how it should fight. Nations could not fight wars of conquest, or just any war that profited them. Paul's advice rang true: the nation's leaders—like these congressmen in Washington—served at God's pleasure, "ordained of God," bearing the sword in God's name as "the minister of God." This war, then, needed to be carried out as "a sacred ministerial office." The United States must pursue war "in the name and with the sanction of God."[61]

Bushnell and Stockton hoped defeat in war would awaken the nation to its religious value. As more blood was shed in battle, Americans would realize that their nation was a sacred cause worth dying for. So, adversity—even defeats like the battle lost at Bull Run—would serve the nation well by sealing the nation's meaning in blood. As Bushnell put it, "True loyalty is never reached, *till the laws and the nation are made to appear sacred,* or somewhat more than human. And that will not be done till we have made long, weary, terrible sacrifices for it."[62]

This was an idea central to the Bible: "Without shedding of blood there is no such grace"—no salvation without sacrifice. So, "There must be tears in the houses, as well as blood in the fields," as the people fought for the nation and cried out in anguish to God. "In these and all such terrible throes, the true loyalty is born. Then the nation emerges, at last, a true nation, consecrated and made great in our eyes by the sacrifices it has cost!" This is the only way "to make a nation great and holy in the feeling of its people." In this civil war, Bushnell surmised, "Victory, when it comes, will even be a kind of religious crowning of our nationality," leaving aside "all the atheistic jargon" of the current government.[63]

Bushnell had grasped something important here—the biblical concept of sacrifice gave religious and moral meaning to otherwise senseless violence. That concept would grow with the death toll as the war progressed.

7

"A Holy Baptism of Fire and Blood"

The Bible marked the landscape of the Civil War—literally. Like Manassas, Shiloh was a name taken from scripture. Shiloh had a tumultuous history in the Bible. It was a central place of worship for Israel, home to the Ark of God—the representation of God on earth, which contained the tablets of the law God delivered to Moses. Shiloh was also a military headquarters (Joshua 18:1, 22:9, 12), but above all, Shiloh was a place of tragedy. The Philistines destroyed Shiloh, a conquest so devastating that the name Shiloh became synonymous with defeat in northern Israel (Jeremiah 7:12–14, 26:6, 9). Shiloh rose again in the United States as many churches took its name. One of those churches stood near the southwestern corner of Tennessee near Pittsburg Landing, which became the site of the war's bloodiest battle yet.[1]

After the Battle of Shiloh, a Baptist in Virginia examined the biblical name of Shiloh, hoping to find "a good omen for our cause." One meaning of "Shiloh," he found, was "the great author of Peace"—ironic, given the amount of blood shed in the battle.[2] Fought on April 6–7, 1862, Americans had never seen a battle with so many casualties—over twenty thousand.[3]

"Our War and Our Religion"

The carnage at Shiloh jolted many Americans back to reality; they had almost forgotten that a war was going on. The previous major conflict had been at Bull Run during the summer of 1861. In the meantime, Lincoln had tried un- successfully to get General McClellan to move against Richmond. The West, however, saw more action. By the beginning of 1862, the Union controlled Kentucky and prepared to move on Tennessee. General Ulysses S. Grant and Admiral Andrew H. Foote maneuvered up the Cumberland and Tennessee Rivers to occupy Nashville and control the railroads, thereby cutting off Confederate supplies.[4]

In February, Union forces defeated two Tennessee forts—Henry and Donelson—that stood just south of the Kentucky state line. In defeating Fort

Donelson, Grant demanded unconditional surrender, serving notice to the Confederacy that he was a tenacious general with sights set on a quick and decisive victory.

As the North came to terms with this exciting news, William Barrows of Reading, Massachusetts, preached *Our War and Our Religion: and their Harmony*. The victories in Tennessee brought mixed emotions, Barrows said. Some Christians "feel that in those splendid successes we lost, in some inexplicable way, the principles and spirit of our Christianity." As a cure for this timidity, he recommended Psalm 109—a biblical attack on a corrupt leader:

> Let his days be few; And let another take his office. As he loved cursing, so let it come unto him. . . . Let there be none to extend mercy unto him. When he shall be judged, let him be condemned. . . . Let his children be fatherless; And his wife a widow.

This was God's warning to the Confederates, especially Jefferson Davis, Barrows said. But was this too harsh? Some Christians could not see how the God of church and sacraments could be the God of "the camp and bayonet, the gun-boat, the deadly assault, and 'garments rolled in blood.'"[5]

Americans needed to move beyond this pacifist faith, Barrows insisted. The Bible and war went together, and wartime revealed some of the most central themes in scripture, themes that were often overlooked in peacetime. It was as if Christians needed war experience truly to understand the Bible. "Times and seasons are profound interpreters of Scripture," he said, "and the hurrying and expository events of the present providences in our land are issuing monthly and almost daily volumes of commentaries" on the Bible. "So the exigencies of the hour may help us to discover a meaning in the sterner and imprecatory parts of God's word that an expounding in times of peace would never furnish us." The war psalms of David, for instance, with "terrible prayers against the enemies of Zion," psalms that had "the very ring and rattle of armor, and the crimson coloring of victims, have not become obsolete."[6]

This was a crucial point for understanding the Bible's place in the Civil War—God "is as glorious when he takes vengeance as when he shows mercy, when he burns Sodom as when he builds Jerusalem. Sinai reflects his excellency as much as Calvary." As Barrows said, "The Old Testament is a fair exposition of the character of God." Also, "The mildness and mercy of the New Testament over the Old are over-estimated and over-stated."[7]

Paul said it well in Romans 13—the civil power was "the minister of God" and "a revenger to execute wrath upon him that doeth evil." Wartime was one of those times "when compassion is out of place, when it is too expensive a luxury and cannot be indulged." Again, paraphrasing Paul, Barrows said, "We bear the sword under the appointment of God, and we must not bear it in vain."[8]

"We've Had the Devil's Own Day"

After the fall of Fort Donelson, General Albert Sidney Johnston had little choice but to give up Nashville to the Union and head south. General Grant then took over the Tennessee Valley. By early April, Grant and his men were at Pittsburg Landing.[9]

The losses of Forts Henry and Donelson stung the South, but Generals Johnston and Beauregard regrouped with plans to retake Tennessee. They wanted to head north and defeat Grant's men before their ranks could be reinforced by General Buell, who was bringing thirty-five thousand Union troops, which would increase the number of Union forces to seventy-five thousand men. The attack had to come soon, Johnston and Beauregard knew, so they planned to surprise the Union troops on April 4. It did not happen, however. Their men were inexperienced marchers, so it was slow going, in part due to bad weather.[10]

The battle finally erupted on the morning of April 6, as Confederates attacked unsuspecting Union forces at Shiloh Church. One of the first divisions hit was under the command of William Tecumseh Sherman. "My God, we're attacked!" Sherman said, and he got his men moving quickly.[11] This would be a monumental day for the war—and for Sherman. He would never be the same, as a man or as a general. He was in constant motion, leading his inexperienced troops through the fighting. By the end of the day, he had suffered minor wounds and Confederates had shot three of his horses from under him.[12]

If Sherman would never be the same after this battle, neither would Grant. The first day was a disaster. When the Confederates attacked, Grant was several miles away having breakfast. After the battle, rumors again spread about Grant's drinking. He must have been drunk, many claimed, which was why he was not at Shiloh when the battle began. Even as complaints about Grant rolled in, President Lincoln brushed them aside. "*I can't spare this man,*" Lincoln reportedly said, "*he fights.*"[13]

Lincoln knew what he was talking about—Grant was a fighter, and too valuable a leader to lose, whatever his faults. Besides, Grant was not drunk at Shiloh; he was sober but overconfident. After victories in Tennessee, Grant had his mind on offense, not defense. He wanted to move south and take Corinth, Mississippi, an essential railroad junction for the Confederacy. A loss at Corinth would devastate the Confederacy's chances in the Mississippi Valley.[14]

That seemed like a lost cause after the first day of fighting at Shiloh. When evening came, several Union commanders, including Sherman, wanted to retreat. Who could blame them? Thunder shook the horrific battlefield. Rain poured down as wild pigs fed on the remains of dead soldiers. Sherman approached Grant as he stood in the rain with a cigar in his mouth. "We've had the devil's own day, haven't we," said Sherman. Grant responded, "Yes. Lick 'em tomorrow, though."[15]

And they did. Overnight, Don Carlos Buell brought fresh troops to reinforce Grant's and Sherman's men. When morning came, Union troops led a surprise assault on tired Confederates who thought they had the battle won. To add insult to injury, the Yankees sang "Dixie" as they attacked. Shocked Confederate troops realized their victory had been snatched away.

The Confederates retreated. In a few hours, they had failed to reassert control in the Mississippi Valley. From that point on, the Union would take the upper hand in this important area. Even more important than the strategic result, however, was the cost. The Union's list of wounded, missing, or killed reached thirteen thousand men; the Confederate list totaled ten thousand. In the two days of this battle, more Americans died than in any battle in American history. Tragically, that record would not last long.[16]

"What Like a Bullet Can Undeceive!"

The Battle of Shiloh "would have cured anybody of war," said Sherman.[17] The battle traumatized everyone. Those who were there had difficulty describing their experiences. Sherman wrote, "Who but a living witness can adequately portray those scenes on Shiloh's field, when our wounded men, mingled with rebels, charred and blackened by the burning tents and underbrush, were crawling about, begging for someone to end their misery?"[18]

The battle stirred crises of conscience among men on both sides. An Illinois private had no desire to kill, but recognized that "fore every secesh that we killed there would be one less to shoot at us. I thought of that several times during the day."[19]

On the Confederate side an Alabama farmer uniquely named Liberty Independence Nixon said, "Here I am ready to take the life of my fellow man when the Scriptures of eternal truth positively declare Thou shalt not kill." He had no choice, however. The Yankees fired, so "We were ordered to fire [and] I became resigned to my fate let it be what it might. My nerve seemed to be as steady as if I was shooting at a beast."[20] A reporter from the *New York Tribune* wrote, "Men lost their semblance of humanity" at Shiloh, "and the spirit of the demon shone in their faces. There was but one desire, and that was to destroy."[21]

The gore of Shiloh inspired biblical comparisons. "The Bloody Field of Shiloh," to some observers, resembled a new Golgotha, the place of Christ's crucifixion.[22] It took a gruesome death for Christ to save humanity. Likewise, observers at Shiloh reflected on the gruesome sacrifice of so many Americans.

A Union soldier reported that he "saw an intelligent looking man with his whole diaphragm torn off. He was holding up nearly all of his viscera with both hands and arms."[23] This same Union soldier saw a pleading "rebel, covered with clotted blood, pillowing his head on the dead body of a comrade. Both were red from head to foot. The dead man's brains had gushed out in a reddish and grayish mass over his face." This brought "to mind one of the hardest principles in warfare—where your sympathy and humanity are appealed to, and from sense of expediency you are forbidden to exercise it."[24]

"What we endured on the field of battle while gathering up the wounded is simply beyond description," said Sister Anthony, a Catholic nun from Cincinnati. She helped pile the wounded aboard boats, so-called floating hospitals, reporting that "at one time there were 700 of the poor soldiers crowded in one boat." They had to move upriver, "being unable to bear the terrific stench from the bodies of the dead on the battlefield."[25]

The thousands of mangled bodies shocked Americans. What could be done with all the dead? Bodies had to be cared for properly, but that did not always happen. Rumors spread that Confederates plundered the corpses of Union soldiers in several battles. "Talk about Southern honor!" proclaimed a Methodist from New Hampshire. "Let them first show some claim to humanity." Confederates "disturbed the graves of our dead on the fatal field of Bull Run, and of those sacred bones carved mementoes of their bravery!"

These rebels allegedly "took the skulls of our brave dead and marked them as drinking cups for their marriage feasts." Whether or not this occurred, the thought of it made this preacher's blood run both cold and hot.[26]

The treatment of the dead after battles was a divisive issue during the war, and both northerners and southerners often quoted a verse from Jesus's ministry. He had called a disciple to follow him, but the disciple asked if he could stay back until he could bury his father. Jesus responded, "Follow me; and let the dead bury their dead" (Matthew 8:22). This text spoke to the gory situation of bloody battlefields and the quandary of what to do with the bodies. Both sides quoted this verse against the other, condemning them for not looking after their dead. A month after the Battle of Shiloh, a newspaper in Mississippi quipped that the Yankees only obeyed one command of Jesus, "Let the dead bury their dead," because they allowed their comrades' "bodies—covered with gore and besmeared with dirt, deprived the conceded right of sepulture," and this injustice called "down imprecations upon their unhallowed heads."[27]

Piety and patriotism blended at Shiloh. "The dead Yankees in front of our regiment," wrote Isaac Tichenor of the Seventeenth Alabama, "were piled three deep" and "most of them were shot in the head." Tichenor was both a chaplain and a sharpshooter who killed Union soldiers at Shiloh. In the heat of the battle, Tichenor said, "I sprang to my feet—took off my hat—waved it over my head—walked up and down the line, and they say, 'preached them a sermon.'" He later reported he was "more than satisfied, with the results of my labors as chaplain of the 17th," believing "that in no other position could I have served the cause of my God or my country so well."[28] He survived the war and later served as president of the future Auburn University and was secretary of the Home Mission Board of the Southern Baptist Convention.[29]

News of Shiloh—including stories like these—spread quickly. Initially, the South celebrated victory. Thomas "Stonewall" Jackson wrote to his wife, "God gave us a glorious victory in the S. W. (Shiloh)." Victory came from virtue in the ranks, he said, praying that his troops would "be an army of *the living God*, as well as of its country." He quoted David, "the ancient warrior-saint," who said, "My flesh crieth out for the living God" (Psalms 84:2).[30]

Then they heard the bad news—initial reports were wrong; the Yankees had won at Shiloh. Some southerners never conceded defeat—perhaps the news was just too hard to accept, given the great cost. But northern readers could not get enough. In Michigan, one teenage newspaper salesman knew that the report from Shiloh would be a bestseller. He borrowed money to buy up all the newspapers he could, then he sold them for a profit. This teenager—Thomas Edison—invested his money, founded a newspaper, studied telegraphy, and became an inventor.[31]

With the news came assessments of the battle and its meaning. None was more accurate than General Grant's report. Before Shiloh, Grant thought—perhaps—the Union could end the war soon. After Shiloh, he "gave up all idea of saving the Union except by complete conquest."[32]

Despair flooded the South. At the end of April, Mary Chesnut heard the war was lost because the Union had the Confederacy outgunned. "Our enemies have such superior weapons of war—we, hardly any but what we capture from them in the fray." It seemed that war was "a game of chess—but we have an unequal number of pawns to begin with."[33]

For some, news of Shiloh brought disillusionment. Did the killing have a point? Even if it did, the tragedy was undeniable. Shiloh was a portent, a sign of the bloodletting to come. As Herman Melville put it in his poem *Shiloh. A Requiem*: "What like a bullet can undeceive!"[34]

"God's Providence Is in This War"

Two days after the battle at Shiloh, Lincoln called for a national day of thanksgiving, calling Americans to "invoke the divine guidance for our national counsels."[35] Although it was common to assume victory meant God's blessing, others disagreed. It "is a very dangerous and a fatal doctrine" to conclude that wartime victories mean that God is on one's side, said Unitarian minister William Orne White. One should be willing to fight for God's purposes without regard for victory or defeat, White said. "We should be content to be losers for two hundred years, without giving up our faith that our cause was precious in his sight." Wasn't Jesus a loser? Anyone looking from the outside would think so. When Jesus's enemies killed him on the cross, Pharisees probably thanked God for the victory, not knowing that Christ was the true victor.[36]

Victory in war, like any kind of success, can be a delusion. God used it to fool sinners into a false sense of security, said White. "Success is one method which Providence seems to employ in order to blind men, and suffer them

to become at last a prey to the snares which they had set for other people."
Paul said as much in his second letter to the Thessalonians: "God shall send
them strong delusion, that they should believe a lie: That they all might be
damned who believed not the truth, but had pleasure in unrighteousness" (2
Thessalonians 2:11–12).[37]

If victory in battle could deceive, so could defeat. Victory at Shiloh did not
mean God favored the Union, just as defeat did not mean God opposed the
Confederacy. So said Joel W. Tucker, a prominent North Carolina Methodist.
He preached from Isaiah: "I form the light, and create darkness: I make peace,
and create evil: I the Lord do all these things" (Isaiah 45:7).

Although many could not imagine that God created evil, it was true because Isaiah said so. Perhaps God only *allowed* evil (which was the usual
interpretation). Either way, God oversaw a world of evil, including the
Confederacy's defeat at Shiloh. One could say, then, that it wasn't the Union
that defeated the Confederates at Shiloh—it was God, because God controlled the war.

"God's providence is in this war," Tucker said. The war would accomplish
some divine purpose. God's providence mystified, but it also consoled. Belief
in providence meant that the universe made sense, if only in the mind of
God.[38] The war would turn out well for God's people, but they would suffer,
as the Confederates did at Shiloh. As Tucker argued, "Whom the Lord loveth
he chasteneth, and scourgeth every son whom he receiveth. If ye are without
chastisement, then are ye bastards and not sons." So defeat could signify
God's favor.[39]

In the Old Testament, God chose Israel, but God did not always bless the
Israelites, allowing them to toil as enslaved people in Egypt. Even after delivering them from slavery, the Lord allowed them to suffer even more losses
to other nations, along with struggles in the wilderness. The same was true
in the American Revolution, Tucker said. "God was with our Revolutionary
fathers in their struggle for independence; but he suffered them often to be
defeated in their seven years conflict with the mother country; but the eagle
bird of Liberty gathered strength while rocked by the storms and tempests of
a bloody Revolution." This cycle continued; God used defeat to improve the
people. To the South, Tucker explained, "God has sent our reverses for our
good. They were necessary to humble our pride; to stop our foolish and absurd boasting, and to make us feel the importance of the conflict in which we
are engaged." Everyone wanted victories, but God honed patriotism through
defeat.[40]

"The Bible Gives a Significance to the Shedding of Blood"

The more blood spilled in the war, the more evidence Americans found for the war's sacredness. "Our cause is sacred," said Tucker. "How can we doubt it, when we know it has been consecrated by a holy baptism of fire and blood." The war "has been rendered glorious by the martyr-like devotion of" Confederates "who have offered their lives as a sacrifice on the altar of their country's freedom."[41]

On the Union side, over a thousand miles from this North Carolina Methodist, a Congregationalist in the Northwest agreed. Shiloh's bloodshed confirmed that this was a sacred war, according to D. C. Sterry of Lake City, Minnesota. We can understand why many Americans called the war sacred—they had lost loved ones, and they wanted to honor those sacrifices. But these concepts of sacred war did not just appear. They had a distinct character and a history, much of it grounded in scripture. "The Bible gives a significance to the shedding of blood, such as no human history ever did or ever will," Sterry preached. Martyrs filled the Bible, and at the center of the New Testament was the ultimate martyr, Jesus, who shed his blood for the world's redemption. Americans should remember the crucifixion when reflecting on Shiloh, Sterry said, remembering how God saved humanity "not with Silver and Gold—but with this precious blood of Christ; thus showing that God's richest gift's [sic] to man—Eternal Life and Immortal bliss—are the fruits of the shedding of blood."[42]

After the bloodbath of Shiloh, Sterry admitted that war was horrible and all too common. World history was a story of one bloody war after another. Even worse, people often liked war. For thousands of years, people "delighted in the carnage of War, and made it their chief business! What blood-thirsty monsters loom up on all those pages of old, monsters bloated with ambition," waging wars "and sending terror to every human heart." There was no glory in this travesty. "None but a FIEND can gaze upon it without the most sickening horror!"[43]

And yet the horror of war should not overshadow the holiness of this war. "The shedding of blood in war, terrible and awful as it is, is sometimes not only justifiable but absolutely demanded by the Almighty," Sterry said. Refusing to fight the Confederates was "a monstrous crime against both man and God."[44]

The blood of Shiloh, although gruesome and tragic, was precious. Sterry quoted Psalms 72:14: "He shall redeem their soul from deceit and violence: and precious shall their blood be in his sight." Sterry applied this scripture to those brave patriots who had sacrificed their lives to defend the United States. Then he made a crucial point: "All the great principles of right—everything from the past worth having—have been the purchase of blood, the best that ever flowed in mortal veins, the best that ever flowed in Heaven!"[45]

Like many biblical reflections on martyrdom, this was a recruitment speech. Sterry asked, if the nation needed "my blood, or the blood of my son, shall I withhold it? God forbid! How should I be a child of His and do so? How a disciple of Him who poured out his blood to save me, and who declares, 'Greater love hath no man than this—that a man lay down his life for his friend?'" (John 15:13).[46]

That was the difficulty, however—laying down one's life. In an age that valued a "good death," death on the battlefield horrified everyone—it was a bad death, one of the worst imaginable, many believed. Not so, said Sterry and many other ministers. They assured soldiers that death in this war was not a bad death; it was an honorable and courageous death. Sterry asserted, "He who lays down his life for such a Government as ours, gives it to a holy cause." The soldier "who dies so, lives forever." Dying in this war was a glorious death, he continued, and "there is a glory in dying for the right in this war.—It is as truly martyrdom for Christ and his truth as was ever endured in any age of the church or the world."[47]

Perhaps this was not just a sacred war, but as sacred as any war ever fought. "Tremendous responsibilities are devolved upon us, the most weighty and solemn that ever rested on a nation under Heaven. We are put in charge of the dearest interests of Humanity, and of the name and honor of God. Sacred trusts! We must never betray them." Further, "Never since time began was there so holy, so just, so righteous a conflict. Never could a people go forward so confident of God's approval." He continued, "We are not only fighting the battles of freedom, but we are fighting the battles of the Lord."[48]

As this remarkable sermon revealed, finding meaning in all the bloodshed was critical for Americans who reflected on the Battle of Shiloh. The struggles of war, said a Baptist from New Haven, would result in a more just and stronger nation—"the stars and stripes all restored, the dear Banner having a new and more precious significance from all its terrible baptism of blood."[49]

"They Are Ceasing to Be Johns and Are Growing to Be Davids"

On April 16, over a week after the Battle of Shiloh, the Confederate Congress passed a conscription act—the first in American history, enabling Jefferson Davis to draft all white men ages eighteen to thirty-five. For pacifists, including Quakers, this draft posed a crisis.

The biblical case for pacifism often rested on Jesus. Quakers in North Carolina said, "We have enlisted under the banner of the Captain of our soul's salvation, Jesus Christ, the Prince of Peace; therefore, . . . we cannot fight, or aid directly or indirectly in any carnal wars."[50]

As pacifists quoted the New Testament to oppose war, more Americans struggled with an Old Testament kind of warfare. Abolitionist minister Levi Paine said after Shiloh: "The precepts of the New Testament seem more in accordance with true Christian feeling and experience." So, "To Christians thus tenderly and peacefully educated, the fierce warfare waged by Joshua against the Canaanites, the warlike hymns of David, and the terrible denunciations of Isaiah and Ezekiel, appear to exhibit little of the spirit of true religion, and less of the spirit of Christianity."[51]

Yet the Civil War confronted American Christians with Old Testament violence. "The thrilling events now transpiring in our country are adding fresh illustration and clearness to the teachings of the Old Testament." The war changed "Christian devotion." Because of the "wicked and powerful rebellion," "Christians begin to understand how the wars of Joshua and the imprecatory psalms of David can properly belong to the Bible." Now "The style of Christian thinking and conversation and devotion is receiving an Old Testament coloring." Christians would "pray in good Old Testament fashion. They are ceasing to be Johns and are growing to be Davids."[52]

Clearly, some people questioned all the Old Testament war arguments, calling them inconsistent with the Gospel. Paine responded, denying any inconsistency between the peaceful Jesus of the New Testament and the warlike Joshua and David of the Old Testament. "We have the authority of Christ's own words in proof of the fact that there is no inconsistency between the Old Testament and the New." The major difference between testaments was that "the New Testament contains the history of *a person* who was himself the model and example for all his followers." In contrast, the Old Testament "is the history of *a nation*, and its lessons are especially applicable to men in their civil and public relations." In the Civil War, therefore, "The Old Testament now possesses for us a new and peculiar interest."[53]

Six days after Shiloh, a similar refrain came from George W. Gardner in the First Baptist Church of Charlestown, Massachusetts. With a sermon titled *Treason and the Fate of Traitors*, he made the shocking claim that they should relish in the bloodletting of the Old Testament and pray for an Old Testament kind of violence on the South. One key example of this Old Testament kind of violence occurred when God sent angels to slaughter the Assyrians. At that time, God's people of Judah had received threats from Assyrian king Sennacherib, who had rampaged the land, defeating other nations and burning their gods. Judah's King Hezekiah prayed to God for deliverance. That night, God sent an angel who killed 185,000 Assyrians, leaving the camp littered with their corpses (2 Kings 19).

Not only was this a bloody scene, but it was a righteous scene. Should Christians praise God for this holy violence? This is a tricky subject for ministers, not wanting to glory in bloodshed. But sometimes bloody victory was God's work. If so, it was sinful *not* to glory in it. Gardner asked, "Is not [the Confederacy's] overthrow, their utter discomfiture, righteous? Shall we not rejoice in it; shall we not give thanks to God for it?" God sent an angel to kill Sennacherib's Assyrian army "on that terrible night of doom," so should not Americans pray that God will "send panic into the ranks of our enemies and scatter them before our advancing armies as chaff before the whirlwind?" Should not the North pray "that he will sow the sunny fields of the South, thick as skulls at Golgotha, with their bleaching bones?" "Do not be shocked," the preacher said. "I shudder as much as you do at the heart-sickening details of a bloody victory." But it is necessary "if the monster will not yield without his hecatomb of human sacrifices." The "weapons" of the Confederacy "must come down; if in no other way, then let them fall from hands made nerveless by the missiles of death."[54]

"The Enemy Must Be Conquered"

If the North needed new Davids and Isaiahs to fight a holy war, the South seemed to need them more. Battle losses—including Shiloh—stung the South, and one of the most-read reflections came from James Henley Thornwell's popular sermon, *Our Danger and Our Duty*. "Providence seems to be against us," Thornwell said, "disaster upon disaster has attended our arms." According to Thornwell, "We must guard sacredly against cherishing a temper of presumptuous confidence."[55]

Providence, not pride, was key to victory. "No nation ever yet achieved anything great that did not regard itself as the instrument of Providence. The only lasting inspiration of lofty patriotism and exalted courage is the inspiration of religion," Thornwell said. The Confederacy suffered defeat because southerners had grown proud. They had made jokes about northerners, calling them cowards, while bragging of the southerners' military expertise. It was as if Confederates had forgotten that Lincoln's armies outnumbered them—the North's "numbers are so much superior, that we are like a flock of kids before him." Pride—it had gone before destruction.[56]

Fear—perhaps that was what the South needed, for it could be that southerners were not terrified enough of losing the war. If the North were to win the war, Yankees would seize southerners' property, and "Our wives and daughters are to become the prey of brutal lust." There would be no southern legacy that any white southerner would want. "The civilized world will look coldly upon us, or even jeer us with the taunt that we have deservedly lost our own freedom in seeking to perpetuate the slavery of others." This humiliation would be worse than all other losses, including property and life.[57]

Surrender? This was not an option for Thornwell—the idea "is monstrous." The Confederacy must defeat the Union at all costs with any possible weapons, even fighting with "axes, and tomahawks; anything that will do the work of death is an effective instrument in a brave man's hand." Southerners needed to be "the fit instruments of a holy Providence in a holy cause."[58]

Before Shiloh, the war was essentially theoretical for many Americans. People had died, but not like they did in that Tennessee field. Before Shiloh, many Americans on both sides held out hope for a short war. After Shiloh, those hopes died, but that was fine for the southerners who refused peace at any cost. "I have always been an advocate of peace," Sarah Morgan wrote in her diary, "but I say War to the death! I would give my life to be able to take up arms against the vandal[s] who are laying waste our fair land!"[59]

The bloodletting that shocked the nation at Shiloh was a foreshadowing of battles to come. A conflict that shed blood on this scale could not easily end, nor could it be easily interpreted. The experience of death moved Americans to reconsider the violence of scripture and set the stage for biblical views of Antietam and Gettysburg.

8

"Welcome to the Ransomed"

Less than a week after the carnage at Shiloh, the Republican-led Congress approved the District of Columbia Compensated Emancipation Act, which proposed to free enslaved people and to compensate slaveowners in Washington, DC. Daniel A. Payne, a bishop of the African Methodist Episcopal Church, visited President Lincoln and encouraged him to sign the bill, which he did on April 16, 1862.

That same week, Payne preached his most influential sermon, *Welcome to the Ransomed, or, Duties of the Colored Inhabitants of the District of Columbia.* He focused on St. Paul's advice to Timothy: give special thanks and prayers "for kings, and for all that are in authority; that we may lead a quiet and peaceable life in all godliness and honesty" (1 Timothy 2:1–4). This meant that those who had been set free should thank God for "the benevolent intention of Congress," which passed the Compensated Emancipation Act. African Americans had been enslaved like the Israelites in Egypt, but God used Congress as "his Moses and Aaron," freeing the people. "Congress has *ransomed* you," Payne wrote, and he urged formerly enslaved people to thank the nation that had liberated them.[1]

But this was also the nation that had enslaved them. As Payne knew, people who had been liberated from slavery had mixed feelings about the United States. Then again, Paul probably had mixed feelings about his political rulers as well. "Paul lived under the reign of Nero, the bloody emperor, who having set Rome on fire, amused himself with drinking and music while the city was in flames; and afterwards, accused the Christians of the crime which he himself had committed, thereby causing many of them to be put to death in the most cruel manner." Nero turned the murdering of Christians into a sport. Still, Paul commanded Christians to pray for the Roman Empire, Payne said. The US government, despite its faults, was much better than Rome under Nero's rule. So "If it was the duty of the ancient Christians to pray for such monsters of wickedness, by how much more is it our duty to pray for a Christian Government."[2]

"A Christian government"? Many African Americans would dispute that label. But Daniel Payne still used it, even though he knew the nation was hardly perfect. African Americans should pray for President Lincoln, his cabinet, the Supreme Court, and Congress. It was "the peculiar privilege of the Colored People in the United States" to offer "supplications, prayers, intercessions, and thanksgiving for these authorities," Payne said.[3]

Speaking of Lincoln, Congress, and other national leaders, Payne prayed, "O, that God may bring them all to the knowledge of the truth as it is in Christ Jesus! O, that every one of these Authorities may become a holy, wise, and just man! Then will the laws be enacted in righteousness and executed in the fear of the Lord." If all these men would follow Jesus, they would see the world as Jesus saw it. Jesus mediated between God and all of humanity— "Black men, red men, white men, are all alike before Him." Payne hoped that God would bless the United States. "If God has blessed this nation, neither internal foes, nor foreign enemies can crush it." But God would only bless the nation if it acted justly, "throwing the broad wings of its power equally over men of every color." Only then "shall justice be engraven on our arms, and righteousness on our star-spangled banners; and our armies shall then be led to battle by the Lord, and victory secured by the right arm of our God."[4]

The future was uncertain, but Lincoln impressed Payne as a man of "real greatness and . . . fitness to rule a nation composed of almost all the races on the face of the globe." High praise from a man that historians call "perhaps the most influential bishop of the nineteenth-century black denominations." But high praise for Lincoln would be in short supply in the coming months, especially from African Americans. Lincoln had wavered on emancipation, many believed, and he needed to pursue a harder war focused on abolishing slavery. The war grew in intensity, and so did debates over slavery's role in the conflict. Through it all, Americans turned to scripture to defend an even more brutal war for and against emancipation.[5]

"The Bloody and Barbarous System"

The emancipation of the District of Columbia in 1862 illustrated an important shift: slavery moved to center stage in the war. More Americans talked about emancipation in public. Abolitionists, deemed dangerous radicals by most Americans, gained more of an audience. When the radical abolitionist Wendell Phillips lectured in Washington, DC, in the spring, large crowds—including congressmen and President Lincoln—came to hear him. That was amazing, considering that in previous years Phillips probably would have been run out of town.[6]

Certainly, millions of Americans still despised abolitionists, even in the North. But much had changed in 1862. Some dreamed that an emancipated Washington, DC, would lead to an emancipated nation. On Easter Sunday, a minister in Salem, Massachusetts, even compared the emancipation of Washington with the resurrection of Christ. "May Christ's resurrection be the type of an awakening to new life in this nation." " '*Christ is risen indeed.*' Let us hope that this country is risen indeed." This was a triumph for the nation, he said. "This great republic, never so great before, makes the important declaration, that it but tolerates slavery where it cannot reach it, and while it cannot; that it does not protect it, nor choose it, nor wish it well."[7]

More Americans than ever blamed slavery for the war and its worst atrocities. In early July, Frederick Douglass said "the monster"—slavery—gave birth to the wars' "shocking practices," including "digging up the bones of our dead soldiers slain in battle, making drinking vessels out of their skulls, drumsticks out of their arm bones, slaying our wounded soldiers on the field of carnage, when their gaping wounds appealed piteously for mercy, poisoning wells, firing upon unarmed men."[8]

Douglass's words rang true for thousands of Americans in 1862. But even those who wanted to abolish slavery disagreed on when and how to do it. Should Lincoln proclaim emancipation immediately, in one dramatic act? This was lunacy, many Americans said. Immediate emancipation would plunge the nation into chaos.

Consider a letter from future president James A. Garfield, a soldier in the Eighteenth Brigade of the Army of the Ohio. He reported on a sermon by Henry Ward Beecher, who blamed Satan and slavery for the war. This, in Garfield's view, was "the best political philosophy Beecher ever wrote." Like Beecher, Garfield hoped that "this war will result fatally to slavery." And yet "I am equally clear that a declaration of emancipation by the administration would be a most fatal mistake."[9] General George B. McClellan, Garfield wrote, was "wickedly conservative" on abolishing slavery, "and the President [was] nearly as bad. But out of the very weakness and timidity of our leaders I draw the hope that thus God has willed it, that He is the commander-in-chief of our armies," and nothing could interfere with God's plan. "If McClellan will discipline and mobilize our people into armies, and let them meet the enemy, God will take care of the grand consequences."[10]

Garfield's letter illustrated just how divided northern whites were on slavery. Even Republicans who opposed slavery split into three groups. On one side were radical Republicans, who wanted the nation to declare emancipation and seize the property of the Confederate traitors. On the other side were conservatives who wanted slavery to die off eventually but only voluntarily when the slave states were ready for it. Freed people would then leave the United States and colonize another territory. In the middle were moderates who hated slavery but worried that sudden emancipation would spell disaster for the war and the nation. As the year progressed and the war raged on, many of the moderates adopted the radicals' view.[11]

As momentum against slavery increased, Republicans passed several laws—not only the law that abolished slavery in the District of Columbia, but an article of war that prevented the Union army from returning formerly enslaved people to bondage. Congress passed this law on March 13. It responded to a critical wartime issue: as Union armies invaded the South, many "contrabands"—people who had escaped from slavery—ran to their camps, hoping to find freedom among Yankee troops.

One such enslaved man, John Boston of Maryland, wrote to his wife on January 12, 1862: "It is with grate joy I take this time to let you know ... i am now in Safety in the 14th Regiment of Brooklyn." He instinctively connected his experience as a fugitive slave with the Exodus: "I had a little truble in giting away But as the lord led the Children of Isrel to the land of Canon So he led me to a land Whare fredom Will rain in spite Of earth and hell." He doubted he would see his wife again, but said "if WE dont met on earth We Will Meet in heven Whare Jesus ranes."[12]

Stories like these multiplied and provoked controversy. Many white soldiers, even those who despised slavery, did not want contrabands living with them. Yet a Republican Congress outvoted their Democratic opponents and settled the matter—any soldier or officer who returned a runaway slave to his or her master would face court-martial.[13]

"A Military Necessity"

As more northerners were debating slavery and emancipation, the Union suffered a setback at the Seven Days Battles, June 25–July 1, 1862. Robert E. Lee's men, although outnumbered, attacked George McClellan's Army of the Potomac close to the Confederate capitol of Richmond. Through a series of skirmishes, Lee prevailed; Richmond was saved. Both sides suffered heavy losses, and one of the major casualties was northern morale, which plummeted.

Meanwhile, southerners celebrated. "The gallantry of the Southern troops has never been surpassed in the world's history, and the North Carolinians have immortalized themselves," reported the *Semi-Weekly Standard* newspaper out of Raleigh, North Carolina. The headline read: "GLORIOUS VICTORY!—MCCLELLAN ROUTED, AND HIS GRAND ARMY BROKEN UP AND IN FULL RETREAT!" The proud McClellan had suffered his worst humiliation— "Exit little Napoleon." In contrast, Robert E. Lee's reputation skyrocketed. Thanks to him and his brave troops, the Union had failed to take Richmond, and Lincoln's men should look for no mercy from the Confederacy. When McClellan asked for "two days to bury his dead," General Lee reportedly quoted one of Jesus's harshest commands: "Let the dead bury the dead" (Luke 9:60).[14]

Northerners responded with harsh words of their own, often directed at Lincoln and his army. In a Fourth of July speech just after the Seven Days Battles, Frederick Douglass called Lincoln and his cabinet "weak" and "incompetent." They had made a mockery out of the war, employing "rebel worshiping Generals in the field," the chief of which was McClellan, "a real pro-slavery Democrat." McClellan had the reputation as a general who refused to fight the rebels. He never seemed to have enough men, and they always needed more training. Not only was McClellan reluctant to attack, he warned against uprisings of enslaved people, and he refused to allow his men to sing "anti-slavery songs in his camp," Douglass said. McClellan was "either a cold-blooded Traitor" or "an unmitigated military Imposter."[15]

Douglass made a point that echoed through the summer of 1862: Lincoln and his armies had "fought the rebels with the Olive branch. The people must teach them to fight them with the sword." No matter what Lincoln intended, he had treated the Confederacy too gently. And because Lincoln refused to wage a strong enough war on the South, he protected slavery, a system he claimed to hate. As Douglass saw it, "We have a right to hold Abraham Lincoln, sternly responsible for any disaster or failure attending to the suppression of this rebellion."[16]

Too many Americans failed to see the link between defeating slavery and defeating the Confederacy, Douglass claimed. Some argued that "we cannot reach slavery until we have suppressed the rebellion." Instead, Douglass argued, "We cannot reach the rebellion until we have suppressed slavery. For slavery is the life of the rebellion." Calling on images from the Exodus, Douglass said, "Let the loyal army but inscribe upon its banner, Emancipation and protection to all who will rally under it, and no power could prevent a stampede from slavery" like "the world has not witnessed since the Hebrews crossed the Red Sea." Americans needed to understand "that this rebellion and slavery are twin monsters, and that they must fall or flourish together."[17]

Lincoln agreed with much of what Douglass said, especially his view of McClellan. After the Seven Days debacle, Lincoln wanted to remove McClellan—many Republicans would have liked that. Rumors circulated that Democrats were trying to recruit McClellan to run against Lincoln in the next election—a rumor that turned out to be true. But again, Lincoln could not just dismiss McClellan. His men loved him; without McClellan in charge, many men would probably have thrown down their rifles.

Lincoln agreed with Douglass on another point: the war had been too soft on the South. The Union needed to pursue a harder war on the Confederacy. To make that happen, Lincoln turned to John Pope, who would command a newly named Army of Virginia. Pope, a strong antislavery man from Kentucky, was a fierce fighter, in stark contrast with McClellan. Also unlike McClellan, Pope wanted to punish the rebels. He'd had enough of southern citizens taking up arms as guerrilla warriors. If they wanted to fight, Pope would give them all the fight they could handle. He commanded his men to shoot any so-called citizens who posed a threat. Also, if his troops ran across southerners who were disloyal to the Union, his troops should take over their property and evict them.

While much of this never happened—Pope's men never shot southern citizens, nor did they force them to leave their homes—Pope did seize property. An enraged Jefferson Davis said Pope's men "are systematically destroying all the growing crops and everything the people have to live on." Davis told General Lee to deal with Yankee officers like they were "robbers and murderers."[18]

Lincoln ramped up this harder war by naming Henry W. Halleck general-in-chief, a position Lincoln had been occupying himself. Halleck had the pedigree to wage a hard war yet keep it within the bounds of morality and just war theory. He was the renowned author of *International Law; or, Rules Regulating the Intercourse of States in Peace and War*. Halleck thus ordered General Grant to deal harshly with rebels. Grant was to "handle that class without gloves, and take their property for public use." The time had come,

Halleck said, "that they should begin to feel the presence of the war." Union armies could seize southern property—especially enslaved people.[19]

Lincoln had moral justification for a harsher war. In May, his administration sent to the Union forces General Orders No. 100, *Instructions for the Government of Armies of the United States in the Field*. They called this manual the "Lieber code" in reference to its author, Francis Lieber, a professor at Columbia College in New York. Before Lieber began writing this document, he knew firsthand about the war's violence—in 1862 one of his sons lost his arm fighting for the Union in the battle for Fort Donelson in Tennessee; that same year, another of his sons died in Virginia while fighting for the Confederacy.[20]

The Lieber code required just treatment of POWs, forbade torture, personal revenge, enslaving prisoners, or returning formerly enslaved people to the enemy. It argued that "men who take up arms against one another in public war do not cease on this account to be moral beings, responsible to one another, and to God." Yet the Lieber code dictated that "military necessity admits of all direct destruction of life or limb of *armed* armies, and of other persons whose destruction is incidentally *unavoidable* in the armed contests of the war." Most critically, the code argued that the most humane wars were often the most violent: "The more vigorously wars are pursued, the better it is for humanity. Sharp wars are brief."[21]

The Union, Lincoln decided, needed to pursue a "sharp war," more intense in fighting the enemy. The Bible helped the North take off the gloves. In July, the *New York World* ran an article titled "The End of Peaceable Warfare." The time for fighting "the rebels with both bullets and sugar-plums, is to cease." Finally, Congress decided that "the rebels must be conquered." Americans in the North had to realize that the rebellion was an act of Satan—"the great arch rebel himself," who authored a war "surcharged with deadliest hate, without hope and yet breathing defiance, remorseless, relentless, insatiate for havoc and spoil and ruin." The danger was that men who had cast aside right and wrong became a mighty enemy in war, "as truly formidable as the very devils of hell." The only way to defeat this enemy was to do what God did when his angels, including Satan, revolted in heaven: he cast them into hell. "Divine *wrath* alone can deal with such crime."

And "divine wrath" should energize Union soldiers. St. Paul said it well: government was "the minister of God, a revenger to execute wrath upon him that doeth evil" (Romans 13:4). The United States was God's "revenger," pursuing revenge on the Confederacy. This meant seizing rebel houses, horses—any property at all. Enslaved people, too, would "be welcomed," and if they can fight "they will be armed and put to that service."[22]

Not surprisingly, this harder war caused an uproar in the South. In response to "the arch fiend and savage, Pope," a Richmond newspaper quoted the Old Testament command "an eye for an eye, a tooth for a tooth, and a life for a life," vowing that Confederates would punish the Yankees for their uncivilized warfare (Exodus 21:24). "They burn down our houses, destroy our property, insult our women, arm the contrabands against us," and yet they call "all this a civilized mode of warfare!" The South would return the favor to "these robbers and murderers with the most scrupulous accuracy." The "atrocities and horrors that may characterize the war hereafter rest upon the heads of the invaders," who have waged "the war" with "a degree of inhumanity and barbarity which has shocked the moral sense of the world."[23]

Southerners were not the only ones outraged by this more brutal warfare; northern Democrats also blasted Lincoln's harsh tactics. Among Lincoln's critics was McClellan. This was an unjust war, McClellan wrote, too cruel to southerners. "It should not be a war looking to the subjugation of the [southern] people," he told Lincoln. It was wrong to seize property, including enslaved people, because doing so would be waging war on civilians. "It should not be a war upon population, but against armed forces." Furthermore, "A declaration of radical views, especially upon slavery, will rapidly disintegrate our present armies."[24]

McClellan wrote down this warning and handed it to Lincoln on July 8, while the president was visiting Harrison's Landing to inspect the army. McClellan stood by while the president read his memorandum, but Lincoln offered no response. His silence spoke volumes.[25]

After ignoring McClellan's rebuke, Lincoln pushed forward in pursuit of a harder war. The Union could not continue to fight the war "with elder-stalk squirts, charged with rose water," said Lincoln. And, like Frederick Douglass, Lincoln understood that the best way to pursue a harder war was to attack slavery. To free enslaved people had become, as Lincoln said privately on July 13, "a military necessity, absolutely essential to the preservation of the Union. We must free the slaves or be ourselves subdued. The slaves were undeniably an element of strength to those who had their service, and we must decide whether that element should be with us or against us."[26] But full emancipation was a bold move, Lincoln knew. He started writing his Emancipation Proclamation, although he said nothing publicly about it.

Many officers in the Union army realized that emancipation would be a good military strategy against the Confederacy. If the North could gain an advantage by freeing enslaved people, so be it, said Ulysses S. Grant. He fought "to put down the rebellion. I have no hobby of my own with regard to the Negro, either to effect his freedom or to continue his bondage." Grant continued, "I don't know what is to become of these poor people in the end, but *it weakens the enemy to take them from them*." This, as James McPherson said, "was abolition in action."[27]

Regardless of how they viewed emancipation, many northerners realized that slavery was not just a moral or economic issue; it was a matter of military urgency. Emancipation was not just about freeing the enslaved people; it was a means of winning the war. Without slavery, the Confederacy would be crippled, its economy devastated, leaving southerners unable to fight an aggressive war.

"King David Used a Slave of the Enemy as a Scout"

When emancipation became a "military necessity," African Americans recognized the irony. One man who saw this firsthand was Henry McNeal Turner, the first black chaplain in the US Army and bishop of the African Methodist Episcopal Church. The irony, as Turner said, was that Confederate victories, not Union victories, drove northern whites toward emancipation. He made this point in July, just after the Seven Days debacle. "McClellan's defeat before Richmond has made a great many emancipational converts," Turner wrote. He noted that "every victory the Southerners gain tends to loosen the chains of slavery, and every one the Northerners gain tends only to tighten them." It seemed that "God's plan of teaching [the North] sense is through Southern victories."[28]

Turner heard rumors "that negroes will be organized into regiments and armed for the war." That would be good, Turner believed. But Lincoln could forget about recruiting black soldiers unless he intended to liberate them. The nation "will have a hard time raising negro regiments to place in front of the battle or anywhere else, unless freedom, eternal freedom, is guaranteed to them, their children, and their brethren."[29]

Many African Americans implored Lincoln to allow them to fight in the war. In July, Frederick Douglass faulted Lincoln and his generals for sacrificing "the brave loyal soldiers of the North by thousands, while refusing to employ the black man's arm in suppressing the rebels."[30] Many Republicans saw Douglass's point. That same month the Thirty-Seventh Congress passed a militia act, which gave Lincoln permission to use "persons of African descent" in "any war service for which they may be found competent," which meant that African Americans could fight for the Union army. This was a daring step, and many northerners were not ready for it. But as some Republicans said, "The time has arrived when . . . military authorities should be compelled to use all the physical force of this country to put down the rebellion." The days of a war of "white kid-glove warfare" had ended.[31]

No issue provoked more outrage in the South than the proposal to enlist formerly enslaved people to fight the war. Many in the North opposed the idea as well. Naturally, then, some northerners turned to scripture to defend the idea. In one key example, the *Chicago Tribune* ran the article "How King David used a Slave of the Enemy as a Scout." This article advised Union generals to put down their tactical manuals and turn to the Bible, where they could learn how King David enlisted a slave in a desperate time of war. "The Amalekites had invaded Judah, burning the city of Ziklag, and carried the women and children away captive, among them David's two wives." David prayed and got God's approval "to pursue the invaders with his army." On the way, David ran across a slave whom the Amalekites had left behind. But David didn't turn the slave away. David fed him, helped him regain his strength, then asked this slave to show him where the Amalekites camped. After David promised that he would not return him to his master, the slave vowed to help David defeat the Amalekites. David went on to win a dramatic victory, but it wouldn't have been possible had he refused to liberate a slave and enlist him as a soldier (1 Samuel 30). "Let us learn" from this scripture, said the *Chicago Tribune*, "that the slaves will not join our side in the great civil war until we swear unto them that we will not return them to their masters."[32]

"God Cares for the Poor and Oppressed"

Readers of the *Chicago Tribune* would not have been surprised to see this extended discussion of scripture in its pages. Newspaper articles and sermons cited the Bible to defend various viewpoints during these months. For every scripture that seemed to justify emancipation, another could be used to reject it. Both sides volleyed biblical texts back and forth.

Occasionally, both supporters and opponents of emancipation centered on a particular biblical text and argued over its details. One important scripture described a violent scene—the fall of Jericho and the sin of Achan. This story fascinated both northerners and southerners alike. The action picked up with Joshua leading the Israelites to battle against Jericho. Before the fighting started, God commanded the Israelites to kill everyone in the city (except "Rahab the harlot"—another story), and to destroy their property. They must not take anything for themselves: "Keep yourselves from the accursed thing, lest ye make yourselves accursed" (Joshua 6:17–19). But one Israelite, Achan, disobeyed. He swiped a garment, along with some silver and gold. This angered God, who retaliated by causing Israel to lose the next battle—a fight against Ai, a lesser opponent that Israel should have easily defeated. After this humiliating loss, Joshua tore his clothing, prayed, and asked God for an explanation. The Lord responded that the people had "taken of the accursed thing," and, as a result, God would depart from the people until they cleansed themselves. Joshua heard God's warning and took action—he had Achan and his family stoned and then "burned them with fire" (Joshua 7:18–26).

This story caught the attention of Methodist minister Sidney Dean of Providence, Rhode Island, and he preached it on July 27, 1862. In the Civil War, the "accursed thing" was slavery, Dean said. Just as Achan's sin caused the Israelites to suffer defeat, so slavery caused the war that devastated the United States. Now the nation needed to follow Joshua and wipe out the "accursed thing." Only violence would work. For years, the nation had been too soft on slavery. "We have reached this crisis in our national history, because we have supposed that a system of kindness could cure an evil of such magnitude and harmonize such diverse and antagonistical principles as liberty and despotism." Now "The blood of one, or possibly five hundred thousand men is to wash anew the alter of American liberty to prevent its crumbling into ruin." The nation would have saved itself this massive bloodshed "had one, or ten, or fifty Achans"—read here, slaveholders—"been hung or stoned at the outset by an indignant nation."[33]

The nation's only hope was "for the sake of God and truth [to] let the edict of *emancipation* come!" If Americans were not ready for emancipation, they had better be ready for a longer and more devastating war. Americans needed to change their view of the war: "We must interpret this war as God's war of emancipation." "Up to the work christian patriots!" If not, "God's angel of vengeance, weary with slaughter," would bring "his dripping sword" to smite the nation because Americans "are wedded to their idols."[34]

Not to be outdone, Confederates responded with their own view of the sin of Achan. In Memphis, Tennessee, a newspaper reported on how some northerners used this scripture against slavery. They had "attempted to fasten the blame of the present unhappy condition of the country upon slavery, as the sin of Achan, which had drawn down upon us the judgments of heaven. But what was the sin of Achan?" Achan "violated the sacred rights of property—he had stolen from the enemy—he had confiscated to his own use that which did not belong to him"—perhaps as the Union army confiscated enslaved people to fight their owners? So this scripture had nothing to do with calling slavery evil. Slavery wasn't even in the text. From a southern perspective, this scripture supported slavery because it supported the right to property—like the rights of slaveholders over their enslaved people.[35]

This comparison shows the conflicting perspectives Americans often brought to the Bible. When Sidney Dean of Rhode Island read this story, he bypassed the fact that slavery was not mentioned in the text. For him, "the accursed thing" was an *analogy* for slavery, a sin that had destroyed the nation in war. He followed Frederick Douglass and other abolitionists in blaming the war and its atrocities on slavery. In contrast, the writer of this Memphis newspaper article took a *literalistic* approach: this story said nothing about slavery, so the "accursed thing" could not be slavery. Again, taking the literalistic reading, this scripture did allude to property rights—the property of Jericho, which the Israelites were forbidden to steal. For this writer, the crime in this story was not slavery; it was theft. So this story could be used to condemn any kind of theft, including the abolitionists' attempted "theft" of southern property by freeing enslaved people. These contrasting viewpoints show how a single biblical text—even one that did not mention slavery—could figure so prominently in debates over slavery and the war.

This debate over Achan also shows how involved newspapers were in applying the Bible to the Civil War in 1862. At about the same time, antislavery newspapers ran an article, "God Cares for the Poor and Oppressed," that stated that God loved lowly people whom the world rejected. God came to earth as Jesus, a poor man. In Jesus, God "entered the brotherhood of poverty, sanctifying it forever." Anyone reading the Gospels could see "how much Jesus loved the poor, how he shared their lot, entered into their sympathies, relieved their wants," said the author of this article.[36]

The story of Jezebel, the infamous evil woman from the Old Testament, helped to make the point. She was the "shrewd and unprincipled wife" of King Ahab, who coveted the vineyard of a poor man named Naboth. Since Ahab had no legal means of acquiring the vineyard, he schemed with Jezebel to seize the vineyard dishonestly. They conspired with others to tell lies about Naboth, falsely accusing him of crimes. In response, people stoned Naboth to death, and dogs licked the blood from his corpse (1 Kings 21). Ahab then seized Naboth's vineyard. This angered God, who sent his prophet Elijah to confront Ahab and Jezebel. Through Elijah, God told Ahab that he was doomed—not only would his kingdom perish, but the dogs would lick his blood as they did Naboth's, and dogs would "eat Jezebel by the wall of Jezreel" (1 Kings 21:23). The message for 1862? "How terrible are the denunciations of the word upon such as wrong the poor, the friendless, the widow, the fatherless, the hireling or the bondman!"

Vengeance—that was God's response to nations that acted as Ahab and Jezebel. Scripture demanded vengeance, and so did the enslaved people. "From thousands of rude altars, from unlighted cabins, from millions of oppressed went up a great, a bitter cry. God heard it. The cry of the oppressed called for vengeance, and it has come." Certainly "The hand of God is seen in this war thus far. He will give us victory if 'we let the oppressed go free.'"[37]

"This Is Our Country as Much as It Is Yours"

Even if many northerners thought the Bible demanded emancipation in the summer of 1862, Lincoln did not. He knew that nearly all Republicans supported emancipation, and nearly all Democrats opposed it. Lincoln could not afford to lose Democrats' support in the war, which could happen if he came out too boldly for emancipation. A direct challenge in 1862 came from the "Peace Democrats"—often called "copperheads"—who opposed the war and wanted to negotiate with the South to end the fighting. To many Republicans, copperheads were traitors, little better than the Confederates. To many southerners, the copperheads offered hope for an end to the war without an end to slavery.[38]

Lincoln still planned to issue his Emancipation Proclamation, but the timing was wrong, he believed. He held out for a major military victory before freeing the enslaved people in the South. He had to proclaim emancipation from a position of strength. That is, the war needed to be going well for the Union. Otherwise, his Emancipation Proclamation would look like a desperate attempt to salvage an unwinnable war.[39]

As Lincoln waited for victory on the battlefield, he endured attacks from abolitionists. In their view, Lincoln had shirked his responsibility as a Republican president; he was doing nothing to free people in bondage. William Lloyd Garrison said the president was "nothing better than a wet rag," and Frederick Douglass called him "the miserable tool of traitors and rebels."[40]

Through all of these conflicts, race dominated many debates. Democrats played on racism at every opportunity, calling the "Black Republicans" a bunch of fanatics who wanted to let loose "two or three million semi-savages" on the North, where these freed slaves would compete with whites for jobs. Among the Democrats was Archbishop John Hughes, who said, "We Catholics, and a vast majority of our brave troops in the field, have not the slightest idea of carrying on a war that costs so much blood and treasure just to gratify a clique of Abolitionists." Rhetoric turned to rioting over the summer, with white workers protesting against African Americans. Some of these turned violent, especially in Cincinnati.[41]

Most whites could not accept a multiracial society in which African Americans lived among them as equals. Even many Republicans who opposed slavery did not want to live among the freedmen. Some even argued that the best way to keep northern whites from having to live with African Americans was to free the enslaved people. After all, African Americans fled the South because they were enslaved there. If they were free, they would stay in the South where they belonged.[42]

Frederick Douglass addressed racist anxieties in his newspaper, *Douglass' Monthly*. African Americans were like people of any other race, Douglass argued. "Take any race you please, French, English, Irish, or Scotch, subject them to slavery for ages," treat them "as property," bound "with chains, scarred with the whip, branded with hot irons, sold" and "kept in ignorance by force of law," and "the same doubt would spring up regarding either of them, which now confronts the negro." African Americans were not an inferior race; they were an enslaved race, and the people of any other race would seem inferior if they had been enslaved. This has happened throughout history—one people enslaved another, and then the oppressors claim the enslaved people deserve slavery because of their "bad character" and inferiority.[43]

After emancipation, then, whites should treat formerly enslaved people fairly. "Pay them honest wages for honest work," Douglass said. This will give them new motivations. While enslaved, their only motivation came from the whip. If treated justly, formerly enslaved people would find "better motives of hope, of self-respect, of honor, and of personal responsibility."[44]

Many northerners agreed with Douglass. Worrying about the calamities that could result from emancipation was the wrong concern. According to a Unitarian minister in Philadelphia, "It is the slave kept in chains, not the slave released from his chains that is to be feared."[45]

Others, including Lincoln, were not so sure. As Lincoln held off on freeing enslaved people, African Americans recalled that Lincoln could, on occasion, sound as racist as most southerners. Back in 1858, he debated Stephen A. Douglas, who proclaimed that Lincoln was a radical who believed that African Americans were equal with whites. This was a controversial issue. If most whites in Illinois thought that Lincoln believed in racial equality, his political career likely would have ended. Lincoln denied the accusation: "I am not, nor have ever been in favor of bringing about in any way the social and political equality of the races."[46]

Yet these public statements did not match Lincoln's private convictions, according to historians. In fact, Lincoln "made the humanity of blacks central to his anti-slavery argument," said James Oakes. There is evidence to support this view. "Let us discard all this quibbling about . . . this race and that race and the other race being inferior," Lincoln said in 1858, urging the people of Chicago to "once more stand up declaring that all men are created equal."[47]

Lincoln knew that most whites believed that their race was superior and that whites and blacks could not live together as equals. Lincoln also knew that these and other racist views were the foundation for slavery. He tried to divide arguments for slavery from arguments for white superiority. He tried to assure whites that they could oppose slavery without accepting the equality of races.[48]

Many antislavery whites proposed colonizing African Americans. That was Lincoln's solution in 1862. He knew that many whites opposed emancipation because they opposed a mixed-race society. The best approach, then, was to free the enslaved people and then export them to a colony outside the United States.

Lincoln explained this view in a meeting with African American leaders in Washington, DC, on August 14, 1862. He was looking for blacks who wanted to leave the United States. Slavery was a great evil, he told them; in fact, it was "the greatest wrong inflicted on any people." But freeing the enslaved people would not extinguish racism. "There is an unwillingness on the part of our

people, harsh as it may be, for you free colored people to remain among us,"
Lincoln said. "Even when you cease to be slaves," Lincoln said, "you are yet
far removed from being placed on an equality with the white race." For all
these reasons, "It is better for us both, therefore, to be separated." Harsh as
they were, these were the facts, Lincoln believed.[49]

The African American response to Lincoln was swift and negative. One
African American from Philadelphia told Lincoln, "This is our country as
much as it is yours." Frederick Douglass agreed, saying that Lincoln had
"contempt for negroes." Lincoln's hypocritical views would motivate "ignorant" whites "to commit all kinds of violence and outrage upon the colored
people." Other advocates of emancipation agreed. As a white Boston minister
put it, "I will not call them *African* slaves. They have no memories of Africa;
they never had homes in Africa; they never saw Africa; they have no longing
for Africa. They have African blood in their veins, diluted, mingled, whit-
ened. They are American slaves." The enslaved people were not fleeing from
America; they were only fleeing from slavery. Those "benevolent" agencies
that wanted to colonize them would be taking them away from their homes.
It would not be liberation; it would be "exile." The enslaved people were "native Americans," and they wanted to remain so.[50]

Lincoln heard the criticism, responded to some of it, but most of all, kept
his mind on his Emancipation Proclamation, biding his time until a military
victory would free him to make it public. Meanwhile, he gave a pointed statement to Horace Greeley's *New York Tribune* in August: "My paramount object in the struggle *is* to save the Union, and is *not* either to save or to destroy
slavery," Lincoln said. "If I could save the Union without freeing *any* slave
I would do it, and if I could save it by freeing *all* the slaves I would do it; and if
I could save it by freeing some and leaving others alone, I would also do that."
These were cagey remarks. Here Lincoln served notice that his main objective was to save the Union, but that he might need to free the enslaved people
in order to do that.[51]

"The Presidential Pharaoh Hardened His Heart"

As we have seen, Daniel Payne called on the Exodus story to praise both
Lincoln and Congress for freeing the enslaved people in the District of
Columbia. The nation's leaders had "ransomed" these enslaved people, Payne
wrote, much as Moses had in the Exodus. Three months later, as Lincoln

stalled on emancipation, another prominent African Methodist Episcopal minister (and future bishop) used the Exodus story to attack Lincoln and other national leaders. On July 12, Henry McNeal Turner defined "a very singular correspondence existing between the war in the United States and the Egyptian plagues." And if the Civil War represented the new plagues of Egypt, then "Abraham Lincoln and not Jeff. Davis becomes the Pharaoh of the mystic Egypt (American slavery)." Lincoln refused to free the enslaved people, so "God calls from heaven, echoed to by five million of mystic Israelites (abject slaves), in peals of vivid vengeance, *let my people go.*" But since the nation refused to free the enslaved people at God's command, the war came—a "series of plagues begins, commencing at Fort Sumter."[52]

Turner then described how the first year of the war looked from his perspective. Not long after Sumter, God sent a message through Union general John C. Frémont. In August 1861, Frémont declared that rebels in Missouri had no rights to their property, so Frémont liberated the enslaved people. He did so without Lincoln's authorization, however, and the president quickly reversed Frémont's order. To Lincoln, Frémont's emancipation of enslaved people threatened to alienate the border states, which would prove disastrous. Henry McNeal Turner disagreed. For him, Frémont was a new Moses, saying, "Let my people go," commanding that "rebels should be shot and their slaves set free." Yet "The presidential Pharaoh hardened his heart and made void all his proceedings," Turner said. So the plagues of war continued.[53]

God had offered Lincoln another chance, Turner said. On May 9, 1862, General David Hunter issued a general order from Hilton Head, South Carolina, that freed the enslaved people in Florida, Georgia, and South Carolina. But again, Lincoln intervened. On May 19 the president rescinded the order, declaring that he had no prior knowledge of the order and that Hunter had no authority to issue it. Turner saw this as another example in which "the presidential Pharaoh hardened his heart, and in one gr[i]m mutter, furious enough to make hell grumble, precipitately hurled" the enslaved people "back into the darkest caverns of oppression, ever felt by a fiendish nerve." The result? Plagues returned with more Union defeats.[54]

Turner then issued his message to Lincoln: "And I tell old mystic Egyptian to-day, *my people must go free.*" The war, these plagues, were God's warning to the nation. "Mystic Egypt, [the United States] with mystic Pharaoh [President Lincoln] at its head, may refuse compliance to Heaven's demand; but the inexpressible tortures inflicted upon ancient Egypt . . . will all hardly bear a comparison to what will befall this nation."[55] The war, Turner reasoned, was a providential ordeal in which God directed events "for the benefit of some portion of discarded humanity." He believed that the world was heading toward a revolution, and that God would reshape the nation on "a platform of more equality and unanimity."[56]

"To Wrest the Bible from the Slave"

Henry McNeal Turner's use of the Exodus story to attack Lincoln's wartime policy points toward two key trends in 1862. First, a harder war against the Confederacy—and slavery—called for more appeals to the Old Testament. That was the opinion of A. L. Stone of Park Street Church of Boston. He called for emancipation—and a shift from the New Testament to the Old. He recognized that the nineteenth century had belonged to the New Testament. "The Old Testament, in our current notions and sympathies, has been almost outlawed from human affairs," he said. "We have turned its leaves for its curious and quaint old histories, but felt as though we were living under a new dispensation." The war had changed that. "Now the days have come upon us, for which these strong-chorded elder Scriptures have been waiting. Their representations of God, as the Rewarder of the evildoer, the Avenger of the wronged, the Asserter of his own trampled prerogatives" denouncing "confederate schemes of fraud and villainy . . . suit the day and the hour of the intense present."[57]

Of course, not all of the Old Testament taught war and vengeance, and some New Testament scriptures also helped to fan the flames of war. Who could forget Paul, who called God "a revenger to execute wrath upon him that doeth evil" (Romans 13:4)? But, as we have seen, Americans often turned to stories of Joshua, Jezebel, and others from the Hebrew scriptures—brutal narratives of a clash between good and evil.

Second, African Americans made some of the most persuasive biblical arguments for war and liberty in 1862. Again, Daniel Payne set the tone in *Welcome to the Ransomed*, when he challenged African Americans to embrace scripture: "Rest not till you have learned to read the Bible. 'Tis the greatest, the best of books." "Meditate" on the Bible "by day and by night," Payne said, learning the perfect law of God, and rejoicing in God's word that converted the soul and enlightened the mind. Scripture was better than "fine gold" and tasted "sweeter also than honey and the honeycomb" (Psalms 19:7–14).[58]

This may not seem controversial, but perhaps it was. It wasn't unusual for preachers to tell congregations to love the Bible—Payne knew that. But Payne also knew many Americans denied that enslaved people and those who had been enslaved *should* read the Bible. Southern states feared a literate slave population, and slave codes made it illegal for anyone to teach enslaved people to read and write. As the *Belmont Chronicle* of Ohio put in June 1862, slaveholders treated enslaved people as "brutes or living machines," believing "that the powers of their souls should be crushed." Slaveholders refused to educate their enslaved people, knowing "that intellectual elevation unfits men for servitude, and renders it impossible to retain them in this condition."[59]

This was a major issue for Christians who opposed slavery. Access to the Bible was a sacred right, they believed. "The gospel, and an open Bible, with the unrestricted privilege of access to them, are designed of God for every human being—every immortal soul—every tribe, race, people," said the *Belmont Chronicle*. "Any thing which withholds the Bible, or seals it up from the benighted," opposed Christ. "Slavery and the slave power" withheld "the Bible and a free gospel from millions of immortal souls," so those who supported slavery "stand against Christ, his gospel and his kingdom." If the nation kept the Bible from African Americans, the nation would be fighting against God—the nation would provoke "divine judgments" for its "Bible withholding policy" in this "age of progress and of the Bible." Anyone who helped "to wrest the Bible from the slave" was doing what it could "to bring this nation into fearful conflict with the uplifted arm of Omnipotence, and court its ruin."[60]

It was this "fearful conflict with the uplifted arm of Omnipotence" that stirred fears in the summer of 1862. Many Americans worried that the nation was courting "its ruin," especially after the Seven Days Battles. Many northerners read their Bibles and looked to Lincoln—some hoping he would declare emancipation and enlist black soldiers, others warning him against doing so. Lincoln, in turn, looked to his generals, hoping for the major victory that would enable him to proclaim emancipation and, hopefully, engage a fiercer war against the rebellion.

9

"Without Shedding of Blood Is No Remission"

Lincoln awaited a major victory, which would give him leverage to announce his Emancipation Proclamation, but he had no idea how long he would have to wait. As everyone soon learned in this war, anything could happen in battle. Strategies went awry when shots rang out. Only solders who had experienced it knew what battle was like. The horror of watching men die at a staggering pace was a bewildering feeling. In the chaos of the battlefield, many soldiers resigned themselves to fate—whatever happened, happened, and there was nothing anyone could do about it.

Others found comfort in providentialism, believing God controlled all events, and their lives were in God's hands. A Pennsylvania soldier wrote to his parents after his brother died in battle: "His time was set by the Almighty Man. He was due to die, and if he hadn't been killed in the battlefield he might have died in the hospital or some other place. I think our time is all set when we shall die and before we want to die, and it makes no difference where we are." It was good that this man had such faith because he met his own death at the battle of Antietam.[1]

Although belief in providence comforted soldiers, people wondered why God would allow such a bloody war to continue. Lincoln made some of his most profound statements regarding providence during this period. Americans had long believed "that God has directed the history of the United States," wrote historian Nicholas Guyatt. The problem is that this idea has become too commonplace, "so thoroughly familiar that one can easily overlook its essential oddness."[2] Providentialism had a long history in the United States, and it "played a leading role in the invention of an American national identity" prior to the Civil War.[3]

The Civil War challenged Americans' belief in providence. Maybe that was why Americans spoke so often about providence in the war—they had to reassure themselves that there was some order in the disorder. They rested on the promise that God directed their history and that their nation was special to God. But what happened when that nation divided? Both northerners and southerners believed in providence, but which side understood it correctly?

Questions like this drove Americans to the Bible, because scripture was their best guide to providence. In the Bible "we have a key to the dispensations of Providence, and need not greatly err in interpreting current events or in speculations as to the future," said Southern Methodist bishop George Foster Pierce. "God is always the same; and the Bible, while it records the actions of men, is really the history of God." In this confidence, "We learn from His past procedure what we may expect as to His present and future government." Pierce delivered this message, *The Word of God a Nation's Life*, in March 1862 at the Bible Convention of the Confederate States. After years of cooperating with the northern American Bible Society, southern ministers felt providence leading them to form a Confederate Bible Society. They believed the South should have its own Bibles, untainted by northern hands, and southerners would discover in them God's true providential message.[4]

The late summer months of 1862 would see a turning point in the war, and the events during this time compelled some of the war's deepest and most self-serving views of providence in scripture.

"Ripe for a Terrible Panic"

Lincoln hoped a harder war would pressure the Confederacy. Yet it seemed that the war was harder on the North than the South. Lincoln looked to his generals for results, especially Halleck (his general in chief) and Pope (general of the Army of Virginia). Lincoln also tolerated McClellan (still general of the Army of the Potomac), although Lincoln knew he couldn't count on McClellan to stand against Robert E. Lee on the battlefield. McClellan, in turn, mumbled in private that he was done with Lincoln and his administration. Halleck, McClellan believed, was "my inferior," and he called Secretary of War Edwin Stanton a "deformed hypocrite & villain." If Stanton "had lived in the time of the Savior," McClellan said, "Judas Iscariot would have remained a respected member of the fraternity of Apostles."[5]

If Stanton was the second coming of Judas Iscariot, in McClellan's view, Pope reminded some of another key biblical figure. Several newspapers, including the *New York Herald*, ran a biblical satire on Pope entitled "A New Apostle in the Shenandoah," comparing the "apostle" John Pope to the firebrand prophet John the Baptist.

John the Baptist dashed on the scene in the Gospels, a wild prophet from the wilderness who wore a coat of "camel's hair, and a leathern girdle about his loins" while eating "locusts and wild honey." Pope didn't wear a camel's hair coat, but he had McClellan's "saddle for his head-quarters." Pope didn't eat locusts and wild honey; he ate anything he could plunder from the people in Virginia. Both John the Baptist and Pope pursued a harsh agenda. John the Baptist cried, "Repent ye: for the kingdom of heaven is at hand"; Pope warned Virginia, "Repent ye, for the army of the Union is at hand." All around John the Baptist were sinners, "confessing their sins" and receiving baptism. All around Pope were rebels "confessing their sins of secession." When John the Baptist saw "Pharisees and Sadducees" he said, "O generation of vipers, who hath warned you to flee from the wrath to come?" The "apostle" John Pope told the Virginia rebels, "O, generation of vipers, who hath warned you to flee from the wrath to come? Bring forth fruits, therefore, meat for repentance." Jesus and John the Baptist warned the Jews they should not think they were invincible because of their relation to Abraham the patriarch. "God is able of these stones to raise up children unto Abraham," John the Baptist said. The "apostle" John Pope had another "Abraham" in mind, warning southerners that they could not trust in an "oath of allegiance" to Abraham Lincoln—they would still have to give up their property to the "apostle" John Pope.[6] Lincoln hoped that the "apostle" John Pope could do what McClellan would not—defeat Robert E. Lee.

Meanwhile, Lee divided his Army of Northern Virginia, sending half to attack federal supplies at Manassas. Stonewall Jackson, a hero at the battle of Manassas just over a year earlier, led his twenty-four thousand men on a rapid fifty-mile march in only two days. They raided the federal supplies at Manassas and then took up positions in the nearby woods. Pope's men tangled with Jackson's troops on August 29. The next day, Lee's army closed in, aided by twenty-eight thousand men commanded by James Longstreet.

After the fighting, the rebels had again defeated the Yankees at Manassas. Lee had accomplished a remarkable feat. A few weeks earlier, Union forces had threatened the Confederate capitol at Richmond. Now Lee had turned the tables. Although McClellan's and Pope's forces were double the size of Lee's army, Lee had defeated them and now seemed on the verge of attacking Washington.[7]

This second defeat at Bull Run devastated the North, summoning bad memories. On September 4, the *New York Tribune* reported, "The Country is in extreme peril." The North must face the fact that "the Union arms have been repeatedly, disgracefully, and decisively beaten."[8]

Somber reports flowed in from the battlefield. Legendary nurse Clara Barton described the scene as they treated the wounded. "The men were brot down from the field and laid on the ground beside the train and so back up the hill 'till they covered acres." Barton joined other nurses in putting down hay for the wounded to lie on. "By midnight there must have been *three thousand* helpless men lying in that hay. . . . All night we made compresses and slings—and bound up and wet wounds, when we could get water, fed what we could, travelled miles in that dark over these poor helpless wretches, in terror lest some one's candle fall *into the hay* and consume them all." It was little wonder why a writer in the *New York Times* asked, "Of what use are all these terrible sacrifices? Shall we have nothing but defeat to show for all our valor?"[9]

The loss at Manassas left Lincoln to deal with military leaders who blamed one another for the debacle. Lincoln blamed McClellan for refusing to support Pope with troops when ordered to do so, and his advisers agreed. Surely McClellan should be court-martialed (said Secretary of War Stanton) or even executed (said Secretary of the Treasury Salmon P. Chase). At the least, Lincoln should dismiss McClellan, said his advisers. They didn't have to convince Lincoln; he wanted McClellan gone at least as badly as they did. But again, he knew how loyal McClellan's men were to him. So instead of dismissing McClellan, Lincoln sent Pope back to the West and assigned McClellan to defend Washington. Besides, few rivaled McClellan at preparing an army for battle. "If he can't fight himself," Lincoln said of McClellan, "he excels in making others ready to fight."[10]

And they would need to be ready to fight and soon. The win at Manassas left Robert E. Lee ready to push north and put the pressure on Lincoln and his army while their morale flagged.[11]

Lincoln's struggles extended beyond the battlefield, however. Midterm elections loomed, and Republicans faced stiff opposition in November from Democrats, many of whom challenged Lincoln's leadership and the war itself. Lincoln also faced challenges on the international front. Would France or England enter the war and side with the Confederacy? It was a possibility, especially since they were running short on the valuable cotton that the southern states had provided. And then there was the Emancipation Proclamation. Lincoln wanted to announce it, but he still needed a victory on the battlefield so that he could do so from a position of strength. But the war seemed to be getting worse, not better.

"Egypt Was the Land of Refuge"

As the Second Battle of Manassas plunged the North into depression, it reassured southerners that God fought on their side. In Raleigh, North Carolina, Presbyterian minister Joseph Atkinson called the Civil War a striking revelation of providence. It was as if God was announcing himself in the war, making it impossible for anyone to deny he controlled all events. "Never in the history of mankind has the wonder-working providence of God been more strikingly manifest than in the successive phases of this contest."[12]

In Richmond, Virginia, Methodist minister and future bishop D. S. Doggett raised the providential stakes even higher. Wars were not like ordinary events; "Wars affect the destinies of mankind and the progress of society. Wars change the current of history. Wars are related to the propagation of the gospel. Wars have the characteristics of a retributive administration. Wars are disciplinary in their results."[13]

Without the Bible, God's providence was a riddle that people had no chance of solving. Southerners needed to rest their hopes on the Bible and nothing else. Just as the Ark of the Covenant represented God among the ancient Hebrews, so for southerners the Bible was "the ark of their safety, and the bulwark of their liberties." If the Confederacy did not follow the Bible's teachings, "Armies, navies, victories, constitutions and laws, will be as unsubstantial as the phantoms of a dream." For the South's own good, "the Southern Confederacy" must "reinstate the Bible to its place," Doggett said.[14]

Providentially, God placed the right people in the right places at the right times. God orchestrated victory on the battlefield, and southerners recognized parallels between heroes in the Bible and heroes in the present day. No biblical hero rivaled David, the man after God's own heart. He could dominate the battlefield and slay hundreds of Philistines. Yet David was not only a courageous warrior, he was also the inspired psalmist. That combination of martial prowess and spiritual character impressed ministers. After Second Manassas, Reverend Atkinson found a new David in Stonewall Jackson. "When we come to our own day, may we not hope that Jackson, the Christian hero, the man of piety and prayer, with a fervency of spirit, like David's in the sanctuary, and a martial ardor like David's in the field, has been graciously given us as the interpreter and impersonation of the Christian element and the Christian consciousness of this grand conflict?" Providentially, God had given the Confederacy a southern David.[15]

Jefferson Davis thought he recognized God's providence at work. After the victory at Manassas, he announced a day of prayer and thanksgiving, scheduled for September 18. In that day's sermon, Episcopalian bishop Stephen Elliott of Savannah pondered providence and victory. He preached from the proverb "Rejoice not when thine enemy falleth, . . . Lest the Lord see it, and it displease him and he turn away his wrath from him" (Proverbs 24:17–18). The moral of this scripture was that, even in the face of victory, the South should not be overconfident because God hated pride. Southerners needed to distinguish "between exulting over an enemy and offering praise and thanksgiving to God for his wrath."[16]

Some may wonder why Elliott wanted the South to thank God "for his wrath." Everyone knew that God's wrath was terrible. It had been over 120 years since Jonathan Edwards preached his sermon *Sinners in the Hands of an Angry God*. But Americans remembered this sermon and generations of others that warned of God's fury. In wartime, however, God's wrath could be a blessing if God directed it at one's enemy. Elliott thanked God for unleashing divine anger on the battlefield at Manassas.[17]

Still, a danger remained: Too much "exultation" would "turn away God's wrath from our enemies," Elliott said.[18] Attitude was everything when it came to prayer and providence; a haughty attitude was poison in wartime. Elliott pointed to a means of managing God's wrath, a delicate exercise but also one of wartimes' most crucial needs—it demanded that Christians respect providence in the war. Modern people tended to ignore providence. They thought natural events always had natural causes, and they disregarded God. But people needed to look to the "infallible book of wisdom and of knowledge, the Holy Scriptures." With the Bible in hand, Elliott's goal was "to justify the ways of God to man," even in this time of violence and war.[19]

Again, to speak this way may seem strange. Wasn't providence supposed to be mysterious? Could anyone ever know what God was planning? Not in full, Elliott knew. But the Bible gave direction, informing people of God's providence, at least partially.[20]

After Second Manassas, Elliott believed God had turned the war to the Confederacy's advantage, and slavery was the reason why. In 1862, southerners had seen slavery attacked like never before in the war, which prompted southern ministers to step up their defenses of slaveholding. Elliott shifted the focus from America to Africa. White missionaries had failed to evangelize Africa, but scripture must be fulfilled, which meant the gospel would spread throughout the world, including Africa. That was the purpose of the enslaved people, Elliott said, and slavery was preparing them for it. Because of slavery, Africans learned the gospel, so they could evangelize their homeland—eventually.[21]

An innovative and self-serving twist on the Exodus story supported Elliott's theory. When discussing slavery, many northerners claimed God would never use slavery to serve a greater good. But they forgot about the Exodus, in which God allowed Egyptians to enslave "his own chosen people . . . for four hundred years, until they were disciplined to go forth and become a nation among the nations." What did God care "for such trivial things as slavery, as toil, as the sufferings of a subject race?"[22]

The sufferings of enslaved people were "trivial things"? Easy for Elliott and other slaveholders to say—they were white, so nobody could enslave them. But in Elliott's view, God had used slavery in Egypt, and now God was using slavery in the South. How blind northern abolitionists were, led away from the Bible, "so blinded by their passions" that they would "overturn a divine missionary scheme." But it was not to be. "The Church of the future will see and confess that as Egypt was the land of refuge and the school of nurture for the race of Israel, so were these Southern States first the home and then the nursing mother of those who were to go forth and regenerate the dark recesses of a benighted Continent."[23]

In this Confederate reading of the Exodus, Elliott called the South the new Egypt, and he meant it as a compliment. Did Elliott forget the rest of the Exodus story? God defeated Egypt, drowning Pharaoh and his men in the Red Sea. But Elliott did not press the analogy that far, focusing instead on the South's divine purpose in keeping slavery alive for the good of Africans.[24]

Slavery survived because of God, who took "providential care" of slavery, and so this was a sacred war that Confederates fought on behalf of enslaved people, Elliott said in an incredible statement. "God has made us the guardians and champions of a people whom he is preparing for his own purposes and against whom the whole world is banded." This responsibility "stretches upwards to the throne of God and links us with immortality."

This so-called divine responsibility protected the South in the war: "What a trust from God! What reliance has he placed upon our faithfulness and our integrity! What a sure confidence does it give us in his protection and favor!" That was why "our arm is nerved with almost super-human strength," and "we are moving forward, as I firmly believe, as truly under his direction, as did the people of Israel when he led them with a pillar of cloud by day and of fire by night."[25]

This explains why the Confederacy would win the war, Elliott believed. Others looked for success in "the valor of our troops" and "the skill of our generals," but "I am looking to the poor despised slave as the source of our security." God put the Africans in the United States, "under our political protection and under our Christian nurture," and no one could interfere with God's plans—not even the Union army.[26]

At about the same time that Elliott preached this vision of a racist, Confederate Egypt, a minister in Philadelphia proclaimed a gloomier view of a northern Egypt. This minister, Edwards Lounsbery, pointed to one of the bleakest scenes in the Exodus story—the final plague. Because Pharaoh refused to free his Israelite slaves, God punished Egypt with plagues, and the final one was the worst: God killed the first-born children of Egypt. Why would God commit such an extreme act? This horrific scene showed how much God hated slavery, Lounsbery reasoned. "The land that had long groaned with the oppressions of the slave, must now be bathed in the blood of the master. Her first-born must die! The devouring sword is commissioned to enter every house in the land, until, in the graphic language of the sacred text, there was not a house in Egypt 'where there was not one dead.'"[27]

Americans could relate. During this dismal period of the war, it seemed every family had lost someone in the devastation. "Now, brethren, in more points than one, our situation is like that of Egypt on that memorial night," Lounsbery said. "A pall of thick darkness has shrouded our once bright and happy land," a devastating war that "is fast drenching our land in the life-blood of her children." Apparently, the nation would suffer as Egypt did— "The wail of Egypt must be heard again, and not a house be left without its sacrifice to the stern exigency of the conflict!"[28]

"The War Is a Divine Retribution"

Abraham Lincoln also pondered providence after the second defeat at Manassas. "The rebel soldiers are praying with a great deal more earnestness, I fear, than our own troops, and expecting God to favor their side"—at least that was the word Lincoln heard from a Union soldier who had been imprisoned with rebels. Like other Americans, Lincoln believed humans may be able to influence God's providential acts. Perhaps the war had taken a turn for the worse because southerners were praying more earnestly than northerners?[29]

Or perhaps the Union's struggles had everything to do with slavery? Nine days before Lincoln would announce the Emancipation Proclamation, ministers from several denominations met in Chicago and presented Lincoln with a memorial, calling for emancipation. "The war is a Divine retribution upon our land for its manifold sins," especially slavery, they said. They added that it was "almost atheism to deny" this link between slavery and the nation's punishments in war losses. They urged Lincoln "to proclaim, *without delay*, NATIONAL EMANCIPATION."[30]

Lincoln replied that he had been thinking a lot about emancipation (little did they know he had already drafted his proclamation). He had asked ministers for advice, but they offered "the most opposite opinions," even though all were "equally certain that they represent the Divine will." Clearly, "Either the one or the other class is mistaken in that belief, and perhaps in some respects both." Lincoln hoped it would not appear "irreverent" to say so, but if God were to "reveal his will to others, on a point so connected with my duty, it might be supposed he would reveal it directly to me." God had not done so. "It is my earnest desire to know the will of Providence in this matter," Lincoln said. "*And if I can learn what it is I will do it!*"[31]

Still, Lincoln knew he was not living in biblical times, so he couldn't expect a divine revelation. He would have to "study the plain physical facts of the case, ascertain what is possible and learn what appears to be wise and right. The subject is difficult, and good men do not agree."[32] "The subject is on my mind, by day and night, more than any other," Lincoln said. "Whatever shall appear to be God's will I will do."[33]

"A National Scourge"

While Lincoln looked for providential direction, ministers offered biblical analogies. Lincoln's situation was like Esther's dilemma in the Old Testament, these ministers said. Esther was a Jew, but she was also the queen of Persian king Xerxes. As a Jew, she was an outsider in the Persian Empire, and yet as the queen, she wielded influence. The crisis came when Esther's cousin, Mordecai, learned of a plot to murder the Jews. He told Esther about the conspiracy and urged her to intervene with King Xerxes to save her people. When Esther hesitated, Mordecai warned that if she did nothing, the Jews would die. She couldn't hold her peace; she had to act. And who knew?

Perhaps she had been placed in this position of power at this time to serve this purpose (Esther 4).

The Esther story was all about providence, these ministers suggested to Lincoln. The ministers were like Mordecai, and Lincoln was like Esther. Under God's direction, Esther became queen to serve one purpose only—to rescue her people. Likewise, providence had placed Lincoln in the presidency for one task—to free the nation's enslaved people, and this was the time. If he did so, Americans would remember him as they honored "George Washington, as the second SAVIOR OF OUR COUNTRY."[34]

If the Esther story would not convince Lincoln to proclaim emancipation, perhaps others would. Ministers across the North brought up other biblical analogies, some of which tried to match the violence of the war with some of the most violent scenes from scripture. Kansas minister James D. Liggett hoped Lincoln and others would take a cue from a biblical parallel to the battles at Manassas (cf. Judges 19–20). In this story, Israel, too, suffered defeat twice on the same battlefield.

The cause of the battle was rape and murder. As the story began, a woman, described as a concubine, traveled with her husband through the land of the Benjamites. When they stopped to spend the night with a man in Gibeah, men pounded on the door, calling for the man to come out so they could have sex with him. But the man sent his concubine out instead. The men raped her through the night and then killed her. When her husband found her the next day, he sliced her body into twelve pieces and sent one piece to each of the tribes of Israel so that they would know about this terrible crime. (Apparently the man did not see his own complicity in this crime—or at least the text does not say so.)

Justifiably angered by this horrific act, men from all over Israel attacked the Benjamites for allowing this crime to go unpunished. And although Israel's cause was righteous, God allowed the Benjamites to defeat them not once but twice on the same battlefield. Then the Israelites finally got the message: they called on the Lord before the battle. They cried out to God, "Shall I again go out to battle against" the Benjamites "or shall I cease?" The Lord responded, "Go up; for to-morrow I will deliver them into thine hand" (Judges 20:27–28). So finally, on the third day, God gave Israel the victory.

This, according to Liggett, was Israel's Manassas. "Israel had one Bull Run disaster, and had passionately resolved to avenge it," but their "pride and unholy ambition . . . made another such disaster necessary. Again, they are defeated and massacred in heaps on the same bloody and fatal field." It was not that they did not have a just cause; they did—they were seeking justice against men who committed a horrible crime. Yet they still lost because they had not looked to God for help. Only when they turned to God, recognizing their own weakness, did God give them victory. If they had won either the first or the second battle, they would have done so out of their own pride and power and, therefore, victory would have been a curse, not a blessing.[35]

This old "history and its lessons" seemed "to us new and profitable," Liggett said. Because "almost the very same history is being acted over again in our country. Thus far the parallel is almost, if not entirely perfect." Slavery was a wicked crime that excited good people in the North against it, just as this rape and murder excited the wrath of Israel. But, like Israel, the Union suffered defeat because it did not fight at God's command for God's cause. Too many in the North fought to restore the Union, but they should fight to end slavery. Until the North fought with this goal in mind, it would lose. "The rebels have resolved to destroy the nation that they may establish Slavery. Shall we hesitate to destroy Slavery that we may preserve the nation?"[36]

Lincoln had led the nation astray by trying "to preserve the national life and slavery too, if he can." The result had been disaster on the battlefield. In those losses, "God thunders in [Lincoln's] ears . . . 'You cannot'" have the Union with slavery intact. The nation needed to fight for the right reason, or God would abandon the United States.[37]

Too many white Americans said, "I hate the Negro, but am willing, for my own safety, to let him shoot a rebel, reserving the privilege of scorning and persecuting him afterwards," Liggett said.[38] God would not bless that war. The problem was not only slavery but racism. "There is yet in the heart of the nation a deep-seated and unjustifiable hatred of the enslaved race of this country," and this is "a spirit which is at once the root and the fruit of Slavery," said Liggett. "Judged by this just rule, we are a nation of slaveholders still." That was why God was "against us, and yet not against us" in the war.[39]

This explanation seemed reasonable because it explained how both sides suffered so severely. "The whole affair appears to be nothing more nor less than a national scourge," said African Methodist Episcopal minister Henry McNeal Turner. "To-day we are gaining great victories, tomorrow we are losing; to-day we are taking prisoners, tomorrow we are being taken prisoners. To-day we are before Richmond, tomorrow the rebels are before Washington." Through all this, "The war is no nearer to an end now than it first began; indeed, the South is stronger now than ever; more disciplined, and more cemented together, in the diabolical traffic." How could this be providential? Turner found a possible explanation in a quotation from another minister: "The head of this rebellion was in the South, and its tail in the North, and . . . God intended to punish the whole as due to its unnumbered crimes."[40]

This was bad news for North and South, and maybe that was the point. This pessimistic idea flooded the North—that this war was God's punishment on the whole nation, although some of its people were guiltier than others. "God deals with us *as a nation*," said Presbyterian minister Alanson Hartpence of Pennsylvania. "He punishes for the existence and practice of evils and sins which belong to us, *as a nation*, whether every portion of the people are guilty of them or not." The war had proven "these States are united by the Maker of heaven and earth in one common weal or wo."[41]

"The Nation Who Will Not Serve Him Shall Perish"

What could be done in this dire situation? Once northerners had turned to scripture and found the reasons for the downturn in the war, they pondered what they could do to reverse their fortunes. The Bible told people that they could know God's providence, at least partially, and they could do God's will. But could they influence providential events?

Americans divided on this question. Some people believed prayer and faith could influence God's treatment of them, perhaps help them to survive the war or even to win it. Others claimed this was sacrilegious—prayer was for spiritual purposes, not personal gain, including survival on the battlefield. "I do not think that I have any right to pray for exemption from physical harm in the discharge of my duty as a soldier," a Confederate soldier from Maryland wrote. In his view, prayer was "only [for] protection from moral wrong and that I may always be prepared to die, come what may."[42]

When pondering human agency and God's providence, Americans found help in the book of Jonah. Everyone knew this adventure about a big fish swallowing a prophet. During these gloomy days after Second Manassas, Reverend Hartpence called on Jonah's adventure to discuss the war.

The story centered on Nineveh, a city so evil that God decided to destroy it. God sent Jonah to warn Nineveh's citizens of their impending destruction. Jonah refused to go, however, so God sent the big fish to swallow him. Once inside the fish's belly, Jonah changed his mind, obeyed God, traveled to

Nineveh, and preached hellfire and brimstone to the people, warning them their days were numbered. Much to Jonah's surprise, the king of Nineveh repented, implored the people to humble themselves, and pleaded to God for mercy. The king told his people, "Who can tell if God will turn and repent, and turn away from his fierce anger, that we perish not?" (Jonah 3:9).

Could the people change God's plans? This was a theological question that interested many in the North. If Americans repented of their sins, could they alter God's providential decree? Could God "repent"?

Not really, Hartpence said. Like most other Christians of the time, he believed God was eternal and unchanging. Yet the Bible said, "God repented of the evil, that he had said that he would do unto [Nineveh]" (Jonah 3:10). What did it mean to say that God may "repent"? "When God is said to repent," Hartpence said, "it means that the visible conduct of Divine Providence *resembles* the conduct of men when they repent; and not that [God] is capable of repentance in a literal sense." God "foresaw" that the Ninevites would repent, so he planned all along to spare them.[43]

After Second Manassas, the people of the North could relate to this question from the book of Jonah: "Who can tell if God will turn and repent, and turn away from his fierce anger, that we perish not?" (Jonah 3:9). As Hartpence said, "The text contains a sentiment that now moves the minds and thrills the hearts of anxious and expectant millions." As Americans struggled with the nation's bloodiest crisis, they—like the people of Nineveh—expressed "a state of suspense between hope and fear," grappling with the nation's "doubtful destiny," and their "utter inability to know the future, when God is moving in some mysterious way his wonders to perform."[44]

The key here was the spiritual direction of the nation. "Do the American people believe in [God's] sovereign sway over the destiny of men and nations?" Do Americans really believe that God controls their future? "Have God and his holy law been duly recognized and regarded in the Constitution and the laws of this nation?" Unfortunately, the answer to all these questions was no. If the nation were to survive, Americans must "remember that *Christ is King*; and that the nation who will not serve him shall perish."[45]

After the second battle at Manassas, therefore, North and South divided in their interpretation of God's providence in scripture. Southerners celebrated, but they did so cautiously. Northerners believed God had turned against them, but could they appeal to God and reverse their fortunes in the war? Jonah's story and other scriptures suggested they could, so they clung to this hope and followed Lincoln in hoping for good news from the battlefield.

10

"The Sword of the Lord"

In 1862, the intellectual and Transcendentalist turned Catholic Orestes Brownson ruminated on the unprecedented bloodshed that gripped the nation. "It is real blood, not red paint that flows, and real life-warm blood must still flow, and flow in torrents." Shedding this blood was a terrible but necessary task, Brownson wrote. The demands of war, therefore, required that "we must have not only the courage to be killed, but we must have . . . *the harder courage to kill*, not simply to bear, but to do harm, to strike the enemy in his tenderest part our quickest and heaviest blows."[1]

In various wars over time, rulers, presidents, generals, soldiers, and even ministers have struggled to inspire this "harder courage to kill." During the same Civil War violence that surrounded Brownson, the renowned minister and theologian Horace Bushnell confronted a Connecticut soldier with the most urgent question: "Killed anybody yet?" Perhaps surprised by the directness of the question, the soldier replied that he did not know. Bushnell's response was just as direct as his question had been: "Time you had, that's what you went out for."[2]

As Drew Gilpin Faust wrote, motivating soldiers to kill in the Civil War was more difficult than inspiring them to die for the cause. Killing "required the more significant departure from soldiers' understandings of themselves as human beings and . . . as Christians."[3] With soldiers "focusing on dying rather than on killing," Faust wrote, it helped "to mitigate their terrible responsibility for the slaughter of others."[4]

Killing was a problem, at least for many soldiers—violence seemed prohibited by the Bible, especially the New Testament. The Old Testament included prohibitions against killing, beginning with the sixth commandment: "Thou shalt not kill" (Exodus 20:13). But as we have seen, the Old Testament also included a lot of God-endorsed killing, especially in war, so it was easier for Americans to read the sixth commandment as a command against murder for a personal grievance, not against killing in war.

By contrast, the New Testament lacked war stories and included Jesus's commands against violence, famously stated in his Sermon on the

Mount: "Resist not evil: but whosoever shall smite thee on thy right cheek, turn to him the other also" (Matthew 5:39). It's no wonder Phoebe Yates Pember from Richmond reportedly claimed she was glad to be Jewish— "born of a nation and religion that did not enjoin forgiveness on its enemies, that enjoyed the blessed privilege of praying for an eye for an eye" (cf. Exodus 21:24). She told her Christian friends that "till the war was over they should all join the Jewish Church, let forgiveness and peace and good will alone and put their trust in the sword of the Lord and Gideon" (cf. Judges 7:20).[5]

Americans turned to scripture to inspire the "harder courage to kill," a concern never more urgent than after the bloodbath at Antietam. Soon after that battle, Lincoln announced his Emancipation Proclamation, which gave northerners additional incentive to fight. It was now a war for freedom. In wrestling with these interrelated concerns—the motivation to kill and the battle for emancipation—Americans struggled with the scriptures in the second half of 1862.

"The Dead of Antietam"

September 17, 1862, was the war's bloodiest day. The fighting raged from daylight to darkness near Antietam Creek, about ten miles from Sharpsburg, Maryland. The battle could have been over for the Confederacy even before it started. Four days earlier, two Union soldiers were passing through a recent Confederate campsite when they found a sheet of paper wrapped around a few cigars. Written on that paper were General Lee's battle plans—his "Special orders No. 191." This was, as James McPherson wrote, "the all-time military jackpot." The orders showed Lee's army was divided and vulnerable. This was McClellan's chance. He was close enough to reach Lee's forces in about a day. Now McClellan could defeat the Army of Northern Virginia and devastate the Confederate cause. McClellan held these plans in his hands, saying, "Here is a paper with which if I cannot whip 'Bobbie Lee,' I will be willing to go home."[6]

But McClellan didn't whip "Bobbie Lee." Once again, McClellan followed his usual pattern: instead of attacking, he delayed, taking extra time to prepare. This allowed Lee time to reunite his army to challenge McClellan in a battle for the ages.

The bloodshed at Antietam astounded observers. A Union private wrote that Antietam "will be put down in history" for its massive casualties, with thousands of soldiers sacrificing "to this holy cause."[7] The numbers were staggering. Almost six thousand died on the battlefield, in addition to seventeen thousand wounded. "The casualties at Antietam numbered four times the total suffered by American soldiers at the Normandy beaches on June 6, 1944," James McPherson reported. To put the numbers in perspective, "More than twice as many Americans lost their lives in one day at Sharpsburg as fell in combat in the War of 1812, the Mexican War, and the Spanish American War *combined*."[8]

The Union claimed victory, with some justification. The battle repelled Lee's forces and sent them back to Virginia, but McClellan failed in doing what Lincoln had charged him to do—"destroy the rebel army." McClellan had more than twice as many men as Lee—80,000 men, compared with Lee's 37,000. But McClellan thought Lee had about 110,000 men, so he played it safe and kept some 20,000 of his own men in reserve. McClellan allowed Lee and his troops to get away, which infuriated Lincoln, though McClellan told his wife he "fought the battle splendidly & that it was a masterpiece of art." Despite his critics, McClellan wrote, "One of these days history will I trust do me justice."[9]

Much of the justice history did in documenting Antietam depended on photography. In 1839, the first photograph went on display in the United States; by the 1850s, Americans had embraced it, taking some twenty-five million portraits. Previously, Americans who wanted a portrait relied on an artist's rendition, which was expensive. Now Americans had photographs—more accurate and less expensive images. With photography, Walt Whitman said, "Art will be democratized." Frederick Douglass had been twenty-three when he first had his photograph taken. "Negroes can never have impartial portraits at the hands of white artists," Douglass said. "It seems to us next to impossible for white men to take likenesses of black men, without grossly exaggerating their distinctive features." Not so for photographs, which explains why Douglass "became the most photographed man in nineteenth century America." In technology—specifically the photograph and the telegraph—Douglass and others found hope for improved communication and representation, which gestured toward a more peaceful, just, and democratic society.[10]

Those hopes faded at Antietam, where photographs provided a record of carnage and war. It was a first for many Americans—they not only heard about the blood and gore at Antietam, they saw them. Photographers Matthew Brady and Alexander Gardner transformed photography into a tool of battlefield journalism.[11] Brady's "The Dead of Antietam" intensified the emotional trauma that the war had caused.[12] *The New York Times* reported, although Brady "has not brought bodies and laid them in our dooryards and along the streets, he has done something very like it."[13]

"God Had Decided This Question in Favor of the Slaves"

Not only was Antietam the nation's bloodiest and most photographed battle to date, it all but ended the South's hopes for diplomatic recognition from Britain and France. But Antietam meant more—for Lincoln, it was a providential sign. Less than a week after Antietam, Lincoln reportedly told his cabinet he "had made a vow, a covenant, that if God gave us the victory in the approaching battle, he would consider it an indication of Divine will, and that it was his duty to move forward in the cause of emancipation." As Lincoln put it, "God had decided this question in favor of the slaves."[14]

On September 22, Lincoln issued his Preliminary Emancipation Proclamation, stating that one hundred days later—on January 1, 1863— "all persons held as slaves within any State, or designated part of a State, the people whereof shall then be in rebellion against the United States shall be then, thenceforward, and forever free." The US government and military would "recognize and maintain the freedom of such persons" held in slavery.[15]

Some African Americans doubted Lincoln's sincerity, recalling he had waffled on slavery and had supported colonization. Yet many defended Lincoln, even some who had criticized him in the past. On October 4, Henry McNeal Turner said, "I differ with a large portion of our people" who doubted Lincoln "wrote his proclamation in good faith." No question, events led to Lincoln's decision. No question, there was a political strategy involved. But those who attacked Lincoln's motives were most likely wrong, Turner said. "Mr. Lincoln loves freedom as well as any one on earth, and if he carries out the spirit of his proclamation, he need never fear hell. GOD GRANT HIM A HIGH SEAT IN GLORY." Lincoln had "silenced the doubt." Now "The Presidential policy is to wage the war in favor of freedom."[16]

The Emancipation Proclamation improved Frederick Douglass's opinion of Lincoln. In July 1862, Douglass had said "Lincoln is no more fit for the place he holds than was James Buchanan." He faulted Lincoln because he "steadily refused to proclaim, as he had the constitutional and moral right to proclaim, complete emancipation to all the slaves of rebels." Soon the nation would "become sick of . . . Lincoln, and the sooner the better."[17] But when Lincoln announced the proclamation, Douglass said, "We shout for joy that we live to record this righteous decree."[18]

"The Character of the War Will Be Changed"

But did the Emancipation Proclamation free anyone? No, as critics pointed out, Lincoln's heralded proclamation freed only the enslaved people of the rebel states as of January 1. But these states did not recognize Lincoln's authority. Meanwhile, the proclamation freed none of the people enslaved in the Union, including border states, where Lincoln still had authority. The *London Times* spoke for many frustrated critics of the president: "Where he has no power Mr. Lincoln will set the negroes free; where he retains power he will consider them as slaves."[19]

The writer in the *London Times* didn't understand the restrictions Lincoln worked under. He lacked the constitutional authority to end slavery in the United States. But in a time of war, the president had war powers, which included the power to confiscate the rebels' property. Come January 1, the Union army would be fighting to defeat the enemy, in part by freeing the enslaved people. Not only that, but the Emancipation Proclamation would call African Americans to join the Union and fight for their freedom.[20]

Most importantly for some Americans, the proclamation had changed the nature of the war. Lincoln said, "The character of the war will be changed" once the new year arrived. "It will be" a war "of subjugation. . . . The [old] South is to be destroyed and replaced by new propositions and ideas."[21] For many northerners, the Emancipation Proclamation sealed God's favor in the war from that point on. Israel Dwinell made this point in Salem, Massachusetts: "Now the Proclamation of the President puts us right. Now we are openly and directly on the side of God; and now we may hope to have his favor."[22]

Many soldiers and officers relished this new incentive for war. A colonel from Indiana said his men would "destroy everything" that gave "the rebels strength," and nothing strengthened the rebels more than slavery. "This army will sustain the emancipation proclamation and enforce it with the bayonet." "The character of the war has very much changed within the last year," said General-in-Chief Henry Halleck to Ulysses S. Grant. "There is now no possible hope of reconciliation," he continued. "We must conquer the rebels or be conquered by them." Furthermore, "Every slave withdrawn from the enemy is the equivalent of a white man put *hors de combat*."[23]

African Americans knew better than anyone that Lincoln's proclamation had reinvigorated the war effort. Speaking of Americans, Henry McNeal Turner wrote, "War they have got to fight, blood they have got to shed" until "they lay waste and desolate every unjustly erected fabrication." Freedom was moving forward, he insisted. "General McClellan may feed the worms of the Peninsula with the bodies of his stagnant army, or rot them upon the suburbs of Harpers Ferry rather than move upon the enemy"—that would not matter. "The great freedom revolution" would accelerate.[24]

Frederick Douglass agreed, and directly linked emancipation to northern success in the war. "Ye millions of free and loyal men who have earnestly sought to free your bleeding country from the dreadful ravages of revolution and anarchy, lift up now your voices with joy and thanksgiving for with freedom to the slave will come peace and safety to your country."[25]

Antislavery soldiers were thrilled with the Emancipation Proclamation. Said a private from upstate New York, "thank God" for the proclamation because "The contest is now between Slavery & freedom, & every honest man knows what he is fighting for." An Iowa sergeant said, "The God of battle will be with us . . . now that we are fighting for *Liberty* and Union and not Union and Slavery."[26]

The Emancipation Proclamation was a sacred cause, and, therefore, the Civil War had become a sacred war—if it were not already. That was the view of many African Americans. The *Christian Recorder*, newspaper of the African Methodist Episcopal Church, justified the war's violence because it accomplished the holy work of ending slavery: "The war is a holy war." Additionally, "God has seen the affliction of the poor slave. He has heard his cry, and has come down to deliver him."[27]

Northern whites who opposed slavery agreed. "I regard it as a *holy* war," said Presbyterian Samuel T. Spear of Brooklyn, New York. "The sword was never drawn in a more sacred cause, and should never be returned to its scabbard till the end is gained."[28] Spear said this, knowing how much the war had cost, especially the blood already shed. But that sacrifice made the war that much more necessary. The Union must destroy the Confederacy, but it would require a harder war.[29] "We have already lost much by *playing* war; and now if we mean to win in this struggle, we must make the rebels *feel* the war in its utmost severity."[30]

Not everyone agreed. Other Union soldiers saw the proclamation as a betrayal. A New York artilleryman said, "I don't want to fire another shot for the negroes and I wish that all the abolitionists were in hell."[31] The remark of a private from Ohio echoed those of many others: "I can tell you we don't think mutch of [the Emancipation Proclamation] hear in the army for we did not enlist to fight for the negro and I can tell you that we neer shall or many of us anyhow no never."[32]

"His Terrible Swift Sword"

A harder war, fought for emancipation, would be an even more violent war with higher casualties, many believed. This again brought up the need to motivate soldiers to kill in the name of a higher cause. For some Americans, however, the highest authority—scripture—condemned killing. Few Americans were strictly pacifist. But Americans who marched to war often found it harder to kill than they thought it would be. Battlefields not only created fighters; they also created pacifists, especially when soldiers faced death and eternal consequences in the afterlife.

"Read all Christ's teaching," wrote an officer from Indiana, "and then tell me whether *one engaged in maiming and butchering men . . . can be saved* under the Gospel." This was just one example among many soldiers in the Civil War who questioned whether scripture justified violence.[33] Nearly everyone had read or heard the Sermon on the Mount, where Jesus preached nonresistance to evil, imploring his followers to turn the other cheek instead of fighting (Matthew 5–7).

This helps to explain why it took a "harder courage" for Christians to kill. Ministers addressed this problem, trying to reclaim Jesus for the war. This had been a difficult task during the American Revolution; it was also difficult in the Civil War, but it was a biblical battle of interpretation that preachers could not give up—they could not allow Jesus to be an obstacle to patriotism.[34]

As these preachers knew, some charged that Jesus would never have joined a war, and they pointed not only to the Sermon on the Mount, but to his interview with Roman officer Pontius Pilate. Jesus had been arrested by the Romans, urged on by "the Jews," according to the Gospel of John. When Pilate asked Jesus what crime he had committed, Jesus responded, "My kingdom is not of this world: if my kingdom were of this world, then would my servants fight, that I should not be delivered to the Jews" (John 18:36). Did this statement prove Jesus's aloofness from worldly matters, especially war?

No, replied an article, "Shall Christians Fight?," that ran in northern newspapers in the fall of 1862. Many people missed Jesus's point. He never rejected violence in war; he only said his servants should not use violence to force the gospel on people.[35] The newspaper article also noted Jesus's statement "Think not that I am come to send peace on earth: I came not to send peace, but a sword" (Matthew 10:34), proving that Jesus endorsed the Christian responsibility "to hate and resist oppression, treason and sin, even unto blood."[36]

From the beginning of the war, other Americans dealt with the pacifist Jesus problem by citing Jesus's words to his disciples just after the Last Supper and just before Judas would betray him (Luke 22).[37] Jesus was trying to prepare the disciples for the trials to come, telling them that if any of them did not have a sword, he should "sell his garment, and buy one." When the disciples replied, "Lord, behold, here are two swords," Jesus said, "It is enough" (Luke 22:36–38).

Even though Jesus advised his disciples to buy swords, it's unclear how or when he wanted them to fight. That same night, when Judas brought the men to arrest Jesus, one of the disciples picked up a sword and sliced off the ear of the high priest's servant. In response, Jesus rebuked the disciple and healed the man's ear. In Matthew's account, Jesus told this disciple, "Put up again thy sword into his place: for all they that take the sword shall perish with the sword" (Matthew 26:51).

Among the preachers who had addressed this problem near the beginning of the war was J. K. Mason, a Congregationalist minister from Maine. He admitted that Jesus's advice on violence seemed to conflict. This was troubling, because it created a "distrust of the Bible," leading people to believe that scripture contradicted itself. That was not so, however; the Bible was "the most harmonious Book in the world." One just needed to understand scripture properly, and this was especially urgent during wartime.[38]

When Jesus said, "All they that take the sword shall perish with the sword," he did not forbid violence, Mason argued. Jesus was speaking about respect for government; he never rebelled against the Roman Empire, and elsewhere he told his disciples to "render unto Caesar" things that belonged to Caesar. Likewise, Jesus forbade the disciples to fight the officials who tried to arrest him. Jesus told his disciple to put up his sword. He would not resist the government; neither would he allow his disciple to do so. Unlike southern outlaws, Jesus would not rebel against legitimate government.[39]

But Jesus was not a pacifist. He told his disciples to buy a sword because he was sending them out on their missions. They would have to defend themselves against wild animals and bandits, so they could use the sword for self-defense, but not to attack the government.[40]

A few days before Antietam, Reverend William Daily pointed beyond the peaceful Jesus of the Gospels to the warlike Jesus of the book of Revelation. The final book in the New Testament, this apocalyptic text was hard for Americans to interpret because it contained a flurry of symbols, colors, wars, beasts, and angels. Many believed the book of Revelation revealed the end of the world, including a period in which Christians would suffer for their faith like the martyrs of the early church.

Reverend Daily preached on the "whore of Babylon," who sat on "a scarlet coloured beast, full of names of blasphemy, having seven heads and ten horns." She was drunk "with the blood of the saints, and with the blood of the martyrs of Jesus." She had joined God's enemies, who "shall make war with the Lamb, and the Lamb shall overcome them; for he is the Lord of lords, and King of kings; and they that are with him are called, and chosen and faithful" (Revelation 17).

This vision illuminated the Civil War, Daily believed, because it displayed "an unprovoked rebellion against a rightful Sovereignty—'the Lamb.'" Everyone knew that "the Lamb" was Jesus; he was the sacrificial lamb who had redeemed humanity.[41] But Jesus was not just a lamb who sacrificed himself; Jesus was also a lamb who waged war. The climax of the Revelation was an apocalyptic battle—the Armageddon, in which Christ would defeat Satan and rescue all Christians who had remained faithful despite persecution (Revelation 17:14). Jesus, then, was no pacifist who let rebels off the hook; Jesus was a mighty warrior. "The Lamb overcomes or subjugates the rebels," Daily said. Jesus was a lamb, but he was also "'the Lion of the tribe of Judah'—a Lion in fight."[42]

Jesus charged into battle riding a white horse and leading a heavenly army. This was a fierce Jesus with "a sharp sword" that he used to "smite the nations: and he shall rule them with a rod of iron: and he treadeth the winepress of the fierceness and wrath of Almighty God" (Revelation 19:14–15).[43] Americans knew these verses—they had inspired Julia Ward Howe's "Battle Hymn of the Republic":

Mine eyes have seen the glory of the coming of the Lord;
He is trampling out the vintage where grapes of wrath are stored;
He hath loosed the fateful lightning of His terrible swift sword;
His truth is marching on.

This image of a militant Jesus appeared frequently in the war, often to in-spire troops. The "Battle Hymn of the Republic"—based, as we have seen, on "John Brown's Body"—was one of the Union's most popular marching songs.

Jesus didn't forbid violence in war, therefore. Jesus fought as a soldier, and he embodied the sacrificial spirit of any good soldier. Many believed Jesus offered the perfect motto for military service—"Greater love hath no man than this, that a man lay down his life for his friends" (John 15:13). In a funeral sermon for Lieutenant Thomas Jefferson Spurr of the Fifteenth Massachusetts Volunteers, who was mortally wounded at Antietam, Alonzo Hill said there was no "sweeter death, than to lay down his life for his friends." Just as Christ showed his "exalted, unselfish devotion" in sacrificing him-self on a cross, so Lieutenant Spurr at Antietam "in the perfection of manly vigor, died for his country's sake."[44] As this young man showed, it was better to suffer any "hardships, wounds and imprisonments, and the carnage of the battlefield, than be guilty of one hour's unfaithfulness to duty, and one act of disloyalty to country and to God."[45]

Jesus demanded sacrifice—he demanded to be placed above all other loy-alties, including families, Hill said. As difficult as it was to send loved ones off to war, Americans needed to know that Jesus called his disciples to leave their families and follow him. This honorable soldier at Antietam answered Jesus's call to " 'leave father and mother' and the endearments of home for freedom and country and Christ's sake." In this view, Jesus's calling to discipleship be-came a divine call to serve in the Union army (cf. Matthew 10:34–39; Luke 14:25–27).[46]

"You Cannot Throw the Bible Away"

As more northerners called the war a holy war for emancipation, they dealt with the controversial reputation of abolitionists, which could hurt the an-tislavery cause. If northern Protestants got the idea that all who opposed slavery were abolitionists—often labeled as atheists, radicals, and fanatics—it would be hard to get church people to support Lincoln's proclamation.

As nearly everyone knew, some abolitionists had criticized the Bible for its alleged proslavery teachings. Even though some abolitionists respected much of scripture, the fact that they attacked some parts of it disturbed many Americans. The key for many northern ministers was to agree with abolitionists on emancipation while rejecting their radical views—especially their pacifism and their attacks on the Bible. In his *Duty of Emancipation* on September 13, Edward Bentley supported emancipation while insisting, "I always have opposed [abolitionists] in the matter of their hostility to the Bible, to the Church, and to the Constitution."[47]

Rarely willing to stand aside from an important issue, Henry Ward Beecher weighed in a couple of weeks later, saying, "I do not stand here to say that if the Bible does not condemn slavery, I will throw the Bible away. I make no such extravagant declaration as that. There are reasons why you cannot throw the Bible away. It clings to you; it is part of your life; it is woven into your memory of father and mother, and of your childhood; and you cannot throw it away."[48]

What Americans often missed, Beecher said, was the difference between slavery in scripture and slavery in the Confederate States. Slavery in the South was much worse than the slavery Paul and Jesus knew, Beecher said. "The American doctrine of slavery," he said, was "the harshest that the world has ever seen."[49] Consequently, the Bible's tolerance for slavery in ancient times meant nothing in the United States.

So-called experts on the letter of scripture—those who used it to defend slavery—missed the central message of the Bible, which condemned slavery. As Unitarian W. Furness put it, "I would a thousand times rather confess myself ignorant of the meaning of the Bible than insult and desecrate and blaspheme it by claiming its authority for treating my brother man not as a brother, but as a chattel and a beast of burden."[50]

To distort scripture in defense of slavery was blasphemy, therefore, a desecration of God's holy Word. Consequently a war against slavery was a holy war, some northern preachers claimed, and they used this argument to overcome soldiers' reluctance to kill. In his sermon to local volunteers, *The Soldier God's Minister*, William L. Gaylord, a Congregationalist minster from New Hampshire, recognized that young soldiers probably hated the idea of killing. This call to kill in battle was "a stern and terrible necessity" in this "just and holy cause."[51] These men needed to remember that the Confederacy was "wholly antagonistic to the spirit of the Bible."[52] Southerners forbade enslaved persons to read scripture because they knew it refuted slavery. Slaveholders "bought and sold their fellow men as they would the dumb brute in the market, and at last baptized the most hideous forms of oppression with the holy name of Christianity."[53] So these soldiers from New Hampshire had a holy calling. "Your sacred mission is to stay— nay, to *strike down* the arm of those bloody destroyers of order and peace, of law, justice, and humanity. And I say the cause is a holy one. It is the cause of Christianity, and of God."[54]

In sending these men off to fight a holy war, Gaylord assured them that if they died, they would die as martyrs. They should fight bravely; a "burning zeal should . . . nerve our arms!" and "a spirit of unshrinking devotion should . . . fire the soul of every hero!" For those who died, an "imperishable glory" would "gild the crown of every martyr!" Their service to the death would be like that of others who have served. "We have given other brothers, husbands, sons, to this holy martyrdom for liberty. Go!"[55] As they went, the Bible would inspire them. "I give you the Bible, God's revealed word, in one hand; and the sword, which I adjure you never to wield in other than a just cause, in the other."[56]

These themes of martyrdom and sacrifice filled the Bible and also appeared in many soldiers' diaries and letters. Soldiers often wrote of sacrificing themselves "on the 'alter' (a frequent misspelling)," McPherson observed.[57] A Confederate sergeant from Georgia wrote, "If my heart ever sincerely desiered any thing on earth . . . It certainly is, to be useful to my Country. . . . I will sacrifice my life upon the alter of my country." His sacrifice would come at Gettysburg.[58] Likewise an Alabama lieutenant wrote to his wife, "I confess that I gave you up with reluctance. Yet I love my country [and] . . . intend to discharge my duty to my country and to my God."[59]

Today this kind of "altar" language sounds like "mawkish posturing, ro- mantic sentimentalism, hollow platitudes," McPherson wrote. Since the end of World War II, "such words as *glory, honor, courage, sacrifice, valor,* and *sacred*" are "vaguely embarrassing if not mock-heroic." In the Civil War, however, "These soldiers, at some level at least, *meant* what they said about sacrificing their lives for their country." McPherson noted, "Our cynicism about the genuineness of such sentiments is more our problem than theirs, a temporal/cultural barrier we must transcend if we are to understand why they fought." He found these patriotic sentiments in the diaries and letters of 66 percent of Confederates he studied and 68 percent of Union soldiers and sailors. Others probably also had these motivations but did not express them in writing.[60]

"My Hands Shall No More Be Raised in Violence"

The pressure to join the war effort was strong enough that many pacifists joined despite their convictions. Consider the Society of Friends, commonly called Quakers, one of the most visible pacifist religious groups. The Civil War put Quakers in a difficult position, especially after Lincoln announced the Emancipation Proclamation. Throughout the war, Quakers found themselves caught between two convictions—they had a long history of opposing slavery, but they also opposed war. Some Quakers compromised on pacifism to fight a war against slavery. "It is my duty to abolish this curse from the nation," said William Stubbs Elliott, a Quaker who volunteered for the war.[61]

Quakers who fought in the war faced stiff penalties, including loss of membership in the Society. Members who wanted to stay in the Society would have to apologize for fighting. Unapologetic Quaker soldiers received written "testifications," stating that their monthly meetings had disowned them. That was the fate of Robert Parker, whose monthly meeting stated that Parker had "so far deviated from the peaceable principles held by our society as to enlist in the Armies of the United States and do military service therein," so "we therefore disown him from being a member with us."[62]

For some, the holiness of the war justified the violence. That was the position of David Wooton, a Quaker who fought for the Union and advocated hanging every rebel, believing "God will also justify us in doing so." He knew the commandment "Thou shalt not kill," yet he also believed God had called him to the battlefield. Through fighting, "I would be serving my God," he said.[63]

"The Fiery Trial"

Soon after the Preliminary Emancipation Proclamation, Lincoln met with a delegation of Quakers led by Eliza P. Gurney. The meeting was "not from any motive of idle curiosity," Gurney promised, nor did they want any political favors. Their motive was spiritual in that they wanted to console Lincoln, given the "heavy weight of responsibility that rested upon him."

Gurney cited 1 Peter 4:12: "Beloved, think it not strange concerning the fiery trial which is to try you, as though some strange thing happened unto you." As Gurney reminded Lincoln, Peter was writing to Christians who endured persecution for their convictions. Lincoln, she said, was in a similar place—being persecuted for his convictions. Like "God's chosen people," Lincoln had to struggle through "trials and persecutions" now that he had supported emancipation. She advised Lincoln to "commit his way unto the Lord by prayer," so that "the peace of God" would fill "the president in heart and mind." Gurney then prayed with Lincoln, and then they all had a time of silent meditation. Those attending later spoke of the "the almost awful silence [that] reigned within that room" and of the "tears running down the cheeks of our honored President as E.P. Gurney solemnly addressed him."[64]

The next month, Lincoln wrote to Gurney and remembered her comments on scripture and persecution. Alluding again to 1 Peter 4:12, Lincoln said, "We are indeed going through a great trial—a fiery trial." Furthermore, President Lincoln called himself "a humble instrument in the hands of our Heavenly Father." Lincoln said that God would "work out his great purposes": "I have desired that all my works and acts may be according to his will, and that it might be so, I have sought his aid." Still, Lincoln acknowledged that he could fail to do God's will. If that happened, "I must believe that for some purpose unknown to me, He wills it otherwise."

Lincoln wished the war were over, "But we find it still continues; and we must believe that He permits it for some wise purpose of his own, mysterious and unknown to us; and though with our limited understandings we may not be able to comprehend it, yet we cannot but believe, that he who made the world still governs it."[65]

This meeting made an impression on Lincoln. In September 1864, Lincoln again wrote to Gurney, "I have not forgotten—probably never shall forget—the very impressive occasion when yourself and friends visited me on a Sabbath forenoon two years ago." Lincoln also never forgot the "fiery trial" metaphor that Gurney used from 1 Peter; he used it often to refer to the war. And he never forgot that this "trial" of war had providential meaning, whatever that meaning might be.[66]

About the same time as this Quaker meeting in September 1862, Lincoln pondered more thoughts on providence and the war in light of the Emancipation Proclamation. "The will of God prevails," Lincoln wrote. In all great wars, both sides claimed to be following God's will. Yet "Both *may* be, and one *must* be wrong. God cannot be *for* and *against* the same thing at the same time." Accordingly, "In the present civil war it is quite possible that God's purpose is something different from the purpose of either party." And yet God depended on humans to accomplish his purposes, including in this war. Lincoln believed that "God wills this contest, and wills that it shall not end yet." God could have ended the war. "Yet the contest proceeds."

Lincoln never published these thoughts; the paper was not found until years after his death, yet he repeated some of these themes in later speeches. It's important to know the timing of these musings on providence. He was thinking these ideas through in 1862 as he reflected on the war and emancipation.[67] For many Americans, including Lincoln, the Preliminary Emancipation Proclamation put God's purposes at the forefront of the war.

11

"We Cannot Escape History"

The Preliminary Emancipation Proclamation, Lincoln hoped, would raise the intensity of the war. It did that, but in some ways that Lincoln had not intended. He wanted a righteous cause that would inspire the North, but the proclamation also inflamed the Confederacy. A typical southern reaction came from Sarah Morgan of Louisiana. "If Lincoln could spend the grinding season on a plantation, he would recall his proclamation," she wrote in November 1862. "As it is, he has only proved himself a fool, without injuring us." She mocked Lincoln, describing how well enslaved people were treated—a typical, self-serving rationalization of slaveholders. The enslaved families on her plantation were so happy they would laugh at abolitionists, Morgan said, describing how she and other women sang to them at night as they warmed themselves by the furnace. "Poor oppressed devils!" she said sarcastically. "Why did you not chunk us with the burning logs instead of looking happy, and laughing like fools? Really, some good old Abolitionist is needed here, to tell them how miserable they are. Cant mass Abe spare a few to enlighten his brethren?"[1]

Critics have attacked the Emancipation Proclamation since the day Lincoln announced it, with historians and others criticizing Lincoln for many reasons, including the nature of the proclamation, its timing, and what it failed to accomplish. Even so, Allen Guelzo is no doubt correct—"The Emancipation Proclamation was the most revolutionary pronouncement ever signed by an American president."[2]

The proclamation directed many Americans to their Bibles—some looking for ammunition to assail it, others looking for barricades to defend it. Did the proclamation align the nation with the Bible, or did it further separate it from God's will? Lincoln hoped, with some confidence, that the proclamation would give the war the cause it needed to inspire more than it repulsed. Only time, and battles, would tell.

"If There Is a Worse Place Than Hell, I Am in It"

After Lincoln announced the proclamation, he wrestled with an unruly war and with generals who wouldn't follow orders. McClellan remained the president's albatross. Why wouldn't McClellan fight like Robert E. Lee? Why wouldn't he fight like Ulysses S. Grant, who commanded the Army of the Tennessee?

McClellan was not the only problem, however. Lincoln wanted General Buell and his Army of the Ohio to move his forces to take East Tennessee, but the general shifted to McClellan mode, offering one excuse after another for why he could not move. Halleck told Buell that Lincoln "does not understand why we cannot march as the enemy marches, live as he lives, and fight as he fights, unless we admit the inferiority of our troops and generals." Lincoln carried the same message to McClellan during a visit with the Army of the Potomac in October. The president told his underperforming general he was too cautious, assuming his army could not cover as much ground and fight as hard as Lee's troops. Your army can overtake Lee, Lincoln told McClellan, "if our troops march as well as the enemy; and it is unmanly to say they can not do it."[3]

Finally, in October, Lincoln removed Buell, replacing him with General William S. Rosecrans. Lincoln held on longer with McClellan, due to his popularity in the ranks, although some newspapers lambasted the tentative general. The *New York Times* ran a headline, "Will the Army of the Potomac Advance," while the *Chicago Tribune* asked, "what devil is it that prevents the Potomac army from advancing?" If the problem was "McClellan, does not the President see that he is a traitor?" Privately, McClellan despised Lincoln, calling him "my inferior socially, intellectually & morally! There never was a Truer epithet applied to a certain individual than that of the 'Gorilla.'"[4]

Lincoln delayed until the fall elections ended before replacing McClellan with General Ambrose Burnside. The timing was important, as Lincoln recognized that those who despised the Emancipation Proclamation would take it out on Republicans at the polls. If he had removed McClellan before the election, Republicans would have taken an even bigger hit than they did. Even with the Democrat McClellan still in command, Republicans lost several governorships, some representatives in state legislatures, and thirty-four congressmen in the House of Representatives. Yet the Republicans still controlled the House and the Senate.[5]

Tired of McClellan's delays, Lincoln wanted a fighter, and he got one with Burnside. But Burnside's willingness to fight could not make up for mistakes in strategy, mistakes that led to a devastating loss at Fredericksburg, Virginia, on December 11–15, 1862. "Fredericksburg," James McPherson wrote, "brought home the horrors of war to northerners more vividly, perhaps, than any previous battle." That was true for Clara Barton. She was used to blood, but Fredericksburg shocked her. Wounded men piled into crowded homes for treatment. One house had over a thousand men lying in it, with blood covering the floors and furniture. "I wrung the blood from the bottom of my clothing, before I could step," Barton recalled.[6]

This setback caused a depressed morale that rivaled any despair the North had experienced. "If there is a worse place than hell, I am in it," Lincoln said.[7] "We are now on the brink of destruction. It appears to me that the Almighty is against us."[8] Henry McNeal Turner agreed, as he waited anxiously for the final Emancipation Proclamation. Writing from Washington, DC, on December 20, Turner said everyone was talking about the catastrophe at Fredericksburg. "Things never looked more gloomy than they do this morning," Turner said. "*God save the nation, is all that I can say.*"[9]

The Union's fortunes seemed to be going from bad to worse, and the last thing Lincoln needed was a distraction, but that was what he got, thanks to an egregious act from one of Lincoln's favorite people, General Grant. Two days after the Battle of Fredericksburg, Grant committed what historians call "the most notorious official act of anti-Semitism in American history." In his General Orders No. 11, Grant expelled "Jews as a class" from a massive area, including parts of Tennessee, Illinois, Mississippi, and Kentucky. Illicit trade was a problem in the war, with smugglers selling cotton from the South in defiance of the Union blockade on southern ports, and Grant blamed much of the problem on Jews. Grant's order came a few weeks before Lincoln was to sign the proclamation. "The irony of his freeing the slaves while Grant was expelling the Jews was not lost on some contemporaries," wrote historian Jonathan Sarna. Due to damage to telegraph lines, it is unclear when Lincoln heard about Grant's order. He certainly heard about it on January 3, when he met with Caesar Kaskel, a Jewish man originally from Prussia but living in Kentucky, who had traveled to the White House to appeal to Lincoln to cancel the order. In response to Kaskel and others, Lincoln turned to the Bible to proclaim his respect for Jewish people, and he wasted no time in retracting Grant's order.[10] It was yet another stressful situation for Lincoln, who was still reeling from the catastrophe at Fredericksburg.

"Was War Ever Intended by Providence . . . ?"

In contrast, southerners celebrated the victory at Fredericksburg, viewing it as a sign that God favored the Confederacy. Robert E. Lee told his army that the victory took place "under the blessing of Almighty God." God had blessed the Confederacy in 1862, giving the South full confidence that God would favor them again in 1863.[11]

What if Lee was right? That question troubled northerners after Fredericksburg, leading many of them to read the book of Job—and understandably so, because Job was the wisdom book of the Old Testament that dealt with unexplainable tragedy.

Job was wealthy and good—a "prince," faithful to God, and full of integrity. The book opened with a conversation between God and Satan about Job. God praised Job for his goodness, and Satan scoffed, saying Job was faithful only because his situation was good. Remove Job's blessings, Satan said, and Job would curse God (Job 1).

God allowed Satan to pillage all Job had, stopping just short of killing him. Satan infected Job with illness, killed his family, and stole his wealth. Devastated, Job hurled hard questions, asking why God had tortured him despite his obedience. Yet Job refused to curse God and vowed to remain faithful.

After Fredericksburg, Reverend Stacy Fowler of Maine called Job the "most ancient and most profound literature of any language." The days of Job seemed to have emerged again in the North. The people could relate to this ancient prince who sat "amid the ruin of his tents," and yet refused to curse God. Instead, Job said, "I know that my Redeemer (or Deliverer) liveth, and that at length he shall appear upon the earth."[12] In Job, the North could find a message of hope despite dreary circumstances. Suffering didn't always result from disobedience. Sometimes God's most faithful people suffered the most devastating evils. With encouragement from Job, therefore, northerners could trust that a loving God controlled all.[13]

Like northerners, southerners also asked questions about God's justice in light of all the suffering. In a funeral sermon for a soldier struck down in the battle of Chickasaw Bayou on December 29, W. W. Lord of Mississippi preached on Psalms 77:3, "I remembered God, and was troubled: I complained, and my spirit was overwhelmed."[14]

This psalmist was caught in a struggle with God. He had "cried to God," had sought God's help "in the day of my trouble," and yet his "soul refused to be comforted" (Psalms 77:1–3). Here Reverend Lord asked a crucial question: was war *ever* worth the sacrifice of so many lives? "Looking upon the harvest which

Death is now reaping in the broad harvest-field of this Southern land," he asked: "Was war ever intended by Providence to be the means of settling national controversies and adjusting the relations of political communities?"[15]

How could war be just, he wondered, since those who fought the wars rarely started the wars. "The ruthless Statesmen" who "created the war, sit secure in places of safety and power, while thousands who are dragged by their action into the disastrous struggle, lie buried, far from domestic graves, in soil that if it could be made conscious of their abhorred presence, would cast them forth, and refuse them sepulture." What an image—if the southern soil knew Yankee soldiers lay buried in it, the dirt itself would throw them out.[16]

As horrifying as it was, God approved of war, Reverend Lord said. God "styles Himself the God of battles, and one of his most frequent names amongst the Hebrews was *Jehovah Sabaoth*—Jehovah of Armies." God "is the Providence of war, and at the same time, blameless for the wars which armies, under His Providential direction wage, and innocent of all the crimes and afflictions of war." Moses said it clearly in the Exodus: "The Lord is a Man of war."[17]

War was here to stay, at least until the end of time. "War is everywhere in the New Testament, as in the Old." War reigns, both literal and metaphorical—military warfare and spiritual warfare. "The Christian is called a Soldier. His service is military, his life a warfare." Even "Christ himself is called the Captain of our Salvation." Christ said, "I come not to send peace but a sword," meaning that he would pursue only wars to bring peace—"wars for the amelioration of war." The young men who died for the Confederacy in this horrific civil war died "in a cause so entirely just and holy."[18]

Lord's sermon reveals the obstacles ministers faced in preaching on war near the beginning of 1863. Especially as the death tolls mounted, more and more Americans questioned the war's value and challenged political leaders who started wars but did not fight in them. These "statesmen" preached the gospel of war, but they did not practice what they preached.

"If My Name Ever Goes into History It Will Be for This Act"

Lincoln looked for better news in Tennessee. He didn't find it quickly, however, because General Rosecrans seemed to be giving his best McClellan impersonation. In October, Halleck warned Rosecrans that he had stayed too long in Nashville. He needed to move his Army of the Cumberland to strike at the enemy, which camped in Murfreesboro, some thirty miles southeast.[19]

Finally, on December 26, Rosecrans moved toward Murfreesboro, where he faced resistance from Confederate general Braxton Bragg. The most intense fighting happened on January 2–3 at the Battle of Stones River (which Confederates called the Battle of Murfreesboro). Rosecrans had won a hard-fought victory, and the cost was high. The federals and Confederates "suffered combined casualties amounting to 32 percent of their strength—the highest percentage for any battle in the war," according to James McPherson. It was worth it for Lincoln, however; he finally had a victory.[20]

This good news came in the wake of Lincoln's signature on the Emancipation Proclamation. Since he had announced it the previous September, many Americans wondered if Lincoln dared to sign the final version. Frederick Douglass wasn't worried, he said. "Abraham Lincoln may be slow, Abraham Lincoln may desire peace even at the price of leaving our terrible national sore untouched, to fester on for generations, but Abraham Lincoln is not the man to reconsider, retract, or contradict words and purposes solemnly proclaimed over his official signature."[21]

Douglass was right; Lincoln had no second thoughts about emancipation. "Fellow citizens, *we* cannot escape history," Lincoln said on December 1. "The fiery trial through which we pass" (again echoes of 1 Peter 4:12) "will light us down, in honor or dishonor, to the latest generation." Not only that, but "In *giving* freedom to the *slave*, we *assure* freedom to the *free*," through which "we shall save the country."[22]

On New Year's Day, Lincoln spent hours shaking hands at a White House event, to the point that his writing hand was tired and trembling. He refused to sign the proclamation with an unsteady hand—since "all who examine the document hereafter will say 'he hesitated.'" He could not allow that, because "I never in my life felt more certain that I was doing right than I do in signing this paper. . . . If my name ever goes into history it will be for this act, and my whole soul is in it." When his hand was no longer shaking, he signed the proclamation.[23] This act shook the nation, especially as Americans saw that this final version called for blacks to fight for the Union. Americans now had no doubt about where Lincoln stood on this controversial issue.[24]

"Good Old John Brown . . . the Nation Is as Mad as He"

On January 4, Urban C. Brewer of New York celebrated the proclamation with a discourse entitled *The Bible and American Slavery*. He pointed back to the two major American authorities—the Bible and the founders, reminding his audience that the Liberty Bell, which "announced to the world 'the Declaration of Independence," had a Bible verse etched on it: "Proclaim liberty through all the land unto all the inhabitants thereof" (Leviticus 25:10). The verse referred to the jubilee year—a time, occurring every fifty years, when God commanded the Israelites to free their enslaved people. Now, God had brought forth a new jubilee in America. With the Emancipation Proclamation, the Liberty Bell had struck again—it had "struck the knell of slavery . . . and now rings out the glad peal of a coming jubilee to four millions of human beings, whose rights have long been trampled in the dust."[25]

When Lincoln signed the proclamation "and reclined himself back in his chair, the Jubilee commenced," said Henry McNeal Turner. "The time has come in the history of this nation, when the downtrodden and abject black man can assert his rights, and feel his manhood."[26] Lincoln had been "ordained by God to free the oppressed." And "The first day of January 1863 is destined to form one of the most memorable epochs in the history of the world." In a reference to Exodus, he said that the Emancipation Proclamation liberated America's "mystic Israelites."[27]

This biblical image of the jubilee also occupied Frederick Douglass's mind. On Sunday, December 28, Douglass spoke at the AME Zion Church in Rochester, New York, on the topic "The Day of Jubilee Comes." "This is scarcely a day for prose," Douglass said, "it is a day for poetry and song, a new song." The cause of the nation (and the war) was now the cause of freedom. "That this war is to abolish slavery I have no manner of doubt," he said. Once Lincoln's historic proclamation—followed by victory in the war—ended slavery in the South, it had no hopes for survival in the border states. "This sacred Sunday," he said, "is the last which will witness the existence of legal slavery in all the Rebel slaveholding States of America."[28]

The Emancipation Proclamation was "the greatest event in our nation's history, if not the greatest event of the century," Douglass said on February 6. The nation had promoted slavery; now it stood for liberty. Douglass couldn't think of a more radical revolution. It would be as if "the Pope turned Protestant." In America, "Color is no longer a crime or a badge of bondage," he said. This was critical for the war. "The brave men now fighting the battles of their country against rebels and traitors are now liberated, and may strike with all their might," and "by thus manfully striking" they will "hurt the Rebels, at their most sensitive point."[29] The Emancipation Proclamation launched a new American Revolution, Douglass said. The date of the Emancipation Proclamation—January 1, 1863—"shall take rank with the Fourth of July."[30]

Emancipation would also help to fulfill the aspirations expressed on the nation's original Fourth of July, Douglass believed. Although many of the revolutionary patriots had been slaveholders, Douglass said that they wanted to see slavery end soon. George Washington "desired to see Slavery abolished, and would gladly give his vote for such abolition." Thomas Jefferson "said he trembled for his country when he reflected that God was just, and that his justice would not sleep forever." And Benjamin Franklin "was President of the first Abolition Society in America."[31]

Scripture, and specifically the biblical idea of millennialism, shaped Douglass's view of the proclamation. "I believe in the millennium," he said, a time in which God would raise humanity to its final stage of "perfection." He hailed the proclamation as evidence of millennial hope. "Born and reared as a slave, as I was, and wearing on my back the marks of the slavedriver's lash, as I do, it is natural that I should value the Emancipation Proclamation for what it is destined to do for the slaves." And yet he saw the proclamation's millennial value "for the nation at large," and "to the cause of truth and justice throughout the world."[32]

To illustrate how much had changed, Douglass resurrected John Brown. He had horrified the nation with his war on slavery, and now the nation was fighting a war on slavery. "Good old John Brown . . . was a madman at Harpers Ferry. Two years pass away, and the nation is as mad as he." All the federal troops and generals would now join the fight John Brown started.[33]

The proclamation stood boldly for truth that cast out slavery. But this was about more than freeing enslaved people. Slavery was not just one sin; it encompassed a full range of evil practices, institutions, and attitudes. Douglass referred to the Gospel story in which Jesus cast out an unclean spirit from a man. When Jesus asked the demon its name, it responded, "My name is Legion: for we are many" (Mark 5:9). For Douglass, this illustrated the nature of evil. "The devil gave his name correctly when he called himself legion—for there are a thousand wrong ways to but one right way." "This world" was "covered with error as with a cloud of thick darkness," filled with "injustice, wrong, oppression, intemperance, and monopolies, bigotry, superstition, Kingcraft, priest-craft, pride of race, prejudice of color, chattel-slavery—the grand sum of all human woes, and villainies."[34]

Looking back on how the nation arrived at this historic moment, Douglass quoted Jesus: "The children of this world are in their generation wiser than the children of light" (Luke 16:8). Worldly people had a worldly knowledge and were often savvy in a way that idealistic people were not. Douglass cited this text to describe how abolitionists—"the children of light"—though principled and moral, had lacked practical knowledge of how the world worked. History would credit abolitionists for their courage, but not for "prophetic vision" because abolitionists did not predict the war and its devastation.[35]

Abolitionists were often naïve in their idealistic pacifism. Until "noble old John Brown" exchanged violence for violence in fights over slavery in "bleeding Kansas," abolitionists did not realize what it would take to defeat slavery. "The grand mistake of the Abolitionists was in supposing the American people better than they were. They did not see that an evil so gigantic as Slavery, so interwoven with the social arrangements, manners, and morals of the country, could not be removed without something like the social earthquake now upon us." In a reference to the great sea monster in the book of Job, Douglass said that abolitionists "ought to have known that the huge Leviathan would cause the deep [oceans] to boil—aye, to howl, and hiss, and foam in sevenfold agony." This horrendous war was practically essential and morally critical. The war was "a school for the moral education of the nation."[36]

As Douglass ruminated on the proclamation, he referred to the Bible's indictment of a slaveholding nation. Americans had corrupted scripture, Douglass believed, and they had done so by rejecting Jesus's golden rule— "All things whatsoever ye would that men should do to you, do ye even so to them: for this is the law and the prophets" (Matthew 7:12). By violating this command, the nation compromised its integrity. Americans called the golden rule impractical, mainly because the golden rule contradicted slavery. Along with the golden rule, Americans also "found the Declaration of Independence very broadly impracticable"—again because it contradicted slavery. Here, then, the words of Jesus and the words of the Declaration challenged slavery, and, therefore, they fell on deaf ears in the United States.[37]

Douglass's connection between the Declaration of Independence and the golden rule made waves in the North. John Brown had made similar statements while he awaited execution, and others followed. In celebrating the eighty-sixth anniversary of the Declaration of Independence in 1862, Unitarian minister W. H. Furness said the Declaration was "identical with the Golden Rule which bids us do to others what we would that they should do to us." This was the central idea of Christianity, and it was also the central idea of the Declaration. It followed, then, that "the Declaration of our

National Independence is substantially a Christian act." The Declaration was "a national confession of faith in the vital principle of Christianity, an echo of the very words of Jesus Christ." It took politics eighteen hundred years to catch up with Jesus. In the Declaration, the founders reaffirmed "the divine wisdom of the Man of Nazareth."[38]

The Emancipation Proclamation had not only proclaimed freedom to enslaved people, it armed them for war. In July 1863, Douglass told an audience of African Americans in Philadelphia, "This rebellion can be put down without your help. Slavery can be abolished by white men; but liberty so won for the black man, while it may leave him an object of pity, can never make him an object of respect." And fight they would, assured Henry McNeal Turner, who encouraged African American troops to "turn their faces South and let the Star-Spangled Banner flaunt in the breeze."[39]

"The Noblest War Measure Known to History"

The Emancipation Proclamation had raised the moral and religious stakes of the war, and more northerners stepped up their biblical calls for a harder war on the Confederacy. In the wake of the proclamation, God demanded a "Christian Patriotism," said Edmund Burke Fairfield, president of Hillsdale College, former state senator and lieutenant governor in Michigan, and future chancellor of the University of Nebraska. In a speech before the Michigan legislature, Fairfield said, "Ages will come to look upon the Proclamation of January 1, 1863, as the noblest war measure known to history." The proclamation was a "magnanimous revenge" because it would help the North achieve revenge on the South.[40]

Revenge is the key word here, and Fairfield cited Romans 13, where Paul called rulers "a revenger to execute wrath upon him that doeth evil." As many in the North saw it, Lincoln was God's revenger, and the Union army executed God's revenge against the Confederacy. God put a sword in Lincoln's hand, and this was a real sword—"not a sword for show, but for use; one whose blade is of steel, and means blood and death to rebels." If any within earshot didn't like the sword, "Don't blame me for this stern word," Fairfield said, "I did not put a sword into this verse"—Paul did, so if you have a problem with it, "You must settle the matter with him."[41]

These were harsh words, to be sure, but necessary in Fairfield's opinion because the Confederacy was barbaric. Just listening to reports of how

Union prisoners were treated, along with other atrocities, Fairfield felt his "blood freeze and boil" at the same time. Prisoners wallowed in filth, starving; he heard of one who "lay upon the stone floor, haggard and ghastly as a living skeleton, his bones had protruded through the broken skin, unable to turn himself over." Confederates no doubt hid worse crimes, knowing that "dead men tell no tales!" It seemed the Confederates were more devils than humans. In the Old Testament, "God commanded an utter extermination of the Hittites and Hivites and Perizzites and Amorites and Jebusites"—did the Confederates deserve the same? "If their utter destruction is the only condition of reinstating the Government in its lawful authority—let it come!"[42]

But who was to say which side, the Union or the Confederacy, was the "lawful authority"? What about the Confederates—didn't they claim to be a sovereign nation, and didn't they claim to be fighting for God as well? They did, but their claims had no merit, said Fairfield. God did not validate *all* nations, requiring Christians to fight any war in his name. This was one of the dangers of Romans 13—it seemed to command Christians to obey *any* ruler, no matter how corrupt or tyrannical. According to this argument, Paul wrote Romans 13 while Nero was emperor, and yet Paul still commanded Christians to obey civil rulers. Did this mean God endorsed any government?[43]

Certainly not. "Paul was a close logician, and anticipated just such an objection," said Fairfield. After Paul said God ordained civil authorities he added, "Rulers are not a terror to good works, but to the evil." Paul was saying that "this is the kind of rulers that I speak of, as ordained of God; if there are those who become a terror to good works and not to the evil, then *they* are *not* ordained of God, and they that resist shall *not* receive to themselves damnation." In Romans 13, then, Paul endorsed only "true governments" that defended "rights" and punish "wrongs." This was "the divine test for discriminating between a *government* and a *tyranny*; between legitimate authority and mere usurpation."[44]

Another key word in Romans 13 was "terror." Godly rulers were a "terror" to evildoers—as Paul said, they wielded the sword—they waged war against evil. Nations and their leaders should "inspire fear in evil-doers," Fairfield said. Jefferson Davis and his renegade government made a mockery of both liberty and law, which was the reason Lincoln's Emancipation Proclamation was so important—it struck at the heart of the Confederacy. This proclamation was the best kind of "revenge; to gain a victory over our enemies by striking off the fetters of millions of oppressed men." This revenge should be swift, with a harder war. As Fairfield said, "It is merciful in war to strike hard blows and fast."[45]

The nation looked forward to a new resurrection, a resurrection of the flag. "The insulted and buried flag shall come forth with a resurrection power, and shall float in prouder triumph than ever, over the very scorners that have heaped indignity upon it!" So said Fairfield, demonstrating how biblical events—like the resurrection in this example—moved from religious to political meanings during the war.[46]

The war had been sacred since its beginning, at least for some Americans. It was sacred because life was sacred, and the war had to be worth the sacrifice of so many Americans. With his Emancipation Proclamation, Lincoln took the war's sacredness to a new level, and that involved the Bible, because without it, no war could be deemed sacred in this biblically infused nation.

12

"Of One Blood All Nations"

Although many hoped that the Emancipation Proclamation would en-list God for the Union's side, it did not seem that God was on any side in 1863. Many northerners were concerned, including Presbyterian Henry Wallace, an Iowa minister whose grandson would later serve as Franklin D. Roosevelt's vice president. "We thought that on and after January 1st, 1863, we should have God on our side," Wallace said. "But we are now saying, is it so?" The problem, Wallace decided, was that Americans had misjudged and disrespected God, believing they could manipulate God into supporting their cause.

How dare Americans try to manipulate God? This concern recalled a fre-quently cited text in the Civil War, in which Isaiah lashed out at Israel for trying to control God with a fast. The people fasted, pled to God, did all the outward works of religion, but they continued to exploit others and quarrel among themselves. Isaiah said God did not honor just any fast. A fast that God approved must be a fast that loosed "the bands of wickedness," removed "heavy burdens," and "let the oppressed go free." Would not God's approved fast be one that would "deal thy bread to the hungry, and . . . bring the poor that are cast out to thy house?" (Isaiah 58:6–7).

Some Americans honored fast days, hoping they would bring God's assis-tance in the war; others complained about fast days, griping that hunger was already rampant in some areas without an obligatory day of fasting. Wallace was preaching on another fast day—April 30, 1863. It was time Americans heard what Isaiah had to say—that fasts could be dangerous, if the people thought "our fasting would place the Almighty under some *obligations* to send us deliverance." This nation, Wallace said, "reels like a drunken giant," calling to God for deliverance while mumbling under its breath "There is no God." The nation fasted and prayed, not because the people "believed much in fasting and prayer, but as if it were 'a war measure,'—'a military neces-sity'"—as if "the Lord of hosts could be deceived" by such schemes.[1]

The only fast God respected had to include justice: the people must commit "to let the oppressed go free, and . . . break every yoke." That meant emancipation, but emancipation was not enough. Also, "It is our duty, as a people, to recognize fully the *manhood of the negro*." Even white Americans who opposed slavery didn't want to live with African Americans, preferring that "the slave should have his freedom" but colonized in Africa. White Americans still held an unchristian "bitter prejudice against a race, inferior though it may be." How were black people inferior? Because they didn't share the advantages of whites. In comparison with a black man, Wallace said, "I stand in advance of him" but only because of "more favorable circumstances." The African American, then, was "sacred—sacred, because God is his father, Christ his brother; sacred, because he bears the image of the Father and the Son, and who then dare deny him?"[2]

What, then, did the Emancipation Proclamation mean for the war and the nation? Americans pondered this quandary endlessly in 1863. As the nation wrestled with emancipation, many Americans called for a reassessment of racism from a biblical perspective.

"Of One Blood All Nations of Men"

Henry McNeal Turner had a theory: maybe the North failed in the war because northerners still resisted the Emancipation Proclamation. Lincoln had endorsed the proclamation, "but the hearts of the people have not. The President has, but the country has not; and it must be done; Else God will blow out the sun, burn up the sea, and thunder his wrath abroad."[3]

Frances E. W. Harper, one of the most prolific African American poets of the day, also had a theory: perhaps Americans should temper their expectations. It could be unrealistic to expect the proclamation to have immediate influence on the battlefield. "What hath God wrought!" she exclaimed. "In the crucible of disaster and defeat God has stirred the nation, and permitted no permanent victory to crown her banners while she kept her hand on the trembling slave and held him back from freedom." "Some may say, why does not God give us full and quick victory?" Harper encouraged her readers not to "despair if even deeper shadows gather around the fate of the nation." Stay firm, she said, even though all seemed to be lost in the war. Now they had the proclamation. "Thank God that the President did not fail us, that the fierce rumbling of democratic thunder did not shake from his hand the bolt he leveled against slavery." The American flag, once a symbol of suffering to enslaved people, now had "become a symbol of protection and freedom."[4]

Some said the nation would draw God to its side by fighting for emancipation, but others argued that was not enough. The nation must move beyond emancipation to fight racism. "Law and the sword can and will, in the end abolish slavery," Frederick Douglass said. "But law and the sword cannot abolish the malignant slaveholding sentiment"; namely, "pride of race, prejudice against color" would persist.[5]

Speaking in Brooklyn, New York, Douglass said the relationship "between the white and colored people of this country" was the "all commanding question for this age and nation to solve." This was the cause of the war, the crisis of the time. And it was a providential work. It was "a divine energy, omniscient and omnipotent," that "forced this mighty question of the negro upon the attention of the country and the world." God's message to white Americans was "Save the negro and you save the nation, destroy the negro and you destroy the nation."[6]

Racism was not confined to the South. "Prejudice is worse in the Northern states than in the Southern," said Edmund Wilson of Massachusetts. "It makes complexion a badge of degradation. . . . It is as bad as slavery, every whit, in spirit. It is the same thing indeed as slavery." The black race was a divine creation, so it was sinful to condemn it. Northerners, Wilson asserted, were hypocritical for attacking slavery while treating "the black race . . . with contempt and scorn" despite Jesus's teachings. "Under every dusky skin is a soul as much [in] the care of God, as is his who issues proclamations from the Presidential seat."[7]

This needed to be said because so many white Americans doubted the humanity of Africans. This had been a major issue in the debates between Abraham Lincoln and Stephen Douglas. Douglas had "no very vivid impression that the negro is a human," Lincoln reported, "and consequently he has no idea that there can be any moral question in legislating about him."[8]

Naturally, then, Americans looked to scripture to assess race and human equality. An important text was Jesus's parable of the Good Samaritan, which condemned racism, according to Urban Brewer of New York. The hero of the story was the Samaritan, who Jews saw "as a mongrel people of very corrupt blood; as having an abominable religion, and as being their implacable enemies" (Luke 10:25–37). But Jesus told everyone to love their neighbors, including Samaritans. He attacked the Jews' "national pride when he extended the provisions of the law of love to a people which they hated with an hereditary hatred." This was racism, and it had a long history. "There are many in this Christian age who would die covered with wounds of blood, before they would accept the humanities of a man who was so unfortunate as to have a black skin."[9]

Racism violated "the Bible doctrine of the unity and universal brotherhood of the human race." It all traced back to Adam and Eve, the first parents, Brewer said. Then he turned to one of the most crucial biblical arguments for racial equality, focusing on Paul's speech in Athens (Acts 17:16–34).[10]

The narrative began with Paul's visit to Athens, a center of politics and philosophy, where he noticed people worshiping many gods. Paul reacted by arguing—he argued with Jews in the synagogue, and he argued with other citizens in the marketplace. Seeing this, philosophers, including Epicureans and Stoics, ridiculed Paul, calling him a "babbler." They led Paul to the Areopagus—the Athenians' high court—where Paul had the chance to preach. He told them he had seen their altar "to an unknown god," and Paul identified this god as the God of the Old Testament and Jesus—the only God, a universal deity they could not represent as a statue.[11] Then Paul said that this universal God created all people from the universal first parents, Adam and Eve. God "hath made of one blood all nations of men for to dwell on all the face of the earth, and hath determined the times before appointed, and the bounds of their habitation" (Acts 17:26).

As Brewer explained it, the Greeks had "great pride of race; they looked upon all other nations as barbarians, and denied the common ancestry of men." This was not just an ancient problem, Brewer knew. Americans followed a lively debate in the 1800s about human origins. One view—represented by Swiss-born Harvard professor Louis Agassiz—supported "polygenism," the belief that different races originated at different times and places. There was no biological relationship between all humans, so physical differences reflected the different origins of races.[12]

In opposition, others argued for "monogenesis," claiming all races had a common origin and so all races shared a common humanity, despite physical differences. Just before the war, abolitionists like Henry David Thoreau turned to a new book, Charles Darwin's *On the Origin of Species*, using it to oppose Agassiz and to argue for a common humanity.[13]

Evidently, St. Paul and Darwin agreed on this issue. According to Reverend Brewer, Paul made "an inspired, authoritative announcement of the *consanguinity* of *all men* and *nations*, made in opposition to the prejudices, philosophy, religion, and politics of one of the proudest nations of antiquity." Paul was clearly talking about race. His "phrase '*of one blood*' means of one *kindred*, *race*, or *family*, for the word" in Greek "translated 'blood,'" meant "*descent, relation, seed,* or *stock.*" According to the Bible, then, all people— slave, free, black, or white—originated from the same parents, Adam and Eve. There was no denying this doctrine without denying scripture itself, Brewer said. And yet slavery contradicted this doctrine. For all the Bible's insistence that all people came from the same origins, slavery denied that enslaved Africans were even human; they were property, "a *chattel,* a *thing,* a *beast of burden*" with "no more name than a *dog* or a *horse,* and no more *family* or *kindred* than the ox."[14]

Paul thus condemned white supremacy, some argued. "If God has made 'of one blood all men,'" said Presbyterian C. F. Worrell of New Jersey, "where does the Southern nabob get his 'boasted blood,' 'better blood,' which exalts him lord over the slave that crouches at his feet . . . whom he would repudiate as an inferior race?" This idea is "anti-national, anti-scriptural, anti-democratic."[15]

Acts 17:26 had been cited against slavery before the Revolutionary era, and it made sense that it became one of the most cited biblical texts during the Civil War. Many antislavery ministers associated Acts 17:26 with the Declaration of Independence. Consider the view of Nathan S. S. Beman, Presbyterian minister whose career ranged from president of the University of Georgia to antislavery pastor in Troy, New York. He called Acts 17:26 a "charter of human rights drawn up by Paul and announced in the cele- brated Areopagus." This was a "prototype" of the statement of equality in the Declaration of Independence. As Beman and many others saw it, the nation was "not less indebted to the apostle Paul than to Thomas Jefferson, for such foundational principles as these: 'We hold these truths to be self- evident—that all men are created equal; that they are endowed by their Creator with certain unalienable rights,'" including "life, liberty, and the pur- suit of happiness."[16] As a Congregationalist minister from Massachusetts put it, "Common parentage proclaims universal brotherhood." If Paul was right that all people were born of one blood, then all were siblings, which implied the equality stated in the Declaration of Independence.[17]

This connection between Acts 17:26 and the Declaration of Independence had appeared in the Constitution of the American Anti-Slavery Society (1835) and in several slave narratives. In the story of their cunning es- cape from slavery, William and Ellen Craft wrote, "HAVING heard while in Slavery that 'God made of one blood all nations of men,' and also that the American Declaration of Independence says, that 'We hold these truths to be self-evident, that all men are created equal; that they are endowed by their

Creator with certain inalienable rights' . . . we could not understand by what right we were held as 'chattels.' Therefore, we felt perfectly justified in undertaking the dangerous and exciting task of 'running a thousand miles' in order to obtain those rights which are so vividly set forth in the Declaration." Whether cited along with this famous quotation from the Declaration or not, Acts 17:26 was one of the most-cited biblical texts in slave narratives before, during, and after the Civil War.[18]

Some viewed Acts 17:26 as a Republican motto. An ad for the *New York Tribune* featured this verse, saying the *Tribune* "is Republican in its hearty adhesion to the great truth that 'God has made of one blood all nations of men.'" After Lincoln was assassinated, Presbyterian minister H. G. Hillman from Ohio said, "Mr. Lincoln has left behind his unequivocal testimony, that he believed in the grand truth promulgated by Paul to the Athenians on Mars' hill, [*sic*] 'And hath made of one blood all nations of men for to dwell on all the face of the earth.'"[19]

"The Great Arian Family"

Southerners countered with a proslavery reading of Paul's statement at Athens. Many of these southerners accepted monogenesis—that God "made of one blood all nations of men"—and they argued for it as fiercely as any antislavery preacher. This was the view expressed by J. C. Mitchell of Alabama in his *Bible Defense of Slavery and the Unity of Mankind*. In his argument against Agassiz, Mitchell quoted Acts 17:26 and remarked, "If the Apostle was a believer in the diverse origin of men, he certainly had a very strange way of expressing himself." Here Paul echoed the Genesis story, which described Adam and Eve as the parents of all humanity. Eve "was the mother of all living," according to Genesis 3:20. "Can it be tortured to mean that Eve was the mother simply of the white race?" No. And it was not just that they did not know about the black race, he said. Surely "Moses, who was born in Egypt," knew "African races existed in Egypt and Ethiopia in his time." Mitchell cited evidence from "paintings and inscriptions of the pyramids and temples" in Egypt to prove that people in Moses's time knew people with black skin.[20]

Yet the common *origin* of races did not imply the *equality* of races, said Mitchell and others. In support, they cited other scriptures, especially "the curse of Ham" (or "the curse of Canaan"), based on Genesis 9, which became one of the most racist and most prominent defenses of slavery long before the Civil War. "Slavery first originated in the family of Ham, the Son of Noah," wrote a North Carolina Methodist minister in an unprinted manuscript, "and in this family has it continued to the present time."[21]

According to this text, Noah got drunk soon after stepping off the ark. As he lay naked in his tent, his son, Ham, saw him and told his brothers, Shem and Japeth, who tried to respect their father's dignity by covering him with a garment without looking at him. When Noah woke and realized Ham had seen him naked, he cursed Ham's son, Canaan, dooming him and his descendants to be servants. Many southerners followed centuries of other interpreters in identifying Africans as the descendants of Canaan who were destined by God for slavery.[22] Those who adopted this view said they were consistent with Paul: God had made "one blood all nations of men"—all races descended from Adam and Eve. But God ruled that some races would be enslaved, and other races would be their masters.[23]

The Curse of Ham (or Canaan) provoked endless debate. Frederick Douglass used this scripture to comment on the many sexual assaults committed by masters against enslaved women. Although racists of the day deplored racial mixing, slavery had mixed races like never before. "If the lineal descendants of Ham are only to be enslaved, according to the scriptures, slavery in this country will soon become an unscriptural institution; for thousands are ushered into the world annually, who—like myself—owe their existence to white fathers and, most frequently, to their masters, and masters' sons."[24]

Often debates over the Curse of Ham included Acts 17:26. In 1862, Cornelius H. Edgar, prolific Dutch Reformed pastor in Pennsylvania, published *The Curse of Canaan Rightly Interpreted*, making three biblical arguments. First, he attacked the claim that Noah's curse on Canaan was divinely inspired. Scripture did not say that Noah spoke for God in declaring this curse. Noah was not under the influence of the Holy Spirit; Noah had been under the influence of fermented spirits. He was angry, not inspired; he was embarrassed and outraged that Ham had seen him naked, and he cursed Canaan out of "chagrin and indignation and self-reproach."[25]

Second, scripture did not say that Canaan's descendants were Africans, nor did it say they were black. These ideas arose from later tradition, which of course did not carry the authority of scripture.[26]

Third, scripture did not say much about skin color, nor did scripture claim that some races arose separately from others. If one could prove that God created different races at different times and places, one could argue that God created some races superior to others, which could justify one race enslaving the other. But Edgar quotes Paul again: "God hath made of one blood all nations of men," which proved that all people were related and, therefore, shared the same human nature.[27]

Regardless of these arguments, there were still other ways to enlist Acts 17:26 in support of slavery. After the Emancipation Proclamation, Reverend James Warley Miles printed Acts 17:26 on the title page of his graduation speech at the College of Charleston in March 1863. Miles's speech took its theme from the second part of Paul's statement: God "hath determined the times before appointed, and the bounds of their habitation." He titled his speech *God in History*, arguing history was not a random sequence of events, ordered only by human actions; history proceeded according to "a rational and providential plan."[28] His interest, then, was not on human equality, nor on the claim that all people shared "one blood." Instead he focused on the plan God put in place for each nation—as Paul put it, God "determined the times before appointed, and the bounds of their habitation."[29]

Although each race had a role to play in "the drama of universal history," Miles said, not all races were equal. Only "the great races" had advanced civilization. The most advanced and influential race, Miles said, was "the great Arian family," which moved west and influenced history more than any other race. This family led in literature and art, science, and philosophy. They ruled history.[30]

As Miles saw it, the Confederacy had a unique destiny. "We have a great lesson to teach the world with respect to the relation of races: that certain races are permanently inferior in their capacities to others, and that the African who is entrusted to our care can only reach the amount of civilization and development of which he is capable." The African had an important role to play—to help the South develop its agricultural resources for the world. If the Confederacy fulfilled its destiny as a Christian nation, then Confederate history would "be another great chapter in the theodicy of nations, justifying the ways of Providence to man."[31]

"A Church of the Devil"

The Emancipation Proclamation had changed the national conversation about race, slavery, and the war. On the war front, Lincoln hoped that the

proclamation would unite the North around a righteous cause and cata-
pult the Union to more victories. That did not happen—at least initially.[32]
The Union was far from winning the war. The Army of the Potomac seemed
in a shambles under Burnside's flailing leadership. On January 26, Lincoln
replaced Burnside with Joseph Hooker, nicknamed "Fighting Joe," a name
Lincoln hoped he would live up to.

Everywhere Lincoln looked, he found disappointment and missed opportunities. Even General Ulysses S. Grant, usually efficient in winning battles,
was having difficulty taking Vicksburg, which was key to controlling the
Mississippi River. Halleck told Grant that control of the Mississippi River
would be better for the Union "than the capture of forty Richmonds."[33] The
problem was that Vicksburg was well protected. It stood at the eastern side
of the river, with protection from swamps and hills around. Grant tried several plans of attack without success, leading to questions about his character
and capability. Newspapers spread rumors of Grant's ineptitude, some accusing him of falling back into his drunken ways. The editor of the *Cincinnati
Commercial* called Grant "a jackass in the original package"—"a poor stick
sober, and he is most of the time more than half drunk."[34]

Diminished morale led to fewer volunteers for military duty. In March,
Lincoln responded by signing off on the first draft in the Union, calling to service men from age twenty to forty-five. These men entered a lottery system,
although a man could purchase exception from the draft for $300—far too
expensive for average Americans. This set off more complaints that this was
"a rich man's war but a poor man's fight."[35]

Southerners made similar statements. Mary Chesnut responded to news of
emancipation: "At last Lincolnton [*sic*] has issued a proclamation abolishing
slavery—here, in the free Southern Confederacy." It was outrageous, in her
view, that Lincoln would presume to free slaves in another nation. Moreover,
she commented on the link between emancipation and a harder war. "They
want more fighting, I mean the government, whose skins are safe." More than
a few folks joined Chesnut in critiquing the government for imposing battles
that others would die in.[36]

Lackluster results on the battlefield, negative reaction to the Emancipation
Proclamation, and Lincoln's conscription law in March all fueled a strong
antiwar movement in the North. This was an internal threat—Lincoln called
it a "fire in the rear" coming from so-called copperheads, who called themselves "Peace Democrats." They had a leader in Clement L. Vallandigham,
who hailed from Ohio and made plans to become its governor.

Vallandigham took his antiwar message to Congress in January, and then toured the country delivering speeches against Lincoln and the war. Americans were dying, he said, not for their country, but for African Americans in a fanatical war for abolitionism. And how was it going? "Let the dead at Fredericksburg and Vicksburg answer," he said. To desert the battle-field in such a war was neither cowardly nor unpatriotic. Several newspapers endorsed desertion, with some quoting a letter from an Illinois man to his son: "Come home, if you have to desert you will be protected" because "the people are so enraged that you need not to be alarmed if you hear of the whole of our Northwest killing off the abolitionists."[37]

The war was unwinnable, said the copperheads. "Stop fighting. Make an armistice. . . . Withdraw your army from the seceded States," said Vallandigham. Slavery would survive, but that was no major compromise to end such a bloody war. "I see more of barbarism and sin, a thousand times, in the continuance of this war" than in African slavery, Vallandigham said.[38]

The copperhead position looked good from the battlefield for some weary soldiers. In May 1863, Adam Bright of Pennsylvania wrote to his uncle, "I guess I am called a copperhead about home, but that will not hurt me. . . . It is very nice to be at home and talk about soldiering, but. . . . A man that never was in the war has no idea of the hardships we have to endure."[39] This soldier's brother, also a Union soldier, disagreed, writing from his camp near Tullahoma, Tennessee: "You cant form the remotest idea what a curse Slavery is to our country unless you travel in a State where it exists."[40]

Many Americans who opposed the war blamed religion for the trouble, calling abolitionists fanatics and religious zealots. The Civil War was a "*quasi religious war*," wrote John Reynolds, Democrat and former governor of Illinois. Voters needed to defeat "the abolition party in the hands of Abraham Lincoln." Reynolds called this "abolition party" demonic and insane, a party that desecrated "religion by preaching politics and singing hypocritical psalms."[41]

This was a major point of debate. What, exactly, was the role of religion in the war? Ministers who supported the war—and often supported emancipation—fired back against copperheads, arguing that both the Bible and the nation's founding pressed Americans to pursue the war. The founders "produced the Declaration of Independence, as the correct political exegesis of the New Testament," argued Universalist minister Willard Spaulding of Salem, Massachusetts. "The Revolution was a religious war; those who fell in it were Christian martyrs," he said. Although the United States was a human government, "It is founded on the Word of God, which has exalted it above all other nations."[42]

To those who blamed political preaching for the war, Spaulding said, "The Pulpit should impart to the people the true spirit of Patriotism, which will constitute their best preparation for the discharge of their civil duties." Patriotism was inseparable from spirituality. "Patriotism is a religious senti-ment," he said.[43]

Spaulding attacked copperheads, many of whom wanted to ban political preaching, and some who wanted to forbid clergy from even praying about the war or slavery. If the church were to cave to these demands, it would no longer be a church, he said. "Such a body cannot be called a Church of Christ. It is a communion of 'copperheads'; it is a nest of traitors; it is a church of the devil."[44]

One of the key scriptures cited in reaction to the copperheads was the prophet Jeremiah's admonition against an unrepentant nation that proclaimed "peace, peace; when there is no peace" (Jeremiah 8:11). God's people were backsliding into injustice and yet fooled themselves into thinking all was well, crying "peace, peace," but there was anything but peace. Pro-war northerners seized upon this scripture warning against the unjust compromise with the South to end the war without ending slavery, the policy of the copperheads. A deal with copperheads could bring an end to the war, but it would not bring a just peace. Several articles published William Lloyd Garrison's *The Liberator* cited this scripture, including one that said those crying "peace, peace" did not want peace, but really wanted "the acquisition of power to themselves and their allies."[45]

"The Proposed Return into Egypt, and Its Consequences"

In response to antiwar advocates, *Harper's* tried to jolt Americans back to wartime reality, reminding them how important this conflict was: "No such war as ours has ever been waged since the Crusades."[46] The stakes were too high to give up.

A biblical attack on copperheads came from George Barrell Cheever. He had made a name for himself by fighting for several reform movements, including temperance. His attack on a distillery in Massachusetts got him horsewhipped and thrown in jail, which earned Cheever widespread noto-riety. If Cheever hated the liquor traffic, he also despised attempts to outlaw

capital punishment, which earned him the reputation as "America's most famous champion of the gallows." But it was Cheever's hatred of slavery that
inspired his biting sermon before the US Senate on February 15, 1863.[47]

This sermon, *The Proposed Return into Egypt, and its Consequences*, focused on the Israelites in the Old Testament, newly liberated from Egyptian
slavery. They fled to the wilderness, led by Moses and inspired by God. Their
path was clear but difficult. The Promised Land of Canaan was their destiny,
but it wouldn't be easy. They could not just move into the land; they had to
conquer it. But many Israelites were not in the conquering mood. They were
more complainers than warriors, griping about the lack of food and various
other hardships. These Israelites sent spies to see what Canaan was like and
found out the people there would be hard to defeat. The war would be impossible, they thought, and they decided to give up and head back to Egypt.
Slavery, they decided, was better than death in the wilderness (Numbers 14),
and they needed new leadership. Moses, God's chosen man who led them
out of Egyptian slavery, had to go; they wanted new captains who would lead
them back to Egypt.[48]

To run back to Egypt was to betray God, however. The Lord had mapped
out their destiny, liberating them to start a new nation—what Cheever
called "a free and holy republic" with "neither slavery nor idolatry." God had
commanded faithfulness and courage. God called on them to conquer the
pagans in a war for liberty and God's people.[49]

The same was true of the Union. To compromise with the Confederacy
would "undo all that you have done for God and humanity." The cost of peace
was too high if it meant backtracking on emancipation, Cheever insisted. The
nation could not treat African Americans as pawns on a chessboard, playing
"fast and loose with four millions of God's souls." The nation could not free
enslaved people only as a means of winning the war, without caring for their
freedom or their lives. If the nation used African Americans like a political
"throw of dice," the United States would condemn itself "to death before
God."[50]

The church was failing the nation, Cheever said. Instead of speaking a
chastising word to correct the nation, the church had been "a servile hanger
on, a camp follower." The church was "a waiter on Providence, not a leader in
duty, or a revealer of principle, or a commander of the right." The northern
church had been conservative, compromising with slavery and obeying
whatever conservative voices demanded. "If we go back to Egypt," he said,
the church "can do us no good."[51]

The only way forward with God was through conquest, Cheever claimed. The Israelites in the wilderness had to attack the pagans, destroy their idols, and claim the promised land for God's people. War was godly; peace was treasonous. The same was true of North and South in 1863. The North must "obey God and take possession of the land for freedom." As Cheever said to the Senate, "Nothing can save us but our saving of the enslaved, at God's command." Compromise with the Confederacy would seal "our own national funeral."[52]

The nation's models should be African American soldiers, he said. "The despised negroes teach us foresight, discipline, purpose, energy." If they had led the way, "The rebellion and war would have been finished."[53] "The enemies of the country respect nothing but power, fear nothing but power." Attack, then, Cheever said. "We must conquer or die."[54]

Some of the strongest attacks on copperheads came from African Americans. Speaking of allowing blacks to serve in the military, Henry McNeal Turner said, "The copperheads were so fearful that a negro would get a crack at a [Confederate soldier], that it appeared they would have been willing to have voted their wives and daughters into the battle rather than allow a negro to take a part."[55]

One of the reasons Turner was so glad that African Americans could serve in the military had to do with the honor that came with military service. Jesus said, "There shall be wars, and rumors of wars" (Matthew 26:4). War was not a good thing, but it was an honor that the enemies of African Americans wanted to deprive them of. The copperheads even spread rumors that enlisting blacks into the war was just Abraham Lincoln's "plan to kill them all off," Turner said.[56]

Despite the Emancipation Proclamation, the war's fortunes had not turned in the Union's favor, which had brought copperheads out of hiding and onto the pages of newspapers everywhere. There was some good news—preachers thanked God that Washington's birthday came on a Sunday in 1863, because it gave them an opportunity to preach on the nation's all-time hero. Now was the time for all Americans "to re-kindle the fires of patriotism," a minister claimed in one of many sermons that capitalized on Washington's birthday to revive enthusiasm for the war.[57] In another sermon to Union troops in Buffalo, New York, the minister spoke On the character and influence of Washington, insisting that Washington, if he could speak from his grave, would quote David from the Psalms: "Through thee will we push down our enemies: through thy name will we tread them under that rise up against us.... blessed be the LORD my strength, which teacheth my hands to war, and my fingers to fight" (Psalms 44:5, 144:1).[58]

These sermons shaped a patriotic ritual when it was needed, when other rituals—like fast days—had been called into question as blatant attempts to manipulate providence. Also, linking George Washington with the Bible was as good a strategy as any to combat the copperhead menace. But there was no mistaking the fact that northern patriotism was in peril, and a substantial number of ministers blamed hypocrisy and compromise, especially on slavery. This made biblical texts like Acts 17:26 even more vital than ever to convince the North to support the war's righteous cause before it was too late.

13

"These Dead Have Not Died in Vain"

Lincoln's Gettysburg Address, delivered on November 19, 1863, included several biblical themes; it even sounded like the King James Bible. The opening—"Four score and seven years ago our fathers brought forth on this continent, a new nation, conceived in Liberty"—recalled texts from the Bible, including the book of Revelation, where a woman in heaven "brought forth a man child, who was to rule all nations" (Revelation 12:5).[1] Lincoln honored the fallen soldiers who had consecrated that ground, vowing to pursue the war so that "these dead shall not have died in vain—that this nation, under God, shall have a new birth of freedom."[2]

The Gettysburg Address assessed a year of unprecedented sacrifice on the battlefield. The year 1863 brought conflicting viewpoints of the war's moral purpose, especially as deaths multiplied and battles continued with no end in sight. Loss cries out for meaning, and Americans sensed that in 1863. When Americans saw loss on a scale like they did that year, they turned to the Bible to give meaning to the war, much as Lincoln did at Gettysburg.

"Our Christian Patriot. Gone!"

During the battle of Chancellorsville on May 2, Thomas "Stonewall" Jackson and several officers took a nighttime ride to investigate the position of enemy forces in the area. As they rode back from this reconnaissance mission, men from the Eighteenth North Carolina Regiment saw Jackson and his men coming and mistook them for Union troops. They shot Jackson three times: once in his hand, and twice in his left arm. A doctor at a nearby field hospital amputated the arm, and initial sights for a recovery looked good. Even so, the news devastated Robert E. Lee. "Any victory is dearly bought which deprives us of the services of General Jackson, even for a short time," Lee said.[3]

A couple of days later, Jackson came down with pneumonia. Mary Anna Jackson rushed to her husband's bedside along with their baby, Julia Jackson.

By Sunday, May 9, it became clear that Jackson was dying. He told his wife that he wanted God's will to be done, whatever that was. He also said, "I always wanted to die on Sunday." He got his wish that afternoon.[4]

Confederates had never grieved more deeply. "On May 10 the General died," wrote Sara Rice Pryor of Virginia, "and we were all plunged into the deepest grief. By every man, woman, and child in the Confederacy this good man and great general was mourned as never man was mourned before." Also from Virginia, Lucy Rebecca Buck wrote, "Oh what a blow is this—Our bravest and best, the most devoted and earnest in the cause in which we all have staked so much—the truest and noblest, our christian patriot. Gone!"[5]

Why did God allow Stonewall Jackson to die? The way he died was bad enough, killed by Confederate soldiers, hardly a good death worthy of such a hero. Beyond that, his death created a dilemma for many whites in the South. As historian Daniel Stowell wrote, "Jackson's death was a spiritual crisis."[6]

Jackson was the man of war many Americans dreamed of, North and South. He was a spiritual man who taught Sunday school, served as a deacon in the Presbyterian church, read his Bible, pondered God's providence in all the war's events, and prayed that revivals would wash over the armies.[7]

In Lynchburg, Virginia, Presbyterian minister James B. Ramsey remembered Jackson by citing David's lament when Jonathan was killed: "How are the mighty fallen in the midst of the battle! O Jonathan, thou wast slain in thine high places" (1 Samuel 1:25; also cited Psalms 91:14). As great as Jonathan was, Jackson was greater, a southern saint, precious to God. "The Church of Christ praised God continually for such a burning and a shining light, and multitudes of souls, especially in our army, high officers and privates, will rejoice eternally in that light." Jackson's "eminence" did not originate in his brilliance; "It was God who made him great, by making him holy."[8]

Jackson defied the usual expectations. The typical image of a soldier did not suggest religious devotion, and army camps overflowed with every variety of sin. But then there was Jackson, who proved that religion made soldiers stronger, not weaker. "True religion has a necessary tendency to produce those qualities that alone can fit men for the highest stations and the noblest deeds," Ramsey said. The fear of God produced "an elevation of character, a purity of motive, a superiority to temptation, a sense of accountability, a submission to lawful authority, that cannot but make men better" no matter what their profession. Religious devotion sharpened the intellect by removing "self-love, passion and prejudice which becloud the judgment."[9]

According to reports that became legend, Jackson faced misfortune with an uncanny trust in the providence of God. When he was mortally wounded and in bed, he reportedly rejoiced when surgeons amputated his arm, then later said, "Many people would regard this as a great misfortune; I regard it as one of the greatest blessings of my life," quoting Paul: "All things work together for good to those that love God" (Romans 8:28). This was a popular biblical text in the Civil War, a statement of absolute trust in providence no matter what happened.[10]

After the war, many southerners pointed to Jackson's death as the moment when the Confederacy began to lose its grip on the war. "From the moment of his death the tide of fortune seemed to turn," wrote Sara Pryor, and "Henceforth there would be only disaster and defeat." Likewise, Confederate soldier John N. Opie said Jackson's "death was the harbinger of the downfall of the Confederacy. When he fell, the Almighty proclaimed the indestructibility of the American Union."[11]

"This War Is a Crusade"

Jackson's death was a blow to the South, but the true turning point in the war came at Gettysburg, Pennsylvania, the site of the war's most famous battle, and its most costly, with forty thousand dead or wounded. The battle lasted for the better part of the first three days in July. When it was over, the beleaguered Army of the Potomac had defeated the Army of Northern Virginia. Robert E. Lee lost the battle. Perhaps just as important, he lost his reputation as an invincible commander.

One of the critical events of the war came on July 3, and it centered on General George Pickett's division from Virginia. Pickett had been a fellow student of McClellan's at West Point. This was Pickett's chance to make his mark in the war. He did, but not in the way he intended.[12] Under Lee's orders, Pickett's men, together with General James Johnston Pettigrew's division, charged with approximately fourteen thousand soldiers against entrenched Union forces, both infantry and artillery. It was a suicide mission. James McPherson put it well: "Pickett's charge represented the Confederate war effort in microcosm: matchless valor, apparent initial success, and ultimate disaster."[13]

Pickett's charge was one of several instances of selfless courage that inspired McPherson to ask: "What made these men do it?" Compared with soldiers in other wars, more soldiers in the Civil War were willing to sacrifice themselves in battle. What was it that inspired this rare brand of selfless courage? We can point to several motivations, and religious faith was one. McPherson found a typical quotation from a Pennsylvania officer: "Sick as I am of this war and bloodshed . . . every day I have a more religious feeling, that this war is a crusade for the good of mankind."[14]

Although some soldiers believed they were fighting for God, this was rarely, if ever, the *only* motive for soldiers to fight.[15] Often they fought for each other, seeing themselves as "bands of brothers," and that was motivation enough to kill the enemy. Scholars call this "primary group cohesion"— soldiers fought for their comrades, sometimes even more than they fought for ideas like freedom or the Union.[16]

An insightful reflection on the comradeship between men at war came from Father William Corby, chaplain to the Irish Brigade at Gettysburg and future president of the University of Notre Dame. "One good result of the Civil War was the removing of a great amount of prejudice," Corby wrote years after the war ended. He spoke from experience, knowing what it was like to live as a Catholic in a nation dominated by Protestants. "When men stand in common danger, a fraternal feeling springs up between them and generates a Christian, charitable sentiment that often leads to most excellent results." War could make people more religious; battle could be a conversion experience.[17]

Father Corby played a legendary role at Gettysburg. On the second day, Corby gave absolution to the men preparing for battle—not just Catholics, and not just Union troops. According to Major General St. Clair Mulholland, colonel in the Irish Brigade, Corby reminded soldiers "of the high and sacred nature of their trust as soldiers and the noble object for which they fought."[18]

We can see why soldiers craved absolution or any comfort in the heat of battle. Fear of death was constant, and fear did not always subside as soldiers gained experience in battle. A Confederate soldier who fought at Gettysburg wrote, "I believe that soldiers generally do not fear death less because of their repeated escape from its jaws. For, in every battle they see so many new forms of death, see so many frightful and novel kinds of mutilation . . . that their dread of incurring the like fearful perils unnerves them for each succeeding conflict."[19]

As battlefield deaths increased, Americans looked to biblical passages that proved how sacred a soldier's sacrifice was. No scripture captured this spirit better than Jesus's words, "Greater love hath no man than this, that a man lay down his life for his friends" (John 15:13). Jesus said this as he contemplated the cross; soldiers heard it as they headed for battle, and their families heard it as their loved ones' bodies headed home from the war.

In the week after the Union victory at Gettysburg, Republican newspapers quoted this scripture text in evaluating the morality of the war, calling the war "a severe test of character" that made heroes of officers and soldiers. War was moral and manly, an antidote of commerce, selfishness, "and the effeminacy that follows it, that emasculates the vigor of a nation." War improved the character of the nation.

War changed people, almost overnight, this newspaper article said. "War is a forcing process; it accelerates development, and abridges time." Think of those who sacrificed their lives. "The brave boys who fell on the late battlefields, whose blood is not yet all washed away by autumnal rains, whose example is immortal." These boys matured beyond their years because of the war. Although young, they experienced a lifetime of discipline. As the Apostle Paul said, these men who died "fought the good fight and finished their course" (cf. 2 Timothy 4:7–8).

Biblical words like these praised soldiers' sacrifices when the Union needed them desperately. More soldiers than ever were refusing to serve as the war stretched into yet another year. Desertions increased as more Americans wanted to give up the fight and look for compromise. This increased the need to pursue the war more intensely than ever. The value of soldiers increased exponentially, and Americans used scripture to praise soldiers and their sacrifices.[20]

"Cursed Is the Peacemaker"

Just as the Union claimed a pivotal victory at Gettysburg, news arrived that Grant had finally captured Vicksburg after a masterful campaign and a siege of almost fifty days. This victory at Vicksburg, quickly followed by the capture of Port Hudson, gave the Union control of the Mississippi River and a decisive advantage in the war. As reports spread about these triumphs, Lincoln proclaimed that August 6 would be a day of thanksgiving.[21] Yet celebrations of Gettysburg and Vicksburg would be short lived. On July 13 anti-draft riots broke out in New York City, with ethnic tensions playing a major role. Many Irish Catholics had no use for emancipation, and they resented being forced to fight a war that favored rich whites and enslaved blacks. Most American

Catholics supported the Democratic Party, if any party at all, and many recognized that some of the same Republicans who despised slavery also despised Catholics. William Lloyd Garrison said Irish Catholics were "the very bitterest enemies of the antislavery cause." This was not the case for all Irish Catholics, but many saw this as a Protestant war, and they grew weary of nativist attitudes among the Protestant mainstream.[22]

Most northern Protestants "*hate* the Catholic religion with an almost satanic hate," said Martin John Spalding, Catholic Bishop in Louisville, Kentucky. These Protestants were warmongers, and theirs was a religion "of demons who make sport of the slaughter." Harsh words, Spalding knew, and he sent them to Rome as part of his "Dissertation on the American Civil War." Written about a month after Lincoln announced the draft, Spalding's "Dissertation" was reportedly read by Pope Pius IX.

Spalding blamed the war on abolitionists and Protestants, "blind fanatics," who had two enemies: slavery and Catholicism, and they attacked both with a vengeance. Most northerners who supported the war had no interest in granting equality to African Americans, no more than they did to American Indians, whom they "have almost exterminated . . . after having stolen their land from them." Spalding went on to describe Lincoln as "bloodthirsty" and the Emancipation Proclamation as "this atrocious proclamation." Spalding urged the Catholic Church to remain neutral in this war. But he was aghast at how Lincoln made neutrality difficult because his conscription law required "that Catholic priests, like the laity, must become soldiers if it falls to their lot!"[23] Spalding's statement was not immediately published, but similar viewpoints were often attributed to Catholics in the northern and border states.

Protestant suspicion of Catholicism was already on high alert, therefore, when the New York mob attacked the draft office, moving from there to other offices and houses, assaulting anyone who had paid the $300 fee to avoid the draft. Rioters even lynched some African Americans, and they set fire to the Colored Orphan Asylum. Union soldiers, on their way back from Gettysburg, restored peace. In all, some 120 people died in the riots.[24]

News of the rioting spread throughout the nation and put Catholic leadership in a difficult position. Archbishop John Hughes, a strong supporter of the Union and the war, published a letter, calling on Catholics to stop the violence. But nothing stopped a Protestant backlash against Catholics, with some Protestant ministers comparing the rioters to the mob that crucified Jesus, and many blaming Catholic priests for participating in the violence.[25]

For supporters of the war, the riots struck at the heart of the nation. Rabbi David Einhorn said the rioters were "like fiends from the lowest pools of hell," and he condemned them for "plundering and murdering, and in their Satanic phrenzy sparing neither age nor sex," attacking people "whose only crime was their dark complexion."[26]

Most Catholics were innocent victims of these attacks, and priests tried to set the record straight. The *New York Herald* reported on a sermon by Father A. J. Donnelly of St. Michael's Catholic Church. He quoted Jesus from the Sermon on the Mount: "Blessed are the peacemakers, for they shall be called the children of God." Implied in this verse is the opposite: "Cursed be the peace breakers, for they shall be called the children of the devil." Reverend Donnelly was relieved that none of his parishioners had rioted.[27]

In a remarkable sermon, *Patriotism, A Christian Virtue*, Rev. Joseph Fransioli of St. Peter's Catholic Church in Brooklyn, New York defended Catholic patriotism by marshalling evidence from scripture and Christian tradition. Jesus was a patriot, he asserted, pointing out that Jesus wept when he drew near Jerusalem and foresaw the devastation the city would endure (Luke 19:41). Jesus loved Jerusalem, proving that "patriotism is not only a social virtue, commanding respect, but a *christian virtue*, to be rewarded by the blessings of God here and hereafter." Not only Jesus, but all the heroes of scripture were devoted to their nations, including Moses, "Joshua, Gideon, [and] Samuel"—"were they not all distinguished patriots?" The same was true of the "the holy Fathers" of the church—all were patriots. The message for Americans was "you shall seek in vain for a Catholic saint that was not a patriot." Any accusation that Catholics "cannot be good patriots, is a deplorable error" that had been "refuted by streams of blood and numberless lives sacrificed to the Union on the fields of battles by heroic Catholic patriotism."[28]

With statements like these, Catholics tried to deflect attacks from many Protestants, but not all Protestants blamed Catholics for the riots. Some, like Methodist minister John Jackson, blamed racism. "That unchristian prejudice against color," Jackson said, provoked violence throughout the land. In the riots, African Americans suffered lynching—"shot, stabbed, and hung, and burned." Christians had a responsibility to "the 'American of African descent.'" Jesus would judge America by how it treated African Americans, Jackson said. In the parable of the sheep and the goats, Jesus condemned those who mistreated the lowly among them (Matthew 25:31–46).[29]

Mostly, this Methodist blamed the riot on so-called peace movements, mainly copperheads. The "peace" they advocated bore fruit in "blood, carnage" and cities "flowing in blood." Jackson accused newspapers—especially "the chief organ of the satanic press, the *New York Herald*"—for covering it all up and calling the rioters heroes.[30]

Americans be warned, said Jackson and others, the war was not over, mainly because there was still a war over the war. As the riots proved, many Americans still despised the war, even as northerners celebrated dramatic victories. That chief copperhead, Clement Vallandigham, still agitated for the movement, prompting attacks from Republicans. A newspaper article titled "The Ohio Copperhead's Latest Hiss" quoted Jesus: "Let the dead bury their dead" (Luke 9:60), referring to Vallandigham and his followers. At last, this author hoped, "Copperheadism" was dying; it "has buried its fangs in its own heart."[31]

Both sides could fight that fight, however, plastering biblical texts across newspapers to support their positions. On July 22, a Democratic newspaper—the *Spirit of Democracy* of Woodsfield, Ohio—displayed the Democratic ticket on the front page, with Vallandigham nominated for governor, and included the biblical text, "The stone which the builders rejected is become the head of the corner" (cf. Psalms 118:22). Also on the front page was a quote from Stephen Douglas: "I hold that this Government was made on the WHITE BASIS, by WHITE MEN, for the benefit of WHITE MEN, and their POSTERITY forever."[32]

Some Democratic newspapers ridiculed the idea that blacks and whites were created equal. One example is a satirical "catechism" for office seekers in the Republican Party, which began with the question, "Who made you?" and the response, "Abraham Lincoln!" There followed,

"What is the noblest work of God"
"A negro . . ."
"What is the object of the war?"
"Negro! . . ."
"Why is the negro the equal of the white man?"
"Because God created them both!"
"On that principle is a jackass the equal of a Brigadier General?"
"Of course."[33]

The more that northern clergy preached war after Gettysburg, the more some Americans questioned any faith that seemed tied too closely to politics.

The *New York News* ran an article, "The Divinity of Fanaticism," that other papers reprinted throughout the northern and border states. The article attacked wartime preaching, which resembled "the ancient Moloch, whose offerings were human beings, who delighted in blood and slaughter." These preachers so lusted for victory that they forgot its price of death. After Gettysburg, churches rang with praise to "God, 'who hath given us the victory through our Lord Jesus Christ'" even as the battlefield remained "drenched with human gore." "This war and the horrid example of the clergy, have done more to set back the progress of real Christianity than all the efforts of the infidel writers that ever lived."[34]

This was a farce, said northern ministers like Union Army chaplain and Methodist John C. Gregg. In a sermon preached at Montgomery Square, Pennsylvania on July 5, he selected as his main text Jesus's famous command, "Render unto Caesar the things that are Caesar's" (Matthew 22:21). Those who complained about political preaching were often traitors and defenders of slavery, he argued. Do people "not know that politics frequently runs into religion," that "Jesus preached against those who sat in Moses' seat and governed Judea?" Also, during the American Revolution patriotic ministers rightly preached against British tyranny. People cannot be naïve—preaching of "the Gospel which did not touch politics, would hardly touch religion." During this critical war, God demanded that clergy support the nation. "The prophets, seers, scribes, and apostles delivered the stern announcement that treason against the government is treachery against God; to disobey the one was to denounce the other." In response to "the traitors and sympathizers with which the North is cursed at this time," Gregg advised them to read "their much-neglected Bible."[35]

"Why Should They Give Their Lives for Us, with . . . Our Purpose to Betray Them?"

In the same month that New York mobs lynched black men, blaming them for the war, black soldiers took to the battlefield. Most famous was the Fifty-Fourth Massachusetts Voluntary Infantry Regiment, which led the attack on Fort Wagner in Charleston. Although it was unsuccessful, news of this attack spread throughout the nation. Hollywood told the story of this attack in the 1989 film *Glory*, starring Denzel Washington, Morgan Freeman, and Matthew Broderick. This film captured what mattered most at the time—the courage and skill displayed by African American troops, an important fact considering that many whites doubted whether black soldiers could fight.

One of the most haunting descriptions of the attack came from Harriet Tubman, well known as "Black Moses" for her leadership in the Underground Railroad: "And then we saw the lightning, and that was the guns; and then we heard the thunder, and that was the big guns; and then we heard the rain falling, and that was the drops of blood falling; and when we came to get in the crops, it was dead men that we reaped."[36]

Tubman was much more than an observer in Union military activities. One month before the attack on Fort Wagner, she had served as a scout, leading three hundred African American troops as they moved along the Combahee River in South Carolina to attack Confederates and free hundreds of enslaved people. Tubman's heroics are reported on the Central Intelligence Agency website, which says: "Gen. David Hunter, commander of all Union forces in the area, asked Tubman to personally guide a raiding party up the river. On the evening of 2 June, Tubman led Montgomery and 150 of his men up the river past Confederate picket lines. In a swift raid, taking the Confederates by surprise, the Union forces destroyed several million dollars worth of Confederate supplies and brought back more than 800 slaves and thousands of dollars in enemy property." The site continues, "Tubman's contribution to the Union cause was significant. When Tubman died in 1913, she was honored with a full military funeral as a mark of respect for her activities during the war." Note also that the CIA recognizes Tubman's biblical title, stating that she was "often referred to by her contemporaries as 'Moses.'"[37]

The sacrifice of African Americans for the Union did not go unnoticed. If this was a sacred war, perhaps black troops were its most righteous soldiers, said some ministers. "Jehovah is a man of war," preached Methodist pastor Daniel Steele in a national thanksgiving sermon preached in Lima, New York on August 6. Steele, future professor at Syracuse and Boston universities, drew on Exodus 15:3, "The Lord is a man of war." Steele believed that this divine warrior supported black troops: "50,000 ebony soldiers are bravely bearing aloft the stars and stripes on Southern battlefields. By their coolness, valor, and heroism, they are silencing the lying tongues that have wagged against them, accusing them of stolidity and cowardice. The glorious record of African courage is written in the trenches of Port Hudson, and on the parapet of Fort Wagner."[38]

Also in August 1863, the North saw one of the most famous celebrations of African American heroism in the funeral for Captain André Cailloux, a free man who recruited a company of soldiers for the Union army in New Orleans. Cailloux served heroically but died in the attack on Port Hudson in May. Because he was black, Confederate sharpshooters threatened to kill any Union soldiers who tried to remove his body from the field. This was another expression of rage against black soldiers—Confederates would not allow them the dignity of a proper burial. So Cailloux's body decomposed on that field until the fort surrendered on July 8, when, finally, Union soldiers were allowed to retrieve his remains.

This was an outrage, many northerners believed, so his funeral was a great event, in part to make up for the Confederates' humiliating treatment of Cailloux. This celebration could also have been a northern response to the southern services in honor of Stonewall Jackson, who was killed shortly before Cailloux.[39]

The Catholic priest who officiated at Cailloux's funeral implored the people "to offer themselves, like Cailloux had done, martyrs to the cause of justice, freedom and good government. It was a death the proudest might envy," he said. Cailloux defended "the sacred cause of Liberty," reported *Harper's Weekly*, and "vindicated his race from the opprobrium with which it was charged."[40]

During that same month of August 1863, President Lincoln wrote a letter to the nation, equivalent to today's televised speeches, and addressed the issue of African Americans in the military. Lincoln directed his comments to those who rioted against the draft: "You say you will not fight to free negroes. Some of them seem willing to fight for you." If the Union finally won this war, Lincoln said, "There will be some black men who can remember that, with silent tongue, and clenched teeth, and steady eye, and well-poised bayonet, they have helped mankind on to this great consummation; while, I fear, there will be some white ones, unable to forget that, with malignant heart, and deceitful speech, they have strove to hinder it."[41]

The brave service of these black troops made it impossible for Lincoln to abandon emancipation. He refused to consider it—"Could such treachery by any possibility, escape the curses of heaven?" As thousands of formerly enslaved blacks fought and died in the war, Lincoln attacked those who "proposed to me to return to slavery [these] black warriors. I should be damned in time & in eternity for so doing. The world shall know that I will keep my faith to friends & enemies, come what will. . . . Why should they give their lives for us, with full notice of our purpose to betray them?"[42]

Would the bloodthirsty radical John Brown be born again in the new policy of enlisting African Americans to fight? This question energized some northerners and terrified others. Former enslaved people in the Union army were not John Brown, said Isaac Newton Sprague, a Presbyterian pastor from New Jersey. John Brown was savage; black troops were dignified. They were not the brutes some whites thought they were, ready at a moment's notice to slit throats and flee to the North. Instead, they "acted with much more forbearance and generosity than . . . white men would have done under the same circumstances," said Sprague. Now the formerly enslaved people were in the military, fighting impressively. God had a purpose in this—likely to give African Americans "such a position of prominence and usefulness, as to call forth the nation's admiration and gratitude."[43]

Like many others, Sprague quoted Paul: God "has made of one blood all the nations of men." Following Paul's teaching, whites and blacks shared "a common brotherhood." One of the great benefits of this war was that it changed attitudes toward race. "This war is rapidly overturning all our pre-conceived ideas about the colored race," said Sprague. Apparently one way to fight racial prejudice was for African Americans to fight a war.[44]

"Selfish and Defective Patriotism"

Despite the victories at Gettysburg and Vicksburg, the prevailing challenges— draft riots, furor over blacks in the military, and copperheads—alarmed many northerners. Perhaps they were enduring a crisis because Americans had forgotten patriotism's religious dimension. "What is patriotism?" asked Sprague. "It is a whole-hearted love of country, preferring *its* welfare to any thing and all things else." In its essence, "patriotism is an active, out-spoken love of country, always willing to lay precious things on that country's altar." Note again the "altar" language, which often appeared in discussions of pa-triotism. The problem, as Sprague and many others saw it, was "the decay of patriotism": "We are, like Sampson [*sic*] shorn of his locks, losing both our beauty and our strength."[45]

Patriotism was one of the central themes of scripture for countless Americans, and they made that point repeatedly during the Civil War. "The Bible is eminently a patriotic book," preached William Barrows to a group of volunteers of the Company D, Fifteenth Regiment of Massachusetts. True patriots could not hear this word often enough in the summer of 1863, many believed. As losses mounted, patriotism waned, and preachers tried to meet the need by stressing the Bible's support for patriotism.

Barrows selected the Absalom story to motivate these soldiers. We have seen how the story of Absalom revealed the tragic results of a rebellion that divided families and nations. In addition, Absalom was a cautionary tale for soldiers: "Absalom in his revolt died as a fool dieth," Barrows told these men, "hung up between heaven and earth, where traitors belong, and thrust through by the three darts, of Joab, as the leader in a rebellion richly deserved." Absalom's fate was not an isolated incident. Throughout scripture, God honored patriots and condemned traitors.[46]

Even traitors and villains were forced to serve God's purposes—that was a message of inspiration for patriots after Gettysburg. President Lincoln heard this message in a thanksgiving service that he attended on August 6. The preacher, whom Lincoln knew well, was Presbyterian minister Phineas Gurley, and he addressed the topic, *Man's Projects and God's Results*. His text was from Proverbs, "A man's heart deviseth his way: but the Lord directeth his steps" (Proverbs 16:9). Gurley prefaced his remarks by saying that God "is in *all* history," and God's "hand and His mercy are exceedingly conspicuous in our own national history; and never more so than in the present eventful and perilous crisis." He followed by reflecting on the mysterious relationship between human responsibility and divine providence. People were free, and responsible for their actions, and yet God was in control, and God accomplished "His fixed and eternal purpose through the instrumentality of free, and accountable, and even *wicked* agents."

Gurley put special emphasis on "wicked," and then relayed biblical examples that showed how God used wicked people to accomplish divine purposes. In the story of Joseph, his wicked brothers sold him into slavery, but God used the situation to elevate Joseph to leadership in Egypt until, eventually, Joseph saved his people. Surpassing all other examples was Christ's crucifixion, an evil act devised by wicked people, but God used it to save the world.

There was plenty of wickedness in the Civil War, with northern conspirators and southern rebels attempting to destroy the nation. But as God did in scripture, he "can provide deliverance for us by methods equally mysterious, and yet equally effective." The God "who made the crucifixion of Jesus by wicked hands the most glorious event" in history "can turn the dark night of our national adversity into a morning of gladness and a day of splendor" that no "nation has ever seen before." God's preference for the nation had been sealed in blood at Gettysburg and other battles, convincing Gurley that the Lord was "the Guardian-God of this Republic." This sermon affected Lincoln, who remarked that he had never heard Gurley preach such a strong endorsement of the North's prospects in the war.[47]

Like northerners, southerners also struggled with patriotism. The war had lasted longer than many thought it would, and staggering losses at Gettysburg and Vicksburg forced southerners to ponder what patriotism demanded of them during these desperate times. Jefferson Davis thought he knew, and he mounted his pulpit to deliver the message. Unlike Lincoln, who called for a day of thanksgiving and praise, Davis called for a day of fasting and prayer, scheduled for August 21. Davis prayed for God's "favor on our suffering country." The Confederacy had angered God, resulting in defeats at Vicksburg and Gettysburg, and southerners had acted with overconfidence after previous military victories. Moreover, the South had loved money more than God, and greed had "eaten like a gangrene into the very heart of the land."[48]

Southerners grasped for their Bibles, looking for lessons from God's people in hard times. Especially popular were stories of Jews after the exile, which reminded southerners of their nation after Gettysburg and Vicksburg. The exile occurred in the sixth century BCE, when Babylonians defeated the Judeans, destroyed Jerusalem, and carried many of them to Babylon. Even though the Babylonians humiliated Judah, that did not mean Babylon was God's chosen empire—far from it. God had not forsaken the people; it just seemed like it. The Jews eventually saw justice done when the Persian Empire defeated Babylon, and Persian kings allowed God's people to return to their homeland, led by God's servants, especially Ezra and Nehemiah.

Several ministers preached sermons on the books named for Ezra and Nehemiah at this point in the war. In Savannah, Georgia, Stephen Elliott preached on Ezra's situation. After the Persian ruler allowed Ezra to lead his people home to Jerusalem, Ezra proclaimed a fast, seeking God's protection for the journey. But would God's protection be enough? It would be a dangerous trip, and Ezra was tempted to ask the king for a security team to accompany them. Ezra then realized his error: if he prayed for God's protection, why did he need protection from Persian soldiers—unless he lacked faith in God?

From his pulpit in Georgia, Elliott found a parallel with the Confederates, who from the beginning of the war had insisted God was on their side. The Confederacy had honored God in its national seal, and southerners had made a big deal about this, insisting that they were a Christian nation, in contrast with the atheistic United States. Confederates claimed they honored

God, and that God would turn "his wrath . . . against all them that forsake him" (c.f. Ezra 8:22). The Confederacy had bound itself to this covenant, "And by it must we now stand or fall." Just as Ezra was embarrassed to ask the king for help, so the Confederacy could not look to any other nation for help—"We should be ashamed to do it."[49]

Everyone understood Elliott's point: he was alluding to the Confederacy's attempt to gain an alliance with Britain or France. That chance ended with the defeats at Gettysburg and Vicksburg. Elliott knew this and found a biblical analogy that spoke to it. The Confederacy was left with God, the southerners' only ally, but that was how it should be, if the Confederates were true to their commitments.[50]

But was it too late? The Confederacy had suffered defeat and came back strong before, but this time was different. "From this recent shock we have not rallied," Elliott said. The South seemed "paralyzed." The best explanation was also the most worrisome: God must have helped the Yankees at Gettysburg and Vicksburg.[51]

But why? Although there had to be a reason, Elliott refused to blame the defeats on slavery. The North was as responsible for slavery as the South, he said. "These slaves were imposed upon us," often "against our wills." If slavery was evil, the North profited from it. And now that slavery was interwoven throughout southern life and its economy, northerners who no longer needed slavery demanded that southerners relinquish it.[52] Now slavery brought fear and war, but it mostly terrorized the South. Southerners lived petrified of slave violence because the North enticed enslaved people away, spreading abolitionist ideas. Enslaved people took care of the slaveholders' children and cooked their meals. "Does the head of any one of us rest less easily upon his pillow? Does any one tremble as he sees his little ones . . . nestled in their bosoms and sung to sleep with their lullabys? Does any one require a taster of his food, an analyser of his drink?"[53]

This war was a Republican "crusade against us," a war that was "unchristian and really atheistic," said Elliott. Northerners "turned their rage against the word of God, and covered it all over with ridicule and with abuse." "They set up liberty, equality, fraternity, as their idols, and virtually dethroned the God of the Bible."[54]

No, slavery could not be the reason for recent defeats, for slavery was not the South's sin. The true culprit was greed. As Jefferson Davis indicated in his proclamation, the South became too focused on money, to the point that men avoided military service to make a profit. As Elliott, Davis, and others saw it, greed invaded the South and sapped the strength from its patriotism. This fast day spoke to an urgent need to "rekindle the sacred fire of patriotism which burned so vividly in the outburst of this revolution."[55]

Many agreed that the South suffered from what a Lynchburg, Virginia, minister called a "selfish and defective patriotism." Too many southerners wanted to enjoy the fruits of victory without risking themselves. One of the signs of waning patriotism was how the people treated their soldiers. The editor of the North Carolina Baptist newspaper *Biblical Recorder* met a destitute soldier making his way home on furlough near Morganton, North Carolina. The soldier was nearly starved, sick with fever, and yet no southerner helped him, either with money or food. "We beg our people every where to be kind to the soldiers," this editor wrote, obeying Jesus's words, "Greater love hath not man than this, that he lay down his life for another" (John 15:13). These soldiers were doing that—fighting for the Confederacy. More to the point, "They are fighting for our negro property," so "slaveholders" had a special responsibility "to be kind, to be generous to soldiers and their families."[56]

The Bible could help here, and southerners searched the scriptures for warnings against avarice. The *Richmond Examiner* published a sermon by Jefferson Davis's pastor, Charles Minnegrode, rector of St. Paul's Church, in which he examined one of the most notorious thieves in the Bible, Gehazi, who cheated the prophet Elisha (1 Kings 5). The story of Gehazi resonated with both northerners and southerners in the Civil War, and both sides used this scripture to condemn selfishness.

As the narrative unfolded, Elisha had bestowed God's healing power on Naaman, a Syrian military hero, healing him of leprosy. Naaman wanted to repay Elisha, but the prophet refused because he did not want to taint his prophetic authority with accusations of greed. But Gehazi, Elisha's servant, coveted the money and tried to steal it, which resulted in his being cursed with Naaman's leprosy. This time in the South was "as serious as those which pressed upon Elisha," according to Minnegrode. "We are standing before God, our Heavenly Master, as Gehazi stood before Elisha, his earthly master."[57]

Gehazi's greed also resonated with many in the North. Famous preacher Phillips Brooks used Gehazi to ridicule stingy northerners. In contrast with southern poverty, the North thrived economically in 1863. "The war is almost three years old," Brooks said, "and industry was never richer, homes were never happier, trade never paid so well, harvests never crowded the bursting barns more fully than in the abundant prosperity of this battle-autumn."[58]

But should not prosperity motivate generosity? "It seems to me every dollar made in these wartimes ought to be sacred," Brooks wrote. Any man who stayed home from the war and prospered financially should take care of poor men who suffered war injuries. Brooks condemned any who made a profit through the war and kept it to themselves. These greedy northerners "must feel so like a very Gehazi."[59]

The story of Gehazi and other scriptures thus helped Americans to examine their patriotism in 1863. The accumulating battles and body count incentivized both northerners and southerners to reassess their commitment to the war and to the legacy of the lives lost—two agendas that Lincoln would address so eloquently at Gettysburg.

"A New Birth of Freedom"

As famous as the Gettysburg Address is, few Americans realize the Bible's influence on it, mainly because people today do not have the Bible so committed to memory as many Americans did in Lincoln's time. Lincoln knew the Bible—the address makes that clear—and most of those who heard and read the address would have recognized its biblical tone.

Lincoln delivered the Gettysburg Address at the dedication of the Soldier's National Cemetery, a new burial ground for those killed on that battlefield. The main speaker at the dedication was not Lincoln but Edward Everett, Unitarian minister and president of Harvard University fifteen years earlier. Lincoln knew Everett well. In 1860, Everett was the vice presidential candidate for the Constitutional Union Party, running with John Bell of Tennessee. Americans also knew Everett as one of the nation's best speakers. They expected a long speech from him and he delivered—literally. Everett spoke for over two hours; Lincoln spoke for less than five minutes.[60]

Reflective of his Harvard pedigree, Everett presented a well-researched history of the battle and its historic significance. He quoted Latin texts, and comparisons to the classical world weighed more heavily than scripture in Everett's speech, one of the ways it differed from Lincoln's address. But Everett did cite scripture sporadically, and he mentioned providence, referring to "the providential inaction of the rebel army" at one point, which proved fortuitous for the Union. And for the victory, he gave credit to providence and the Army of the Potomac's "spirit of exalted patriotism that animated them, and a consciousness that they were fighting in a righteous cause."[61]

Unlike Lincoln, Everett blamed the Confederacy for the war and all its suffering. Not only was the rebellion treasonous, it also was a crime against Christendom—an injustice, "an imitation on earth of that first foul revolt of 'the infernal serpent,' which emptied Heaven of one-third part of its sons." This was Everett's reference to Revelation 12, suggesting that the southern rebellion against the United States paralleled Satan's rebellion against heaven.[62]

Even with all the animosity and even hatred on both sides, Everett believed a reunited nation was possible because of the blood shed at Gettysburg and other battlefields. These men lay together in death. They rose to battle at the sound of a trumpet from their armies, but they would rise to new life at the sound of the angel's trumpet at the final resurrection, he said. "God bless the Union! It is dearer to us for the blood of those brave men shed in its defense." This is a key point, which Americans would repeat for the remainder of the war—the nation had always been special to God, but it was even more holy because of those who died to defend it in this war. He concluded by bidding "farewell to the dust of these martyr-heroes." Americans would never forget them; in American history, "There will be no brighter page than that which relates THE BATTLES OF GETTYSBURG."[63]

While he spoke, Everett stood in front of Lincoln on the platform, which gave him the uncomfortable choice of turning his back either to the audience or to the president. He adjusted his position as he spoke, alternating between facing Lincoln and the audience. A couple of times Lincoln chimed in to help Everett when he confused Lee and Meade in his speech.[64]

When Lincoln stood up to speak, he donned reading glasses and read his prepared text. He knew the Bible well, and had often used it to cast a sacred aura, but never more effectively than at Gettysburg.[65] Lincoln began with a reference to the Declaration of Independence that sounded like scripture: "Fourscore and seven years ago, our fathers brought forth on this continent a new nation . . ."

This was biblical language; "fourscore and seven years ago" echoed biblical texts such as "threescore years and ten" (Psalms 90:10) and "an hundred and fourscore days" (Esther 1:4). Lincoln didn't have to use biblical language; he could have just said "eighty-seven years." But he wanted to give "the passage of time since the founding of the Republic weight and solemnity." As historian Robert Alter observed, Lincoln wanted to sound "a strong note of biblical authority at the beginning of the Gettysburg Address."[66]

This nation, Lincoln added, was "conceived in Liberty, and dedicated to the proposition that all men are created equal." In this sentence, then,

Lincoln cited the Declaration of Independence and alluded to scripture. At the end of the sentence, we see Lincoln's quote from the Declaration—"all men are created equal"—and the beginning of the sentence recalled the book of Revelation, where a woman in heaven "brought forth a man child, who was to rule all nations" (Revelation 12:5). Or perhaps Lincoln had in mind the birth of Christ, when an angel told Mary, "behold, thou shalt conceive in thy womb, and bring forth a son, and shall call his name Jesus" (Luke 1:31). As historian A. E. Elmore said, Lincoln drew a parallel between Christ, the savior of the world, and the United States, "the savior of liberty, equality, and representative government for the entire world."[67]

Americans had never agreed that "all men are created equal," as Lincoln knew. Slavery contradicted the Declaration, from the nation's founding until the Civil War, when many Americans could no longer live with that contradiction. The nation claimed to be a nation of liberty, and that claim was on Lincoln's mind at Gettysburg.[68]

The Civil War was the nation's great trial, "testing whether that nation, or any nation so conceived and so dedicated, can long endure." Could the United States pass the test of time? Many Europeans doubted it, scoffing at the notion of a nation founded on the principle of equality. Would the Civil War prove them right? Not according to Lincoln. The Civil War was proving them wrong, he believed, in a great trial that required great sacrifice, none greater than the sacrifices at Gettysburg.

This was holy ground, but not because Lincoln's address or other speeches made it holy. "We can not dedicate—we can not consecrate—we can not hallow—this ground," Lincoln said, using biblical terms his audience would recognize. But the soldiers who risked their lives on that field had already "consecrated it far above our poor power to add or detract." Lincoln's biblical phrasings and biblical allusions drew attention to their sacrifice—the men who died had offered a sacrifice that was sacred because the nation was sacred.[69]

The dead of Gettysburg issued a command to the living, Lincoln believed. "It is for us, the living . . . to be dedicated here to the unfinished work which they who fought here have thus far so nobly advanced." Further, "We here highly resolve that these dead shall not have died in vain; that this nation, under God, shall have a new birth of freedom; and that government of the people, by the people, for the people, shall not perish from the earth." Again Lincoln was using religious ideas. Anyone at the time would know that "new birth" often referred to conversion in evangelical churches, as when a sinner received the "new birth" of life with Christ.[70]

This "new birth of freedom" was not yet complete; it would demand additional sacrifices like those commemorated at Gettysburg. And although Lincoln did not mention slavery, his audience did not miss that his "new birth of freedom" related to his Emancipation Proclamation. A nation reborn in its commitment to freedom had no place for slavery. Above all, God was watching. As Lincoln made clear, "this nation" was "under God," and events would occur as God's will dictated.[71]

Lincoln's address began with a phrase that *sounded* biblical—"four score and seven years ago"—and it ended with an almost exact *quotation* from the Bible—"shall not perish from the earth." We find this phrase in three places in the King James Bible, except the "not" is missing, as in Job 18:17: "His remembrance shall perish from the earth." Here again Lincoln sought to give his speech a biblical aura, a sacred tone.[72]

In the Gettysburg Address, therefore, Lincoln referred to the nation's founding—specifically the Declaration of Independence—and he did so with biblical language. If someone asked many Americans of the day what was most sacred to them, the Bible and the nation's founding would probably make the short list, and Lincoln knew it. Perhaps that is why, as one historian said, the Gettysburg Address "weaved together the biblical story and the American story."[73] Of course he did, because, as Lincoln saw it, both the nation's revolutionary legacy and the Bible supported liberty for all. In this address, Lincoln reflected on American history and scripture as he looked back on a year of the Emancipation Proclamation, hard-fought victories on bloody fields, and courageous African American soldiers.[74]

14

"Cursed Be He That Keepeth Back His Sword from Blood"

"It is cowardly to shuffle our responsibilities upon the shoulders of Providence," Frederick Douglass said in January 1864. "Our destiny is not to be taken out of our own hands." He was speaking in New York City, and the title of his address was "The Mission of the War"—apt because the war's purpose, its "mission," was unclear to many Americans. Debates abounded about the war's meaning and necessity. "We are now wading deep into the third year of conflict with a fierce and sanguinary rebellion," a war that many thought would be over "in less than ninety days." Hardly. In its "destruction of human life and property" this war "rivalled the earthquake" and the "whirlwind," Douglass said—a war that "filled our land with mere stumps of men, ridged our soil with 200,000 rudely-formed graves, and mantled it all over with the shadow of death." All this death had ignited a crisis for many Americans, Douglass knew. "I know that many are appalled and disappointed by the apparently interminable character of this war."[1]

He was right. Americans were bewildered by the war. In what direction was it heading? Although Americans typically believed in providence, convinced that God had a plan, they grasped for clues to discover what it was. As renowned southern minister Benjamin Morgan Palmer wrote in 1864, "Providence is always hard to be interpreted, when we are in the very current of events, drifting and whirling us along too rapidly for the comparison and thought which are necessary to scan the mysterious cypher in which God writes his will upon the page of human history."[2] Americans related to this statement in 1864—they felt like they were "drifting and whirling" much "too rapidly" to understand what God was doing in this war.

Americans turned to scripture to address various wartime needs in 1864. In the South, Confederates executed deserters while reminding soldiers that the Jesus story was in part an execution story marked by betrayal. The biblical theme of betrayal also came into play in the South as Lincoln tried to entice southerners into signing a loyalty oath in exchange for pardon. Loyalty and morale were not just southern problems, however. 1864 was the year Grant and Lee faced off in some of the war's fiercest combat. Americans had seen Shiloh, Antietam, and Gettysburg—surely the worst was over, they had thought. Yet the devastation of 1864 surprised them again with expanding lists of casualties that seemed only to get longer. Americans grew more war weary than ever, which prompted Frederick Douglass and others to call on the Bible to remind Americans of the war's sacred meaning.

"The Unholy and Hellish Work"

By the beginning of 1864, the war had drained the southern economy and workforce, and southerners faced catastrophic inflation. A southerner in Richmond listed the skyrocketing prices: potatoes were going for $25 per bushel and bacon was $9 per pound. Before the war, a typical family spent less than $7 per week on food. By 1864, the same foods cost $68.25.[3]

Much of the blame fell on Jefferson Davis. The *Southern Literary Messenger* criticized him as "cold, haughty, peevish, narrow-minded, pigheaded, *ma-lignant*."[4] "The tide is against us, everything is against us," wrote a North Carolina resident to Governor Zebulon Vance in January. "I fear the God who rules the destinies of nations is against us." This North Carolinian expressed a common view among poor whites. "We want this war stopped; we will take peace on *any terms* that are *honorable*."[5]

Attacks on the war were especially strong in North Carolina, where many citizens wanted the state to begin its own negotiations for peace with the Union.[6] By 1864, western North Carolina was one of the most pro-Union areas of the South, and a clandestine, yet popular peace organization developed in the area, calling itself the Order of the Heroes of America.[7] The war's most influential critic in the state was William V. Holden, editor of the *North Carolina Standard* newspaper, which Holden used to criticize Davis and the war. Holden, like many others, believed rich men started the war and benefited from it, while poor people did the fighting, and the dying. He met with citizens who favored peace negotiations, even though many accused him of treason. In September 1863, a Confederate brigade ransacked the office of the *North Carolina Standard*.[8]

Morale was low among Confederate troops, but the Confederacy was desperate for more men. In February 1864, the Confederacy approved an updated Conscription Act, drafting men between the ages of seventeen and fifty.[9] Throughout the South, numerous soldiers avoided combat when they could, and some—perhaps as many as 10 percent of Confederates—deserted.[10] Such widespread losses in an already depleted Confederate army created a crisis that officers dealt with harshly. Chaplains in the field and ministers at home employed the Bible to counteract the epidemic of desertions.[11]

The punishment for desertion was execution, at least in many cases. In an age concerned with dying a good death, executions were horrible, one of the worst ways to die, and yet Drew Gilpin Faust noted that executions "were more frequent in the Civil War than in any American conflict before or since." Executions were not just punishments for crime, Faust observed. Instead, executions "were rituals customarily staged before assemblies of troops and were designed to make a powerful impression and serve a distinct disciplinary purpose."[12]

Consider a case in North Carolina in which Confederates executed twenty-two deserters by hanging in February 1864. Methodist minister John Paris, chaplain of the Fifty-Fourth Regiment of North Carolina Troops, counseled the deserters before their execution and preached a sermon to the soldiers of General Robert Hoke's brigade, who witnessed the executions.[13]

It all began on February 1, when Hoke's brigade pursued federal troops near Newbern and captured dozens of prisoners, only to discover among them "fifty native North Carolinians, dressed out in Yankee uniform, with muskets upon their shoulders." Of these men, Hoke's men recognized twenty-two soldiers "who had deserted from our ranks, and gone over to the enemy." Speedy courts-martial ensued, convicting the men and sentencing them to death.[14]

After the hangings, which occurred in front of Hoke's men, Paris preached his sermon—more a warning for the living soldiers than a eulogy for the deserters. He preached so "that the eyes of the living might be opened, to view the horrid and ruinous crime and sin of desertion, which had become so prevalent."[15]

Reverend Paris reminded these soldiers that loyalty and betrayal—crucial military concerns—were central to the New Testament. Although Jesus preached a spiritual gospel, he lived a harsh, political reality, and he died by execution at the hands of the state. Jesus expected loyalty from his closest friends, his disciples, who were closer to him than brothers, but they repaid him with disloyalty and betrayal. Paris read to the soldiers from Matthew 27:3–5, which described the fate of Judas Iscariot, who betrayed Jesus to the authorities. Stricken with remorse, Judas tried to return his bounty—"thirty pieces of silver"—to the elders and chief priests, confessing "I have sinned in that I have betrayed the innocent blood." The chief priests and elders had no concern with this—"What is that to us?" they said. Distraught, Judas threw the silver on the temple floor, then ran out and hanged himself, which must have resonated with these soldiers who had just witnessed the hanging of the deserters.

Judas was a fascinating study, Paris said. He was among the worst criminals in world history and yet, as a disciple of Jesus, he had occupied one of the most sacred positions in history. Paris compared Judas with Benedict Arnold, traitor in the American Revolution. Like Judas, Arnold at one time moved in elite circles—he held the confidence of George Washington. These two traitors were "grand prototypes of desertion, whose names tower high over all on the scroll of infamy."[16]

The traitorous spirit of Judas and Arnold haunted the Confederacy. "Every man who has taken up arms in defense of his country, and basely deserts or abandons that service, belongs in principle and practice to the family of Judas and Arnold." Did that include "those twenty-two deserters whose sad end and just fate you witnessed across the river in the old field?" Paris wanted these men to feel the betrayal. These twenty-two traitors betrayed their brothers-in-arms. These men "went boldly, Judas and Arnold-like," to "assist in the unholy and hellish work of the subjugation of the country which was their own, their native land!" "They were citizens of our own Carolina." Yet they abandoned "every principle of patriotism, and sacrifice every impulse of honor."[17]

Why betray the Confederacy? Paris probed for the answer in his conversations with these deserters shortly before the hangings. Surely, they would be honest, he thought. They had "death staring them in the face, and only a few short hours between them and the bar of God." But the men were not as forthcoming as he had hoped. If it had only been these twenty-two men, the problem would not have been so severe. But since the Confederacy was dealing with an epidemic of desertions, it was imperative for Paris to find out what the motivations were.[18]

"From all that I have learned in the prison, in the guard house, in the camp, and in the country," Paris blamed the desertions on a "disloyal influence that is at work in the country at home." If the Confederacy were to lose the war, this influence would be the main reason, he said. Everyone had seen citizens of North Carolina gather in meetings, supposedly to rally for peace, but really to weaken the Confederacy. These "malcontents" could have met to support the war, to encourage the population to remain steadfast, but instead they damaged the war effort. Citizens could identify these troublemakers by the terminology they used, as they constantly said, "This is the rich man's war and the poor man's fight," or "We are whipt!" and "We might as well give up!" Even the press and the pulpits have gotten into the act, Paris said, trying to end the war and take down the Confederacy.[19]

Lest they forget, desertion was not only a crime against the nation; it was a sin against God. "There are few crimes in the sight of either God or man, that are more wicked and detestable than desertion." When God handed down the Ten Commandments, God told the people he was "a jealous God, visiting the iniquities of the fathers upon the children unto the third and fourth generations of them that hate me" (cf. Exodus 20:5). Not only did these men shame themselves, they also shamed their families, who would carry the stigma with them forever. "Disloyalty is a crime that mankind never forget and but seldom forgive; the grave cannot cover it."[20]

Everyone wanted peace, but at what price? As Paris saw it, there were only two ways to peace—either give up the fight and surrender to Lincoln, "the tyrant at Washington," or "fight it out to the bitter end, as our forefathers did in the revolution of 1776." The latter choice was the only honorable one.[21]

Paris played on racist fears to generate support for the war. If Lincoln's Union armies won the war, blacks would "be declared free, and placed upon a state of equality with the whites." Meanwhile, southern whites would become the enslaved people of the North, with "bands of negro soldiers stationed in almost every neighborhood, to enforce" northern tyranny. "Tell me to-day, sons of Carolina, would not such a peace bring ten-fold more horrors and distress to our country than this war has yet produced?" This would not do for a true patriot, Paris said. Confederates could not have "peace without independence."[22]

But not all men in the Confederate armies were true patriots, Paris knew. He claimed to know more about cowards—"skulkers"—than most people. He had studied them to learn what made them cowards, concluding that the main flaw that infected their characters was a lack of religious faith. He had known many deserters, but only three of them were Christians. His conclusion? "The true Christian is always a true patriot. Patriotism and Christianity walk hand in hand." Christians knew the Bible, which told them there was no neutrality in life or war. One was either on the side of God or Satan. A Christian knew that "*if a man is not for his country, he is against it.*" Referring back to Revolutionary times, he said, "There is no toryism in a Christian's heart. The two principles cannot dwell together."[23]

In closing, Paris told his men that there was no higher calling that to serve the Confederacy on the battlefield. He was a chaplain—ordained of God, which was a high calling indeed. But it was an even higher calling because he served in battle for the Confederacy. Paris expressed pride in his courage under fire. "At Fredericksburg, Williamsport, Mine Run, and Batchelor's Creek, I was under the fire of both artillery and musketry, and I will here add that if ever my country calls upon me to fall into ranks in her defense with a musket on my shoulder, my answer shall be, 'Here am I.' " Times were tough, he admitted, and the Confederacy was in peril. "But are we not men? Have we not buckled on the armor, putting our trust in the Lord of hosts, as the arbiter of our destiny as a nation?" They could not surrender before the fight was done. "Sons of Carolina, let your battle-cry be, Onward! Onward!"[24]

"Rather the Spirit of Moloch than of Jesus"

This issue of Confederate loyalty had come to a head, not only because of dire conditions in the South, but because Lincoln had extended an olive branch to war-weary southerners in his Proclamation of Amnesty and Reconstruction, dated December 8, 1863. Lincoln offered to pardon southerners and to restore their property—except enslaved people, of course.[25]

In order to qualify, southerners had to swear—"in presence of Almighty God"—an oath of loyalty to the United States.[26] If 10 percent of voting citizens of a southern state took this oath, Lincoln would recognize these loyal citizens as leaders of that state, allowing them to reconstruct the state government. This offer of pardon, Lincoln hoped, would motivate southerners to defect, thereby further weakening the Confederate war effort.[27]

Understandably, Lincoln's "10 percent plan" caused a stir in the South, especially during this time when the Confederacy was already weakened. Outraged responses came from some clergy, including William Henry Ruffner of Virginia, who cited scripture to convince Virginians to throw Lincoln's plan back in his face. Ruffner, a Presbyterian minister and future first superintendent of public schools in Virginia, led with one of the Ten Commandments: "Thou shalt not take the name of the Lord thy God in vain; for the Lord will not hold him guiltless, that taketh his name in vain" (Exodus 20:7). People had forgotten the true biblical meaning of an oath, he said, commonly using this verse to forbid cursing, and otherwise expressing "ignorance and bewilderment" about what oaths implied.[28]

Before southerners rushed off to sign Lincoln's oath, they needed to know that an oath did not just involve Lincoln and Congress; an oath involved God—it made God "not only a witness, but a party." An oath "is a religious transaction," really "an act of worship." To make an oath is to "covenant *with* God, rather than with man, and lay our souls under the tremendous sanctions of eternity!" An oath is "a sacrament." If southerners swore Lincoln's oath, they would be signing a covenant with God, binding themselves to Lincoln and his government.[29]

In swearing loyalty to Lincoln, southerners would be devoting themselves to a nation that had pursued a barbaric "mode of warfare worthy only of the dark ages." Even more dire, the North had corrupted the church as well as the state—northern Christianity, in supporting the aggressive war, had been "perverted into a religion breathing rather the spirit of Moloch than of Jesus," he said.[30]

Even if southerners agreed with Ruffner in principle, principle was not at issue here—survival was. Although most southern whites despised Lincoln, his offer tempted them. These were desperate times. Could southerners forgive their neighbors for swearing Lincoln's oath under duress? No, said Ruffner, for this oath was not a valid escape from suffering. Persecution and martyrdom were central to scripture and the Christian life. Christ himself "was made perfect through suffering," as were Daniel and countless others who "have been tempted to abandon their principles by means of persecution."[31]

What about those who swore the oath to escape suffering and planned to recant it later? Even they violated the third commandment by taking God's name in vain, and they were no better than the Apostle Peter when he "saved himself from the perils of threatened duress by profane cursing, and *swearing* that he knew not the man Jesus Christ." When asked to swear this oath, only one option would "keep the soul clear under the burning eye of God and that is to refuse it—yes, *to refuse it*, though a thousand bayonets were pointed at his breast."[32]

"Who Are Worthy to Carry On This War"

Courage ran in short supply in the South. People were hungry, broke, discouraged—and General Ulysses S. Grant loomed with a reputation for fighting and winning. On March 9, Lincoln placed Grant in command of all the Union armies, and Grant relocated to the Army of the Potomac with its 115,000 men, still commanded by General Meade. Grant's forces would now challenge the full force of the Confederate armies.[33]

Jefferson Davis thought the time was right for a day of "Humiliation and Prayer," scheduled for April 8. Davis put the best spin he could on a divided situation: "Our armies have been strengthened; our finances promise rapid progress to a satisfactory condition; and our whole country is animated with a hopeful spirit and a fixed determination to achieve independence."[34]

This was wishful thinking. As Davis boasted of the Confederacy's military strength, he was still fending off critics of his administration, and deserters racked his army. To speak to these dire times, on April 8, Bishop Stephen Elliott of Savannah preached from one of the most inspiring biblical texts on military loyalty, the story of Gideon (Judges 6–8).

We can see why this scripture seemed fit for the times: here was a case in which God defied military logic, preferring a smaller army to a larger one. Gideon was a reluctant hero, called by God to command the Israelites against the Midianites. The problem was that Gideon's army was *too* large. "The people that are with thee are too many for me to give the Midianites into their hands," God told Gideon. Most arresting was the reason God wanted Gideon to reduce his numbers: God did not want Israel to boast that it could win its battles without divine intervention (Judges 7:2). This was a major theme in scripture—and in the Civil War: the people needed to know that only God gave the victory. To trust too much in military might was to risk disaster.

Gideon, then, had the unusual task of sending many of his troops home. He started by asking for volunteers. Any who were afraid of battle should leave. That cost Gideon twenty-two thousand men, leaving him ten thousand to fight. But that was still too many, God said, so he directed Gideon to observe how his men drank water—those who lapped water like a dog would be Gideon's army, while those who "bowed down upon their knees to drink water" could go. That left Gideon with three hundred men, which were more than enough to defeat the Midianites, but only because they had God's help.

Could this Gideon story ease southern anxieties? Elliott was not blind—he knew "the enemy has been steadily gaining upon us, and every year finds him in possession of some new territory which weakens us and gives him confidence of final success." But the past did not determine the future. The Union could not keep up the pace of war, nor could it take on the rising cost of the conflict. Union forces had to take the war to the South, which would be a long and expensive undertaking. Rumors gave Elliott confidence that Lincoln's people were as weary of the war as southerners were; they would not put up with an unending conflict. Many of them yearned for peace.[35]

Maybe the Union army was not as mighty as they thought. Even though African American troops had proven their mettle in battle, many southerners refused to admit it. "No man will quail, I trust, before any number of negroes," Elliott said. Black troops were brought in only "to swell the numbers of our adversary, and to make false impressions abroad, but they can never be depended upon, and like the elephants of the Eastern wars, will be as apt to trample down their friends as their enemies."[36] The South should celebrate the North's enlistment of black troops, Elliott reasoned. Not only were black troops poor warriors, but they misled Union generals into thinking their armies were more powerful than they were. The more Lincoln, Grant, and his officers trusted in their military might, the better for the Confederacy. "One of the great mistakes which our enemies have made," Elliott said, "has been in supposing that mere numbers and material power were to decide this conflict—that right was nothing—that moral power was nothing." They forgot that the South fought for "a mighty principle."[37]

This "mighty principle" was slavery, a holy cause for the South.[38] "When the cause is a holy one such as this," Elliott said, the Lord does what he did with Gideon; he cuts the number of troops, so that they rely on God and not on multitudes of soldiers. Like Gideon, the South needed to be wary of some of its own people, on guard against disloyalty in the ranks: "We must not permit the serpents which are to crush us and our children to creep out of our own altars."[39]

Davis and his generals needed to know who was really with them in the conflict. Since times were hard, "We are now about to learn who are worthy to carry on this war; who are eager and earnest for the work of the Lord; the men who are ready to lap water with their mouths as a dog lappeth; the men who are to be set apart by themselves for battle and for history."[40]

Elliott called down God's curse on any southerner who shirked responsibility in this holy cause. He cited the famous curse from the story of Deborah, the great Judge of Israel:

"Curse ye Meroz, curse ye bitterly the inhabitants thereof, because they came not to the help of the Lord, to the help of the Lord against the mighty" (Judges 5:23).

The people of Meroz were cursed because of their cowardice, and so would those southerners be cursed who did not stand behind Jefferson

Davis, Robert E. Lee, and all of the other brave patriots of the Confederacy. Take courage, Elliott told his people, because the Yankees fought "not only against us, but against God."[41]

"War with Amalek!"

Elliott was correct: they were "about to learn who are worthy to carry on this war." In the spring of 1864, the Confederacy's strength resided in an eastern force—Lee's Army of Northern Virginia—and a western force—Johnston's Army of Tennessee. Grant knew that he needed to coordinate attacks on both armies at once. If not, Confederates would move troops between the two armies where they were needed to keep both armies viable. Grant couldn't allow this. He knew the Confederacy would survive as long as these two armies survived, so he planned "to use the greatest number of troops practicable against the armed force of the enemy, preventing him from using the same force at different" times and places. Additionally, Grant intended "to hammer continuously against the armed force of the enemy and his resources, until by mere attrition" the Confederates' only option would be "submission." This plan pleased Lincoln.[42]

Grant wanted to force the war into a decisive, bloody climax. Worries about the upcoming clash between Grant and Lee drove many soldiers to religion. "With the approach of spring in 1864," McPherson wrote, "men on both sides recognized that the forthcoming military campaigns would be more terrible than anything that had gone before. The most frequent word in soldiers' letters as they anticipated this fighting was 'dread.'" Religious zeal kept many men on the battlefield. "Heightened religiosity helped to prevent the collapse of both armies during the terrible carnage of 1864," McPherson noted, and southern revivals may have "enabled Confederate armies to prolong the war into 1865."

Even in the Union armies, where revivals were rare, soldiers who had never been religious found religion during these punishing months. In May 1864, a corporal from Ohio expressed the first stirrings of religious commitment: "I feal confident that I have found grace in the sight of god why then should we be afraid to die."[43]

The war not only drove soldiers to religion, it also drove many northerners to ensure that the United States was a Christian nation. On December 9, 1863, Secretary of the Treasury Salmon Chase had approved adding the motto "In

God We Trust" to the national currency. As he wrote on November 20, 1861, "No nation can be strong except in the strength of God, or safe except in His defense. The trust of our people in God should be declared on our national coins." This was a motto that the nation needed, many believed, if they were to keep God on their side in the conflict. Congress made it official by passing the Coinage Act of 1864.[44]

But it was not enough to add "In God We Trust" to coins, at least for many Christians. By 1864 a group of ministers—calling themselves the National Reform Association—lobbied Lincoln and Congress for a constitutional amendment that would proclaim the United States a Christian nation. A delegation from the National Reform Association approached Lincoln on February 10 with a formal proposal for the amendment.[45]

This was cause for alarm, said Rabbi David Einhorn, a Bavarian-born leader of Reform Judaism who led Congregation Keneseth Israel in Philadelphia. This would ruin the nation's commitment to civil and religious liberty, Einhorn warned. If the founders could, they would "rise from their graves" and protest this proposal. It would turn the United States into a new Rome and turn the president "into a Pope." The result would not be peace but war, a conflict for supremacy within Christian denominations and between them and other religious groups.

Most importantly, adopting this constitutional amendment would be catastrophic for the war effort. Einhorn shook his head at the suggestion that such an amendment would give the North the edge in its war with the South. Hardly, Einhorn said. Was not the South itself claiming to be a Christian nation as well? Of all wars, this war did not result from a lack "of Christian belief." This amendment would make the nation's military weaker, not stronger, because it would alienate all the courageous patriots from other religions who had served so bravely in Lincoln's armies.[46]

Einhorn implored Christians to respect patriotism outside their churches. Even if faith in God was vital for the nation, faith in Christ was not. Jews were some of the nation's most devout patriots. He called on American Jews to "display, in this hard struggle for our national existence, sentiments of brilliant patriotism."

With northern patriots from various religions pulling together, the North was on God's side in the Civil War, which Einhorn compared to Israel's ancient "war with Amalek." God was a warrior, and he expected his people to be at war continually. As Moses said, "The LORD hath sworn that the LORD will have war with Amalek from generation to generation" (Exodus 17:16).

"Amalek is represented in the Bible as the arch-foe of Israel," and God's people would continue fighting with new "Amalekites" or "Amalek's seed, wherever the evil and wicked rule"—wherever "rude violence with cheaply bought courage makes war upon defenseless innocence." These wars with Amalek continued—the Civil War was just the latest version—and the Confederates were the new Amalekites. This was "a war for the existence of God's people, and hence a war for God Himself." This was "a war against the Enslavement of Race, which has brought the Republic to the verge of destruction, against an Amalek-seed which is turned into a blood-drenched dragon-seed."[47]

As far as the "Christian Amendment" was concerned, Einhorn had little to worry about—Lincoln listened politely but did not support a constitutional amendment to proclaim the United States a Christian nation. Not that Lincoln opposed biblical rhetoric in politics—he quoted scripture as much as most any politician, and he was the president who established a yearly Thanksgiving Day each November. "The general aspect of your movement I cordially approve," Lincoln told these ministers, but then cautioned that "the work of amending the Constitution should not be done hastily." He promised to "carefully examine" the proposal and to "take such action upon it as my responsibility to my Maker and our country demands." Apparently, God led Lincoln to put the document aside.[48]

"Mother Needs Abraham's Faith in Laying Me upon the Altar of God and Her Country"

Grant's assault on Lee began with a battle at the Wilderness, May 5–7, 1864. Grant had the numerical advantage, but the rebels knew the terrain better, which meant a lot in this densely wooded area with heavy underbrush. This was bloody, sometimes chaotic combat with heavy casualties on both sides. Grant lost almost eighteen thousand men, compared with eleven thousand Confederate casualties, with neither side gaining any significant advantage. Grant's aide-de-camp reported that "it seemed as though Christian men had turned to fiends, and hell itself had usurped the place of earth."[49]

Next, Grant moved South and engaged Lee's Army of Northern Virginia in an equally intense battle at Spotsylvania Courthouse, which lasted on and off for more than two weeks. Although Grant still had the advantage in number of troops, Lee helped to negate that by entrenching his men, which made Grant's charges less effective. During one twenty-two-hour period, men lashed out at one another in some of the most vicious hand-to-hand fighting of the war. An observer from Mississippi said, "The field presented one vast Golgotha in immensity of the number of the dead."[50]

Everyone recognized the reference to "Golgotha" as the place of Jesus's crucifixion—a horrific scene of death. For many in the Civil War, battlefields paralleled Golgotha because they also were places of sacrifice. No one believed a soldier's sacrifice in battle equaled Jesus's sacrifice on the cross, but troops were following his example in obeying God's command to die for a sacred cause.

As bloody as the war had been up until 1864, this was violence on yet another level. The massive killing was horrific, especially because it offended Americans' view of a good death, which they had learned from Christian traditions of *ars moriendi*. As Christians had taught for centuries, there was an art to dying, which involved detailed practices and expectations of a good death. Most people wanted to die at the right time, when they were spiritually ready for it, and they much preferred to die surrounded by loved ones at home. As Drew Gilpin Faust observed, "As late as the first decade of the twentieth century, fewer than 15 percent of Americans died away from home." Not in the Civil War, however, when the desire to die at home crashed on the harsh realities of warfare, where loved ones perished on distant battlefields, after which their bodies were shoveled into pits or trenches.[51]

In the chaos of war, Americans improvised. Doctors joined nurses and chaplains to give dying soldiers a good death, even on the battlefield, at least to the extent it was possible. They wrote to the loved ones of dead soldiers, putting their deaths in the best possible light.[52]

Newspapers also consoled those whose loved ones died on the battlefield, sometimes by pointing to biblical figures like Ruth and Samson, who died away from home but did so for a higher cause. It was better, the papers said, to die courageously on a battlefield for a righteous cause than to die at home.[53] This pastoral need was especially important in the South, where a frequently cited text during the war was from the book of Job: "Naked came I out of my mother's womb, and naked shall I return thither: the Lord gave, and the Lord hath taken away; blessed be the name of the Lord" (Job 1:21). This verse appeared often in obituaries to commemorate deaths—many related to the war, some unrelated—and on at least one occasion it was cited, hopefully "not irreverently," to mourn the loss of a ship at sea.[54]

Typical was a newspaper article from Staunton, Virginia, paying tribute to "brother Elliott," a soldier slain in July 1863, who was "a noble and brave defender of" the Confederacy's "rights and liberties." Yet "the Providence of God . . . doeth all things right," and "The Lord gave and the Lord hath taken away, blessed be the name of the Lord."[55]

Another moving example appeared in a newspaper report from a North Carolina soldier the previous month—an article that some credit with giving North Carolinians the nickname "Tar Heels." According to Sergeant G. W. Timberlake, North Carolina troops had recently faced "terrific fire of grape and canister" and yet held firm in battle while solders from other states retreated. Afterward, "Troops from other States call[ed] us 'Tar Heels,'" and "I am proud of the name, as tar is a sticky substance, and the 'Tar Heels' stuck" tight in battle. He hoped it would console "bereft mothers, fathers, wives, sisters" to know that their men "fell upon the field of battle in a just cause," and "Their names will ever live with those who saw them gallantly fall on the field of battle." This soldier wrote to the families, "[God] bless you, and enable you to say as Job did, 'The Lord gave and the Lord hath taken away; blessed be the name of the Lord."[56]

As casualties mounted in 1864, thousands more parents coped with the loss of their sons in battle. Funeral sermons filled churches and newspapers, putting pressure on ministers to reassure mothers and fathers that their children had not died in vain. In this crisis, ministers, soldiers, and their parents often recalled a major theme from scripture: God often commanded people to sacrifice their children.

In perhaps the most famous example, God called Abraham to sacrifice his son, Isaac. This command devastated Abraham, but he obeyed, bound Isaac to the altar, and prepared to slay him until God stopped Abraham's knife at the last moment (Genesis 22). Although God rescued Isaac, the point was that God called Abraham to sacrifice his son and Abraham obeyed. The "Binding of Isaac" made an impression in the Civil War. At the end of 1863, Sergeant Edward Amos Adams of the Fifty-Ninth Massachusetts wrote in his journal, "Mother needs Abraham's faith in laying me upon the altar of God and her country. May Heaven bless her in making this great sacrifice and preserve me." God preserved Isaac, but he did not preserve this soldier; he died in the battle of Petersburg.[57]

In the funeral for a soldier killed at Spotsylvania, the Reverend Perkins K. Clark of Deerfield, Massachusetts spoke of the sacrifice of Isaac and other instances in which God called parents to sacrifice their children, ending with the ultimate sacrifice, when God gave Jesus to be executed for the world's sins.[58] Parents were devastated by watching their children slaughtered for a war that seemed to have no end in 1864. As the mortality rate increased with Grant's pursuit of Lee, northerners needed to be reminded of the stakes. In this sermon, Clark served up both rewards and punishments. First the reward: God blessed the deaths of martyrs. In the battle at Spotsylvania Court House, when a bullet summoned this soldier "to 'that better land,' " it was "a glorious transition!" He joined "with the multitude of Christian heroes that have gone up from battle-fields to glory." But heaven was not the only reward; heroes were remembered on earth as well. "It is through suffering that noble characters are formed and national greatness attained," Clark said.[59]

Then there was the threat of retribution: God punished cowards who refused to fight in God's wars. As we have seen, Bishop Stephen Elliott asserted this warning earlier in the year to his Savannah congregation. Like Elliott, this northern preacher cited one of the most popular scriptures in colonial American wars: "Curse ye Meroz, saith the angel of the Lord; curse ye bitterly the inhabitants thereof, because they came not to the help of the Lord . . . against the mighty!" (Judges 5:23). Here the people of Meroz "did not respond to the call made upon them for troops for the war!" They refused to "send their young men! And that refusal was followed by one of the most awful curses on record."

When Lincoln called parents to send their sons to war, they should remember God's willingness to sacrifice Jesus. "Did not God give up His Son to suffering and death for us? and shall we withhold ours when He calls us to give them up for our country and suffering humanity? No! No!" Clark and other preachers of funeral sermons were not alone in making such statements. Some soldiers did link their deaths in battle with Christ's. Shortly before his death, Edward Amos Adams wrote, "As the Saviour's blood was shed to save sinners, so may mine in part for my country."[60]

"The World Has Not Seen a Nobler and Grander War"

The intense fighting continued on June 3 at Cold Harbor, about eight miles from Richmond. Grant's and Lee's men clashed head-on. Some of the men on the Union side remembered the violence at Spotsylvania and attached name tags to their clothing in hopes that survivors could identify their bodies after the battle. A wise move, as it turned out. An astounding seven thousand men fell dead or wounded in less than an hour of intense fighting. If ever it was true that battles stimulated religious devotion, it was true at Cold Harbor. "In that dreadful place," a Delaware soldier wrote, "I resolved to forsake my evil ways and to serve god."[61]

The level of violence at this point of the war was unprecedented and would have been unimaginable at the beginning of the conflict. Before the first Bull Run, General Winfield Scott said "no Christian nation" could rightly fight a "war in such a way as shall destroy five hundred and one lives, when the object of the war can be attained at a cost of five hundred. Every man killed beyond the number absolutely required is murdered." Lives seemed not so valuable in 1864, when so many thousands of lives seemed expendable.[62]

The increasing intensity of the war brought an increased justification of violence. Earlier in the war, most Americans insisted that vengeance was not an acceptable motivation in war. That changed as the war raged on into 1864. "Vengeance came to play an ever more important role," said Drew Gilpin Faust, "joining principles of duty and self-defense in legitimating violence." Faust quoted South Carolinian Hugh McLees, who fought to control his desire to seek vengeance on Union prisoners of war in Atlanta. "As I looked at our poor Boys there with their grisly wounds and some of them cold in death," he said, "I could much more easily have taken a dagger" and murdered the Yankee prisoners. Yet, he prayed, "May God give me grace to live a Christian."[63]

Grant's campaign in 1864 reminded some Americans of this violent verse from Jeremiah: "Cursed be he that keepeth back his sword from blood" (Jeremiah 48:10). This threat was the main text in a funeral sermon for two Vermont soldiers, one killed at the Wilderness and the other at Cold Harbor. These men were safe from that threat, of course—they had done their duty. Others, however, ran away from battle and avoided the military altogether in these violent days. They needed to heed Jeremiah's command, said Reverend A. W. Wild of Greensboro, Vermont. "Cursed be he that keepeth back his sword from blood"—cursed be any northerner who failed in God's "solemn personal charge in the fulfillment of divine vengeance. It was the Lord's work."[64]

These were hard words, even in these dire days in the North. This preacher knew that this was "the sterner side of the Old Testament," but the nation needed that sterner side. These warnings, though vicious and seemingly out of synch with the times, "have not even now lost their power." In fact, "The martial scenes of the present day"—scenes like those at the Wilderness and Cold Harbor—"bring out and enforce the spirit of these old prophetic words, and intensify their meaning," despite those who scoff at them and call them "unchristian."[65]

Grant realized he could not conquer Richmond, at least not yet, so he moved on Petersburg, hoping to sever an important rail line for the Confederacy, but again he failed to take the city. He then prepared for a siege that would last nine months.[66] Serving as a chaplain, Henry McNeal Turner wrote on July 9, 1864, about the attack on Petersburg: "A man thinks very little about the niceties of literature when bombs and balls are flying around his head." As he said, "Nothing less than the pen of horror could begin to describe the terrific roar and dying yells of that awful yet masterly charge and daring feat."[67]

Although Lee had stymied Grant with his defensive fighting within entrenchments, some northern newspapers reported that Grant was winning easily, and they celebrated victories. "Lee's Army as an effective force has practically ceased to exist," wrote the *New York Tribune*. When northerners saw the long lists of casualties, however, they changed their perspective. Suddenly Grant went from hero to "the fumbling butcher" in the minds of many, especially Democrats. Although many northerners may not have noticed it, Grant had won a major victory by keeping Lee busy, making it difficult for him to send troops to assist General Johnston in Georgia.[68]

As the nation commemorated Independence Day on July 4, celebrations were few as Americans wondered if the cause was worth the bloodshed. In a discourse commemorating the nation's independence, well-known Unitarian and founder of the Transcendentalist movement Frederick Henry Hedge tried to turn the North's attention to Exodus 20:5: "I the Lord thy God am a Jealous God, visiting the iniquities of the fathers upon the children." This was the same divine threat that Confederate chaplain John Paris used to warn his North Carolina troops against desertion. This threat served just as well when directed to Union troops. As Hedge said, "The consequences of our actions extend to our posterity; what is sown by one generation is reaped by another," and this was no more true than in war. Just as many northerners were ready to give up the fight, and they must remember that this battle was not only for them and their time. If this war were only fought for "ourselves and our own time," Hedge said, "I would say, let treason do its worst; let the schism spread; let the Union slide; let the flag of our pride be trampled in the dust!" The bloodshed was not worth it. But the war was not only for their time; it was for the future—for their children. For their sake, he said, we must "strike the blow which shall either kill the serpent Secession, or disfang and disable it for future harms."[69] For all its suffering and despair, therefore, the war had purpose—this was a war for the future.

This chapter opened with Frederick Douglass, who said "many are appalled and disappointed by the apparently interminable character of this war." But Douglass quickly followed, "I am neither appalled nor disappointed." This was a war between "Slavery and Freedom," and it would "be fierce, long and sanguinary." The war *was* long, but "I say the longer the better if it must be so—in order to put an end to the hell black cause out of which the Rebellion has risen."[70]

Not that Douglass was "indifferent to the horrors and hardships of the war. I am not indifferent." But this was a war above all wars. This was a war to free "the whole world from Slavery—for when Slavery falls here—it will fall everywhere." The temptation was to end the war prematurely, to seek a copperhead peace that kept slavery alive. But the North should push on and "offer no peace, accept no peace, consent to no peace, which shall not be . . . an Abolition peace."[71]

That was Douglass's fear, a peace without emancipation, and he feared a president who might even support it. Douglass loved the Emancipation Proclamation, but "It settles nothing," and he detested "the motive and principle upon which it is based," which allowed those loyal to the Union to keep people enslaved. More seriously, Lincoln had said several times that "the abolition or non-abolition of Slavery was a matter of indifference to him," said Douglass, because Lincoln's goal was to "save the Union with Slavery or without Slavery." Even after all the bloodshed, Lincoln was "uttering substantially the same heartless sentiments" as before the war—that the Union mattered, not emancipation. Even he had not understood the war's "true mission"—abolition.[72]

This reminded Douglass of Jesus's warning against putting new wine into old bottles (Matthew 9:17). The nation was trying "to impose old and worn-out conditions upon new relations." The old Union, complicit in slavery, was over, never to return. To restore the old Union would blaspheme the blood spilled in the war. This was a war for a new Union, "a free country," one that "shall not brand the Declaration of Independence as a lie." This country, this war, had a "manifest destiny," which was "to unify and reorganize the institutions of this country," and that was "the sacred significance of this war." Without that sacred mission, this war was no more "than a gigantic enterprise for shedding human blood."[73]

How that mission fared would depend on what happened in November, for it was an election year. Only November would tell, Douglass said, whether the nation would have "a sound Anti-Slavery man as President," or whether the nation would "be in danger of a slaveholding compromise." The nation could only be great if it followed that scriptural truth: "Righteousness alone can permanently exalt a nation," Douglass said, paraphrasing without citing Proverbs 14:34.[74]

The war desperately needed supporters in 1864, as Douglass knew, and he relished that role—proclaiming to the nation that this war did have a mission of ultimate importance. This was a bloody but sacred war, on this point Lincoln and Douglass agreed. This speech, "Mission of the War" was, according to David Blight, Douglass's "radical abolitionist Gettysburg Address, a rhetorical sword into the Confederacy's heart, and a statement of the war's meaning as ancient as the Old Testament." Douglass concluded with an uncited paraphrase of Isaiah 48:18, "Such, fellow-citizens, is my idea of the mission of the war. If accomplished, our glory as a nation will be complete, our peace will flow like a river, and our foundations will be the everlasting rocks." Blight notes that this conclusion "anticipates Martin Luther King, Jr.'s 'I Have a Dream' speech a century later," where King had echoed Amos 5:24, "Let judgment run down as waters, and righteousness as a mighty stream."[75]

This speech was also important because Douglass knew how far morale had dipped in the North. This was bad news for Lincoln—not that the South fared any better. Jefferson Davis saw his nation crumbling, and yet his armies remained in the field, so far unconquered. All indications were that Lincoln's bid for reelection was nearly hopeless. Again, Lincoln looked to success on the battlefield to keep his administration viable.[76]

15

"Woe to That Man by Whom the Offense Cometh"

In the fall of 1864, "Democrats launched the most racist presidential campaign in American history," according to historian David Goldfield. Democrats coined a new term: "miscegenation." They called Republicans the miscegenation party and the Emancipation Proclamation was "the Miscegenation Proclamation." Democratic newspapers defended white supremacy with so-called science. Newspapers reprinted a cartoon, "Miscegenation Ball," which showed whites and blacks dancing in a party for Abraham Lincoln's mission of "Universal Freedom, One Constitution, One Destiny." A vote for Lincoln, these Democrats claimed, was a vote for racial equality, whites losing jobs to blacks, and white women raped by black men.[1]

The problem for Lincoln was that these racist attacks seemed to be working—in part because many whites believed the Bible supported them. Lincoln's opponents attacked him with racist biblical satire, including some of the fiercest rhetoric of the war. This political use of scripture contrasted with Lincoln's own reflections on the Bible, which viewed the war as God's judgment on both North and South for the sin of slavery.

If the war was God's judgment, it was a fierce judgment in 1864, and Americans took stock of the unprecedented death and devastation. As horrific as the battles were, other atrocities also shocked Americans, including the massacre of African American troops who had surrendered at Fort Pillow, Tennessee, and the inhumane conditions at Andersonville Prison in Georgia. Death tolls rose, bringing with them shouts for revenge, but also pleas for Americans to remember that every human life was sacred to God—a biblical idea that may have been the war's most troubling casualty.

The Lincoln Catechism

When Frederick Douglass arrived at the White House, he found a distressed president. It was August 25, 1864, and Lincoln agonized over the war, his bid for re-election, and the future of emancipation. If Union fortunes on the battlefield didn't improve, he was looking at almost certain defeat in November. And if that happened, emancipation was doomed—as was a constitutional amendment to declare slavery illegal. Time was short to free as many people from slavery as possible. Lincoln had hoped that the Emancipation Proclamation would inspire more enslaved people to flee plantations and run for freedom behind the Union lines.

"The slaves are not coming so rapidly and so numerous to us as I had hoped," Lincoln said. Douglass reminded Lincoln that many enslaved people had not heard of the proclamation. In that case, Lincoln said, "I want you to set about devising some means of making them acquainted with it, and for bringing them into our lines." Douglass agreed. He would enlist a team of African Americans who would travel through the South, delivering news of emancipation.[2]

Douglass never had to carry out his mission, but this meeting left a lasting effect on him. Lincoln impressed Douglass with "a deeper moral conviction against slavery than I had ever seen before in anything spoken or written by him." Several times during this meeting, Lincoln's secretary interrupted the conversation, urging the president to wrap it up so the governor of Connecticut could meet with him. "Tell Governor Buckingham to wait," Lincoln responded, "I wish to have a long talk with my friend Douglass." And so they had a long talk, keeping the governor waiting for another hour. "In his company," Douglass later said of Lincoln, "I was never in any way reminded of my humble origin, or of my unpopular color."[3]

Douglass had not always felt that way about Lincoln—far from it. For years he had attacked Lincoln, questioning his commitment to emancipation. But their friendship warmed in the fall of 1864, which was good for Lincoln; he would need all the friends he could get. Months of unprecedented bloodshed provoked cries for peace and against Lincoln, who had a November face-off against George McClellan, the Democratic nominee for president.[4]

A vote for McClellan was a vote to end the war without emancipation, an issue that played well with many whites. McClellan was a dangerous opponent, and Lincoln knew it. His troops had loved him in the war. Would they support him again in the election, especially if he could end their misery?

The idea of peace without emancipation enraged and worried African Americans. In September 1864, Henry McNeal Turner attacked the so-called Chicago platform, which said the only "indispensable condition" for peace was a restored Union. Anything else—including emancipation—was up for negotiation. The men who proposed this platform should "be hung till dead by the neck, or shot till riddled like Napoleon's lion," said Turner.[5]

On this point, Lincoln had held firm—there would be no peace without emancipation—but he faced opposition, not only from Democrats, but from some within his own party as well.[6] Lincoln's enemies attacked him with the Bible, as in the satirical *Lincoln Catechism*, claiming to be "A Guide to the Presidential Election of 1864." Featuring a picture of a black Lincoln on the cover, the *Catechism* called him "Abraham Africanus the First" and listed Lincoln's "Ten Commandments":

> Thou shalt have no other God but the Negro. Thou shalt make an image of a negro, and place it on the Capitol as the type of the new American man. Thou shalt swear that the negro shall be the equal of the white man. . . . Thou shalt not honor nor obey thy father nor thy mother if they are Copperheads; but thou shalt serve, honor and obey Abraham Lincoln. Thou shalt commit murder—of slaveholders. Thou mayest commit adultery—with the contrabands. Thou shalt steal—everything that belongeth to a slaveholder.[7]

Also in the *Lincoln Catechism* was Lincoln's "Sermon on the Mount" with satirical "beatitudes":

> Blessed are they that do hunger and thirst after the blood of slaveholders, for they shall be filled. . . . Whosoever does not smite thee on one cheek, smite him on both. And if he turns away from thee, turn and hit him again. . . . Give to a negro that asketh not, but from the poor white man turn thou away. Be ye therefore unkind, spiteful, and revengeful, even as your father the devil is the same. Take heed that ye give alms in public to the negroes, otherwise ye have no reward of your father Abraham, who is in Washington. . . . Do not forgive men their trespasses, for if you do God will not forgive your trespasses. . . . Every man can serve two masters, the devil and the Abolitionists.[8]

The *Catechism* hoped to sting Lincoln by comparing him to Jesus, who said, "Blessed are the peacemakers" and commanded his followers to turn the other cheek. Not Lincoln, he insisted on a bloody war against slavery. The *Catechism* even had a satirical "Lord's Prayer" to Lincoln:

> Father Abram, who art in Washington, of glorious memory—since the date of thy proclamation to free negroes. Thy kingdom come, and overthrow the republic; thy will be done, and the laws perish. Give us this day our daily supply of greenbacks. Forgive us our plunders, but destroy the Copperheads. Lead us into fat pastures; but deliver us from the eye of detectives; and make us the equal of the negro; for such shall be our kingdom, and the glory of thy administration.[9]

"War Is Cruelty, and You Cannot Refine It"

Lincoln's re-election appeared almost hopeless until September 3, when a message arrived from General Sherman to Lincoln: "Atlanta is ours, and fairly won."[10] This was a crushing blow for the Confederacy—Atlanta was a center of industry and transportation that supported the war. But Atlanta did not surrender easily. Sherman's campaign took four months, beginning on May 4, when Sherman marched his 110,000 troops south from Chattanooga. Both Sherman and Johnston did almost as much maneuvering around each other as they did fighting. After a series of skirmishes, Sherman finally backed Johnston into Atlanta in July.[11]

It was a desperate situation, and on July 17, Jefferson Davis replaced Johnston with Texan John Bell Hood, whom Davis hoped would be more aggressive. Davis got the hard-hitting leader he wanted. Hood attacked Sherman's men in a series of battles on July 20–28. The Confederates fought bravely, impressing Union commander Giles Smith, who said the rebels brawled with "splendid abandon, and reckless disregard of danger," rushing into "our line of fire, of iron and cold steel" with a ferocity that had "no parallel during the war." But the attacks backfired. Hood lost twenty thousand troops in about a week, and his men evacuated the city after the final defeat at Jonesboro.[12]

After he took Atlanta, Sherman launched his famous "March to the Sea," beginning in November. It became the war's most famous campaign, devastating and intimidating the South, and earning Sherman's reputation as one of the nation's most famous military leaders—admired in the North and detested in the South. Before he left Atlanta, Sherman destroyed much of the city and forced its citizens out, telling Atlanta's mayor that "war is cruelty, and you cannot refine it: and those who brought war into our country deserve all the curses and maledictions a people can pour out."[13]

Sherman's harsh realism bred religious cynicism. "When preachers clamor," Sherman said, "don't join in, but know that war, like the thunderbolt, follows its own laws, and turns not aside even if the beautiful, the virtuous and charitable stand in its path."[14]

Many northerners welcomed war like a "thunderbolt" on the South, and so they welcomed the news from Atlanta. It was right for Sherman to wreak devastation on the South, some ministers claimed, because this was a fight between good and evil. Not only did several ministers make this point in the summer and fall of 1864, but they did so by citing Paul's famous statement from Acts 17:26, God "hath made of one blood all nations of men."

First, a well-known Presbyterian minister in Pittsburgh, Pennsylvania, reminded his people that this was not just a war against the South; this was a war against Satan. This war was "far above the petty interests of politics and parties. It is a war of principalities and powers, and the rulers of the darkness of this world, and spiritual wickedness in high places, no less than a war of flesh and blood" (cf. Ephesians 6:12). He reasoned, "Where government ordained of God is at stake—where law, fair form of liberty, and liberty, the soul of law, are at stake—where equality and brotherhood in Christ are at stake—where the principle that God hath made of one blood all the nations of the earth is at stake, there Satan is not idle." Paul's statement that God "made of one blood" all nations was a biblical endorsement of human equality. The Confederacy attacked this biblical teaching, posing a satanic threat, and the seriousness of that threat justified "the violence and carnage and cost." In scripture, God warned that victory over Satan would never be easy. Instead, God warned, "Thou shalt break them with a rod of iron; thou shalt dash them in pieces like a potter's vessel" (Psalms 2:9).[15]

Second, if this was a fight between God and Satan, it was also a fight to see if a Christian nation could survive—so preached a Methodist minister in Washington, DC. It was just under two weeks after the fall of Atlanta, and Reverend B. H. Nadal said this was war was "a dire and deadly conflict between Christian and anti-Christian forces, between the representatives of the civilization of the New Testament . . . in the nineteenth century, and the lawlessness of a dark age, supposed to be long since dead." At stake in this war was the nation's Christian character. "The United States," Nadal preached, "is a Christian nation, in such a sense that Christianity is absolutely essential to its identity; the life-blood, the very essence of our civilization is Christianity." Yet the Confederacy challenged this Christian nation at its core. The war "is a stupendous effort to overturn the very foundations of Christian morality, to blot from existence Christ's doctrine of the universal and real brotherhood of men, and to deny and dishonor the declarations of Scripture, that God hath made of one blood . . . all the nations of men that dwell on all the face of the earth."[16]

Third, the title of a sermon from Vermont during these weeks said it all: *Our Country's Mission, or The Present Suffering of the Nation justified by its Future Glory*. The preacher, J. W. Hough, also cited Paul's famous "one blood" statement, and linked it with the nation's founding. "The Declaration of Independence, though penned by the freethinker Jefferson, was really an inspiration of that Gospel, which declares that 'God hath made of one blood all nations of men.' "[17]

These three sermons, all preached after Sherman's defeat of Atlanta, justified the violence by calling on the highest ideals of the nation, and all used Paul's "one blood" statement to make the argument. Many agreed with the statement of a preacher from Massachusetts who said in November 1864: "Republican America was in God's purpose when He 'made of *one blood* all the nations of men.' Ours is the first human government whose organic law enunciates that doctrine."[18]

"Fresh Courage and Additional Madness"

The perspective was radically different in the South. As they faced Sherman's brutal march, citizens of Georgia and South Carolina turned to the Bible to cope, and their interpretations divided. Some held out hope that God would stop Sherman in his tracks. We see this view eleven days after Atlanta fell, from a Baptist minister in Augusta, Georgia, who turned to Jeremiah's image of the potter and the clay (Jeremiah 18). God controlled nations as a potter controlled the clay, shaping them according to his will. "A nation is, to Him, as a ball of plastic clay." Even the mighty Union army, therefore, could be dashed to pieces.[19]

Four days later in Savannah, Episcopalians conceded that Sherman would overtake them—just as Union forces had wreaked havoc in other southern states. The war was "a dispensation of death" with "no results but slaughter and bloodshed," said Episcopal Bishop Stephen Elliott.[20] Had not Louisiana,

Mississippi, Virginia, and Arkansas suffered defeats as well? But these states had recovered, "unconquered," and so would Georgia. "We are only passing through the fiery trial which has tried most of our sister States," said Elliott.[21] Sherman's punishment would make Georgia better, Elliott believed, and he cited the Revolutionary War as evidence. The states that suffered the most in the Revolution earned the most respect for their heroic patriotism. By suffering through Sherman's march, Georgia would add to its patriotic credentials.[22]

Elliott didn't downplay his people's suffering, however. "War and its attendant horrors have come very near our own homes," and these horrors had ushered his congregation into church on this fast day.[23] Desperate times in Georgia called up desperate times in the Old Testament. Elliot turned to the Exodus story, specifically to the Israelites' complaining to Moses near the Red Sea: why did you free us from Egypt? "For it had been better for us to serve the Egyptians, than that we should die in the wilderness?" But no; God told Moses to admonish the Israelites to push on.[24] That was the situation of Georgia. The people needed to stand firm, resolved. We need "to awake and buckle on the armor of heroic citizenship! God works by means; we must not expect in these days, to receive help from Him through miracle."[25]

Forget miracles in Georgia. God would help the Confederates who helped themselves. They must "rally around the Government" and fling "back, into the face of our enemies, his insults and his cruelty." Elliott chose a scripture that made his point: Psalms 60:11–12: "Vain is the help of man. Through God we shall do valiantly; for He it is that shall tread down our enemies." In other words, "This is God's war," and he would end it on his terms.[26]

And God's terms were bloody. "This war, continued now for more than three years with unparalleled bloodshed, is the mode in which God is accomplishing his purposes. Our punishment," Elliott preached, was "a dispensation of death. This war has produced no results but slaughter and bloodshed." Neither side has emerged as the victor; only "death has reigned triumphant."[27]

Victory and defeat in battles had been mirages, fooling either side that they would at last win the war. But that did not happen. "And so will it continue until God's wrath is satisfied, and therefore have I not been disturbed by our recent reverses. They mean blood and death and nothing more."[28] Here Elliott sounded as Lincoln would in the Second Inaugural Address the following year—the war would continue until God's wrath was satisfied, until the nation had suffered enough for its sins. But there the similarities ended.

In Lincoln's view, the national sin was slavery, whereas Elliott contended that the national sin was the North's opposition to slavery.

Both sides suffered, but eventually the North would turn its weapons on itself. Northerners will face their own "dispensation of death." They bragged that the war was not harming them as badly, but "they are only fattening in a large place as a lamb for the slaughter. Their feet shall slide in due time." Here Elliott quoted part of Deuteronomy 32:35, in which God said of his sinful people, "To me belongeth vengeance, and recompence; their foot shall slide in due time: for the day of their calamity is at hand, and the things that shall come upon them make haste."[29]

Over a century earlier, this had been the main verse in Jonathan Edwards's famous sermon, *Sinners in the Hands of an Angry God*. Edwards warned his congregation that God was angry and eager to destroy them for their sins. They were like clueless spiders hanging by a thin web over a raging fire, never knowing how close they were to the flames. If they kept sinning and refused to repent, "Their foot shall slide in due time." Elliott here made a similar point about the Union. Sherman may overrun Georgia, but, mighty as his army was, "Their foot shall slide in due time." God's vengeance would consume them—"in due time."

How much time? Elliott didn't know, but he offered an unexpected interpretation, especially for a southerner—God *wanted* Lincoln to win the election, which was why God allowed Sherman to defeat Atlanta. Although most southerners saw this as terrible news, Elliott said Lincoln's re-election was necessary "for our deliverance; any other result should be disastrous to us. We need his folly and his fanaticism for another term; his mad pursuit of his peculiar ideas. It is he that is ordained to lead his people to destruction." Lincoln's "re-election will give him fresh courage and additional madness." Lincoln's pursuit of "the war with redoubled fury" will be his undoing; it will awaken the sane people of the North to turn against him, and that "conflict" will be their downfall, and "shall deliver us." So "all things are working together for our good [Romans 8:28]. The fall of Atlanta, the victories at Mobile, our reverses of whatever kind, are so many links in the re-election of Lincoln, and therefore, so many links in the chain of our deliverance. Every thing which gives them confidence, is so much in our favor, because it goads them on in their career of madness."[30]

Elliott and other ministers voiced the best possible interpretation of the worst possible defeat. Few ministers were more devoted to the Confederacy than Benjamin Morgan Palmer, but by 1864, even he doubted that the

Confederacy could win. He consoled friends, reminding them that "this poor world is not our final home." In September, he preached in Richmond, breaking the bad news. Mary Chesnut heard the sermon. "It was hard to listen and not give way," she wrote. "Despair was his word—and martyrdom. He offered us nothing more in this world than the martyr's crown."[31]

As if to confirm the South's martyred status, the election in November, which before seemed to be a clear win for McClellan, was not close. Lincoln beat McClellan by over four hundred thousand votes, with a decisive 221–21 electoral advantage.[32]

"Plea for the Sacredness of Human Life"

When Sherman said, "War is cruelty," many agreed—in theory. But events in 1864 pushed the boundaries of cruelty tolerable even in war. One of the men who accounted for the war's cruelty was Confederate cavalry commander Nathan Bedford Forrest, whom Sherman called a "devil" who needed to be "hunted down and killed if it costs 10,000 lives and bankrupts the Federal treasury."[33]

On April 12, Forrest's men captured Fort Pillow, located on the Mississippi River in Tennessee, and then committed one of the most horrific acts of the war by murdering black troops who had surrendered. A few days later, Forrest reportedly said that "the river was dyed with the blood of the slaughtered for two hundred yards." One Confederate soldier who saw what happened said, "Human blood stood about in pools and brains could have been gathered up in any quantity."[34] Similar mass murders of mostly black troops occurred elsewhere, including at Fort Wagner the previous July. Although most Americans didn't know the details of these massacres until later, enough news spread that black soldiers knew military service was riskier for them than for their white comrades. If Confederates captured them, they probably wouldn't be imprisoned; they'd be enslaved or murdered.[35]

As the North reeled with the news from Fort Pillow, Lincoln stood by his vow not to exchange prisoners of war until the Confederacy agreed to exchange black prisoners. From the time that Lincoln began enlisting black troops to fight for the Union, Confederates fumed. There would be no prisoner-of-war exchanges for black soldiers, Jefferson Davis said. When the Confederates captured black soldiers, they were "slaves captured in arms," and Confederates claimed the right to execute them.[36]

Many southerners were as shocked as northerners about such atrocities. Preaching just a few days before the Fort Pillow travesty, Bishop Stephen Elliott said black troops "are to be pitied, not feared." "I trust that whenever mercy can be shown them with justice to ourselves it will be extended to them." African American soldiers weren't to blame; nefarious Union officers fooled them into fighting. These Union officers were "the proper objects of vengeance," said Elliott.[37]

Some Union soldiers took revenge for Fort Pillow. A lieutenant reported the following after a Mississippi conflict: "We did not take many prisoners. The Negroes remembered 'Fort Pillow.'"[38] Some religious leaders spoke out against revenge, however. On June 30, Henry McNeal Turner condemned "the killing of all the rebel prisoners taken by our soldiers. True, the rebels have set the example, particularly in killing the colored soldiers; but it is a cruel one, and two cruel acts never make one humane act." Fighting this way, Turner wrote, was "an outrage upon civilization and nominal Christianity." Confederates expected the Yankees "to carry out a brutal warfare," so Union soldiers should "disappoint our malicious anticipators" by fighting a just war that the world could not condemn.[39]

As Americans processed what happened at Fort Pillow, another harsh reality hit them: news of inhumane conditions at Andersonville Prison in southwest Georgia. Without regular prisoner exchanges, the number of captured troops multiplied, forcing the Confederacy to open the prison camp at Andersonville in February 1864. Originally the camp spanned across sixteen acres, room enough for about ten thousand captives; it had a population of approximately thirty-three thousand by August, which forced an expansion to twenty-six acres. That was not nearly enough room. Even with the expansion, James McPherson estimated that there was only "an average of thirty-four square feet" for each prisoner, compared with "an average of 180 square feet" for each prisoner in the worst Union prison. Even worse, the prison had virtually no shelter. Prisoners were exposed to the elements, and many of them tried to assemble makeshift coverings out of rags and sticks. A stream ran through the prison and since it was the only source of water men used it as a latrine and also drank from it. Disease ran rampant and flies swarmed over the putrid water. At Andersonville, therefore, thousands of men crammed into a prison with almost no shelter, living without clean water and subsisting on paltry rations.[40]

The prisoners at Andersonville were no more than "walking skeletons, covered with filth and vermin," reported an eyewitness. As many as one hundred prisoners per day died in the summer of 1864, McPherson reported, totaling thirteen thousand deaths out of forty-five thousand prisoners—a rate of 29 percent. By comparison, the highest mortality rate of a northern prison camp was 24 percent at Elmira, New York. "The camp at Andersonville," McPherson wrote, "became representative in Northern eyes of Southern barbarity."[41]

At Andersonville, Elmira, and other prisons, men suffered immeasurably, cursed the war, and questioned the God who commanded it. A Confederate prisoner, nearly starving and subsisting on wormy crackers, wrote, "Dam Old Abe and old Jeff Davis," and "dam the day I 'listed."[42] Some prisoners found solace in the scriptures. Paul's words, "I have learned in whatsoever state I am therewith to be content," spoke to three Connecticut soldiers as they looked through the scriptures one June morning. "We all felt it was for us," one soldier said about this verse. Often men clung to the Bible as they died. The last entry on one soldier's diary at Andersonville read, "My bones ached so I could not lay any longer and so got up and am sitting on a log. I have got so weak that I can't get my coat on without help." Even so, he wrote. "A lovely morning. My only trust is in Christ." Four days after writing this he was dead. Some of the soldiers at Andersonville believed God urged them to "prepare for death, bidding us to purify our hearts & Lives & let the Master find us ready & waiting when he calleth for us."[43]

Reports spread through the North and South about the conditions at Andersonville. Kate Cumming stopped by the camp at the height of the misery in 1864. "My heart sank within me at seeing so many human beings crowded so closely together," she wrote. She blamed Abraham Lincoln: "O how I thought of him who is the cause of all this woe on his fellow-countrymen—Abraham Lincoln. What kind of a heart can he have, to leave these poor wretches here? . . . May Heaven help us all! But war is terrible."[44]

Lincoln also felt the wrath of northern citizens for the suffering of their countrymen at Andersonville. "For God's sake, interpose!" begged a representative of several physicians and ministers. "We know you can have them exchanged if you give your attention to it." To neglect to do so would be equivalent to murder, they said. Republicans also advised Lincoln to reconsider his hard stance on prisoner exchanges. They cautioned that northerners would "vote against the President, because they think sympathy with a few negroes" caused Lincoln to leave his citizens suffering in that sweltering prison. But Lincoln refused to betray the black recruits who fought for the nation.[45]

Although the refusal to exchange prisoners led to unimaginable suffering, it also helped the Union cause. The Federals knew that the Confederate armies needed every man available, so every man taken prisoner was one less man on their side of the battle. In contrast, the Federals had more men available, so they could afford to replenish their forces when they lost prisoners of war. "It is hard on our men held in Southern prisons not to exchange them," General Grant said, "but it is humanity to those left in our ranks to fight our battles. We have got to fight until the military power of the South is exhausted, and if we release or exchange prisoners captured it simply becomes a war of extermination."[46]

As horrific as they were, the atrocities at Fort Pillow and Andersonville just reinforced what all Americans knew too well by the end of 1864: if war was "cruelty," then this war was crueler than any they had imagined. Many Americans who lost family members in the war had nothing to bury—their loved ones' remains lay unidentified, often in a mass grave near some battlefield. This was especially traumatic in the nineteenth century, when Christians typically believed in a bodily resurrection and thought it was important to have a proper burial of the beloved's body. Such comfort was impossible for thousands of Americans who lost loved ones whose bodies were never found.[47]

All of this death had cheapened human life, many believed, and they turned to the Bible's teachings on the sacredness of the body and life in this world, not just in the hereafter. This was the point of a sermon titled *A Plea for the Sacredness of Human Life*, preached in January 1865. The preacher, George Bacon of Orange Valley Church in New Jersey, cited Jesus's defense of his ministry to the disciples of John the Baptist. "Go your way," Jesus said, "and tell John what things ye have seen and heard; how that the blind see, the lame walk, the lepers are cleansed, the deaf hear, the dead are raised, to the poor the gospel is preached" (Luke 7:22).[48]

When called on to prove his ministry was authentic, therefore, Jesus did not mention his great spiritual works, including his saving of souls. Instead, Jesus spoke of *bodily* works—his healings of disease, disability, and even raising the dead. Jesus had "tender pity" for people, and "not only for the souls of men, but also for their bodies," Bacon said. Jesus expressed "divine recognition of the value and the sacredness" of human life. Too often, Christians spoke of their faith in spiritual terms, or they spoke of the next life as more important than life in the body. But Jesus cared about the body; so should Christians, because the body was sacred. Christianity never neglected the body to save the soul. Christianity never looked only to the afterlife while disregarding this life. "This life is sacred too; this hour, this moment is of consequence."[49]

The Genesis story made this clear—God made humans in God's image, which meant "our life is a copy of his life," Bacon said (Genesis 1:26–27). Paul also taught the sacredness of human life when he wrote that God would "sanctify you wholly," praying that "your whole spirit and soul and body be preserved blameless" (1 Thessalonians 5:23). Paul also urged Christians to "present your bodies a living sacrifice, holy, acceptable unto God" (Romans 12:1). These verses made clear the biblical view that "the whole man was sacred, for the whole man was Christ's."[50]

Was life sacred in the Civil War? How could it be, with so much death? "It is one of the innumerable evils of war," Bacon said, "that it has a tendency to undermine our sense of this sacredness of human life." When Americans saw thousands of lives slaughtered in a day's battle, they should have cringed in horror at the priceless loss. But the opposite was true—when people saw killing on such a major scale, they thought that life "is a cheap and worthless thing."[51]

Taking of life, therefore must be sacred, or it must not be done. One should draw the sword "only for interests that are more sacred, for truths that are more precious, even than the lives which are laid down for them." In this war, then, Americans should not "prize human life the less, but only that we prize the divine unity of the nation, and the sacredness of the truths and liberties that are given us in trust, the more."[52] The war had to be worth the bloodshed—a sacred cause worthy of the loss of sacred lives. But as the death toll rose to the hundreds of thousands, with many dying senselessly at Andersonville, Fort Pillow, and elsewhere, many Americans questioned whether the nation—and the churches—had moved past the biblical view of life's sacred value.

"Both Read the Same Bible"

In September 1864, a group of African American ministers from Baltimore presented President Lincoln with a Bible, on which they inscribed: "To Abraham Lincoln, President of the United States, the Friend of Universal Freedom."[53] Lincoln responded, "In regard to this Great Book, I have but to say, it is the best gift God has given to man. All the good the Saviour gave to the world was communicated through this book. But for it we could not know right from wrong. All things most desirable for man's welfare, here and hereafter, are to be found portrayed in it."[54]

Lincoln was being polite. The occasion called for him to express appreciation for a meaningful gift. But he was not *only* being polite. He believed what he said. Lincoln wasn't an evangelical; he wasn't even a church member. But he had a "profound understanding of the Bible," as historian Joseph R. Fornieri has shown. The Bible, for Lincoln, had political value and power.[55]

But Lincoln didn't exploit the Bible for political gain, intentionally distorting its message. As we've seen in previous chapters, Lincoln knew his Bible and he pondered its meaning. But he took that pondering to a new level in his Second Inaugural Address on March 4, 1865. This was Lincoln's most insightful assessment of the war's meaning—and the Bible figured prominently in his reflections.

For such a profound speech, the Second Inaugural Address had a less than profound introduction. Before Lincoln stood to speak, the audience suffered through a speech from an intoxicated vice president-elect, Andrew Johnson of Tennessee. Johnson, who apparently had taken whiskey for medicinal purposes to treat typhoid fever, rambled on and made an embarrassing spectacle of himself. Finally, former Vice President Hannibal Hamlin put the audience out of its misery by pulling on Johnson's coat and convincing him to pipe down. Johnson ended by waving a Bible around and, according to reports, "slobbered the Holy Book with a drunken kiss." The intermission gave everyone a chance to recover as they moved outside to the East Portico of the Capitol for Lincoln to take the oath of office. On the way out, Lincoln told the marshal in charge, "Don't let Johnson speak outside."[56]

As the president stepped up to speak, sunlight finally broke through; it had been a rainy week in Washington. The address was brief—703 words—compared with 3,700 words in his First Inaugural Address. There was not as much to say, Lincoln pointed out. Everyone knew how the war was going, and that it had gone well for the Union lately. Since Lincoln had nothing new to report about the war, he turned instead to the more important goal of interpreting the war.[57]

Although Lincoln never made a public profession of faith, he had profound theological insight into the war, and it was on full display in this address. Mark Noll argues that Lincoln's reflection on the war's meaning was more insightful than that of esteemed ministers and theologians of the day. The Second Inaugural Address, in Noll's view, stands as "among the small handful of semisacred texts by which Americans conceive their place in the world."[58]

Lincoln began with a look back over the previous four years, reflecting on his first inaugural, when "all thoughts were anxiously directed to an impending civil war. All dreaded it, all sought to avert it." But all efforts failed. "Both parties deprecated war, but one of them would make war rather than let the nation survive, and the other would accept war rather than let it perish, and the war came."[59]

"The war came," and it was a war over slavery. Enslaved people constituted one-eighth of the nation's population, Lincoln said, and "these slaves constituted a peculiar and powerful interest. All knew that this interest was somehow the cause of the war." There was no doubt in Lincoln's mind that slavery caused the Civil War, and he said everyone knew it. It was a war over the survival of slavery, and the survival of the nation.[60]

This war over slavery also involved a war over the Bible. The holy scripture, trusted by so many Americans, did not speak a definitive word on the war. The irony was tragic—"Both [North and South] read the same Bible and pray to the same God, and each invokes His aid against the other," Lincoln said. The Bible had one meaning in the South and another meaning in the North—it all depended on one's place. The Bible could be shaped to fit any agenda.[61]

Did that mean the Bible had no relevance? Lincoln refused to take such a cynical view, refused to throw up his hands and declare that the Bible was an empty text that has been so misconstrued that no truth remained. Instead of rejecting the scripture, Lincoln used it even more, quoting and alluding to biblical texts throughout his address—so much so Frederick Douglass said the Second Inaugural Address "sounded more like a sermon than a state paper."[62]

"It may seem strange that any men should dare to ask a just God's assistance in wringing their bread from the sweat of other men's faces," Lincoln said, alluding to Genesis. This verse described God's punishment for the first sin in the Garden of Eden. Because Adam sinned, God cursed him with work in the fields: "In the sweat of thy face shalt thou eat bread" (Genesis 3:19). People shall work for their bread, God said, but slavery violated this commandment. Slaveholders wrung "their bread from the sweat of other men's faces." Slavery corrupted labor.[63]

Even though slaveholders did "dare ask a just God" to endorse slavery, Lincoln warned the North: "Let us judge not that we be not judged," quoting

Jesus (Matthew 7:1). There was no place for self-righteousness in this war, no space for one side to judge the other. As Lincoln had said before, slavery was not only the sin of the South; it was the sin of the nation.[64]

Then Lincoln turned to prayer and providence. Throughout the war, Americans prayed, frequently commemorating days of fasting, prayer, and thanksgiving in which both northerners and southerners prayed that God would take their side. Yet "The prayers of both could not be answered. That of neither has been answered fully," Lincoln said.[65]

Many Americans believed that God had a providential plan, and that all events somehow fulfilled God's purposes, even the war. Americans prayed to seek knowledge of God's mysterious plan, and frankly they prayed to influence God, to implore God to guide their armies to victory. The war proved, however, that "the Almighty has His own purposes." No matter how much Americans prayed, God did not obligate himself to answer their prayers— and he refused to cater to either side in the war.[66]

From prayer and providence, the president moved to sin and judgment. Once more Lincoln quoted Jesus: "Woe unto the world because of offenses; for it must needs be that offenses come, but woe to that man by whom the offense cometh" (Matthew 18:7). Here Jesus spoke to his disciples, warning them that sin had a great cost. So, if your feet caused you to sin, you should cut them off, Jesus said. Likewise, with the eye—pluck it out if it causes you to sin. It was better, he said, "to enter into life with one eye, rather than having two eyes to be cast into hell fire." Sin offended God, and it had a great cost. Grace was not cheap.[67]

What if slavery offended God, Lincoln asked, and God punished the nation with this Civil War as God's way to end slavery? As Lincoln put it, "If we shall suppose that American slavery is one of those offenses which, in the providence of God, must needs come, but which, having continued through His appointed time, He now wills to remove, and that He gives to both North and South this terrible war as the woe due to those by whom the offense came, shall we discern therein any departure from those divine attributes which the believers in a living God always ascribe to Him?" Neither northerners nor southerners in 1865 had invented slavery; they were born into it. But that did not excuse either side from the guilt of slavery.[68]

The war was not over. God's punishment continued. Lincoln hoped and prayed, and he implored Americans to do the same—"Fondly do we hope, fervently do we pray, that this mighty scourge of war may speedily pass away." But again, God may not answer these prayers because he may have more punishment in store for the nation. "If God wills that [the war] continue until all the wealth piled by the bondsman's two hundred and fifty years of unrequited toil shall be sunk, and until every drop of blood drawn with the lash shall be paid by another drawn with the sword, as was said three thousand years ago, so still it must be said 'the judgments of the Lord are true and righteous altogether.' "[69]

Here Lincoln paraphrased Psalms 19:9, which said all God's judgments were harsh but righteous. Americans had suffered in this war as they had never suffered before, so if all this suffering was God's judgment, we can see how many Americans may have wanted nothing to do with this God. But Lincoln did not question God; he affirmed that this punishment in blood was what one could expect from the God of scripture in response to so great a sin as slavery.

This view of the Civil War as God's judgment for slavery echoed John Brown's prediction, expressed just before his hanging: "I, John Brown, am now quite *certain* that the crimes of this *guilty land* will never be purged away but with *blood*."[70] As we have seen, Lincoln wanted nothing to do with Brown or his violent attack on slavery. But as he examined the war that Brown virtually predicted, he reached a similar conclusion: this was a judgment of God. Despite his religious skepticism, Lincoln's God was a mysterious God of judgment—righteous judgment, but judgment nonetheless.

Judgment belonged *only* to God, however. Neither North nor South had cause to blame the other, Lincoln said as he looked beyond the war to reconstruction. "With malice toward none, with charity for all, with firmness in the right as God gives us to see the right, let us strive on to finish the work we are in, to bind up the nation's wounds, to care for him who shall have borne the battle and for his widow and his orphan, to do all which may achieve and cherish a just and lasting peace among ourselves and with all nations."

These concluding words cautioned the North against arrogance and especially against seeking vengeance on the South. If the nation were to reunite, it would need to do so in humility and charity, healing "the nation's wounds" by caring for the widows and orphans left behind in the wake of many bloody battles. Lincoln did not quote scripture here, but biblical commands to care for widows and orphans were plentiful (e.g., James 1:27).

As Lincoln finished his speech, applause rose from the solemn crowd, and Salmon Chase administered the oath of office. Before Lincoln stepped down, he kissed the Bible.[71]

Lincoln's providential view of the nation was unusual—and it was different from the view he held earlier in the war. In 1861, Lincoln had a more conventional view of God's plan for the nation. "Intelligence, patriotism, Christianity, and a firm reliance on Him, who has never yet forsaken this favored land, are still competent to adjust, in the best way, all our present difficulty," he said.[72]

Yet, by the following year, Lincoln expressed a different view. After the Second Battle of Bull Run, he wrote, "It is quite possible that God's purpose is something different from the purpose of either party." Lincoln acknowledged that God's providence was mysterious, and that there was no indication that God had selected the United States as God's chosen nation. Because of this view of providence, combined with his doubt about the nation's divine ordination, Mark Noll called the Second Inaugural Address "a theological statement of rare insight." These views set Lincoln apart from most ministers and theologians who endured the Civil War and tried to fathom its meaning. As Noll concluded, "The contrast between the learned religious thinkers and Lincoln in how they interpreted the war poses the great theological puzzle of the Civil War." Lincoln was an unchurched theological amateur, and yet he "propounded a thick, complex view of God's rule over the world and a morally nuanced picture of America's destiny" that stood in stark contrast with most ministers and theologians, who touted a "thin, simple view of God's providence and a morally juvenile view of the nation and its fate."[73]

At the time, Lincoln's address had a mixed reception. In reply to a letter that praised it, Lincoln wrote, "Every one likes a compliment," and thanked the writer while admitting that the address was "not immediately popular." He understood why, explaining that "men are not flattered by being shown that there has been a difference of purpose between the Almighty and them. To deny it, however, in this case, is to deny that there is a God governing the world. It is a truth which I thought needed to be told." God was not completely on either side in this war, contrary to what many of the clergy on both sides had claimed repeatedly. Either God had judged both North and South, or there was no God—not a God that deserved to be worshiped anyway.[74]

Lincoln's views on God's will and the war were complex and unique. Granted, others, including ministers, had questioned whether God was on their side in the war. With texts such as Isaiah 58, preachers questioned national fasts, suspecting that Americans used them to try to manipulate God rather than to repent. Others also expressed horror over war's violence and its bloody price, and wondered if the blood was the point, and that perhaps

God wanted the nation to pay a heavy price because of its sins. Others also wondered at how both sides read the scriptures and called on the same God for deliverance. In almost every case, however, ministers who expressed these views used them as part of the jeremiad—as a way of calling people to account for their sins—but then they ended their sermons with an assuring statement that God really would be on their side if the people repented. Lincoln, it seemed, did not see this happy ending; he remained transfixed by the mystery of God's judgment, and that set him apart from most religious leaders of his time.

16

"Baptized in the Blood of Their President"

When President Lincoln arrived at Ford's Theatre, the play stopped, the audience applauded, and the band played "Hail to the Chief." It was not a surprise appearance—a local newspaper had advertised Lincoln's attendance at the evening performance of *Our American Cousin*.[1] Security for the president was nothing like what Americans expect today. There was no Secret Service securing the area and monitoring the Lincolns' every move. The president, Mary Todd Lincoln, and their guests, Clara Harris and her fiancé, Major Henry Rathbone, entered and climbed the stairs to the president's box, which was to the left of the stage and had been decorated in anticipation of the president's arrival.

Our American Cousin was a comedy, which is why the audience was laughing just before John Wilkes Booth shot the president from behind. At first, the audience was confused. Some assumed that the gunshot was a sound effect in the performance. But then they saw a man jump from the president's box to the stage. He landed awkwardly. Observers said he had caught his boot spur in the swag that decorated the president's box. Some remarked later the irony that a US flag had injured the assassin—"the outraged flag of our country" seized the assassin "by the spur and causing him to fall crippled on the stage," as one newspaper account read.[2] The crowd recognized the man as Booth, the Shakespearean actor, but they knew he wasn't supposed to be in this play, especially not while brandishing a knife and shouting before dashing offstage.

Five days separated General Robert E. Lee's surrender at Appomattox and Lincoln's assassination at Ford's Theatre. For Christians, it was Holy Week: Lee surrendered on Palm Sunday; Booth shot Lincoln on Good Friday. For many in the North, jubilation turned to mourning and calls for retribution. For many in the South, anger and mourning turned to muted celebration with anxiety over possible repercussions. Almost everyone struggled for explanations and worried about what would come next. How could the nation move forward after this tragedy? The war seemed to be ending, but was it really? In addition to Lincoln's assassination, conspirators planned—but failed—to murder Secretary of State William Seward and Vice President Johnson. Clearly the war was not over for everyone. As Mary Bushnell Cheney of Connecticut wrote to her sister, "We were preparing in peace and forgiveness to smooth over and forget" the South's crimes in the war, but after Lincoln's murder, "God has given us a sword again."[3]

"The Civil War was a revolutionary war," Martha Hodes wrote, "and Lincoln's assassination complicated its ending." It shocked everyone, and on some level it still shocks and fascinates. Hodes compared reactions to Lincoln's assassination with Americans' reactions to 9/11. The comparison is appropriate. Both events shook the nation; both events changed history. If the American Revolution began with "the shot heard round the world," the shot that killed Lincoln was at least as infamous.[4]

Ministers concentrated on Booth's bullet, almost obsessing over it. How could such a tiny piece of lead wreak such national damage? As one Methodist minister preached, "The bullet that entered the head of our noble President has settled in the people's heart, and we are not the only nation that will feel the wound."[5] Likewise, "The bullet that murdered him was aimed at our national life," said a Presbyterian minister in Friendsville, Illinois.[6]

That hated bullet may have wounded African Americans worst of all. As one white minister lamented, the bullet "that pierced his brain, pierced [African Americans'] hearts more deeply, if possible, than ours."[7] Jacob Thomas, an African American from New York, agreed. "We, as a people, feel more than all others that we are bereaved. We had learned to love Mr. Lincoln as we have never loved man before. We idolized his very name. We looked up to him as our saviour, our deliverer. His name was familiar with our children, and our prayers ascended to God in his behalf."[8]

Did God send—or at least allow—this hated bullet to kill Lincoln? Was it providential? Perhaps not. "It was not the hand of Providence that did this stupendous wrong; it was the great, black hand of the Devil," said a Methodist minister in Boston.[9] For many Americans, however, everything that happened was providential. A few weeks before, when Edwin Stanton wanted to increase security around the president, Lincoln reportedly said, "Stanton it is useless. If it is the will of Providence that I should die by the hand of an assassin, it must be so."[10] Evidently it was the will of Providence, many Americans believed, but why?

For most Americans, the best guide to providence was the Bible. Although many agreed that God was mysterious, they also agreed that Scripture was the best guide to God's will. The circumstances of the assassination made the

Bible especially visible for Christians. Again, it was Holy Week: Booth shot Lincoln on Good Friday; he died on Saturday, so many preachers addressed the assassination on Easter Sunday. As news of Lincoln's death shook the nation, preachers scrapped their Easter sermons and took on the task of addressing the crisis. Many ministers could relate to the Unitarian pastor in Detroit, Michigan, who complained of having only "a few brief hours for preparation, with body and mind exhausted by a week of excitement."[11]

The pressure was on, as preachers knew they would be speaking before large crowds. As Martha Hodes wrote, "Pews always filled to capacity on Easter, but no one had ever seen anything like April 16, 1865." Both "black churches and white churches were jammed," and there was "not an inch of floor space to spare."[12] Three days later, thousands of Americans attended additional sermons preached on the day of Lincoln's funeral, Wednesday, April 19. Many preachers addressed Lincoln's life and death again on April 23, the Sunday following the assassination, and on June 1, the Day of National Humiliation in honor of Lincoln. In addition to the thousands who heard the sermons preached, many others read them when they were either published separately or in newspapers.[13]

With crowds looking to them for words of consolation, ministers sensed the importance of their task. As a Brooklyn Episcopalian put it:

It is made the duty of the pulpit, beyond any other organ of public sentiment, to deal with the overwhelming sorrow of the hour, to guide and temper the nation's grief, to teach it how and for what to weep, to interpret the sober philosophy of the grave, and to press home upon the softened, pain-stricken sensitivities of the people those gifts, privileges, and destinies which the world can neither give nor take away.[14]

Many Americans looked to the ministers and to the Bible for answers, consolation, even retribution. Especially in the North, Americans turned to the Bible to honor Lincoln's legacy as they coped with his assassination.

"The Modern Moses"

When northerners reflected on Lincoln's life and legacy, they found resemblances between him and many heroic figures in the Bible. Each comparison revealed some aspect of Lincoln's legacy that ministers believed was important for the nation's future. Lincoln was wise, like Solomon; a great leader, like David; and willing to sacrifice for his people, like Samson—and the list goes on. But the biblical hero whose life and character most resembled Lincoln was Moses. Preachers drew numerous comparisons between Lincoln and Moses in their sermons. The *Boston Daily Advertiser*, the *Milwaukee Daily Sentinel*, the *Daily Cleveland Herald*, and San Francisco's *Daily Evening Bulletin* were among the newspapers that compared Lincoln and Moses after the assassination. On April 18, the Jewish synagogue Mikveh Israel compared Lincoln to Moses in an ad in the *North American and United States Gazette*, published in Philadelphia.[15] Many Jews respected Lincoln because he had a closer relationship with Jews than any previous president. At the time of Lincoln's birth there were only about 3,000 Jewish Americans; at the time of his assassination, there were 150,000 Jews, mostly due to European immigration. As the number of Jews increased, so did anti-Semitic feelings, but not so with Lincoln. He insisted on appointing Jews to various positions, including assigning the first Jewish chaplains to the army, and he backed off the usual proclamations of the United States as a "Christian nation."[16]

A Methodist from Ohio spoke for many when he said, "Abraham Lincoln was the chosen of God, the modern Moses, to lead the four millions of slaves from a worse than Egyptian bondage into the Canaan of Freedom."[17] But this new American Moses was a divisive figure, mostly loved in the North and hated in the South. So assassination sermons were not just commemorations; they were assertions of Lincoln's greatness in retaliation against those who despised him and secretly celebrated his murder.

Often these sermons argued for Lincoln's worthiness to stand alongside both the biblical Moses and America's founding "Moses," George Washington. During Lincoln's lifetime there was no question that Washington was the golden standard for presidential greatness. As the nation descended into civil war, comparisons between Lincoln and Washington escalated. Ministers saw Washington and Lincoln as God's chosen leaders. One Union chaplain even called them "the two greatest men that ever lived."[18] A Presbyterian from Jacksonville, Illinois, joined many in calling Lincoln "the second father of his country."[19]

Lincoln shared Washington's most respected trait: moral integrity. "It was said of him as of the immortal Washington, that he never told a lie," preached an Episcopalian from Philadelphia. Lincoln was an incorruptible politician, rare in such a corruptible profession. This honesty was a mark of Lincoln throughout his life, even from his childhood, when he famously worked for days to pay back the owner of a book he had borrowed and accidentally ruined. Lincoln remained true to his convictions throughout his life. What made this so remarkable was the turmoil of his presidency. He was at war the entire time he was in office, and yet he remained honest despite constant attacks and ridicule.[20] This kind of integrity distinguished Lincoln, as it had Washington. Americans could trust them with power because they were not obsessed with power—it did not corrupt them.[21]

Some ministers made the radical claim that Lincoln was greater than Washington. A Union chaplain in New Orleans said,

> Washington was the founder of a republic, Lincoln the emancipator of a race. Washington who redeemed us from tyrants abroad, Lincoln who delivered us from traitors at home. Washington who gave us civil liberty, Lincoln who preserved the Union. Washington the Father of his Country, Lincoln the Savior of the Nation. Washington liberated us, Jackson defended us, but Lincoln *died* for us. And we hail in him, at once, the hero, the patriot, and the martyr.[22]

Many preachers agreed. In his comparison of Washington with Lincoln, a Methodist from Ohio said, "The first was patriotic and heroic—the last was Christ-like and divine."[23]

Divine? That was a strong claim for any president. But it was an important claim because ministers insisted that national leaders be godly leaders. This was the case for the Civil War, just as it was for the American Revolution. Constantly ministers said, as a Union chaplain preached, "The best citizen, the best soldier, the best man, and the best magistrate is the true Christian." Those who try "to subvert religion would thereby sacrifice all claim to patriotism."[24]

But *was* Lincoln a Christian? And, for that matter, was Washington? These heroic presidents perplexed ministers because neither Washington nor Lincoln discussed his faith in detail, at least not publicly. American Christians looked for ways to put aside this obstacle, but it was not easily cleared. Decades after the war Americans still discussed Lincoln's religion, or lack thereof, along with comparisons with Washington. The author of an article in the *Arkansas Democrat* from 1899 admitted that Lincoln was "somewhat skeptical," although never so radical as "Tom Paine." He added that "Lincoln had as much faith in the efficacy of prayer during the Civil War as George Washington had during the Revolutionary War."[25]

This problem became especially acute just after Lincoln's assassination. Many ministers insisted that he was a Christian, just as they insisted that he compared to Washington in presidential greatness. Sometimes the two agendas combined. Lincoln may not have said much about his religious beliefs, but he said a lot about divine providence. Even better, ministers retold a story in which Lincoln discussed George Washington's faith in providence. As Lincoln left Springfield for Washington soon after his election, he reportedly said: "A duty devolves on me which is perhaps greater than has devolved upon any other man since the days of Washington." President Washington's success, Lincoln added, would have been impossible without "the aid of a divine providence upon which he always relied." Likewise, Lincoln said, "I can not succeed without the same divine aid which sustained him, and in the same almighty Being I place my reliance for support." Lincoln then asked for prayer that he would receive that support because he would fail without it. But with it, Lincoln said, "Success is certain."[26]

An even more popular story reported that the Battle of Gettysburg influenced Lincoln's conversion to Christianity. As Union chaplain Nelson Brakeman preached, when Lincoln was elected president and took on the great weight of war, he needed "wisdom and strength from God," but he still "was not then a Christian." When Lincoln's son died, "the severest trial of my life," he saw "it as a chastening from God's hand, but still did not devote myself wholly to Him." But Gettysburg changed everything. Lincoln said, "When I went to Gettysburg, and looked upon the graves of our dead heroes, who had fallen in defense of their country, I then and there consecrated myself to Christ; and now *I do love Him*."[27] A Presbyterian preacher in the Nebraska territory agreed, adding that the Gettysburg experience converted Lincoln because there he "saw the holocausts of a nation's offering on the altar of liberty, and beheld how the Christian soldier could cheerfully lie wounded and bleeding in his country's cause." This made Lincoln think about "how little he had given to that Saviour, who had done so much for him."[28]

Most likely Lincoln never told this story. It was probably a fabrication, created by ministers, and based on Lincoln's general comments about being moved by the soldiers' sacrifice at Gettysburg.[29] Regardless of this story's authenticity, however, stories like this played an important role for preachers: they supplied testimony in Lincoln's own words to his Christian faith.

As he had for Washington, Moses reinforced Lincoln's religious authority. We see this clearly in a sermon entitled *The Assassinated President*, from

Joseph Seiss, a Lutheran minister from Philadelphia. Lincoln was America's true Moses, Seiss asserted as he went to great lengths to draw out the parallels between them. Both Moses and Lincoln were born poor. When he was a baby, Moses's mother placed him in a basket and floated it down the Nile. Lincoln's infancy was less dramatic, but equally humble. He was born to a poor Kentucky family. Both Moses and Lincoln lacked formal education, but learned "in the school of humble life." Their roots caused them to despise the rich people who filled their pockets with slave labor. Neither Moses nor Lincoln craved honor and glory. When God called them into service, both had reservations. If Moses felt inadequate to be God's chosen leader, saying, "Who am I" to "go unto Pharaoh . . . O my Lord, I am not eloquent," so did Lincoln doubt his own eloquence. In his debates with Stephen Douglas, the humble, backwoods Lincoln faced one of the nation's leading politicians, a man who possessed "all the powers of extraordinary genius, adroitness, and forensic skill." Were their famous debates not "a re-enactment" of the "contest between the shepherd of Midian and the Magicians of Egypt?"[30]

Moses and Lincoln were most alike in their opposition to slavery. Both liberated enslaved people from bondage, and both did so against incredible odds. The mighty Egyptians never dreamed "that, within her own borders, there was a young mind maturing, who, with no ally but God," would defeat Egyptian slavery.[31] "When God wanted a Moses, there was a Moses ready, hidden" in the desert. Clearly, Seiss preached, "The same has been repeated, in our day, in our country." The parallels were so obvious that "the picture rises to your view without my aid to call it up."[32]

For both Moses and Lincoln, heroism had its price. Despite strong opposition, Moses fought with an "endurance which outwearied even Pharaoh's hardness." Moses even had to endure his own people, who criticized him and "conspired against him." But Moses persevered. "How like Moses, in these respects, was our late President? Who ever encountered more or greater perplexities, difficulties, provocations, and discouragements than those which beset his way? And yet, with what earnest but passionless calmness did he grapple with them!"[33]

Was Lincoln even greater than Moses? To say that Lincoln's greatness surpassed Washington was a major statement. But to claim that Lincoln superseded Moses was an even more radical claim. And yet that topic was addressed at Lincoln's burial service in Springfield, Illinois. Matthew Simpson, friend of Lincoln and a Methodist bishop, said: "Moses stands preeminently high" among "the sacred characters" that "we have all been taught to revere." Moses was God's lawgiver, "honored among the hosts of heaven," but was not his "greatest" accomplishment "the delivering of three millions of his kindred out of bondage?" In comparison, Lincoln was even greater. Not only did Lincoln free more enslaved people than Moses, but Moses freed his own people, whereas Lincoln accomplished the greater moral good by freeing "those not of his kindred or his race."[34]

If Lincoln and Moses shared many similarities in their lives, the timing of their deaths seemed even more remarkable. Henry Ward Beecher connected Lincoln's assassination with the dramatic scene of Moses's death before entering the Promised Land. "No historic figure" was "more noble" than Moses, Beecher preached. Moses' death was touching because God barred him from the promised land even though he had led God's people there. Understandably, Moses yearned to enter the Promised Land—it was "the consummation of every desire, the reward of every toil and pain." But God prohibited Moses from entering, and Moses looked on the Promised Land "with eager longing, with sad resignation," for "it was now to him a forbidden land."[35]

The clear parallel to Moses was Lincoln—"a great leader of the people" who "has passed through toil, sorrow, battle, and war, and come near to the promised land of peace, into which he might not pass over."[36] He was a hands-on military president who did all in his power to win the war. Once the war was almost won, however, he died before he could experience the peace brought by his sacrifices. The promised land was within reach, but, like Moses, he only saw it from a distance.

Frances E. W. Harper drew this same comparison between Lincoln and Moses. Lincoln led the nation "through another Red Sea" to the "land of triumphant victory," yet "God has seen fit to summon for the new era another man. It is ours then to bow to the Chastener and let our honored and loved chieftain go."[37]

"How Are the Mighty Fallen!"

If ministers looked to Moses to honor Lincoln's life, they looked to more tragic biblical heroes to cope with his horrible death. For all the similarities between Moses and Lincoln, there was one key difference: Moses died peacefully; Lincoln died violently. So ministers looked through the Bible to find deaths that better compared with Lincoln's. Here preachers had a lot to choose from, because the scriptures contain many killings, some of them gruesome. And yet, of all the deaths in scripture, the two most often compared to Lincoln's murder were from the book of 2 Samuel: the tragic death of King Saul (2 Samuel 1), and the murder of Abner (2 Samuel 3). These scriptures were so popular that they made the book of 2 Samuel the most cited biblical book in the main texts of sermons on Lincoln's assassination.

It's easy to see why. Saul and Abner died tragically during a civil war between the kingdoms of David and Saul. Earlier, Saul, Israel's first king, had befriended David. Eventually, however, Saul became jealous of David, and the relationship crumbled as David's stature among the people, and favor with God, surpassed Saul's. Civil war erupted between the houses of Saul and David, therefore, and American preachers in the North could relate to it. The conflict between them was, as Ohio Baptist Samuel Gorman said, an "unnatural war," and an "unholy war of brethren against brethren, and against God's ordained government." It was, like the American Civil War, a war that "wasted the people, and filled the land with sadness and distress."[38]

We could argue that King Saul's death was more assisted suicide than murder. But David viewed it as murder, and ministers agreed as they compared Saul's killing to Lincoln's. The account opens at the beginning of 2 Samuel, with David having just returned from a military victory over the Amalekites. After three days, an Amalekite man came into the camp and fell at David's feet. The man reported to David that he had just left the battlefield where Saul had been fighting the Philistines, Israel's archenemies. The man reported to David that the Philistines had defeated Saul's army, and that Saul and his son, Jonathan, were dead. When David asked how he knew this, the man responded that he had come upon Saul on Mount Gilboa. Saul had been mortally injured in battle, and the Philistines were in pursuit with chariots and horses, giving Saul no chance for survival. In desperation, Saul commanded the man to kill him. The man obeyed—he killed Saul, took his crown and amulet, and delivered them to David. If the man expected David to be grateful, he was disappointed—David had him executed for daring to kill God's anointed ruler. Then David sang:

> The beauty of Israel is slain upon thy high places: *how are the mighty fallen!*
> Tell it not in Gath, publish it not in the streets of Askelon; lest the daughters
> of the Philistines rejoice, lest the daughters of the uncircumcised triumph.
> (2 Samuel 1.19–20, emphasis added)

The "mighty" *had* fallen, the mighty Lincoln, so David's words of mourning fit the experience of many on Easter. Some preachers just quoted these lines, while others reflected more deeply on Saul's assassination in relation to Lincoln's. As they did, some ministers expressed amazement at David's harsh treatment of the man who killed Saul. Surely this assassin did David a favor, they reasoned. "You should remember that the only obstacle between David and the throne was removed by the death of Saul," preached Warren Hathaway, a Methodist minister from New York. Saul had been cruel to David, "seeking his life with relentless hatred."[39] Saul, once a hero, had failed as a king, and the nation was better off without him. The natural reaction to Saul's death, therefore, should have been celebration. Saul's killer went to David expecting a reward, a reasonable expectation, considering the personal and political rivalries that divided Saul and David. But David was better than that. Although Saul ruined the nation, hated David, and even tried to kill him, David avenged Saul's death by executing his assassin.[40]

David's brutal and swift action appealed to northern ministers after Lincoln's assassination. How dare anyone kill God's anointed leader! David had reacted admirably, just as he did after the death of Abner, recorded just two chapters later (2 Samuel 3).

If Saul's killing was, arguably, an assisted suicide, there was no question about Abner's fate. Abner was brutally murdered, killed by Joab, David's military captain. Abner was a tragic figure in this biblical civil war. After starting out as a commander in Saul's army, Abner had defected to David's side. Joab, however, hated Abner. Not only had Abner previously killed Joab's brother, but Joab also suspected that Abner was a spy. Joab tricked Abner into a meeting with him, and when Abner let his guard down, Joab killed him. When David heard this, he was devastated and furious with Joab. He proclaimed that Abner's blood was on Joab's head, and asked God to curse Joab's family with poverty, leprosy, disability, and murder. David then cried, "Know ye not that there is a prince and a great man fallen this day in Israel?" (2 Samuel 3:38).

When preachers addressed the Lincoln assassination, this was the verse they cited most often in their main sermon texts. One of these preachers, African American Methodist Jacob Thomas of New York, said this "text is a fitting one" for Lincoln's assassination because truly "a great man has fallen."[41] Many preachers agreed. For some ministers this verse was a motto, an expression of grief. This verse was, of course, appropriate for Lincoln's assassination, or any great leader's death, for that matter.

Ministers saw some of Lincoln in Abner's work as a peacemaker. "Abner was chiefly influential in translating the kingdom from the house of Saul and setting up the throne of David over all the land," said a Methodist from Springfield, Massachusetts. The tragedy was that Abner had no sooner secured peace in the land when Joab murdered him in a cruel manner— without warning, and under the guise of friendship. This tragedy spoiled what would have been a lasting peace. As in America upon the death of Lincoln, so with Abner "The joy of the nation, at the prospect of permanent peace, was turned to universal grief."[42]

"As a Man Falleth before Wicked Men"

To assassinate is to humiliate. Assassination is politically inspired murder. Assassins take down the powerful, and they do so in the most degrading way. That was what David meant when he said Abner died "as a fool" died, "as a man falleth before wicked men." That was also what David meant when he questioned why the man who killed Saul had dared to raise his hand to kill the Lord's anointed.

When ministers reacted to Lincoln's death, they found humiliation all around. They despised the fact that he was killed in a theater. This embarrassed some ministers and horrified others. Lincoln's assassination in a theater meant that he was, like Abner, slain "before wicked men." As a Baptist minister asked about Lincoln's death in the theater: "What Christian man, what thinking man would seek to meet his end in such a scene?" Most ministers agreed that "the theater is a place of vain and expensive amusement, a place unfriendly to piety, and hurtful to morality," most often frequented by "lovers of pleasure more than lovers of God."[43]

Why did Lincoln, a man of such impeccable character, spend Good Friday in a theater? It was horrible, ministers knew—so horrible that they looked for excuses to account for Lincoln's theater attendance. A Presbyterian in Penn Yan, New York, preached that the president was overwhelmed with the stresses of war, constantly meeting with "hundreds of visitors in a day," and worn down by the pressures he was under. Lincoln went to the theater to get a well-deserved break. By doing so, Lincoln "set a personal example" that would corrupt citizens if they followed it. Lincoln mingled with a low class of people, the entertainers. They claimed to be respectable and to be examples of virtue, but they were in fact "the most depraved, vicious and unprincipled" people in the nation.[44]

Some ministers, in contrast, tried to turn Lincoln's theater attendance into a virtue. A Baptist in Hartford, Connecticut, said the president didn't really want to go to the theater, but the people expected him to be there, and he didn't want to disappoint them. Lincoln went "at a personal sacrifice, and for the sake of the people whom he loved."[45] Likewise, a Dutch Reformed minister in Schenectady, New York, said Lincoln's "kindness of nature" led him "to the theater, so that the people who expected to see General Grant there might not be disappointed."[46] So even in Lincoln's theater attendance, he was a martyr.

Excuses aside, preachers knew that Lincoln's death was doubly bad—bad because of the manner of his death, and bad because it happened in a theater. Lincoln's death violated American views of a good death. As historian Drew Gilpin Faust wrote, "The concept of the Good Death was central to mid-nineteenth-century America, as it had long been at the core of Christian practice." According to this idea, "Dying was an art."[47] Christian ideas about the resurrection of the dead had conditioned nineteenth-century Americans to focus in on the moment of death. How people died said something about their character, and implied something about their eternal home. As Faust wrote, "How one died thus epitomized a life already led and predicted the quality of life everlasting." So "the hour of death . . . had therefore to be witnessed, scrutinized, interpreted, narrated—not to mention carefully prepared for by any sinner who sought to be worthy of salvation."[48]

Abraham Lincoln deserved a good death if anyone did, most northerners believed. Instead he suffered one of the worst deaths imaginable. Like Abner, he died among "wicked men," and the most wicked was his assassin, John Wilkes Booth. As Presbyterian Frederick Starr of New York preached, "We could wish that our noble martyr had met his death in almost any other place than a theatre—by almost any hand rather than that of a depraved actor." Booth was, as another Presbyterian minister from Illinois put it, a "product of the theatre, the drinking saloon, and the gambling hell." These "dens of vice and infamy" shaped his views on life. Such men easily transformed "into monsters of crime."[49]

Some ministers speculated that Booth's training as an actor turned him into an assassin. Villains often were heroes in plays, and Booth stepped into this role. Booth's love of acting motivated him to leap to the stage and "to proclaim his guilt in the traditional dramatic style" before a horrified audience, preached a Presbyterian minister from New Jersey. Booth had played the villain on that stage, and he merely stepped into the role when he killed Lincoln.

Lincoln's assassination was God's means of warning people to despise the theater, for it had a corrupting influence on morality.[50]

"Wehr-Wolves or Fiends Incarnate"

Booth may have been "a depraved actor," but the wickedness that killed Lincoln went far deeper than the immorality of the theater. Jacob Thomas, an African Methodist Episcopal Zion minister, said that Lincoln "was brutally murdered—shot down by the cowardly hand of an assassin." Booth was an "execrable wretch who committed this, the blackest of all crimes." Lincoln was "the father and friend of the oppressed, the champion of universal freedom," and tragically "a victim to Southern malice and revenge."[51]

Booth was demonic, many preachers asserted. As a Congregationalist from near Buffalo, New York, preached, Booth's inspiration came from "the Prince of darkness," who sent him "to perform the last grand master-piece of hell in the murder of Abraham Lincoln."[52] Booth was no man; he was "the emissary of the devil," argued John Drumm, an Episcopal minister from Pennsylvania. Booth was no longer fully human. "A being of true human constitution could never" have killed a man like Lincoln, nor could a human kill so scandalously. Booth "shot him like a dog!" Booth had neither heart nor conscience—"the fire of hell" had burned it away.[53]

Evil as he was, the most terrifying truth was that Booth was one among many. The satanic power that possessed him inspired the South. As a minister from Lafayette, Indiana preached, the conspiracy to kill Lincoln was "of the same heart that roasted soldiers alive at Fort Pillow; that starved them to the death of living skeletons at Andersonville; that froze them to death on Belle Isle and in Libby Prison; that robbed their dead pockets and made finger-rings of their skull-bones."[54] As John Drumm put it, the Confederates were "wehr-wolves or fiends incarnate."[55]

Satanic, fiendish, "wehr-wolves"—these were just a few of the terms ministers used as they struggled to express Confederate evil. Presbyterian Marvin Vincent, later professor at Union Theological Seminary in New York, quoted Milton's Satan, proclaiming that the Confederates preferred to "rule in hell than serve in Heaven."[56] The Confederates were demonic, he argued. "The mutilation of the dead" was part of "the civilized warfare of the chivalrous South," with "our murdered sons and brothers dug from their graves, and their bones hacked into pieces to furnish amulets for dainty Southern dames."[57]

Booth was part of a "hellish clan" that included Confederates and copperheads, preached Ohio Methodist Rolla Chubb. "This slimy monster was coiling its loathsome carcass with deadly folds around the Genius of Liberty, essaying to crush, in its snaky embrace, the spirit of Freedom and the life of the nation. This spawn of perdition," Chubb continued, "is the living embodiment and personification of all that is mean on earth, of all that is de-testable this side [of] the dark domains of the damned."[58] So, "If they are not ultimately hanged, hemp will have lost its virtue, and if not finally damned, Hell ought to be abolished for having violated its charter."[59]

"The Avenging Sword Is at His Heels"

Attacks on Booth were ecumenical, seething from Protestants, Catholics, and Jews. Rabbi Morais of Synagogue Mikveh Israel in Philadelphia called Booth "the execrable wretch who has robbed liberty of its staunchest defender, and nature of its noblest creation." Booth should beware, Rabbi Morais warned, because "the avenging sword is at his heels. It shall never return to its scab-bard until it has consumed, with the assassin, his accessories and abettors." The United States insisted on justice, the rabbi said. "The mournful nation shall be avenged; they shall behold the dastardly hand which spilled innocent blood, severed from its venomous body."[60]

Northern religious leaders found this call for vengeance throughout the scriptures. And again, the murders of Saul and Abner provided popular illustrations. In calling for vengeance, David was the perfect model. Not only did he condemn Joab and his entire family for killing Abner, but he executed the man who dared to kill Saul. "God raised up a David to avenge the fearful crime," preached a minister in Washington, DC, because Saul was God's anointed.[61]

If Saul was sacred to Israel, Lincoln was even more sacred to the United States—and to God.[62] Saul may have been Israel's first king, but Lincoln was his superior, both in character and in leadership, ministers argued.[63] So if Saul's executioner deserved God's vengeance, how much more did John Wilkes Booth? After all, unlike Saul's death, which blessed Israel, Lincoln's assassination was disastrous for the United States.[64]

Were southerners celebrating Lincoln's murder? Even the suggestion in-censed northern ministers. They could relate to David's warning against spreading the news of Saul's death to the Philistine cities of Gath and Askelon, lest the Philistines celebrate the murder of God's anointed ruler. Southerners were the modern Philistines, so "If there be still a Gath or an Askelon in the territory of rebellion, let not their inhabitants know of this calamity," insisted a minister in Waitsfield, Vermont. "Let not the enemies of the Republic have one moment of triumph," for surely Booth did not act alone. No doubt Jefferson Davis, "the arch traitor and official head of the rebel government has shared with the murderer of our President" in "a tragedy intended to be more extended and fatal."[65]

The cry for vengeance in retaliation for southern crimes was so critical that, according to many preachers, it was the reason God allowed Booth to murder Lincoln. This was awkward for many of the northern clergy. They loved Lincoln, but they thought that God allowed his murder because Lincoln did not seek retribution on the South. He wanted to put the nation back together and to heal the wounds of division. For northern ministers, this meant that Lincoln was "*too lenient* to rebels and assassins" who sought to destroy the nation.[66] Lincoln would not punish the South. As a Presbyterian in Friendsville, Illinois, preached, Lincoln had an "inborn goodness" that made him "poorly qualified to act as judge, and dispense the awful awards of justice and law upon the perjured and blood-stained leaders in treason." His assassination "relieved" him from this duty.[67]

A sore point for clergy was that Lincoln had not sufficiently punished the Confederates for their crimes involving Union casualties and prisoners of war. One minister lamented about their "sunken eyes, and hard and shriveled and ashy skins, and wasted forms." They were like "living skeletons." Can anyone think about them "and not feel your blood grow hot like fire in your veins?"[68] Another minister said, "I see rising from the dead a host of wounded, mangled bodies," which were "the forms of" Union soldiers who died in war, who "starved to death by a slow but sure process in Belle Isle and Andersonville." The preacher saw "their skeleton fingers pointing to" Confederates and Confederate sympathizers who are walking around free. "I see them thus rise from the dead and demand of this Republic: Is this the fruit of our labors; the reward of our suffering?" They also seemed to be saying, "You asked our blood to save the country, while you spare the blood of these men who have tried to destroy it!"[69] As another minister said about Confederate leaders, "Are we to stand here to-day and clasp their blood-stained hands in ours, and welcome back to fellowship those who only want the opportunity to renew their devilish work! For one, I say *no!*"[70]

"Vengeance Is Mine; I Will Repay, Saith the Lord"

The North yearned for vengeance, but didn't scripture demand forgiveness? It was a dilemma, and one minister who addressed it had an unfortunate last name—Booth. Presbyterian Robert Russel Booth of New York addressed Lincoln's assassination in a sermon titled, *Personal Forgiveness and Public Justice*. "There are two distinct sentiments which have been struggling together in our national councils," Booth said. As they mourned their president, Christians grappled with how to harmonize "the Divine law of *forgiveness* and good will to our enemies, and the Divine law of *punishment* in the interest of justice for the welfare of society." This was not a new dilemma, and Booth found it expressed well in Paul's letter to the Romans.[71]

First, Paul told the Roman Christians "avenge not yourselves" because it is written, "vengeance is mine; I will repay, saith the Lord" (Romans 12:19). The key word here is "yourselves"—Christians were not to avenge sins against themselves. They were to leave that vengeance up to God.[72]

Next, Booth turned to the following chapter, which must have been familiar to everyone because it was the ever popular Romans 13, which begins, "Let every soul be subject unto the higher powers; for there is no power but of God," a text that called every civil ruler to be the "minister of God, a revenger to execute wrath upon him that doeth evil" (cf. Romans 13:1–4). Here God placed the responsibility for executing vengeance in the hands of civil rulers.[73]

These two statements from Paul appeared contradictory, Booth admitted, but they were complementary. When one person sinned against another, vengeance belonged to God, and not the offended person. But when people committed crimes against the state, vengeance belonged to the civil ruler. The golden rule and Jesus's teachings in the Sermon on the Mount—like turn the other cheek—applied only to personal morality. But the golden rule had no place in politics. If it did, no nation could wage war, "no matter how righteous the cause for which it was waged." Not only that, no city or state could punish a criminal or enforce its laws. Cities, states, and nations would be chaotic.[74]

The United States had a God-given responsibility to execute vengeance on the South for Lincoln's assassination, he said. Americans watched in horror "at the cruel fate of our Martyr-President." And Americans had every right to expect the state to dispense justice. The nation's "majesty has been defied" and its "very life has been put in peril." It was time to take Paul's advice in both

Romans 12 and Romans 13. "We may obey the voice of the holy Apostle, in the first of these passages, while we insist that the State shall obey his precepts in the second." He continued, "At this point our responsibility is drawn, not from the 12th but from the 13th chapter of the Epistle to the Romans. It is drawn not from the gentle impulses of personal piety, but from the stern mandate of the external law of God."[75]

Booth filled his sermon with documentation of the brutality the South had inflicted on the nation. "Secession and slavery, the twin horrors" that destroyed the nation, must die. They explained why "300,000 men or more are lying cold beneath the sod to-day, or bleaching under a Southern sky," not to mention thousands more who came home "maimed, mutilated and suffering." Now patriots must bury secession and slavery "in the grave of our murdered President," and they should never "be spoken of with approval hereafter by a true patriot or Christian man."[76]

Although Booth preached from the New Testament, he said the nation needed "an infusion of the Old Testament severity rather than of the New Testament tenderness."[77] There was no shortage of "Old Testament severity" after Lincoln's assassination; northern ministers found the Old Testament filled with calls for retribution. In a sermon titled, "Southern Chivalry, and What the Nation Ought to Do with It," Alonzo Quint, a Congregationalist minister from Massachusetts, chose a text from Isaiah: "We have made a covenant with death, And with hell are we at agreement."[78] This scripture fit the situation, Quint said, because the South had "made a covenant with death," a deal with the Devil. The southern "customs, their laws, their practices, were all of hell."[79]

God used the assassination "to startle the nation out of its weakness," Quint argued. For years the North had admired "Southern chivalry" and the "Southern Gentleman" as "the perfection of humanity." But this was delusional. Southern chivalry was nothing more than a cover for slavery. And southerners fought the war to protect "the rights of the Southern Gentleman, which were to breed babies for a market, trade in helpless victims of lust, whip and maim human bodies, and starve human souls."[80]

Above all, "Southern Chivalry killed the President." The assassination was a "last lesson to tell you what Southern Chivalry is."[81] The North, led by Lincoln, was "too kind. You have played at war. Barbarians respect only force." So when Confederates "hung men in Tennessee, you should have hung men in Louisiana." And "When they burnt Chambersburg, you should have burned Huntsville. When they shot black prisoners at Pillow, you should have shot white prisoners in South Carolina. That is hard? It is war. War is not play; it is not for women; it is not a lullaby for your children." War commands the North: "Be the instrument in God's hand of cleansing the land of its pollution."[82] He concluded with the plea, "Let us swear eternal hatred to Southern Chivalry," and by quoting and paraphrasing several violent scriptures, including part of this one from Jeremiah: "Pour out their blood by the force of the sword; and let their wives be bereaved of their children, and be widows; and let their men be put to death; let their young men be slain by the sword in battle."[83]

The message was clear: Lincoln's death should inspire vengeance. As a Presbyterian minister from New Jersey put it, "The nation, baptized in the blood of their President, will rouse itself to self-assertion and to a final and terrible termination of this war. The blood of Abraham Lincoln dripping down from the 'high places' of the land upon the hearts of this people will cement them into one heart, into one purpose."[84]

One of the major questions was what to do with Confederate military officers. Some radical Republicans, including ministers such as Methodist Erastus Wentworth, wanted Robert E. Lee and others to be executed.[85] Lincoln's assassination, they hoped, would motivate the people to punish "the traitors, both North and South." If this happened, Lincoln would have served "his country as much by his death as by his life."[86] As a Presbyterian in Batavia, New York, put it, the assassination should convince the nation that "the rebellion must pay in blood."[87]

God's plan for the nation seemed to point away from Lincoln toward Vice President Andrew Johnson, who would deal more sternly with the South. Before the assassination, ministers had mixed feelings about Johnson. He was, after all, a southerner. And who could forget that he made a spectacle of himself at the second inaugural with his embarrassing, drunken speech? Obviously, it did not look good to see an intoxicated vice president making a fool of himself. And yet in the desperate days after Lincoln's assassination, Johnson became the ministers' hero. If Lincoln was America's Moses, "Andrew Johnson is the Joshua whom God has appointed to consummate the work which our dead Moses so nobly commenced,"[88] preached a Baptist from Connecticut. Many preachers agreed that the biblical parallel fit, because Moses led the Israel to the Promised Land, but Joshua conquered it. "Who knows but God permitted the removal of the lenient Lincoln, that the chair of state might be filled by the sterner Johnson," preached a Congregationalist minister in Niagara City. The South would now have to answer to Johnson, "And his little finger will be heavier than Lincoln's whole hand."[89]

As it turned out, President Johnson was no Joshua. In the view of most Republicans and northern Protestant ministers, his plan for Reconstruction was disastrous. It was far too easy on the southern establishment and it reinforced the oppression of African Americans. Republican leaders' perception of Johnson's failures ultimately resulted in his impeachment (although he was acquitted).

America's Cain and an American Christ

After he shot Lincoln, John Wilkes Booth hid in Zekiah Swamp, Maryland, near the Potomac River. Although he was on the run, he opened his diary and reflected on his situation—and his reputation. He had read newspaper accounts of the assassination, and they offended him. He was no coward. "I struck boldly and not as the papers say," he insisted. "I walked with a firm step through a thousand of his friends, was stopped, but pushed on" toward Lincoln's box at Ford's Theatre. Contrary to reports, Booth claimed, "I shouted *Sic* semper *before* I fired," not after; then "in jumping broke my leg." Booth claimed to have escaped by riding "sixty miles that night, with the bones of my leg tearing the flesh at every jump." Booth then turned to religious justifications of the assassination. "We hated to kill," he wrote, but "our country owed all her troubles to" Lincoln, so "God simply made me the instrument of his punishment."[90]

Five days later, still on the run in Maryland, Booth turned again to his diary. He had read more newspapers, which made him bristle at being labeled "a common cutthroat," chased "like a dog through swamps." He had acted only for his country, "Yet now behold the cold hand they extend to me." He yearned to have his name cleared. As he prepared to make another attempt to cross the river, he thought of Cain, the Bible's first murderer, whom God cursed for killing his brother, Abel (Genesis 4). "I think I have done well," he wrote, and yet "I am abandoned, with the curse of Cain upon me." Only he hoped to avoid the legacy of Cain. "If the world knew my heart, *that one* blow"—killing Lincoln—"would have made me great." Insisting that he had "too great a soul to die like a criminal," Booth prayed that God might "let me die bravely," but he conceded that "God's will be done."[91]

God's will *was* done, according to many Americans, four days later when a Union soldier killed Booth in a barn in Port Royal, Virginia. He did not get the heroic death he wished for—far from it. In the eyes of Americans, then and now, Booth was one of the nation's most hated villains. The comparison with the despised Cain proved to be accurate. In Des Moines, Iowa, a Presbyterian minister spoke for many: "if Cain deserved to be punished sevenfold, surely [Booth] deserves to be punished seventy and seven fold."[92]

Many agreed that Booth was an American Cain. Not only preachers, but newspapers mentioned this comparison, including articles in the *Daily National Intelligencer,* the *New Haven Daily Palladium,* and the *Boston Daily Advertiser,* published in the weeks following the assassination.[93] It was no wonder, as the story of Cain inspired a call for vengeance that Americans could relate to. Cain killed his brother but did not get away with it because Abel's blood cried to God from the ground. The same was true for Lincoln's blood and that of the other Union patriots in the war. "The voice of the blood of our patriots crieth unto God from the ground for vengeance," preached John Chester in a sermon at Capitol Hill Presbyterian Church.[94]

The Cain and Abel story made its presence known in another way in the wake of Lincoln's murder. One of the most preached scriptures from the New Testament referenced the Bible's first murder: "By faith Abel offered unto God a more excellent sacrifice than Cain, by which he obtained witness that he was righteous, God testifying of his gifts: and by it he being dead yet speaketh" (Hebrews 11:4). Abel, though dead, lived on because of his righteousness—although dead, he spoke.

This scripture was popular because preachers believed that Lincoln still spoke to the nation after his death. If scripture was clear about anything, preachers believed, it was that there was some form of life after death. Lincoln would live on; his legacy would endure, and it would help to shape the nation's future.

Lincoln's legacy was on the minds of many Americans in the days after his death. Twenty-five thousand people stood in line at the White House to view Lincoln in his casket, and still others visited his body as it lay in state at the Capitol. Add to those numbers the thousands who gathered to see his train pass through seven states on the seventeen-hundred-mile trip from Washington, DC, to Springfield, Illinois, where he was buried nearly three weeks after the assassination.[95]

As Lincoln's funeral train moved through the nation, Henry Ward Beecher called on Hebrews 11:4 and its reference to Abel. "Now the martyr is moving in triumphal march, mightier than when alive." True—Lincoln was dead. But "Dead—dead—dead—he yet speaketh!" Lincoln had given up his body. But "His life now is grafted upon the Infinite, and will be fruitful as no earthly life can be." Lincoln, in death, had "new influence. Dead, he speaks to men who now willingly hear what before they refused to listen to." Americans would "receive a new impulse of patriotism for his sake, and will guard with zeal the whole country which he loved so well."[96]

The assassination made Lincoln's legacy even more vital for the nation. If Booth had not killed Lincoln, Americans still would have remembered their president for his honesty, his kindness even to his enemies, and especially for his work in liberating the enslaved people of the nation. But Lincoln's "image would not have struck so deeply into the heart of the nation, and the force of his example, and the purity of his life, and the grandeur of his character" would not have been as celebrated, wrote a minister from Leavenworth, Kansas.[97] A minister from Freeport, Illinois, also commented on Lincoln's enduring legacy. His "character remains an active, beneficent force in our history, and among the richest of our possessions."[98] This minister also said that Lincoln would yet illumine the nation "with undiminished lustre forever," and he would be "a permanent spiritual force into our national life" that should bid future leaders to follow this "hero and martyr."[99]

This emphasis on Abraham Lincoln's legacy was one of the most important messages in the assassination sermons. It was not enough to say that Lincoln was a great president, nor was it enough to say his political contributions to the nation would endure. Lincoln was sacred, and his righteousness and sacrifice contributed to the sacredness of the nation and its future. In arguing for the sacredness of Lincoln, preachers could find no better evidence than the fact that God allowed Booth to assassinate him on Good Friday. There could be no clearer comparison between Abraham Lincoln and Christ. God had aligned it providentially.

Preachers worried that comparisons between Lincoln and Christ veered dangerously toward blasphemy. But they did it anyway, making apologies as they thought necessary. The parallel between Lincoln and Christ was important because Lincoln's sacrifice was unique. To be sure, they agreed that in some sense the Union soldiers who sacrificed on the battlefield were martyrs. But Lincoln was special—his sacrifice to reunite the nation paralleled Christ's sacrifice to reunite God with a sinful world.

"If I am unwittingly blasphemous, forgive me," preached a Baptist minister from Connecticut. But just as only God's son could offer a sacrifice sufficient to reconcile "apostate humanity" with God, so only Lincoln, "he who was dearest to all loyal hearts should be offered in sacrifice" to reconcile an apostate South with the nation.[100] Only Lincoln was sacred enough to offer the sacrifice, and only this assassination was tragic enough to parallel Christ's crucifixion. "As on the first Good Friday peace was secured between an apostate race and God, so we will trust that on the last Good Friday peace was secured between the contending regions of our distracted country."[101]

In the hands of these ministers, the Bible helped to shape a legacy of Lincoln as a sacred president. Lincoln was almost *too* sacred for some northern ministers. We find one indicator of just how sacred Lincoln was by noting the anxiety that some preachers expressed about it. There was a concern that Lincoln had become too deified in the American mind, and ministers expressed this anxiety by bringing up scriptures that warned against idolatry.[102] Lincoln, they worried, had moved beyond an American president to become an American idol. "Perhaps we were inclined to hero-worship," preached a Presbyterian minister in New York. "Perhaps we were inclined to exalt the man above the Almighty Supporter."[103]

Likewise, a Congregational pastor from Connecticut said that Lincoln was killed because he "was the idol of the nation." Americans believed he had "the wisdom and the power of Ommnipotence [*sic*]." Too much trust in Lincoln was "idolatry," and "natural atheism."[104] So, God "stepped forth from His sacred pavilion and touched our idol, and it withered into dust."[105] On April 14, Lincoln started the day as the nation's most powerful man, but the end of the day "saw him weltering in blood." Now Lincoln, "the hope and the heart of millions," lay "in the dust." Lincoln "was too much loved and too much trusted in," and given his success, "We had almost forgotten that he was mortal."[106]

If the sacredness of Lincoln's legacy created theological anxieties for some ministers, it was only because northern ministers had been so successful in securing Lincoln's reputation as America's savior, the Christlike martyr for freedom.

When preachers addressed Lincoln's assassination, they took on an important responsibility. They knew that the stakes were high, and the job could be risky. As the North mourned Lincoln's death, most southern clergy dared not speak a word against him for fear of retribution. Preaching after the assassination could be precarious, even in the North. In Medway, Massachusetts, one visiting minister made the mistake of not mentioning Lincoln's assassination during his sermon in a Baptist church on Easter Sunday 1865. This neglect infuriated the congregation. When the service ended, they demanded that he leave town within fifteen minutes.[107]

Such severe reactions were unusual, but not unheard of. One study of newspapers published after Lincoln's assassination cited "eighty mobbings and arrests of persons who had used 'treasonable language,' " that is, "any language that was deemed disrespectful to Lincoln."[108] Martha Hodes is right to compare the days after Lincoln's assassination to the anxious days that followed 9/11. People dealt with fear, grief, fury, and uncertainty.

In these high-pressure days, ministers did not have time for careful and prolonged interpretations of the Bible. As Mark Noll wrote, "When religious leaders turned to the Scriptures at moments of unusual crisis, their biblical usage was instinctive, and so revealed deep habits of thought, fundamental convictions, and commonly accepted conventions of interpretation." The sheer prominence of these sermons, given the vast audiences of people who heard them, makes these occasions some of the more significant displays of the Bible in the United States during the Civil War era.[109]

The Old Testament dominated. Obviously, that was not the plan for sermons on Easter Sunday; preachers had planned to celebrate Christ's victory over evil, concentrating on the empty tomb and resurrection. But the horrible events of Good Friday made that plan impossible. When ministers revised their Easter sermons to preach on Lincoln, many of them also shifted from the Easter story of the New Testament to Old Testament scriptures.[110] In my collection of 367 assassination sermons that listed at least one main biblical text, I found 380 biblical texts, of which 81 (21.3 percent) were from the New Testament and 297 (78.1 percent) were from the Old Testament (two were from the Apocrypha). When they heard that Booth had shot Lincoln, preachers scoured the Old Testament to secure Lincoln's reputation as a great leader, explain the humiliating details of his murder, condemn his murderer (and the South) as demonic, and call for vengeance in retaliation for this heinous crime.

For all these texts of Old Testament heroism and vengeance, the New Testament also had a prominent place in Americans' views of Lincoln. When they heard the news of Lincoln's death, preachers did not throw out their Easter sermons; they politicized them. Instead of preaching on Christ's death and resurrection, they preached the martyrdom of Lincoln—a death that signaled a new resurrection of God's chosen nation after the war. As a Methodist from Ohio put it, the American flag had been "made sacred by the blood of a martyred Lincoln," so "I press it to my heart."[111]

In various scriptures from both testaments, therefore, northern ministers helped to shape Lincoln's legacy as a sacred leader. That legacy persists today. When pollsters ask Americans today who the nation's greatest president was, Lincoln is always at or near the top of the rankings. A *New York Times* story during the COVID-19 pandemic in May 2020, said, "Abraham Lincoln may have died 155 years ago, but everyone still wants his endorsement." Historian Richard Wightman Fox wrote, of all presidents, "Lincoln is cherished and loved—more deeply, by more people—than any other." Lincoln also "persists as a moral exemplar, a man of saintly disposition." Describing Lincoln's symbolic presence in the nation, Fox quoted a historian from the 1940s who spoke of a "cult" around Lincoln that was "almost an American religion."[112] Few doubt that he was one of America's greatest presidents, and for some, he retains a sacred aura. Many factors contributed to this legacy of a sacred Lincoln, but the Bible, especially as preached by northern clergy, was a significant one. If the Bible was America's most sacred book, it helped to shape Lincoln's legacy as perhaps America's most sacred president.

Epilogue

"Pyrotechnics of Providence"

The United States "has come out of the war by far more powerful than when it began it," proclaimed Rabbi Samuel Adler in December 1865. His sermon, published in the *New York Times*, had a weighty title: "The Structure of Our Union a Temple of God." The Hebrew scriptures, as we have seen, were full of stories of war, devastation, and exile, and one of the greatest casualties of war was the temple in Jerusalem. With God's help, the people rebuilt it, and the Second Temple was even greater than the first. Rabbi Adler compared the rise of Jerusalem's Second Temple with the second rise of the United States after its victory over the Confederacy. Jerusalem's first temple had been destroyed, just as the United States had been ruptured by war and unprecedented devastation. Adler quoted Haggai the prophet: " 'The latter glory of this house will be greater than the former,' says Yahweh of Armies; 'and in this place will I give peace' " (Haggai 2:9).

This verse leapt off the page. "Does not this appear as if spoken to our time and to our people?" Rabbi Adler asked. "We also are in the act of rebuilding a temple and what a temple!" Indeed "the structure of our States . . . is a temple of God." Just as the nation was born in war, so it would be reborn in war. The nation of the founders had many faults, but the new nation, "consecrated by the blood of so many brave and noble men, now is rendered safe and lasting for ages to come, a fact unalterable." "This great land . . . has risen again from its fall, has risen a mighty giant," expanding "from ocean to ocean"—so who could doubt the United States would "illuminate the whole earth?" The nation has never been "so powerful," nor "so honored, because so feared" in the world.[1]

Rabbi Adler's sermon exemplified three prominent convictions that Americans invoked from the Bible during the Civil War era: confidence in a clear analogy between a biblical text and the war; faith in the war's redemptive outcome, which, for many in the North, charged the United States with a divine mission in the world; and above all, reverence for the sacred sacrifice of the dead, whose blood "consecrated" the nation. Adler's main image is critical to the sermon: the nation was a *temple*, and temples were places of sacrifice. Whatever else this war was, it was a massive sacrifice—on that everyone agreed. Blood had been shed on an unprecedented scale, but the sacrifice was not futile. As Lincoln said at Gettysburg, "We here highly resolve that these dead shall not have died in vain."[2]

Southerners felt the same. After the First Battle of Manassas, Bishop Stephen Elliott of Georgia said, "God does not permit his creatures, especially those who are bound to him in the bond of the Christian covenant, to be slaughtered as they have been slaughtered in this war without meaning to produce effects adequate to the punishment. . . . What a terrible reckoning! It cannot be for nothing!"[3]

When Americans went to war, they often cited biblical images of blood sacrifice and martyrdom. They had done it during the Revolutionary War, as many Americans recalled. But the Civil War shocked them with sacrifice on a new level. This was the war of Shiloh, Antietam, and Gettysburg—the names still heavy with meaning because of the massive death tolls. Pickett's charge was a suicide mission, with thousands of Confederate soldiers advancing against heavy fire. Yet these men charged, even though they knew the odds. Religious faith was one among several factors that inspired this kind of selfless courage. James McPherson found a typical quotation from a Pennsylvania officer: "Sick as I am of this war and bloodshed . . . every day I have a more religious feeling, that this war is a crusade for the good of mankind."[4]

Words like "crusade," "holy war," and "sacred war" were used throughout the Civil War, although it's not always clear what people meant by these labels. Often Americans didn't distinguish between a holy war and a just war. Technically, just wars were secular wars that fit the criteria of just war theory—wars of self-defense fought against combatants, not civilians. But some just wars had deeper religious meaning, and Americans used terms like "sacred war" and even "crusade" to express that meaning. This "war is not only just, but is a nation's most sacred duty," said a minister from Massachusetts. For support he cited a text from the Old Testament, "The battle is not yours, but God's" (2 Chronicles 20:15).[5]

Whether they called it a just war, a sacred war, or a crusade, many Americans looked to the Bible for guidance. Through all the death and injury, endless debates over slavery, defenses of secession, and proclamations of patriotism, the Bible was a constant reference. The American Civil War may not have been "a war of religion," James McPherson wrote, but we should not forget "the degree to which it was a religious war." In similar way, the American Civil War was not primarily a war over the Bible, but for many Americans it was a biblical war.[6]

"The Scroll of God's Purposes"

In the Bible, Americans found evidence that wars had a providential purpose. "Wars affect the destinies of mankind and the progress of society," wrote D. S. Doggett in Richmond, Virginia. "Wars change the current of history. Wars are related to the propagation of the gospel. . . . Wars are disciplinary in their results." God used wars to shape history according to his will. God was mysterious; but wars revealed God's will, just as the Bible did. The Bible was not only a book of war—filled with heroic Davids and villainous Judases—but the Bible resembled war in another way: *both war and the Bible revealed God's providential plan to the world*. Going to war "is the most direct method of unrolling the scroll of God's purposes; of removing the veil by which He hides His eternal counsels," said Massachusetts minister J. E. Rankin in 1863.[7]

Note the imagery here: war unrolls "the scroll of God's purposes." Just as God revealed his will on the written scrolls that became the Bible, so also did God write his will on the scrolls of war. Perhaps the only way to know God's will, therefore, was to fight it out, Bible in hand, and see how the battles unfolded.

The Bible and war went together, and wars revealed some of the most crucial truths of the Bible, truths that often got lost in peacetime. "Times and seasons are profound interpreters of Scripture," said Reverend William Barrows in 1862, "and the hurrying and expository events of the present providences in our land are issuing monthly and almost daily volumes of commentaries" on the Bible.[8]

Every bullet fired in the war had a sacred purpose, many Americans believed. A Presbyterian minister in Harlem, New York, called the booming cannons of the Civil War the "pyrotechnics of Providence," all "pre-arranged by a superintending hand" and communicating a biblical message: "Righteousness exalteth a nation," and God's will reigns in heaven and earth (cf. Proverbs 14:34).[9]

War was a revealer of God's providence that only the Bible could decipher. In the Bible, Southern Methodist bishop George Pierce said, "We have a key to the dispensations of Providence, and need not greatly err in interpreting current events or in speculations as to the future."[10] His southern colleague Benjamin Palmer said, "All history is but an exposition of Providence, as Providence is the interpretation of history. They are the two poles of the same truth: Providence aside from history is a blind enigma—history apart from Providence is a senseless fable."[11]

As the war revealed, God willed victory for the Union and defeat for the Confederacy—so Americans delved into the Bible to determine its meaning. And there they found not just one meaning, but many competing meanings. Lincoln was right: "Both sides read the same Bible." But they read the same Bible in many ways. They read the Bible differently, in part, because they experienced the war differently, and their struggles with the war shaped how they read the war through scripture.

"A Revenger to Execute Wrath"

"War is hell," said William Tecumseh Sherman. Of all people, he would know, and no one who suffered through the Civil War disagreed with his assessment. Hell was a biblical reality, and so was war. For many Christians, however, war's violence was more in Satan's domain than Christ's. Reluctance to fight created problems in the field. Val C. Giles, who fought with the Fourth Texas Infantry, once "saw a fellow shooting straight up in the air and praying" rather than aiming his gun at the Yankees. When reprimanded by a superior officer, the man "paid no attention to him whatever." When "Captain Joe Billingsley threatened to cut him down with his sword if he didn't shoot at the enemy," the man responded, "You can kill me if you want to, but I am not going to appear before my God with the blood of my fellow man on my soul."[12] Most Christians of the day thought of themselves as a New Testament people, and Jesus taught his disciples to turn the other cheek when attacked, not to kill.

In motivating soldiers to fight, therefore, American Christians often turned to the Old Testament. They knew this was an important shift for them, however, and they marveled at it. "The thrilling events now transpiring in our country are adding fresh illustration and clearness to the teachings of the Old Testament," said abolitionist minister Levi L. Paine. The war changed "Christian devotion," he said—it thrust Americans back to the Old Testament, teaching them to "pray in good Old Testament fashion. They are ceasing to be Johns and are growing to be Davids."[13]

But that was not broadly true. "By the second half of the nineteenth century," historian Eran Shalev argues, "the Old Testament's influence on the American political imagination had dramatically diminished." Americans had turned to the New Testament.[14] My study of biblical citations during the Civil War supports Shalev's argument. As I noted in a previous chapter, the Bible of the American Revolution was more of an Old Testament Bible than the Bible of the Civil War. According to my calculations, fifteen of the twenty most-cited texts during the American Revolution were from the Old Testament (75 percent), while only of eight of the twenty most cited texts during the Civil War were from the Old Testament (40 percent).

When it came to motivating soldiers to fight—and justifying the violence of war—one of the strongest New Testament texts was Romans 13, which Americans cited to support militant patriotism and endorse violence in God's name. Threats and violence appear frequently in this text: Paul threatened with "damnation" anyone who "resisteth the power"; he said rulers were "a terror" to "evil"; rulers bear "the sword" with God's endorsement—they were "a revenger to execute wrath" on evildoers.

Romans 13 was popular because the turn to the Old Testament to justify violence only went so far. While it was fine for American Christians to draw from the Old Testament to inspire their soldiers to fight, they had to show that the Old Testament did not contradict the New Testament on this point. They had to justify violence from the New Testament as well as the old. As Methodist minister D. D. Buck said in 1863, many thought that "all the portions of the Bible that seem to justify war, must be sought for in the Old Testament." Yet the Union's war on the Confederacy "is not only *permitted* by the New Testament but *required*." This war was one of those situations that made "the infliction of revenge just as much a religious duty, as refraining from it at other times."[15]

Americans in the Civil War era found vengeance in the New Testament. In Romans 12, Paul warned, "Vengeance is mine, saith the Lord." But Paul followed up quickly in Romans 13, saying that the Lord gave rulers the authority to execute divine vengeance. Ministers noted the contrasts between Romans 12 and Romans 13, "the one *prohibiting* revenge; the other *providing* for it. The one *removing the right of revenge from man to God*, the other *restoring the right from God to man*. The one making revenge to be *sinful*; the other making it not only *rightful*, but *dutiful*."[16]

This was helpful because it called on the state to avenge its enemies in God's name. Whether it was killing one's enemies on the battlefield or punishing

John Wilkes Booth and his co-conspirators, revenge was not forbidden—it was commanded by God. Vermont minister A.W. Wild, preaching in 1864, said, "The magistrate . . . says the word of God, 'beareth not the sword in vain'; 'he is the minister of God, a revenger to execute wrath.' " so "The sword of the magistracy is to be wielded with a holy purpose."[17] Wartime was one of those times, William Barrows of Massachusetts said, "when compassion is out of place, when it is too expensive a luxury and cannot be indulged." Paraphrasing Paul, Barrows proclaimed, "We bear the sword under the appointment of God, and we must not bear it in vain."[18]

To what extent did revenge motivate Civil War soldiers? This is a question that has been the subject of some debate, with a recent historian denying that "revenge" was "a significant factor in explaining the behavior of most Civil War troops." James McPherson disagrees, citing various expressions of vengeance in soldiers' diaries and elsewhere. Confederates fumed about "thieving hordes of Lincoln," calling them the "lowest and most contemptible race upon the face of the earth." Some southerners wanted their children to learn, as one father put it, "a bitter and unrelenting hatred to the Yankee race" because they "invaded our country and devastated it," murdering "our best citizens." A Union soldier from East Tennessee expressed similar hatred for Confederates, saying that he would like to "draw their blood and mutilate their dead bodies and help send their souls to hell."[19] Mississippi cavalry private Edwin H. Fay wrote to his mother, "*We* will not live under Yankee domination for we will go to Brazil or some other South American country and live free from the accursed race. I shall never cease to hate them." Such expressions of hatred were common. After the defeat at Bull Run, Ellen Ewing Sherman, a devout Catholic and the wife of General William Tecumseh Sherman, expressed "loathing and hatred of the men that are desolating our country without cause." "For the first time in my life," she wrote, "I wish that I had a man's strength that I night use it against the traitors."[20]

Robert E. Lee sensed that the desire for revenge was a problem among Confederate soldiers. After Gettysburg, Lee announced, "Soldiers! We have sinned against Almighty God." The Confederate army had "cultivated a revengeful, haughty and boastful spirit." The army needed to pray for "a higher courage, a purer patriotism, and more determined will." The same tone was struck almost two months before Gettysburg in the *Biblical Recorder*, a Baptist newspaper printed in North Carolina, which warned southerners against "Hatred of our Enemies." "Blood-thirsty ferocity" was "unnecessary to the achievement of Southern independence." Southerners needed to remember Jesus's command that Christians must "love their enemies" (Matthew 5:44), just as they should remember Jesus's words on the cross, when he said of his tormenters, "Father, forgive them; for they know not what they do" (Luke 23:34). To hate one's enemies is not only wrong, it is bad strategy. How could the South hope to receive God's help in the war if they disobeyed his commands?[21]

Earlier in the war, many Americans insisted that vengeance was not an acceptable motivation. That changed as the war raged into 1864. "Vengeance came to play an ever more important role," said Drew Gilpin Faust, "joining principles of duty and self-defense in legitimating violence."[22] This drive for vengeance helps to explain why the Bible became a book of war, just as it helps to explain why Romans 13 became one of its most-read pages. Americans knew that it was wrong to seek personal revenge, just as it was wrong to hate, but they also knew that war bred both of these sinful impulses. Better, then, to purify the desire for vengeance by finding biblical warrants for it—shifting the call for vengeance from the individual to God.

"Of One Blood All Nations"

Most white Americans believed that the Bible supported white supremacy. "Nobody at the North, we think, would defend Slavery, even from the Bible, but for this color distinction," said Frederick Douglass before the war. "Color makes all the difference in the application of our American Christianity," Douglass continued. "To the whites it is full of love and tenderness. To the blacks it is full of hate and bitterness. The same Book which is full of the Gospel of Liberty to one race, is crowded with arguments in justification of the slavery of another."[23]

Biblical arguments in support of slavery, based on a literalist, common-sense view of scripture, were common sense mainly for whites. As many African Americans read the Bible, it opposed both slavery and racism—and it was not even a difficult argument to make. Scriptures abounded in opposition to both, including Paul's frequently cited assertion that God "hath made of one blood all nations of men for to dwell on all the face of the earth, and hath determined the times before appointed, and the bounds of their habitation" (Acts 17:26). This was one of the most-cited biblical verses in Civil War sermons and newspapers. Antislavery advocates found here an argument against racism and slavery—if all races shared the same blood, how could one enslave the other? Many associated this verse with the Declaration of Independence's statement that "all men are created equal," thereby making Paul and Thomas Jefferson speak in unison.[24]

Also pervasive was the golden rule, cited by Douglass and many others to expose as ridiculous any claim that scripture enforced slavery. The golden rule was hostile to slavery, in Douglass's view, because it demanded that one treat others as they wanted to be treated, and no one wanted to be enslaved. "There is not a man beneath the canopy of heaven that does not know that slavery is wrong for him," Douglass said. Did he really have "to argue that it is wrong to make men brutes, to rob them of their liberty, to work them without wages . . . to beat them with sticks, to flay their flesh with the lash . . . to sunder their families . . . ?" And did he really have to argue that God opposed slavery? If slavery is "inhuman," it "cannot be divine!"[25]

Frances E. W. Harper's "Bible Defense of Slavery" also dismissed any claim that the Bible approved slavery; to argue otherwise was blasphemy against the Word of God:

> Take sackcloth of the darkest dye,
> And shroud the pulpits round!
> Servants of Him that cannot lie,
> Sit mourning on the ground.
> Let holy horror blanch each cheek,
> Pale every brow with fears:
> And rocks and stones, if ye could speak,
> Ye well might melt to tears!

She chastised proslavery preachers—who sacrificed "truth" at "the shrine of Slavery." To enforce slavery, "the Word of life" had been forced to lie. Finally, she attacked the southern idea that slavery was a missionary effort, providentially approved to convert enslaved people to Christianity:

> Oh! When ye pray for heathen lands,
> And plead for their dark shores,
> Remember Slavery's cruel hands
> Make heathens at your doors![26]

Like Douglass, Harper dismissed any "common sense" arguments from the Bible in support of slavery. The overall spirit of scripture opposed slavery, which is why God had brought the war to punish the nation. "I am not un-easy about the result of this war," Harper said. "We may look upon it as God's controversy with the nation; His arising to plead by fire and blood the cause of His poor and needy people."[27]

"The Mission of the United States Republic"

War, as Jill Lepore has written, involves "wounds and words."[28] War requires both violence and interpretation—words to justify killing, words to cope with destruction, and words to make sense of victory and defeat. After the Civil War was over and the North had mourned a martyred president, Americans assessed the previous four years of destruction—not just counting the cost of war, but trying to see it in biblical and providential perspective.

One of the key moments of interpretation came on the Fourth of July 1865. Addressing a crowd in Augusta, Georgia, African American preacher James Lynch delivered a speech titled *The Mission of the United States Republic*. Lynch celebrated the heroes of the American Revolution and embraced the Declaration of Independence, specifically its declaration that "all men are created equal." "That is a gospel," he said, and "America's mission is to preach it" in pulpits as well as in Congress. The sin of the Confederacy was to attack this American gospel. The nation only emerged victorious after Lincoln's Emancipation Proclamation, when the nation "realized that Divine Providence had united the destiny of both races and God had made the de-liverance of the slave from bondage the *sine qua non* of the deliverance of the nation from the consuming fires of rebellion."[29]

According to Lynch, many whites said, "The colored man is too ignorant to vote," but then whites used to say African Americans were "too ignorant to fight," and yet the war proved that theory wrong. "Why hate the colored man? God made him—Jesus died for him—Heaven is prepared for him," Lynch said. "Slavery is the cause of prejudice, its virus has poisoned the feelings you have toward the colored race."[30]

Southerners had to see reality for what it was: God's purposes would be fulfilled, as they had been in the war. African Americans asked for justice from whites; whites could refuse, but not for long—"For there will be an army marshalled in the Heavens for our protection, and events will transpire by which the hand of Divine Providence will wring from you in wrath, that which should have been given in love."[31]

"The Nation's Second Birth"

In another Fourth of July speech, John Williamson Nevin called the Civil War the "Nation's Second Birth." A graduate of Princeton Theological Seminary and leading proponent of the Mercersburg theology, Nevin was critical of American evangelicalism. In his view of the war, however, Nevin shared the providential view of many others: The Civil War paralleled the Revolution—it was a new beginning for the nation. This Civil War, Nevin said, was "not simply of historical significance in the ordinary meaning of the term"; this war's "character is *world-historical.*"

Offering a variation on a famous quote from Jesus, Nevin said, "Render here unto Caesar . . . the things that are Caesar's, and to Satan the things that are Satan's, that we may be better able, through all, to render unto God with full faith the things also that are God's—whose province is to bring good out of evil, and to make all things work together gloriously for the accomplishment of His own infinitely excellent will."[32] Nevin believed in providence, but he did not believe God directly caused every event. Humans had free will, and they influenced events. And many of these human actions were evil—literally influenced by Satan. And yet Nevin also cited Paul's promise that "all things work together for good," which he paraphrased—despite evil human actions and free will, God made "all things work together gloriously for the accomplishment of His own infinitely excellent will" (cf. Romans 8:28). Evil intentions were real; but God brought good out of evil in the end, a classic teaching of Christian theology and theodicy.

In this Civil War, "Our national deliverance has been wrought out for us, as a world-historical act, by God himself, and," therefore, "it deserves . . . our most joyful confidence and trust." God's accomplishment in the war came through "the use of means," human effort, but it was a "mighty drama" that, in the end, "seemed to be the result of divine agency more than human." The war reunited the nation, making it stronger than ever.[33]

"Without Shedding of Blood, There Is No Remission"

War as sacrifice, war as redemption—these ideas circulated during the conflict, but even more so after the war. This interpretation made sense of the war in biblical perspective; it also made sense of the immense losses. In the

Civil War, "Men slaughtered each other with a zeal we still grope to comprehend," wrote Mark Schantz. "In ways that continue to startle even avid students, the sheer destructiveness of the Civil War worked profound transformations on American society." We fail to understand soldiers' willingness to die, Schantz argues, because we do not share their views of life and death. They acted within "a wider cultural world that sent them messages about death that made it easier to kill and to be killed." Death was not the end for them; heaven awaited for the faithful. Some say that today's American society is "a death-denying culture," but "we may say with greater certainty that nineteenth-century America was a death-embracing culture."[34]

Scripture was part of that. The Bible reinforced views of killing and dying that prepared America for the violence of the war. The Bible also helped to equip Americans to deal with catastrophic losses. The most cited biblical texts of the Civil War included Jesus's statement in a parable, "Well done, thou good and faithful servant," which Americans cited in honor of soldiers who had served faithfully to the death (Matthew 25:21). Heaven awaited them for their service, as it awaited Abraham Lincoln, said several ministers who cited this verse to console the nation after the assassination.[35] The book of Job, also, was popular, including "the LORD gave, and the LORD hath taken away; blessed be the name of the LORD," which recognized God's justice even in the face of devastating loss.

One of the most riveting assessments of death in the aftermath of the war came from Horace Bushnell's commencement speech at Yale, titled "Our Obligations to the Dead," specifically "the dead who have fallen in this gigantic and fearfully bloody war." Bushnell quoted from Hebrews, "Without shedding of blood, there is no remission" (Hebrews 9:22), a verse that expressed the value of sacrifice, a value Americans found throughout scripture during the Civil War. As Bushnell expressed it, "Without shedding of blood, there is almost nothing great in the world, or to be expected for it." War was essential to God's providence. "God could not plan a Peace-Society world, to live in the sweet amenities, and grow great and happy" without conflict. "There must be bleeding also," and "there must be heroes and heroic nationalities, and martyr testimonies." Here, then, was the value of the war's dead. They have accomplished "for us a work so precious"—"they have bled for us; and by this simple sacrifice of blood they have opened for us a new great chapter of life."[36]

In this sacrifice of death, the heroes of the Civil War reunited the Union and "sanctified" it. The fallen patriots of the Revolution started the work, but the states had not been truly unified. "We had not bled enough, as yet, to merge our colonial distinctions and make us a proper nation." After the Civil War, the nation "will be no more thought of as a mere human compact"; instead, "it will be that bond of common life which God has touched with blood; a sacredly heroic, Providentially tragic unity," in which "the sense of nationality becomes even a kind of religion."[37]

Bushnell spoke "of the new great history sanctified by this war, and the blood of its fearfully bloody sacrifices." This was God's way; "History cannot live on peace, but must feed itself on blood." Without bloodshed, "There is really nothing great enough in motive and action, taking the world as it is, to create a great people or story." "Nations can sufficiently live only as they find how to energetically die." The Civil War "is the grandest chapter, I think, of heroic fact, and tragic devotion, and spontaneous public sacrifice, that has ever been made in our world. The great epic story of Troy is but a song in comparison. There was never a better, and never so great a cause," Bushnell said.[38]

This view of national sacrifice redeemed the deaths so many Americans mourned in 1865. Even losses had been gains, indeed the greatest gains. "In these rivers of blood we have now bathed our institutions, and they are henceforth to be hallowed in our sight. Government is now become Providential,— no more a mere creature of our human will, but a grandly moral affair."[39]

Another minister, taking this verse from Hebrews—"Without shedding of blood, there is no remission"—agreed with Bushnell that the value of the war was sacrifice, but added that the nation's destiny was still in doubt. In Massachusetts, Baptist James T. Robinson asked, "What then is the meaning of this tremendous war; what is the value of this transcendent victory . . . ?" The war meant "Punishment, Retribution for National guilt . . . North and South." This war administered "the awful retributive vengeance of heaven," he said. He agreed with "the prophecy of Lincoln" in his Second Inaugural Address: God would match the blood drawn by the lash with blood drawn by the sword.[40]

Robinson compared the blood of American martyrs shed as the price for victory with the blood of Christ shed as the price of salvation. "There is no remission of sins, except by the shedding of blood [Hebrews 9:22]. Before all salvations there must be Calvary—the cruel spear, the vinegar, and the gall. . . . So with us. This terrible sacrifice must be made of the brave and noble, before the Genius of Liberty could burst the doors of that tomb," he said. "We must suffer. Blood must flow." Even now, only justice for African

Americans could save the nation, he said. The war should have taught the nation that "there is a God of Justice, and that the weakest black hand in the Carolinas uplifted in prayer to that God, may call down a power 'in the midst of which the iron hearts of your warriors shall be turned into ashes.'"[41]

Sacrifice was central to the Bible—Americans knew this in principle, but the Civil War thrust it into their consciousness. We misunderstand the Bible's role in the war—its pastoral role of comforting loss, and its patriotic role in inspiring patriotism—if we devalue the biblical images of sacrifice that surrounded the war.

"Atonement Is More Difficult Than Damnation"

Recalling again Jill Lepore's point—that war involves "wounds and words," violence and interpretation—naturally raises a question: Who gets to do the interpreting? Who has the authority to define a war's meaning? Normally, that might lead us to the cliché, "History is written by the victors." Not in the Civil War, however. The losers probably wrote as much as the winners about the war's meaning. After the war, many southerners denied they had fought to preserve slavery. Instead, they claimed, the war was about states' rights, honor, and other values. Yet many southerners stood by their conviction that slavery was God's providential plan to convert Africans to Christianity. "Slavery, as opening to us a missionary field of four millions of souls, to whom we were bound to preach the gospel, was an institution having moral and religious aspects of the most conspicuous and manifest importance," wrote John Adger, professor of church history at the Columbia Theological Seminary in South Carolina. "Slavery was to the Church, indeed, a sacred and solemn trust," and "God, in his providence, did commit this trust to the Southern Church."[42]

If slavery was providential, why did the Confederacy lose? That question was grounded in what some southerners saw as a mistaken notion, "that God must surely bless the right." Southern ministers who subscribed to that idea had not read their Bibles carefully, southern postwar interpreters argued, and had not remembered how God sometimes allowed "the righteous to be overthrown." This, they claimed, was what happened in the Civil War. Southern patriots had done their duty in fighting for a righteous cause, but they should have realized that "the result was with God alone," who "had not revealed his own plans or purposes." Now there was a great disappointment and disillusionment in the South among men and women. Many "have been tempted to doubts about the whole doctrine of divine providence."[43]

Yet southerners must overcome this temptation to disillusionment and doubt, Adger said. "We accept the failure of secession, as manifestly providential." The Confederacy's revolution was "a just cause," but God allowed northern victory in order to punish the South for its sins. This was the classic jeremiad—God punished the people God loved in order to correct them. "Yes! The hand of God, gracious though heavy, is upon the South for her discipline." Now the North should take heed, because if their victory in war taught northerners "pride and self-confidence" that inspired them to treat the South severely, they would soon suffer the same fate. Make no mistake, "It is not true that the South is ashamed of the war, or penitent for her noble, though unavailing, defense of constitutional liberty." This interpretation expanded after the war, as southerners celebrated their Confederate heroes, and their sacred honor and culture, as a "Lost Cause." In their view, they were still God's chosen nation.[44]

Much of this was typical language of the jeremiad, and southerners combined it with biblical attacks on northern patriotism, calling it idolatrous—not just at the end of the war, but throughout the conflict. One of the most scathing biblical assessments came from southerner Calvin Wiley, an attorney and the superintendent of public schools in North Carolina. In 1863, he published *Scriptural Views of National Trials: Or the True Road to Independence and Peace of the Confederate States of America*, a 213-page book filled with hundreds of biblical citations. Wiley was no stranger to publishing. He had worked was a newspaper editor and had published an attack on Harriet Beecher Stowe's *Uncle Tom's Cabin* in 1852.[45] His goal was to defend the Confederate States against northern aggression in "one of the most bloody and terrible wars known in the history of the human race." There was no way to understand this war by looking at battles, soldiers, officers, and presidents. Those were external actors in the war, but God controlled all through his providence. God is "the Author of the Drama of Life" and controls "the casting of the plot and arrangement of the actors." God worked through war, as in scripture, and "God does not permit revolutions to happen without a moral purpose"—they "are the voice of the Almighty, pursuing His certain plans." Wiley drew on Job—"Affliction cometh not forth of the dust, neither doth trouble spring out of the Ground"—all afflictions had a providential meaning and purpose (Job 5:6).[46]

Americans needed to admit that "all wars are God's wars: that this revolution is His work . . . and that this wicked enemy whom we abhor, is His
sword." The war was God's judgment on North *and* South. Most critically,
Americans had grown arrogant, believing "the United States are the hope of
the World"—an "infidel idea" that had "penetrated the hearts of the people."
The nation had embraced a perverse idea of itself, a form of self-worship.
"American history was a great Pantheistic Temple where incense was daily
burned at a thousand idol shrines—the American idea was a grand falsehood," Wiley argued. America deceived itself in its arrogance, gave glory
to itself instead of to God, and God had struck down the nation's pride in
return.[47]

Northern pride would therefore come before a northern fall—a point
driven home by southerners, especially after the war. This message fell on
deaf ears for many in the North as they celebrated victory and demonized
the South. But others looked for a deeper meaning to the war that would
value all the war's sacrifices, even those of the Confederacy. This was a point
of a thanksgiving discourse by F. R. Abbe, delivered on December 7, 1865, in
Massachusetts. "The glory of the noblest things is in their crosses," he said.
"Costless patriotism is as worthless as costless piety." All of the sacrifices of
the war would be redemptive—all have "been needed . . . from the blood of
our dear, good President, to the blood of the most unknown in rebel graves.
And even the sacrifices of the South," which, "though made in the interests of
crime, by the good providence of God have been used and will be used, like
plowshares of vengeance and mercy, to root out infernal wrongs and plant
better things in a glorious land" (cf. Isaiah 2:4). "Atonement is more difficult than damnation," he said. Atonement was what the nation needed, even
though this was the harder work. Atonement required wisdom, which was
the point of his discourse. His scripture was also his title: "Wisdom Better
Than Weapons of War" (Ecclesiastes 9:18). "There will be much to reap from
these bloody fields" he said, "but the richest harvest will be wisdom. Courage,
patriotism, glory, prosperity, freedom have grown rank in soil so fertilized
with death; but wisdom overtops them all."[48]

"Both Read the Same Bible"

When Lincoln said both North and South "read the same Bible," he was probably more accurate than he knew—both sides did read the same Bible, and

often read the same biblical texts, and for both sides the Bible was their most sacred authority. Reared on the Revolution, Americans in the North and the South saw the United States as a biblical nation, and the Bible as the nation's book.[49] For the most part, both sides opposed pacifism, and viewed the Bible as a book of war—filled not only with military warfare, but spiritual warfare as well. The Bible was a narrative of good versus evil, and that conflict was a war, sometimes on literal battlefields, sometimes in an apocalyptic Armageddon at the end of time, and sometimes in the struggles within each soul. Both sides believed in a patriotic Bible—God's word preached civic virtue against vice and freedom against tyranny, although they disagreed radically on the limits and nature of freedom. Above all, both sides believed that the Bible valued sacrifice, courage, and loyalty—from Abraham's willingness to sacrifice Isaac, to Jesus's sacrifice on the cross, to the courage of faithful martyrs in the book of Revelation.

Americans drew much of this from the Bible of the American Revolution, but they spoke even more of biblical sacrifice in the Civil War because that war brought so much more violence into their lives. So much more blood was shed, which demanded more justification and consolation from scripture. In the Civil War, the Bible served the urgent demands of death. There was more pain, more despair, and more defeat. The Bible was the balm for these wounds. The sacrifices of the Civil War became sacred when viewed through a biblical lens, as did patriotism (North and South). The Civil War intensified and expanded civil religion in the United States, as historians have shown, and this could not have occurred without the thousands of biblical texts that surrounded the war.

"Both sides read the same Bible"—again Lincoln's short remark said much. In the Civil War, the national vision of a patriotic Bible was in crisis—both the Union and the Confederacy claimed loyalty to scripture, but they enlisted it to kill each other. America's patriotic Bible had grown divided and, therefore, faced unprecedented challenges. Never had Americans seen so much disagreement over scripture on a national scale. If the Bible was, as Phoebe Palmer said, "a wonderfully simple book," then why the war?[50] Not only did the Bible fail to prevent the war, both sides enlisted the Bible's support, believing their side was in the right, so the divisions themselves became sacred and the Bible intensified the war. The Civil War saw biblical patriotism at its height, but the war also strained the limits of the Bible's political relevance for some Americans. Much of the damage to America's Bible was done in the debates over slavery, which introduced Americans to questions about the Bible's authority and its historical validity well before most of them had heard of higher criticism or the theory of evolution.[51] Did the martial use of scripture in wartime fade after the Civil War? Perhaps, but not for all and not only because of the war. The Bible remained as a source of analogies and symbols that continue to reappear in times of crisis, especially wartime.

The Americans who fought and endured the Civil War brought with them a bewildering array of agendas and experiences. They were men, women, and children; they were northern, southern, black, white, Catholic, Protestant, Jewish, Mormon, and more. Yet, as George Rable wrote, few among them doubted God's role in "the causes, course, and consequences" of the war. And few among them doubted that the Bible was their best source for knowing the war's place in God's providential design. The Bible was a constant in the Civil War, but it was also constantly debated, its meaning shifting with each interpreter in response to every crisis. Americans were never in more disagreement over the Bible, and yet never more in agreement that the Bible proved the sacredness of war.[52]

Biblical Citations in the Civil War Era

Abraham Lincoln was correct that both North and South "read the same Bible," but which parts of the Bible did they read most often? This book examines this question in part by revealing data on biblical citations in the Civil War era, including the secession crisis, the war, and its aftermath (1860–1865). As in my previous book, *Sacred Scripture, Sacred War: The Bible and the American Revolution*,[1] I based much of this work on databases of biblical citations, uncovering the Bible's presence in a selection of various sources, including sermons, newspapers, diaries, tracts, letters, and slave narratives.

I was able to locate thousands of biblical citations in these sources with the invaluable technical assistance of Lincoln Mullen, a historian and expert in digital humanities. Mullen uses the methods of machine learning (based on the R programming language) to search documents for biblical citations. During my research on the Civil War, I converted my collection of sources to text files, sent them to Mullen, and he scanned them with his application. To assess data on newspapers, I have used Mullen's *America's Public Bible: Biblical Quotations in U.S. Newspapers*, soon to be published as a digital project with Stanford University Press. This massive database "uncovers the presence of biblical quotations in . . . nearly 11 million newspaper pages" from the nineteenth century.[2] In this book, therefore, I have used data from this newspaper project, combined with data from my sources (including sermons, diaries, tracts, letters, and slave narratives), all totaling thousands of biblical citations from over two thousand sources.

I have organized the data into three tables, listing most-cited texts in the Confederacy, the Union, and combined. Each table has three columns: the first lists the biblical reference (e.g., Romans 8:28), the second lists the number of sources (e.g., sermons, newspaper articles) that cite that verse, and the third column is the text of the verse (e.g., "And we know that all things work together for good to them that love God"). Although I have attempted to be as comprehensive as possible, I have filtered out citations from newspapers that, as far as I could tell, were not often cited in the context of the war. For example, "Suffer little children to come unto me" (Luke 18:16), was all about death but had little to do with the Civil War. Newspapers often printed it with notices of children who had died.[3] I have included other verses, such as Job 1:21, which were often cited in direct connection with the war, but not always—they sometimes appeared in other contexts, including obituaries for people who did not serve in the war. Overall, the Union citations far outnumbered the Confederate citations mainly because the population in the North was much higher, and a larger population produced more newspapers, sermons, and other sources.

Some of these verses listed in these tables were often cited but rarely discussed. Others received extensive attention and became central to major disagreements and debates, and I have focused mostly on these texts in the book. Together, these rankings of often-cited verses provide an unprecedented perspective on the biblical context of the American Civil War.

Table A.1 The Confederate Bible

Reference	Texts Cited in	KJV
Job 1:21	63	Naked came I out of my mother's womb, and naked shall I return thither: the Lord gave, and the Lord hath taken away; blessed be the name of the Lord.
Matthew 25:21, 25:23	48	Well done, thou good and faithful servant: thou hast been faithful over a few things, I will make thee ruler over many things: enter thou into the joy of thy lord.
Romans 8:28	41	And we know that all things work together for good to them that love God, to them who are the called according to his purpose.
Job 3:17	38	There the wicked cease from troubling; and there the weary be at rest.
Genesis 13:9	36	Is not the whole land before thee? separate thyself, I pray thee, from me: if thou wilt take the left hand, then I will go to the right; or if thou depart to the right hand, then I will go to the left.
Psalms 46:7	34	The Lord of hosts is with us; the God of Jacob is our refuge.
Ruth 1:16	32	And Ruth said, Intreat me not to leave thee, or to return from following after thee: for whither thou goest, I will go; and where thou lodgest, I will lodge: thy people shall be my people, and thy God my God:
2 Corinthians 5:1	32	For we know that if our earthly house of this tabernacle were dissolved, we have a building of God, an house not made with hands, eternal in the heavens.
Psalms 46:1	31	God is our refuge and strength, a very present help in trouble.
Romans 8:31	30	What shall we then say to these things? If God be for us, who can be against us?

Note: Biblical citations in the South (1860–1865), ranked by number of documents that include the verses listed. Documents include sermons, newspaper articles, journals, and slave narratives.

Table A.2 The Union Bible

Reference	Texts Cited in	Verse (KJV)
Acts 17:26	231	And hath made of one blood all nations of men for to dwell on all the face of the earth, and hath determined the times before appointed, and the bounds of their habitation
Isaiah 58:6	134	Is not this the fast that I have chosen? to loose the bands of wickedness, to undo the heavy burdens, and to let the oppressed go free, and that ye break every yoke?
Leviticus 25:10	133	And ye shall hallow the fiftieth year, and proclaim liberty throughout all the land unto all the inhabitants thereof: it shall be a jubilee unto you; and ye shall return every man unto his possession, and ye shall return every man unto his family.
Matthew 25:21, 25:23	132	Well done, thou good and faithful servant: thou hast been faithful over a few things, I will make thee ruler over many things: enter thou into the joy of thy lord.
Matthew 7:12	131	Therefore all things whatsoever ye would that men should do to you, do ye even so to them: for this is the law and the prophets.
Romans 13:2	120	Whosoever therefore resisteth the power, resisteth the ordinance of God: and they that resist shall receive to themselves damnation.
Jeremiah 8:11	120	For they have healed the hurt of the daughter of my people slightly, saying, Peace, peace; when there is no peace.
Romans 13:1	111	Let every soul be subject unto the higher powers. For there is no power but of God: the powers that be are ordained of God.
Matthew 25:40	103	And the King shall answer and say unto them, Verily I say unto you, Inasmuch as ye have done it unto one of the least of these my brethren, ye have done it unto me.
Romans 13:4	98	For he is the minister of God to thee for good. But if thou do that which is evil, be afraid; for he beareth not the sword in vain: for he is the minister of God, a revenger to execute wrath upon him that doeth evil.

Table A.3 Biblical Citations during the American Civil War Era: Union and Confederacy

Reference	Texts Cited in	Verse (KJV)
Acts 17:26	244	And hath made of one blood all nations of men for to dwell on all the face of the earth, and hath determined the times before appointed, and the bounds of their habitation
Matthew 25:21, 25:23	180	His lord said unto him, Well done, thou good and faithful servant: thou hast been faithful over a few things, I will make thee ruler over many things: enter thou into the joy of thy lord.
Matthew 7:12	145	Therefore all things whatsoever ye would that men should do to you, do ye even so to them: for this is the law and the prophets.
Jeremiah 8:11	144	For they have healed the hurt of the daughter of my people slightly, saying, Peace, peace; when there is no peace.
Isaiah 58:6	143	Is not this the fast that I have chosen? to loose the bands of wickedness, to undo the heavy burdens, and to let the oppressed go free, and that ye break every yoke?
Leviticus 25:10	137	And ye shall hallow the fiftieth year, and proclaim liberty throughout all the land unto all the inhabitants thereof: it shall be a jubilee unto you; and ye shall return every man unto his possession, and ye shall return every man unto his family.
Romans 13:1	126	Let every soul be subject unto the higher powers. For there is no power but of God: the powers that be are ordained of God.
Job 1:21	125	And said, Naked came I out of my mother's womb, and naked shall I return thither: the LORD gave, and the LORD hath taken away; blessed be the name of the LORD.
Romans 13:2	123	Whosoever therefore resisteth the power, resisteth the ordinance of God: and they that resist shall receive to themselves damnation.
Proverbs 14:34	118	Righteousness exalteth a nation: but sin is a reproach to any people.
Matthew 25:40	117	And the King shall answer and say unto them, Verily I say unto you, Inasmuch as ye have done it unto one of the least of these my brethren, ye have done it unto me.
Luke 2:14	115	Glory to God in the highest, and on earth peace, good will toward men.

Table A.3 *Continued*

Reference	Texts Cited in	Verse (KJV)
Romans 13:4	104	For he is the minister of God to thee for good. But if thou do that which is evil, be afraid; for he beareth not the sword in vain: for he is the minister of God, a revenger to execute wrath upon him that doeth evil.
Romans 8:28	101	And we know that all things work together for good to them that love God, to them who are the called according to his purpose.
Luke 23:34	96	Then said Jesus, Father, forgive them; for they know not what they do. And they parted his raiment, and cast lots.
Job 3:17	96	There the wicked cease from troubling; and there the weary be at rest.

Abbreviated Titles

Accessible Archives	https://www.accessible-archives.com
CA	*Chronicling America: Historic American Newspapers*, Library of Congress. https://chroniclingamerica.loc.gov/
Douglass, *FDP*	Frederick Douglass. *The Frederick Douglass Papers. Series One: Speeches, Debates, and Interviews.* Edited by John W. Blassingame. New Haven: Yale University Press, 1979.
Lincoln, *Works*	Abraham Lincoln. *The Collected Works of Abraham Lincoln.* 9 vols. Edited by Roy P. Basler. New Brunswick, NJ: Rutgers University Press, 1953. https://quod.lib.umich.edu/l/lincoln/
19th Century US Newspapers	19th Century US Newspapers, https://www.gale.com/c/nineteenth-century-us-newspapers
OECW	William L. Barney. *The Oxford Encyclopedia of the Civil War.* New York: Oxford University Press, 2011.
RACW	Robert R. Mathisen, editor. *The Routledge Sourcebook of Religion and the American Civil War: A History in Documents.* New York: Routledge, 2015.

Notes

Introduction

1. Abraham Lincoln, "Second Inaugural Address," in *God's New Israel: Religious Interpretations of American Destiny*, ed. Conrad Cherry (Chapel Hill: University of North Carolina Press, 1998), 202.
2. Frederick Douglass, *The Life and Times of Frederick Douglass: From 1817–1882* (London: Christian Age Office, 1882), 318. See also Ronald C. White Jr., "Lincoln's Sermon on the Mount: The Second Inaugural," in *Religion and the American Civil War*, ed. Randall M. Miller, Harry S. Stout, and Charles Reagan Wilson (New York: Oxford University Press, 1998), 223.
3. Given the overwhelmingly Christian context of the United States in the 1860s, I often use the term "Old Testament" instead of "Hebrew Bible."
4. "During the generation that culminated in the Civil War," Mark Noll observed, "no society on earth was as preoccupied with Scripture as the United States." Mark A. Noll, *America's God: From Jonathan Edwards to Abraham Lincoln* (New York: Oxford University Press, 2002), 16. As Paul Gutjahr wrote, "The Bible [was] the most imported, most printed, most distributed, and most read written text in North America up through the nineteenth century." Paul C. Gutjahr, *An American Bible: A History of the Good Book in the United States, 1777–1880* (Stanford: Stanford University Press, 2002), 1.
5. B. H. Nadal, *A Christian Nation's Ordeal: A Fast-Day Sermon* (Washington, DC: M'Gill & Witherow, 1864), 7.
6. Mark A. Noll, *The Civil War as a Theological Crisis* (Chapel Hill: University of North Carolina Press, 2006), 14. Henceforth abbreviated *CWTC*.
7. George C. Rable, *God's Almost Chosen Peoples: A Religious History of the American Civil War* (Chapel Hill: University of North Carolina Press, 2010), 18–19. Rable's excellent book is the best and the most comprehensive religious history of the Civil War. In addition, I have learned much from the groundbreaking book by James H. Moorhead, *American Apocalypse: Yankee Protestants and the Civil War, 1860–1869* (New Haven, CT: Yale University Press, 1978). Also essential is the excellent and comprehensive work of David B. Chesebrough, especially *"God Ordained This War": Sermons on the Sectional Crisis, 1830–1865* (Columbia: University of South Carolina Press, 1991); David B. Chesebrough, *No Sorrow Like Our Sorrow: Northern Protestant Ministers and the Assassination of Lincoln* (Kent, Ohio: Kent State University Press, 1994); and David B. Chesebrough, *Clergy Dissent in the Old South, 1830–1865* (Carbondale: Southern Illinois University Press, 1996).

8. Drew Gilpin Faust, *This Republic of Suffering: Death and the American Civil War* (New York: Alfred A. Knopf, 2008), 172.

9. James McPherson, "Afterword," in Miller, Stout, and Wilson, *Religion and the American Civil War*, 409. See also James M. McPherson, *For Cause and Comrades: Why Men Fought in the Civil War* (New York: Oxford University Press, 1997), Kindle edition, especially chapter 5, "Religion Is What Makes Brave Soldiers." Note that pagination in Kindle editions often differs slightly from print versions. Drew Gilpin Faust, "Christian Soldiers: The Meaning of Revivalism in the Confederate Army," *Journal of Southern History* 53, no. 1 (February 1987): 64; Robert J. Miller, *Both Prayed to the Same God: Religion and Faith in the American Civil War* (Lanham, MD: Lexington Books, 2007), 41; and Timothy L. Wesley, *The Politics of Faith during the Civil War* (Baton Rouge: Louisiana State University Press, 2013), 11.

10. On death and destruction in the Civil War, see Mark S. Schantz, *Awaiting the Heavenly Country: The Civil War and America's Culture of Death* (Ithaca, NY: Cornell University Press, 2008) and Faust, *This Republic of Suffering*. See also James M. McPherson, *The War That Forged a Nation: Why the Civil War Still Matters* (New York: Oxford University Press, 2015), Kindle edition, 1–2; J. David Hacker, "A Census-Based Count of the Civil War Dead," *Civil War History* 57, no. 4 (December 2011): 307–48.

11. Sherman quoted in McPherson, *The War That Forged*, 32; William Meade, *Address on the Day of Fasting and Prayer, Appointed by the President of the Confederate States, June 13, 1861* (Richmond: Enquirer Book and Job Press, 1861), 6. I have edited some of the longer titles of primary sources, especially sermons.

12. According to Mark Noll, the Bible "was, without a rival, the most widely read text of any kind in the whole country." Noll, *CWTC*, 4. Corwin E. Smidt wrote that the Bible "likely serves as the text that has most fully shaped American culture." Corwin E. Smidt, "The Continuing Distinctive Role of the Bible in American Lives: A Comparative Analysis," in *The Bible in American Life*, ed. Philip Goff, Arthur E. Farnsley II, and Peter Thuesen (New York: Oxford University Press, 2017), 203.

13. Eran Shalev, *American Zion: The Old Testament as a Political Text from the Revolution to the Civil War* (New Haven, CT: Yale University Press, 2013), 5–6. On biblical authority in modernity, see Michael Legaspi, *The Death of Scripture and the Rise of Biblical Studies* (New York: Oxford University Press, 2010).

14. Frances Ellen Watkins Harper, "Bible Defense of Slavery," in *Poems on Miscellaneous Subjects* (Philadelphia: Merrihew & Thompson, 1857), 8–9.

15. On Douglass's use of the jeremiad, see David W. Blight, *Frederick Douglass: Prophet of Freedom* (New York: Simon & Schuster, 2018), 157. On the jeremiad in American history, see Sacvan Bercovitch, *The American Jeremiad* (Madison: University of Wisconsin Press, 1978); Andrew R. Murphy, *Prodigal Nation: Moral Decline and Divine Punishment from New England to 9/11* (New York: Oxford University Press, 2009); Perry Miller, *The New England Mind: From Colony to Province* (Cambridge, MA: Belknap Press of Harvard University Press, 1983), 27–39; Harry S. Stout, *The New England Soul: Preaching and Religious Culture in Colonial New England* (New York: Oxford University Press, 1986), 62–63, 75–76. Stout's *New England Soul*

remains the definitive work on preaching in the colonial era and has greatly informed my approach to sermons and their contexts.

16. Nathan O. Hatch, "Sola Scriptura and Novus Ordo Seclorum," in *The Bible in America: Essays in Cultural History*, ed. Nathan O. Hatch and Mark A. Noll (New York: Oxford University Press, 1982), 59–78; Noll, *America's God*, 367–85. See also James P. Byrd, "The New World of North America and Canada and the Globalization of Critical Biblical Scholarship," in *Hebrew Bible / Old Testament, vol. 3: From Modernism to Post-modernism. Part I: The Nineteenth Century—a Century of Modernism and Historicism*, ed. Magne Sæbø (Bristol, CT: Vandenhoeck & Ruprecht, 2012), 175.

17. Phoebe Palmer, "Witness of the Spirit," *Guide to Holiness* 47 (June 1865): 137, as quoted in Noll, *CWTC*, 20.

18. Paul Harvey, "The Bible in the Civil War," in *The Oxford Handbook of the Bible in America*, ed. Paul Gutjahr (New York: Oxford University Press, 2017), 358. As Mark Noll observed, "Hans Frei's description of earlier Bible reading as 'strongly realistic, i.e., at once literal and historical,' remained true for most Americans far into the nineteenth century." *America's God*, 371. See Hans W. Frei, *The Eclipse of Biblical Narrative: A Study in Eighteenth and Nineteenth Century Hermeneutics* (New Haven, CT: Yale University Press, 1974), 1. For an outstanding assessment of Frei's analysis as it applies to the United States in the nineteenth century, see Peter J. Thuesen, *In Discordance with the Scriptures: American Protestant Battles over Translating the Bible* (New York: Oxford University Press, 1999), 6–11. The transitions in biblical authority, both theological and cultural, through the latter eighteenth and early nineteenth centuries are well analyzed in Jonathan Sheehan, *The Enlightenment Bible: Translation, Scholarship, Culture* (Princeton, NJ: Princeton University Press, 2005). See also Robert E. Brown, "Navigating the Loss of Interpretive Innocence: Reading the 'Enlightenment' Bible in Early Modern America," in Goff, Farnsley, and Thuesen, *Bible in American Life*, 63–68. For an excellent overview of Bible debates over slavery, see E. Brooks Holifield, *Theology in America: Christian Thought from the Age of the Puritans to the Civil War* (New Haven, CT: Yale University Press, 2003), 494–97; James P. Byrd, *Sacred Scripture, Sacred War: The Bible and the American Revolution* (New York: Oxford University Press, 2013), 7–8, 176 n. 19.

19. Mark Noll argued that "Bible was not so much the truth above all truth as it was the story above all stories. . . . That is, ministers preached as if the stories of Scripture were being repeated, or could be repeated in the unfolding life of the United States." Mark A. Noll, "The Image of the United States as a Biblical Nation, 1776–1865," in Hatch and Noll, *Bible in America*, 43. See, for example, Henry Ward Beecher, *Patriotic Addresses in America and England from 1850 to 1885, on Slavery, the Civil War, and the Development of Civil Liberty in the United States*, ed. John R. Howard (New York: Fords, Howard and Hulbert, 1887), 342–43.

20. See Exodus 20:13; Matthew 5:38–43.

21. See Joseph R. Fornieri, *Abraham Lincoln's Political Faith* (DeKalb: Northern Illinois University Press, 2005), 37–38.

22. Nicholas Guyatt, *Providence and the Invention of the United States, 1607–1876* (New York: Cambridge University Press, 2007), 6.

23. Charles Pettit McIlvaine, *Pastoral Letter of the Bishops of the Protestant Episcopal Church in the United States of America* (New York: Baker & Godwin, 1862), 4–5.

24. Charles Hodge, *President Lincoln. From the Princeton Review, July 1865* (Philadelphia: Philadelphia, P. Walker, 1865), 435–36; Noll, *CWTC*, 83.

25. William Barrows, *Honor to the Brave* (Boston: John M. Whittemore & Co., 1863), 5–7.

26. Quoted in Rable, *God's Almost Chosen Peoples*, 356.

27. William T. Brantly, *Our National Troubles* (Philadelphia: T. B. Peterson & Brothers, 1860), 17–18.

28. Thomas Smyth, *The Battle of Fort Sumter: Its Mystery and Miracle* (Columbia, SC: Southern Guardian Steam-Power Press, 1861), 19.

29. Rable, *God's Almost Chosen Peoples*, 3.

30. McPherson, *For Cause and Comrades*, 1, 3, 11; see also chapter 5, "Religion Is What Makes Brave Soldiers."

31. D. C. Sterry, *A Sermon in Memory of the Heroic Dead, Who Have Fallen in the Battles of Freedom* ([Lake City]: [Weekly times], 1862), 2.

32. J. W. Tucker, *God's Providence in War* (Fayetteville [NC]: Presbyterian Office, 1862), 10–11.

33. Elizabeth R. Baer, ed., *Shadows on My Heart: The Civil War Diary of Lucy Rebecca Buck of Virginia* (Athens: University of Georgia Press, 1997), 16.

34. Faust, *This Republic of Suffering*, xi–xii. As stunning as these statistics are, the Civil War death toll was even worse. Historians have increased the casualty estimates since Faust's book was published, from 620,000 to at least 750,000.

35. Faust, *This Republic of Suffering*, 39–41.

36. Faust, *This Republic of Suffering*, 6, 62–63 and overall chapter 3, "Burying." On Lincoln exhuming his son's coffin, see David Goldfield, *America Aflame: How the Civil War Created a Nation* (New York: Bloomsbury, 2012), 240–41; George B. Bacon, *A Plea for the Sacredness of Human Life. A Sermon Preached at Orange, New Jersey, January 8th, 1865* (New York: John F. Trow, printer, 1865).

37. Orestes A. Brownson, *The Works of Orestes A. Brownson*, vol. 17 (New York: AMC Press, 1966), 214. See also Faust, *This Republic of Suffering*, 32. Many worried about the disconnect between Christianity, especially ministry, and violence. In an unprinted letter, Leila Callaway of Georgia wrote to her husband, a Methodist minister, "I am greatly delighted to hear that there is a probability of your being Chaplain. I do believe that it would kill me to know that you were fighting." Leila Callaway to Morgan Callaway, April, 1962, Morgan Callaway Papers, 1831–1899, Stuart A. Rose Library, Emory University.

38. Faust, *This Republic of Suffering*, 32.

39. Examples include a tract first published in 1863: John M. Brenneman, *Christianity and War* (Elkhart, IN: John F. Funk, 1868). For more see James O. Lehman and Steven M. Nolt, *Mennonites, Amish, and the American Civil War* (Baltimore: Johns Hopkins University Press, 2011).

40. As quoted in McPherson, *For Cause and Comrades*, 69–72, emphasis in source. This emphasis on a suffering Jesus fit with Catholic devotions of the time. Noll, CWTC, 131; John T. McGreevy, *Catholicism and American Freedom: A History* (New York: Norton, 2003), 28.

41. Phoebe Yates Pember, as quoted in Robert N. Rosen, *The Jewish Confederates* (Columbia: University of South Carolina Press, 2000), 300; Rable, *God's Almost Chosen Peoples*, 164. See William M. Daily, *The Great Rebellion, a Discourse* ([Madison, IN]: [s.n.], 1862), 2.

42. Joseph A. Seiss, *The Assassinated President* (Philadelphia: [s.n.], 1865), 11.

43. John F. W. Ware, *Manhood, the Want of the Day* (Boston: Leonard C. Bowles, 1863), 3–4.

44. Rable, *God's Almost Chosen Peoples*, 1.

45. John H. Caldwell, *Slavery and Southern Methodism* ([Newman, GA?]: Printed for the author, 1865), 49.

46. Leila Callaway to Morgan Callaway, April 1862, in the Morgan Callaway Papers, 1831–1899, Stuart A. Rose Library, Emory University.

47. Richard Johnson, "Letter to William, March 6, 1862," Johnson Family Papers, South Carolina Historical Society, Charleston, South Carolina. Johnson may have intended this sentence as a question, but I have quoted it as written.

48. Jill Lepore, *The Name of War: King Philip's War and the Origins of American Identity*, vol. 1 (New York: Knopf, 1998), x; Byrd, *Sacred Scripture, Sacred War*, 20; Rable, *God's Almost Chosen Peoples*, 5; Wesley, *Politics of Faith*, 11.

49. Harry S. Stout, *Upon the Altar of the Nation: A Moral History of the American Civil War* (New York: Viking, 2006), 48, 475 n. 5.

50. James H. Otey, "Sermon on Exodus 17:11–12," James Hervey Otey Papers, 1823–1885, Collection no. 00563, Southern Historical Collection at the Louis Round Wilson Special Collections Library, University of North Carolina at Chapel Hill. Otey preached this sermon twice in 1862: November 9 and December 14.

51. Kenneth Moore Startup, *The Root of All Evil: The Protestant Clergy and the Economic Mind of the Old South* (Athens: University of Georgia Press, 1997), 4–5. On sermon analysis in the nineteenth century, see David B. Chesebrough and Lawrence W. McBride, "Sermons as Historical Documents: Henry Ward Beecher and the Civil War," *History Teacher* 23, no. 3 (1990): 275–91.

52. Sarah Morgan Dawson, *The Civil War Diary of Sarah Morgan*, ed. Charles East (Athens: University of Georgia Press, 1991), 269.

53. Emma Holmes, *Diary of Miss Emma Holmes, 1861–1866*, ed. John F. Marszalek (Baton Rouge: LSU Press, 1994), 57, 111, 127.

54. We find evidence for preaching's influence in the number of people who blamed ministers for inciting the war. William G. "Parson" Brownlow, Methodist minister and editor of the *Knoxville Whig* in Tennessee, defended slavery as biblical but sided with the Union. He stated in 1862, "Here, as in all parts of the South, the worst class of men are preachers. They have done more to bring about the deplorable state of things existing in the country than any other class of men." Quoted in Chesebrough, *Clergy Dissent*, 55. See also Chesebrough, chapter 1.

55. Shalev, *American Zion*, 151, also discussed in chapter 5; A. L. Stone, *Emancipation* (Boston: Henry Hoyt, 1862), 4.

56. Shalev, *American Zion*, 2–3, 8. See also Philip Gorski, *American Covenant: A History of Civil Religion from the Puritans to the Present* (Princeton, NJ: Princeton University Press, 2017), chaps. 2–3.

57. McPherson, *The War That Forged*, 9.

58. See "The Star-Spangled Banner, and the Duty of Colored Americans to that Flag," *Christian Recorder*, April 27, 1861, Accessible Archives. See also Stout, *Altar of the Nation*, 26; Linus Parker, "Fast day sermon, Joel 2:12, November 15, 1861," in Linus Parker Papers, 1853–1886, Manuscript Collection no. 091, Pitts Theology Library, Emory University.

59. George Duffield Jr., *Courage in a Good Cause* ([Philadelphia]: T. B. Pugh, 1861), 8. The Revolutionary War sermon cited was Robert Cooper, *Courage in a Good Cause, or The Lawful and Courageous Use of the Sword* (Lancaster: Francis Bailey, 1775). For a similar view of the Revolution's importance see E[dward] S[umner] Atwood, *The Purse, the Knapsack and the Sword* (Boston: Bazin & Chandler, 1861), 20–21. Bishop William Meade said, "Many sermons preached in behalf of the Revolution have been placed in my hands." William Meade, *Sermon Preached by Bishop Meade at the Opening of the Convention* (Richmond: Charles H. Wynne, 1861), 23.

60. Noll, *CWTC*, 8.

61. *The Lincoln Catechism Wherein the Eccentricities & Beauties of Despotism Are Fully Set Forth.: A Guide to the Presidential Election of 1864* ([New York]: J.F. Feeks, 1864), 12.

62. James C. Furman, Thos. S. Arthur, Wm. H. Campbell, and Wm. M. Thomas, "Letter to the Citizens of the Greenville District," transcribed by Lloyd Benson from the *Southern Enterprise* (Greenville, SC) 22 (November 1860), 21, http://history.furman.edu/~benson/docs/scgese112260.htm.

63. Mark A. Noll, *In the Beginning Was the Word: The Bible in American Public Life, 1492–1783* (New York: Oxford University Press, 2015), 1; Nadal, *Christian Nation's Ordeal*, 7.

64. As quoted in Drew Gilpin Faust, "Without Pilot or Compass: Elite Women and Religion in the Civil War South," in Miller, Stout, and Wilson, *Religion and the American Civil War*, 252.

65. A. B. Longstreet, *Fast-Day Sermon: Delivered in the Washington Street Methodist Episcopal Church* (Columbia, SC: Townsend & North, 1861), 13.

66. Harvey, "Bible in the Civil War," 359.

67. John Fea, *The Bible Cause: A History of the American Bible Society* (New York: Oxford University Press, 2016), 78–81; Harvey, "Bible in the Civil War," 359.

68. Fea, *Bible Cause*, 78–81; Harvey, "Bible in the Civil War," 359. See also Steven E. Woodworth, *While God Is Marching On: The Religious World of Civil War Soldiers* (Lawrence: University Press of Kansas, 2001), 68–69. Leeser quoted in Jonathan D. Sarna, "The Bible and American Judaism," in Gutjahr, *Oxford Handbook of the Bible in America*, 507.

69. Quoted in Rable, *God's Almost Chosen Peoples*, 118; see also 130–31; Woodworth, *God Is Marching On*, 70–71.

70. McPherson, *For Cause and Comrades*, 62–63; Rable, *God's Almost Chosen Peoples*, 166.
71. William A. Moore as quoted in Woodworth, *God Is Marching On*, 71–72. Other soldiers noted that a deck of cards could stop a bullet just as well as a Bible. Woodworth, 72.
72. Mary Boykin Chesnut, *Mary Chesnut's Civil War*, ed. C. Vann Woodward (Norwalk, CT: Easton Press, 1998), 1:71.
73. Thanks to the technical expertise of Lincoln Mullen, a historian and scholar in digital humanities, I was able to locate many of these biblical citations. Lincoln used the methods of machine learning to help locate biblical citations in my collection of sources. I have also used Mullen's groundbreaking database of biblical citations in American newspapers, *America's Public Bible: Biblical Quotations in U.S. Newspapers*, http://americaspublicbible.org/.
74. "The Great Rebellion. Part of a Letter to President Lincoln from Rev. Granville Moody," *Christian Advocate and Journal*, August 29, 1861, 273.
75. *Semi-Weekly Standard* (Raleigh, NC), November 18, 1862, *Chronicling America: Historic American Newspapers*, Library of Congress, https://chroniclingamerica.loc.gov/. Henceforth abbreviated CA.
76. *Staunton Spectator* (Staunton, VA), July 21, 1863, CA. See also *American citizen*. (Canton, MI), December 7, 1861, CA.
77. Aristides Spyker Smith, "Sermon on Job 16:22," Harrison and Smith Family Papers, 1857–2005, Collection no. 05144, Southern Historical Collection at the Louis Round Wilson Special Collections Library, University of North Carolina at Chapel Hill.
78. Seth Perry, *Bible Culture and Authority in the Early United States* (Princeton, NJ: Princeton University Press, 2018), 3. I am grateful to a peer reviewer of the manuscript for helping me to make this point.

Chapter 1

1. Lincoln, "Second Inaugural Address," 201.
2. "Declaration of Independence, July 4, 1776," Avalon Project, Lillian Goldman Law Library, Yale University, https://avalon.law.yale.edu/18th_century/declare.asp.
3. Noll, *CWTC*, 31; Frederick Douglass, *My Bondage and My Freedom* (New York: Miller, Orton & Mulligan, 1855), 355; Blight, *Prophet of Freedom*, 104.
4. William Lloyd Garrison, *Selections from the Writings and Speeches of William Lloyd Garrison: With an Appendix* (Boston: R.F. Wallcut, 1852), 95.
5. Garrison, *Selections*, 95–96.
6. Garrison, *Selections*, 221–24.
7. Garrison, *Selections*, 224–26.
8. Garrison, *Selections*, 225–29.
9. Noll, *CWTC*, 32, 36–37.
10. Richard Allen, *The Life, Experience, and Gospel Labours of the Rt. Rev. Richard Allen* (Philadelphia: Martin & Boden, 1833), 17. For an explanation of why African Americans, including enslaved people, preferred evangelical denominations, see

Albert J. Raboteau, *Slave Religion: The "Invisible Institution" in the Antebellum South* (New York: Oxford University Press, 1978), 128–49.

11. See Dennis C. Dickerson, *The African Methodist Episcopal Church: A History* (Cambridge: Cambridge University Press, 2020), chap. 1.

12. David Walker, *Walker's Appeal, in Four Articles* (Boston: David Walker, 1830), 65–66. https://docsouth.unc.edu/nc/walker/walker.html. See also Peter P. Hinks, *To Awaken My Afflicted Brethren: David Walker and the Problem of Antebellum Slave Resistance* (University Park: Pennsylvania State University Press, 2010), 65–66.

13. Heather Andrea Williams, *American Slavery: A Very Short Introduction* (New York: Oxford University Press, 2014), 55.

14. Walker, *Walker's Appeal*, 9–10.

15. Walker, *Walker's Appeal*, 10–11.

16. Walker, *Walker's Appeal*, 11–12, 20.

17. Walker, *Walker's Appeal*, 42–43.

18. Walker, *Walker's Appeal*, 47.

19. Walker, *Walker's Appeal*, 37, 66–67.

20. Walker, *Walker's Appeal*, 45.

21. Walker, *Walker's Appeal*, 23, 43, 45, 49.

22. Walker, *Walker's Appeal*, 82.

23. Williams, *American Slavery*, 56–58.

24. Maria W. Stewart, *Meditations from the Pen of Mrs. Maria W. Stewart* (Washington, DC: W. Lloyd Garrison & Knap, 1879), 4; Maria W. Stewart and Marilyn Richardson, *Maria W. Stewart, America's First Black Woman Political Writer: Essays and Speeches*, Blacks in the Diaspora (Bloomington: Indiana University Press, 1987), xiii. See also Valerie C. Cooper, *Word, Like Fire: Maria Stewart, the Bible, and the Rights of African Americans* (Charlottesville: University of Virginia Press, 2011).

25. Stewart, *Meditations*, 24.

26. Stewart, *Meditations*, 33.

27. Stewart, *Meditations*, 33.

28. Patrick H. Breen, *The Land Shall Be Deluged in Blood: A New History of the Nat Turner Revolt* (New York: Oxford University Press, 2015), 21.

29. Nat Turner and Thomas R. Gray, *The Confessions of Nat Turner: The Leader of the Late Insurrection in Southampton, Va.* (Baltimore: T. R. Gray, 1831), 11.

30. Turner and Gray, *Confessions*, 11.

31. Kenneth S. Greenberg, *Nat Turner: A Slave Rebellion in History and Memory* (New York: Oxford University Press, 2003), 120, 122, 126.

32. Ethan J. Kytle and Blain Roberts, *Denmark Vesey's Garden: Slavery and Memory in the Cradle of Confederacy* (New York: New Press, 2018), 72; Louis P. Masur, *The Civil War: A Concise History* (New York: Oxford University Press, 2011), Kindle edition, 7; John C. Calhoun, "Speech on the Reception of Abolition Petitions, February, 1837," in *Speeches of John C. Calhoun* (New York: Harper & Brothers, 1843), 225.

33. Masur, *Civil War Concise History*, 8; Sven Beckert, *Empire of Cotton: A Global History* (New York: Alfred A. Knopf, 2014), xiii; Andrew A. Lipscomb, *Substance of*

a Discourse Delivered before the Legislature of Georgia (Milledgeville, GA: Boughten, Nisbet & Barnes, 1860), 19; Nadal, *Christian Nation's Ordeal*, 12.

34. C. C. Goen, *Broken Churches, Broken Nation: Denominational Schisms and the Coming of the American Civil War* (Macon, GA: Mercer University Press, 1985).

35. Richard Carwardine, "Methodists, Politics, and the Coming of the American Civil War," *Church History* 69, no. 3 (September 2000): 588–89.

36. Larry E. Tise, *Proslavery: A History of the Defense of Slavery in America, 1701–1840* (Athens: University of Georgia Press, 1990), 79; Stephen R. Haynes, *Noah's Curse: The Biblical Justification of American Slavery* (New York: Oxford University Press, 2002).

37. Noll, *CWTC*, 36–37; Richard Fuller and Francis Wayland, *Domestic Slavery Considered as a Scriptural Institution: In a Correspondence between the Rev. Richard Fuller, of Beaufort, S.C., and the Rev. Francis Wayland, of Providence, R.I.* (New York: Sheldon & Co., 1860), 4–7, 13–34. See also Elizabeth Fox-Genovese and Eugene D. Genovese, *The Mind of the Master Class: History and Faith in the Southern Slaveholder's Worldview* (Cambridge: Cambridge University Press, 2005), chap. 15, especially 490–91.

38. Fuller and Wayland, *Domestic Slavery Considered*, 3.

39. Quoted in Masur, *Civil War Concise History*, 10–11.

40. Andrew Delbanco, *The War before the War: Fugitive Slaves and the Struggle for America's Soul from the Revolution to the Civil War* (New York: Penguin Press, 2018), 5–6.

41. Delbanco, *War before the War*, 2, 5. See Moses Stuart, *Conscience and the Constitution* (Boston: Crocker & Brewster, 1850), 3–5, 112. For southern uses of Romans 13 to attack the act, see the *Daily Dispatch* (Richmond, VA), July 6, 1855, CA; *Weekly North Carolina Standard* (Raleigh), October 30, 1850, CA. See Lincoln Mullen, "The Fight to Define Romans 13," *The Atlantic*, June 15, 2018.

42. James M. McPherson, *Battle Cry of Freedom: The Civil War Era* (New York: Oxford University Press, 1988), 38. Henceforth *BCF*.

43. David S. Reynolds, *Mightier Than the Sword: "Uncle Tom's Cabin" and the Battle for America* (New York: W. W. Norton, 2011), 125–28.

44. McPherson, *BCF*, 89–90.

45. Quoted in Reynolds, *Mightier Than the Sword*, 117–18, 129.

46. McPherson, *BCF*, 89; Reynolds, *Mightier Than the Sword*, ix.

47. See Harriet Beecher Stowe, *Uncle Tom's Cabin*, vol. II (Boston: John P. Jewett, 1852), 123, 133–34; Stephen Railton, "Uncle Tom's Cabin & American Culture," http://utc.iath.virginia.edu/sitemap.html. See especially "The Bible and the Novel," http://utc.iath.virginia.edu/christn/kjb_utc.html.

48. Lyman Beecher, *A Plea for the West* (Cincinnati: Truman & Smith, 1835), 142. See also her brother's book, Edward Beecher, *The Papal Conspiracy Exposed and Protestantism Defended in the Light of Reason, History, and Scripture* (Boston: Stearns, 1855); and Susan M. Griffin, *Anti-Catholicism and Nineteenth-Century Fiction* (Cambridge: Cambridge University Press, 2004), 224 n. 20.

49. Reynolds, *Mightier Than the Sword*, 32, 37–38.

50. Harriet Beecher Stowe, *Uncle Tom's Cabin*, vol. 2 (Boston: John P. Jewett, 1852), 243–44; Reynolds, *Mightier Than the Sword*, 35–37.

51. Reynolds, *Mightier Than the Sword*, 1, 29.

52. Quoted in Reynolds, *Mightier Than the Sword*, 41–42.

53. Blight, *Prophet of Freedom*, xiv.

54. "Douglass," according to Blight, "rooted his own story and especially the story of African Americans in the oldest and most powerful stories of the Hebrew prophets." Blight, *Prophet of Freedom*, xvii, 157.

55. Blight, *Prophet of Freedom*, xiii, 157.

56. Blight, *Prophet of Freedom*; D. H. Dilbeck, *Frederick Douglass: America's Prophet* (Chapel Hill: University of North Carolina Press, 2018).

57. Frederick Douglass, *Narrative of the Life of Frederick Douglass* (Boston: Anti-Slavery Office, 1845), 118–19.

58. Quoted in Blight, *Prophet of Freedom*, 115.

59. Dilbeck, *Douglass*, "Introduction"; Blight, *Prophet of Freedom*, 231.

60. Blight, *Prophet of Freedom*, 229–30.

61. Frederick Douglas, *Great Speeches by Frederick Douglass*, ed. James Daley (Mineola, NY: Dover Publications, 2013), Kindle edition, 32.

62. Douglass, *Great Speeches*, 32.

63. Douglass, *Great Speeches*, 30.

64. Douglass, *Great Speeches*, 32–33.

65. Douglass, *Great Speeches*, 33–34.

66. Douglass, *Great Speeches*, 34.

67. Douglass, *Great Speeches*, 35–36.

68. Douglass, *Great Speeches*, 41–42.

69. Douglass, *Great Speeches*, 43–44. Douglass was one of many who made this connection between Acts 17:26 and the Declaration of Independence. See Noll, *CWTC*, 41–42.

70. As quoted in Goldfield, *America Aflame*, 139–40.

71. Frederick Douglass, *The Frederick Douglass Papers. Series One: Speeches, Debates, and Interviews*, ed. John W. Blassingame (New Haven: Yale University Press, 1979), 3:165. Henceforth *FDP*.

72. Douglass, *FDP*, 3:167, 170; Blight, *Prophet of Freedom*, 278–79.

73. Quotation and commentary in Milton C. Sernett, *Harriet Tubman: Myth, Memory, and History* (Durham, NC: Duke University Press, 2007), 78. See also Goldfield, *America Aflame*, 159.

74. Blight, *Prophet of Freedom*, 283–84.

75. John Stauffer and Zoe Trodd, eds., *The Tribunal: Responses to John Brown and the Harpers Ferry Raid* (Cambridge, MA: Belknap Press, 2012), 119.

76. As quoted in David S. Reynolds, *John Brown, Abolitionist: The Man Who Killed Slavery, Sparked the Civil War, and Seeded Civil Rights* (New York: Alfred A. Knopf, 2005), 24.

77. Richard J. Hinton, *John Brown and His Men* (New York: Funk & Wagnalls, 1894), 637–43; Ted A. Smith, *Weird John Brown: Divine Violence and the Limits of Ethics*

(Stanford, CA: Stanford University Press, 2014), 88–91; Jill Lepore, *These Truths: A History of the United States* (New York: W. W. Norton, 2018), 283.

78. Hinton, *Brown and His Men*, 640–43.
79. As quoted in Goldfield, *America Aflame*, 160. See also Mark S. Weiner, *Black Trials: Citizenship from the Beginnings of Slavery to the End of Caste* (New York: Vintage, 2004), 180.
80. Louis DeCaro Jr., *John Brown Speaks: Letters and Statements from Charlestown* (Lanham, MD: Rowman & Littlefield, 2015), 123–28.
81. McPherson, *BCF*, 84, 152.
82. Stauffer and Trodd, *Tribunal*, 67–68, 119.
83. Stauffer and Trodd, *Tribunal*, 73.
84. Smith, *Weird John Brown*, 41; Lepore, *These Truths*, 285.
85. Noll, *America's God*, 427.
86. Stauffer and Trodd, *Tribunal*, 104. I previously published material in these paragraphs on Brown in a review article, James P. Byrd and Alan Murphy, "Keep John Brown Weird: Moral History without Facile Moralizing," *Syndicate*, https://syndicate.network/symposia/theology/weird-john-brown/.
87. Stauffer and Trodd, *Tribunal*, 107, 109. Longfellow as quoted in Lepore, *These Truths*, 284–85.
88. William Edward Burghardt Du Bois, *John Brown* (Philadelphia: G. W. Jacobs, 1909), 8, 375–76, 386, 396.
89. David S. Reynolds, "Freedom's Martyr," *New York Times*, December 1, 2009. https://www.nytimes.com/2009/12/02/opinion/02reynolds.html.
90. Sean Wilentz, "Homegrown Terrorist," review of *John Brown, Abolitionist: The Man Who Killed Slavery, Sparked the Civil War, and Seeded Civil Rights*, by David S. Reynolds, *New Republic*, October 24, 2005, http://www.newrepublic.com/article/homegrown-terrorist.
91. Reynolds, *John Brown, Abolitionist*, 467–69.
92. John Stauffer and Benjamin Soskis, *The Battle Hymn of the Republic: A Biography of the Song That Marches On* (New York: Oxford University Press, 2013), iii, 73–74.
93. Reynolds, *John Brown, Abolitionist*, 469.
94. Reynolds, *John Brown, Abolitionist*, 467–69.
95. Stauffer and Soskis, *Battle Hymn*, 5–8; 86–87.

Chapter 2

1. Robert L. Dabney, "The Christian's Best Motive for Patriotism. A Sermon Preached in the College Church, Hampden Sydney, Va., on a General Fast Day, November 1, 1860," in *Fast Day Sermons: Or the Pulpit on the State of the Country* (New York: Rudd & Carleton, 1861), 81, 83–87.
2. Wise as quoted in Jonathan D. Sarna and Benjamin Shapell, *Lincoln and the Jews: A History* (New York: St. Martin's Press, 2015), 77–78.

3. Allen C. Guelzo, *Fateful Lightning: A New History of the Civil War and Reconstruction* (New York: Oxford University Press, 2012), 127.

4. Guelzo, *Fateful Lightning*, 127.

5. Gilbert Haven, *Te Deum Laudamus. The Cause and the Consequence of the Election of Abraham Lincoln* (Boston: J. M. Hewes, 1860), 25–26.

6. Abraham Lincoln, "Abraham Lincoln's First Inaugural Address," in *The Routledge Sourcebook of Religion and the American Civil War: A History in Documents*, ed. Robert R. Mathisen (New York: Routledge, 2015), 22 (henceforth *RACW*); Haven, *Te Deum Laudamus*, 5–6, 25–26. Lincoln's remarks on Brown quoted in Goldfield, *America Aflame*, 161.

7. Lincoln, *The Collected Works of Abraham Lincoln*, 9 vols., ed. Roy P. Basler (New Brunswick, NJ: Rutgers University Press, 1953), 4:147 (henceforth Lincoln, *Works*); McPherson, *BCF*, 179–80.

8. *Wilmington* (NC) *Herald*, "A Few Reflections on Secession," in *RACW*, 4.

9. Guelzo, *Fateful Lighting*, 126–29; Goldfield, *America Aflame*, 178–79.

10. B. M. Palmer, *The South: Her Peril, and Her Duty* (New Orleans: Office of the True Witness and Sentinel, 1860), 6.

11. Palmer, *The South*, 10. Like Palmer, southern ministers often insisted that in attacking slavery the North threatened the South's existence. See H. A. M. Henderson, *The Religion and Politics of the Crisis* (Marion, AL: George C. Rogers, 1860), 6–7.

12. Palmer, *The South*, 10–13, 17.

13. Palmer, *The South*, 13; Rable, *God's Almost Chosen Peoples*, 35–36.

14. George H. Clark, *The Union. A Sermon* (Savannah: George N. Nichols, 1860), 7, 12–15.

15. John Cotton Smith, *Two Discourses* (New York: John A. Gray, 1861), 3–4. See also Truman M. Post, *Our National Union* (St. Louis: R. P. Studley and Co., 1860), 16.

16. William O. Prentiss, *A Sermon Preached at St. Peter's Church* (Charleston, SC: Evans & Cogswell, 1860), 3, 17.

17. Benjamin Morgan Palmer was among those who made this point. *Nashville* (TN) *Union and American*, December 13, 1860, CA.

18. *Daily Nashville* (TN) *Patriot*, December 5, 1860, CA.

19. William Adams, "Prayer for Rulers, Or, Duty of Christian Patriots. A Sermon," in *Fast Day Sermons: Or the Pulpit on the State of the Country* (New York: Rudd & Carleton, 1861), 334–35. There is a period, not a question mark, in the source. William Adams, "Prayer for Rulers, or, Duty of Christian Patriots," in *RACW*, 14. Note that the *RACW* version has "lie" in place of "be." I've opted for "be," which is the wording in the original.

20. Adams, "Prayer for Rulers," 329–30.

21. Adams, "Prayer for Rulers," 330–31, 333. Adams's "partizanship" corrected to "partisanship."

22. James Buchanan, "Fourth Annual Message to Congress on the State of the Union, December 3, 1860," *The American Presidency Project*, UC Santa Barbara, https://www.presidency.ucsb.edu/documents/fourth-annual-message-congress-the-state-the-union.

23. Henry Jackson Van Dyke, *The Character and Influence of Abolitionism* (Baltimore: H. Taylor, 1860), 6, 10–12, 18.

24. Joseph R. Wilson, "Mutual Relation of Masters and Slaves as Taught in the Bible," in *RACW*, 15–16. Wilson cited Ephesians 6:5–9.

25. Rabbi Bernard Illowry, "Fast Day Sermon," in *RACW*, 13. See also Rabbi Morris J. Raphall of the Jewish Synagogue of New York,M. J. Raphall, *Bible View of Slavery* (New York: Rudd & Carleton, 1861), 232–35; Noll, *CWTC*, 3–4.

26. As quoted in Rosen, *The Jewish Confederates* (Columbia: University of South Carolina Press, 2000), 38.

27. McPherson, *BCF*, 242. For figures on slave ownership, see Masur, *Civil War Concise History*, 9.

28. James Dunwoody Brownson De Bow, *The Interest in Slavery of the Southern Non-Slaveholder* (Charleston, SC: Presses of Evans & Cogswell, 1860), 5, 7–9; Lepore, *These Truths*, 292.

29. De Bow, *Interest in Slavery*, 21. See also Bishop John Hopkins, "Bible View of Slavery," *Newark Advocate*, March 15, 1861, 19th Century US Newspapers.

30. Quoted in McPherson, *BCF*, 243.

31. Furman et al., "Letter to the Citizens," 5; McPherson, *BCF*, 243.

32. Furman et al., "Letter to the Citizens," 17, 21.

33. Furman et al., "Letter to the Citizens," 21; Noll, *CWTC*, 54.

34. Noll, *CWTC*, 55; Noll also cites Luke E. Harlow, "Antislavery Clergy in Antebellum Kentucky, 1830–1860," MA thesis, Wheaton College, 2004.

35. John Gregg Fee, *The Sinfulness of Slaveholding Shown by Appeals to Reason and Scripture* (New York: Printed by John A. Gray, 1851), 28–29; Noll, *CWTC*, 55.

36. Fee, *Sinfulness of Slaveholding*, 5; see Noll, *CWTC*, 55.

37. Lincoln, *Works,* 3:445; see Noll, *CWTC*, 56–57.

38. Furman et al., "Letter to the Citizens," 17.

39. Furman et al., "Letter to the Citizens," 19–20.

40. As quoted in McPherson, *BCF*, 237; see also McPherson, *BCF*, 234, 236–38; Guelzo, *Fateful Lightning*, 131; Goldfield, *America Aflame*, 187–89.

41. B. F. Brooke, *The Olive Branch* (Winchester, VA: Printed at the Republican Office, 1861), 8, 13–14, 16–18.

42. Goldfield, *America Aflame*, 185–86.

43. See also Psalm 118:22. In addition to Mark 12:10, several other New Testament passages refer to this statement. See Matthew 21:42; Luke 20:17; Acts 4:11; 1 Peter 2:7.

44. A. H. Stephens, "Speech of A. H. Stephens," in *The Rebellion Record: A Diary of American Events*, vol. 1, ed. Frank Moore (New York: G. P. Putnam, 1861), 45–46.

45. Goldfield, *America Aflame*, 186–87.

46. Lincoln, *Works*, 4:240.

47. Thomas Smyth, *Sin and the Curse; Or, The Union the True Source of Disunion* (Charleston, SC: Evans & Cogswell, 1860), 13–14.

48. Smyth, *Sin and the Curse*, 13; William L. Harris, "Address," in *Journal of the Senate of the State of Mississippi* (Jackson: E. Barksdale, State Printer, 1860), 16, 19; Goldfield, *America Aflame*, 182; Judge William L. Harris as quoted in G. Edward

White, *Law in American History*, vol. 1: *From the Colonial Years through the Civil War* (New York: Oxford University Press, 2012), 387–88; see also Prentiss, *Sermon Preached*, 12–13.

49. Jefferson Davis, "Farewell Address in U.S. Senate," in *RACW*, 18.
50. Lepore, *These Truths*, 290–91.
51. Lincoln, "First Inaugural Address," 22–25.

Chapter 3

1. "War as a Schoolmaster," *Harper's Weekly*, October 19, 1861, 658.
2. On Anderson, see David Detzer and Gene Smith, *Allegiance: Fort Sumter, Charleston, and the Beginning of the Civil War* (New York: Houghton Mifflin Harcourt, 2002), chapter 2.
3. Guelzo, *Fateful Lightning*, 134–37.
4. Anderson quoted in Benjamin Franklin Morris, *Christian Life and Character of the Civil Institutions of the United States: Developed in the Official and Historical Annals of the Republic* (Philadelphia: G. W. Childs, 1864), 674; Rable, *God's Almost Chosen Peoples*, 52.
5. Goldfield, *America Aflame*, 199–201.
6. Ralph Waldo Emerson and James Elliot Cabot, *The Works of Ralph Waldo Emerson: Miscellanies* (Boston: Houghton, Mifflin, 1883), 312. As James McPherson observed, "Abraham Lincoln was the only president in American history whose entire administration was bounded by war." James M. McPherson, *Tried by War: Abraham Lincoln as Commander in Chief* (New York: Penguin, 2008), xiii, 2.
7. As quoted in McPherson, *Tried by War*, 14–15.
8. McPherson, *BCF*, 265–68; 270–71; McPherson, *Tried by War*, 20.
9. As quoted in Guelzo, *Fateful Lightning*, 140; McPherson, *BCF*, 274,
10. As quoted in Goldfield, *America Aflame*, 205, 203.
11. Ann Stevens, "May God Direct us All," in *RACW*, 28–29.
12. W. H. Isely, "The Sharps Rifle Episode in Kansas History," ed. John Franklin Jameson and Henry Eldridge Bourne, *American Historical Review* 12 (October 1906–July 1907): 547–48.
13. See also Charles Eliphalet Lord, *Sermons on the Country's Crisis* (Milford NH: Boutwell's Newspaper, Book and Job Office, 1861), 5–6.
14. Henry Ward Beecher, "The Battle Set in Array," in *Freedom and War* (Boston: Ticknor and Fields, 1863), 84–110. See also Henry Ward Beecher, "Peace, Be Still. A Sermon Preached at Plymouth Church, Brooklyn, on the Day of the National Fast, Jan 4., 1861," in *Fast Day Sermons: Or the Pulpit on the State of the Country* (New York: Rudd & Carleton, 1861), 265–92.
15. Beecher, "Battle Set in Array," 86–87.
16. Beecher, "Battle Set in Array," 86–88.
17. Beecher, "Battle Set in Array," 88–89.
18. Beecher, "Battle Set in Array," 90.
19. Beecher, "Battle Set in Array," 93–94, 101.

20. Beecher, "Battle Set in Array," 95. For another sermon in the days after Sumter that drew on the legacy of Exodus in the American Revolution, see Silas McKeen, *Heroic Patriotism* (Windsor, VT: Chronicle Press, 1861), 9–10.

21. Guelzo, *Fateful Lightning*, 141; McPherson, *Tried by War*, 10–11.

22. McPherson, *Tried by War*, 23.

23. McPherson, *Tried by War*, 23; Guelzo, *Fateful Lightning*, 142.

24. Cf. Matthew 26:52; "President Lincoln a Usurper," *Charleston Mercury*, April 22, 1861, Accessible Archives.

25. McPherson, *Tried by War*, 23; Guelzo, *Fateful Lightning*, 142.

26. McPherson, *Tried by War*, 23–24, 30; "Lincoln to A. G. Hodges, April 4, 1864," in Lincoln, *Works*, 7:281.

27. As quoted in McPherson, *Tried by War*, 25.

28. "Jonathan Worth to D. G. Worth, May 15, 1861," in *The Correspondence of Jonathan Worth*, vol. 1, ed. Joseph Grégoire de Rhoulhac (Raleigh: Edwards & Broughton, 1909), 144. See also McPherson, *BCF*, 277.

29. McPherson, *BCF*, 283.

30. Guelzo, *Fateful Lightning*, 146.

31. McPherson, *BCF*, 275.

32. McKeen, *Heroic Patriotism*, 4, 9.

33. McPherson, *Tried by War*, 23.

34. Noll, *Beginning*, 52; William B. Kurtz, *Excommunicated from the Union: How the Civil War Created a Separate Catholic America* (New York: Fordham University Press, 2015), 2–3.

35. Kurtz, *Excommunicated from the Union*, 30; Father Creedon, "A Catholic Priest's War Speech," in *RACW*, 30; Noll, *CWTC*, 127; Randall M. Miller, "Catholic Religion, Irish Ethnicity, and the Civil War," in Miller, Stout, and Wilson, *Religion and the American Civil War*, 261.

36. Brownson as quoted in Kurtz, *Excommunicated from the Union*, 1; see also p. 31.

37. As quoted in *The Oxford Dictionary of American Quotations*, ed. Hugh Rawson and Margaret Miner (New York: Oxford University Press, 2006), 703; also see Ralph Waldo Emerson, *The Complete Works of Ralph Waldo Emerson: With a Biographical . . .*, vol. 11, ed. Edward W. Emerson (Boston: Houghton Mifflin, 1904), 579.

38. Louisa May Alcott, *Little Women: Annotated Edition*, ed. Daniel Shealy (Cambridge, MA: Belknap Press, 2013), 37; Stout, *Altar of the Nation*, 36.

39. George E. Woodbury, *Nathaniel Hawthorne* (Boston: Houghton Mifflin, 1902), 282; Stout, *Altar of the Nation*, 36.

Chapter 4

1. Stout, *Altar of the Nation*, 28; soldier quoted in McPherson, *For Cause and Comrades*, 16.

2. Benjamin Morgan Palmer, *National Responsibility before God* (New Orleans: Price-Current, 1861), 24–25. See also John H. Rice, "The Princeton Review on the State of the Country," *Southern Presbyterian Review* 14 (April 1861): 38–39.

3. Barrows, *Honor to the Brave*, 7.

4. Byrd, *Sacred Scripture, Sacred War*, chap. 5.

5. Samuel T. Spear, *Two Sermons for the Times* (New York: Nathan Lane & Co., 1861), 12–13.

6. Spear, *Two Sermons*, 9–10, 16.

7. Spear, *Two Sermons*, 9–10, 16.

8. Spear, *Two Sermons*, 16–17.

9. Spear, *Two Sermons*, 20–21.

10. Spear, *Two Sermons*, 18, 26–27. Similar references to "Paul's politics" appeared throughout the North and in some border states. See Joseph T. Duryea, *Loyalty to Our Government: A Divine Command and a Christian Duty* (Troy, NY: A. W. Scribner & Co., 1861), 28.

11. W. W. Lord, *Our True Government* (Vicksburg, MS: Christ Church Vestry, 1861), 1.

12. Lord, *Our True Government*, 4–5, emphasis added.

13. Lord, *Out True Government*, 5.

14. Lord, *Our True Government*, 6, 8, emphasis added.

15. Beecher, *Patriotic Addresses*, 291–94.

16. Beecher, *Patriotic Addresses*, 291–92.

17. Smith, *Two Discourses*, 5–6; McPherson, *For Cause and Comrades*, 16.

18. Smith, *Two Discourses*, 3–15, 17–18; see also J. J. Bowden, *A Voice for the Union* ([Pittsfield, MA]: Pittsfield Sun Print, 1860), 7.

19. Albert Barnes, *The Love of Country* (Philadelphia: C. Sherman & Son, 1861), 5, 12–13, 32.

20. "The Star-Spangled Banner, and the Duty of Colored Americans to that Flag," *Christian Recorder*, April 27, 1861, Accessible Archives.

21. Joel Tyler Headley, *The Chaplains and Clergy of the Revolution* (New York: Charles Scribner, 1864), 158. See also John Wingate Thornton, *The Pulpit of the American Revolution: Or, The Political Sermons of the Period of 1776* (Boston: Gould and Lincoln, 1860); Frank Moore, *The Patriot Preachers of the American Revolution. 1776–1783* ([New York]: Printed for the subscribers, 1860). See also Jon Butler, *Awash in a Sea of Faith: Christianizing the American People* (Cambridge, MA: Harvard University Press, 1990), 195; Byrd, *Sacred Scripture, Sacred War*, conclusion.

22. Quotation and statistics in Rable, *God's Almost Chosen Peoples*, 108–10. Morgan Callaway quotation is in an unprinted letter dated April 24, 1862, Morgan Callaway Papers, 1831–1899, Stuart A. Rose Manuscript, Archives, and Rare Book Library, Emory University.

23. Duffield, *Courage*, 4; the Revolutionary War sermon cited was Cooper, *Courage*; Duffield, *Courage*, 29. See also Atwood, *Purse*, 20–21.

24. Duffield, *Courage*, 8.

25. Duffield, *Courage*, 24.

26. Daniel C. Eddy, *Liberty and Union* (Boston: John M. Hewes, 1861), 24–25.

27. Eddy, *Liberty and Union*, 25.

28. Duffield, *Courage*, 24–26.

29. Duffield, *Courage*, 23, 27.

30. Duffield, *Courage*, 8, 18.

31. Duffield, *Courage*, 17–20.

32. As quoted in C. Michael Hawn, "History of Hymns: 'Stand Up, Stand Up for Jesus,'" United Methodist Church, https://www.umcdiscipleship.org/resources/history-of-hymns-stand-up-stand-up-for-jesus.

33. Diana Hochstedt Butler, *Standing against the Whirlwind: Evangelical Episcopalians in Nineteenth-Century America* (New York: Oxford University Press, 1995), 136–37.

34. Atwood, *Purse*, 6; McPherson, *BCF*, 238; see also William J. Rogers, *A Southern Writer and the Civil War: The Confederate Imagination of William Gilmore Simms* (Lanham, MD: Lexington Books, 2015), 89; Drew Gilpin Faust, *Mothers of Invention: Women of the Slaveholding South in the American Civil War* (Chapel Hill: University of North Carolina Press, 1996), 12–13; Stout, *Altar of the Nation*, 40.

35. C. D. Helmer, "The War Begun," in *RACW*, 30–31.

Chapter 5

1. J. H. Elliott, *The Bloodless Victory. A Sermon* (Charleston, SC): A. E. Miller, 1861), 4–5.

2. Elliott, *Bloodless Victory*, 5–9.

3. As quoted in Faust, *Mothers of Invention*, 179.

4. As quoted in Faust, *Mothers of Invention*, 180.

5. Chesnut, *Chesnut's Civil War*, 48, April 13, 1861.

6. Ada White Bacot, *A Confederate Nurse: The Diary of Ada W. Bacot, 1860–1863* (Columbia: University of South Carolina Press, 2000), 26.

7. McPherson, *BCF*, 238.

8. As quoted in Goldfield, *America Aflame*, 206. Also in "Speech of Ex-Gov. Henry A. Wise," in Moore, *The Rebellion Record*, 824.

9. Reported by Confederate war clerk J. B Jones in John B. Jones and Earl Schenck Miers, *A Rebel War Clerk's Diary at the Confederate States Capital*, vol. 1 (Philadelphia: J.B. Lippincott & Co., 1866), 22–23; Stout, *Altar of the Nation*, 26.

10. As quoted in McPherson, *For Cause and Comrades*, 12–13.

11. McPherson, *BCF*, 280–81.

12. John William Jones, *Personal Reminiscences, Anecdotes, and Letters of Gen. Robert E. Lee* (D. Appleton, 1875), 136–37; McPherson, *BCF*, 281.

13. "Letter from Robert E. Lee to Winfield Scott," in *Life and Letters of Robert Edward Lee*, ed. J. W. Jones (New York: Neal Publishing, 1906), 132–33. See also McPherson, *BCF*, 281.

14. Chesnut, *Chesnut's Civil War*, 217, October 1861.

15. As quoted in Rosen, *The Jewish Confederates*, 38–39.

16. As quoted in McPherson, *For Cause and Comrades*, 96.

17. Brantly, *Our National Troubles*, 16–21; Rable, *God's Almost Chosen Peoples*, 36; McPherson, *The War That Forged*, 97.

18. Smyth, *Battle of Fort Sumter*, 19.

19. See Daniel 3.

20. Smyth, *Battle of Fort Sumter*, 19.
21. Palmer, *National Responsibility*, 15.
22. Smyth, *Battle of Fort Sumter*, 20
23. Smyth, *Battle of Fort Sumter*, 6–7. See also Palmer, *National Responsibility*, 15; Mitchell, *Government Street*, 7.
24. Chesnut, *Chesnut's Civil War*, 154–55, August 1861.
25. Palmer, *National Responsibility*, 13.
26. Ferdinand Jacobs, *A Sermon, for the Times* (Marion, AL: s.n., 1861), 3. This exchange with Hamilton probably never occurred. See Matthew Harris and Thomas Kidd, *The Founding Fathers and the Debate over Religion in Revolutionary America: A History in Documents* (New York: Oxford University Press, 2012), 15. Southerners often criticized the founders for their failure to create a Christian nation. See Meade, *Sermon Preached by Bishop Meade*, 13.
27. Stephen Elliott, "God's Presence with the Confederate States. A Sermon Preached in Christ Church, Savannah, on Thursday, the 13th June," in *Two Sermons Preached in Christ Church, Savannah* (Savannah: W. Thorne Williams, 1861), 21.
28. Palmer, *National Responsibility*, 12.
29. Daniel I. Dreher, *A Sermon Delivered by Rev. Daniel I. Dreher* (Salisbury, NC: Watchman Office, 1861), 13.
30. Morgan, *Civil War Diary*, 67, May 10, 1862; Smyth, *Battle of Fort Sumter*, 32; Dreher, *Sermon Delivered*, 13.
31. "Constitution of the Confederate States; March 11, 1861," *The Avalon Project: Documents in Law, History and Diplomacy*, Lillian Goldman Law Library, Yale Law School, http://avalon.law.yale.edu/19th_century/csa_csa.asp; Palmer, *National Responsibility*, 13.
32. Otto Sievers Barten, *A Sermon Preached in St. James' Church* (Richmond: Enquirer Book and Job Press, 1861), 8.
33. T. L. De Veaux, *Fast-Day Sermon* (Wytheville: D. A. St. Clair, 1861), 11.
34. Dreher did not capitalize "christian." Dreher, *Sermon Delivered*, 6.
35. Longstreet, *Fast-Day Sermon*, 6–7.
36. Dreher, *Sermon Delivered*, 4–5, 14.
37. Dreher, *Sermon Delivered*, 6.
38. Mitchell, *Government Street*, 6.
39. Smyth, *Battle of Fort Sumter*, 19.
40. Stephen Elliott, *The Silver Trumpets of the Sanctuary* (Savannah: John M. Cooper & Co., 1861), 3, 11. He quotes the following biblical texts, though he does not cite chapter and verse: Deuteronomy 32:35; Romans 12:19; Numbers 10:9.
41. Elliott, *Silver Trumpets*, 11.
42. J. R. Kendrick, *Lessons from an Ancient Fast* (Charleston, SC: Evans & Cogswell, 1861), 15.
43. H. N. Pierce, *Sermons Preached in St. John's Church, Mobile* (Mobile: Farrow & Dennett, 1861), 10–11.
44. Mitchell, *Government Street*, 11.
45. Mitchell, *Government Street*, 11–13.

46. Mitchell, *Government Street*, 17.

47. See Byrd, *Sacred Scripture, Sacred War*, 12–14; Mitchell, *Government Street*, 11–13; James H. Otey, "Sermon on Exodus 17:11–12," The James Hervey Otey Papers, 1823–1885, Collection No. 00563, Southern Historical Collection at the Louis Round Wilson Special Collections Library, University of North Carolina at Chapel Hill. Otey preached this sermon twice in 1862: November 9 and December 14.

48. Smyth, *Battle of Fort Sumter*, 3. Like many preachers, Smyth called on examples from ministers in the revolutionary era. *Battle of Fort Sumter*, 32–33.

49. Lincoln, "Second Inaugural Address," 202.

50. Smyth, *Battle of Fort Sumter*, 3–4. See also Kendrick, *Lessons*, 14.

51. Thomas Atkinson, *Christian Duty in the Present Time of Trouble. A Sermon Preached at St. James' Church, Wilmington, N.C., on the Fifth Sunday after Easter, 1861* (Wilmington, NC: Fulton & Price, 1861), 7.

52. Pierce, *Sermons Preached*, 6.

53. Kendrick, *Lessons*, 14, 16–17.

54. E. B. Long, *The Saints and the Union: Utah Territory during the Civil War* (Urbana: University of Illinois Press, 2001), 6–7.

55. Elder John Taylor, "Safety of the Saints at Home," April 28, 1861, in *Journal of Discourses Delivered by President Brigham Young*, vol. 9 (Liverpool, England: s.n., 1862), 234–35.

56. Taylor, "Safety," 234, 236–37. For background on Elder Taylor, see "The Life and Ministry of John Taylor," The Church of Jesus Christ of Latter-Day Saints, https://www.lds.org/manual/teachings-john-taylor/the-life-and-ministry-of-john-taylor?lang=eng. Taylor's account of the attack is part of LDS scripture, recorded in *Doctrine and Covenants*, Section 135, https://www.lds.org/scriptures/dc-testament/dc/135?lang=eng; see also Long, *Saints and the Union*.

57. Taylor, "Safety," 235–36.

58. Taylor, "Safety," 236.

59. Brigham Young, "True Testimony," in *Journal of Discourses*, 3–4.

Chapter 6

1. Mary Boykin Chesnut, *A Diary from Dixie* (Cambridge, MA: Harvard University Press, 1980), 58; McPherson, *BCF*, 332–33.

2. McPherson, *BCF*, 308–9.

3. Guelzo, *Fateful Lightning*, 149–50; McPherson, *BCF*, 313.

4. As quoted in Guelzo, *Fateful Lightning*, 150. As James McPherson wrote, "The Civil War was preeminently a *political* war, a war of peoples rather than of professional armies." McPherson, *BCF*, 332.

5. McPherson, *BCF*, 312.

6. McPherson, *BCF*, 313.

7. McPherson, *BCF*, 318–19.

8. McPherson, *BCF*, 332–35.

9. Goldfield, *America Aflame*, 219–20; Guelzo, *Fateful Lightning*, 151.

10. Guelzo, *Fateful Lightning*, 154; McPherson, *BCF*, 335.

11. McPherson, *BCF*, 340–41, 343.

12. S. S. Cox, "Speech of Hon. S. S. Cox of Ohio," in *The Army of the Potomac, and Its Mismanagement*, ed. Charles Ellet (New York: Ross & Tousey, 1862), 4; McPherson, *BCF*, 345.

13. McPherson, *BCF*, 346–47.

14. McPherson, *BCF*, 347.

15. Mary Anna Jackson, *Life and Letters of General Thomas J. Jackson* (New York: Harper & Brothers, 1892), 177–78.

16. Jackson, *Life and Letters*, 177–78; cf. Thomas J. Jackson, "The Credit Goes to God," in *RACW*, 75–76.

17. *New Orleans Daily Crescent*, August 12, 1861, CA.

18. *The HarperCollins Study Bible* (New York: HarperCollins Publishers, 1993), 62, emphasis added.

19. R. C. Grundy, "Manassas—Its True Signification," *Memphis Daily Appeal*, August 18, 1861, CA.

20. *New Orleans Daily Crescent*, August 12, 1861, CA.

21. John Fletcher, "The Bible and the Sword," in *Political Sermons of the American Founding Era, 1730–1805*, ed. Ellis Sandoz (Indianapolis: Liberty Fund, 1998), 560; Byrd, *Sacred Scripture, Sacred War*, 120.

22. Union army chaplain, Decatur, Alabama, as quoted in Albert J. Raboteau, "African-Americans, Exodus, and the American Israel," in *Religion and American Culture: A Reader*, ed. David Hackett, 2nd ed. (New York: Routledge, 2003), 84.

23. *New Orleans Daily Crescent*, August 12, 1861, CA.

24. Elliott, *God's Presence with our Army at Manassas!* (Savannah: Thorne Williams, 1861), 10–11.

25. John T. Wightman, *The Glory of God, the Defense of the South* (Portland, ME: B. Thurston & Co., 1871), 9, https://archive.org/details/gloryofgoddefens00wigh. On the pillar of fire and cloud, see Exodus 13–14 and Numbers 14, among other texts. Wightman cites Isaiah 4:5.

26. Most helpful for me is the excellent book by Eugene D. Genovese and Elizabeth Fox-Genovese, *Fatal Self-Deception: Slaveholding Paternalism in the Old South* (Cambridge: Cambridge University Press, 2011).

27. Wightman, *Glory of God*, 13.

28. T. S. Winn, *The Great Victory at Manassas Junction. God the Arbiter of Battles* (Tuskaloosa, AL: J. F. Warren, 1861), 2, 6. https://archive.org/details/greatvictoryatma00winn.

29. William C. Butler, *Sermon: Preached in St. John's Church, Richmond, Virginia, on the Sunday after the Battle at Manassas* (Richmond: Charles H. Wynne, Printer, 1861), 5, 7, 11, 13.

30. Wightman, *Glory of God*, 10.

31. Wightman, *Glory of God*, 8–9.

32. Wightman, *Glory of God*, 3.
33. Thomas Smyth, "The Victory of Manassas Plains," *Southern Presbyterian Review* (Columbia, SC) 14 (1862): 612–13.
34. Smyth, "Victory of Manassas Plains," 612–13.
35. Smyth, "Victory of Manassas Plains," 605.
36. Smyth, "Victory of Manassas Plains," 610–11.
37. Smyth, "Victory of Manassas Plains," 613.
38. George D. Armstrong, *"The Good Hand of Our God upon Us." A Thanksgiving Sermon* (Norfolk, VA: J. D. Ghiselin Jr., 1861), 7–8.
39. Armstrong, *Good Hand*, 8.
40. Smyth, "Victory of Manassas Plains," 600, 603. For their citations of Exodus 15:3, see Armstrong, *Good Hand*, 3; Smyth, "Victory of Manassas Plains," 6.
41. Smyth, "Victory of Manassas Plains," 610.
42. Greeley as quoted in John George Nicolay and John Hay, *Abraham Lincoln: A History*, vol. 4 (New York: Century Company, 1914), 365–66; McPherson, *BCF*, 347.
43. Hughes quoted in Kurtz, *Excommunicated from the Union*, 46.
44. For example, see *Bedford* (PA) *Inquirer*, September 13, 1861, CA.
45. Abraham Lincoln, "Lincoln and the First National Fast Day," in *RACW*, 79.
46. John F. Ware, *Our Duty under Reverse; a Sermon Preached* (Boston: John Wilson and Son, 1861), 9–10.
47. As quoted in McPherson, *BCF*, 354.
48. As quoted in McPherson, *BCF*, 354.
49. McPherson, *BCF*, 355.
50. McPherson, *BCF*, 356–58.
51. Horace Bushnell, *Reverses Needed* (Hartford: L. E. Hunt, 1861), 9–10.
52. Bushnell, *Reverses Needed*, 10–13.
53. Bushnell, *Reverses Needed*, 13.
54. Bushnell, *Reverses Needed*, 14–15.
55. Bushnell, *Reverses Needed*, 19–21.
56. T. H. Stockton, *American Sovereignty: A Short Sermon Delivered in the National Hall of Representatives, Sabbath Morning, July 28, 1861* (Washington, DC: Printed by H. Polkinhorn, 1861), 3. Newspapers citing Romans 13 included the *Daily intelligencer* (Wheeling, WV), August 30, 1861, CA; *The Highland Weekly News* (Highland County, OH), August 22, 1861, CA; *Centre Democrat* (Bellefonte, PA), August 1, 1861, CA. On Stockton, see J. M. Buckley, *A History of Methodists in the United States* (New York: Scribner's, 1903), 607–8.
57. Stockton, *American Sovereignty*, 3–4.
58. Stockton, *American Sovereignty*, 3–4.
59. Stockton, *American Sovereignty*, 4–5.
60. Stockton, *American Sovereignty*, 5.
61. Stockton, *American Sovereignty*, 6.
62. Bushnell, *Reverses Needed*, 23, emphasis added.
63. Bushnell, *Reverses Needed*, 23–25.

Chapter 7

1. Commentary on Genesis 49:10, *HarperCollins Study Bible*, 73.

2. J. Lansing Burrows, *Shiloh. A Sermon* ([Raleigh, NC]: [General Tract Agency], 1862), 2–3, 5–6.

3. Robert R. Mathisen, "From Shiloh to Emancipation," in *RACW*, 127. With reference to Shiloh and other battles, some historians have called the Civil War a total war, but Mark E. Neely Jr., James McPherson, and others have corrected this view, arguing that the Civil War did not fit the technical definition of a total war. McPherson, *The War That Forged*, 47–49. But Shiloh was a "baptism" in brutal warfare for Americans. On the Civil War as a total war question, see Mark E. Neely Jr., "Was the Civil War a Total War," *Civil War History* 37, no. 1 (March 1991): 5–28.

4. Goldfield, *America Aflame*, 225.

5. William Barrows, *Our War and Our Religion: And Their Harmony* (Boston: J.M. Whittemore & Co., 1862), 3–4.

6. Barrows, *Our War*, 5.

7. Barrows, *Our War*, 6–7.

8. Barrows, *Our War*, 9, 11, 18.

9. Goldfield, *America Aflame*, 226.

10. McPherson, *BCF*, 406.

11. Quoted in McPherson, *BCF*, 408–9.

12. McPherson, *BCF*, 409.

13. Quoted in McPherson, *BCF*, 414.

14. McPherson, *BCF*, 406, 414.

15. As quoted in Guelzo, *Fateful Lightning*, 206–7.

16. McPherson, *BCF*, 413–15; Goldfield, *America Aflame*, 230; Guelzo, *Fateful Lightning*, 207.

17. Quoted in McPherson, *BCF*, 413.

18. Quoted in Goldfield, *America Aflame* 234.

19. Quoted in McPherson, *For Cause and Comrades*, 71. The Illinois soldier was Edgar Embley.

20. As quoted in McPherson, *For Cause and Comrades*, 71.

21. As quoted in Faust, *This Republic of Suffering*, 36.

22. Frank Moore, *The Civil War in Song and Story, 1860–1865* (New York: P.F. Collier, 1865), 438. See also George Barton, "George Barton's Battlefield Angels," in *RACW*, 134; Goldfield, *America Aflame*, 230; Stephen William Berry, *Weirding the War: Stories from the Civil War's Ragged Edges* (Athens: University of Georgia Press, 2011), 1.

23. Moore, *Song and Story*, 64–65.

24. Moore, *Song and Story*, 64.

25. As quoted in Barton, "George Barton's Battlefield Angels," 134.

26. J. H. McCarty, *The American Union* (Concord, NH: Fogg, Hadley & Co., 1862), 20–21. He quoted Leviticus 26:14–36.

27. *American Citizen* (Canton, MS), May 16, 1862, CA.

28. Isaac T. Tichenor, "I have Served the Cause of My God," in *RACW*, 138–39; letter from Isaac T. Tichenor to Alabama attorney general T. H. Watts.

29. Rable, *God's Almost Chosen Peoples*, 116; "Isaac Taylor Tichenor," Southern Baptist Historical Library and Archives, http://www.sbhla.org/bio_ittichenor.htm.

30. As quoted in Robert Lewis Dabney, *Life and Campaigns of Lieut.-Gen. Thomas J. Jackson, (Stonewall Jackson)* (New York: Blelock & Company, 1866), 329–30.

31. Goldfield, *America Aflame*, 235.

32. Grant quoted in Goldfield, *America Aflame,* 234–35.

33. Chesnut, *Chesnut's Civil War*, 331–32, April 29, 1862.

34. Herman Melville, *Battle-Pieces and Aspects of the War* (New York: Harper & Brothers, 1866), 63.

35. Abraham Lincoln, "Trusting that God Will Bring Us Safety," in *RACW*, 136.

36. William Orne White, *"Our Struggle Righteous in the Sight of God." A Sermon* (Keene, NH): G. & G. H. Tilden, 1862), 6.

37. White, *Our Struggle Righteous*, 6–7.

38. Tucker, *God's Providence in War*, 5–6.

39. Tucker, *God's Providence in War*, 7.

40. Tucker, *God's Providence in War*, 7–8.

41. Tucker, *God's Providence in War*, 10–11.

42. Sterry, *Sermon in Memory*, 2.

43. Sterry, *Sermon in Memory*, 1–2.

44. Sterry, *Sermon in Memory*, 2.

45. Sterry, *Sermon in Memory*, 1, 3, 6.

46. Sterry, *Sermon in Memory*, 7.

47. Sterry, *Sermon in Memory*, 7, 9.

48. Sterry, *Sermon in Memory*, 11–12.

49. S. D. Phelps, *National Symptoms* (New York: Sheldon & Co., 1862), 14–15.

50. *Semi-Weekly Standard* (Raleigh, NC), April 26, 1862, CA.

51. Levi L. Paine, *Political Lessons of the Rebellion. A Sermon* (Farmington: Samuel S. Cowles, 1862), 5.

52. Paine, *Political Lessons*, 5–6.

53. Paine, *Political Lessons*, 6.

54. George W. Gardner, *Treason and the Fate of Traitors* (Boston: Davis and Farmer, 1862), 12–13.

55. James Henley Thornwell, *Our Danger and Our Duty* (Columbia, SC: Southern Guardian Steam-Power Press, 1862), 9, 12–13.

56. Thornwell, *Danger and Duty*, 9–10. See also J. H. Thornwell, "Our National Sins," in *Fast Day Sermons* (New York: Rudd & Carleton, 1861), 9–10, 13.

57. Thornwell, *Danger and Duty*, 3–4.

58. Thornwell, *Danger and Duty*, 9–11.

59. Morgan, *Civil War Diary*, 213, August 13, 1862.

Chapter 8

1. Daniel A. Payne, *Welcome to the Ransomed* (Baltimore: Bull & Tuttle, 1862), 5–7, 11.
2. Payne, *Welcome to the Ransomed*, 11.
3. Payne, *Welcome to the Ransomed*, 11–12.
4. Payne, *Welcome to the Ransomed*, 15–16.
5. Milton C. Sernett, ed., *African American Religious History: A Documentary Witness*, 2nd ed. (Durham, NC: Duke University Press, 1999), 232.
6. McPherson, *BCF*, 494–95.
7. Edmund B. Wilson, *Reasons for Thanksgiving: A Sermon* (Salem, MA: Observer Office, n.d.), 4–5.
8. Douglass, *FDP*, 3:525.
9. James A. Garfield, *The Wild Life of the Army: Civil War Letters of James A. Garfield* (East Lansing: Michigan State University Press, 1964), 65, February 12, 1862.
10. Garfield, *Wild Life*, 65, February 12, 1862.
11. James McPherson describes these three "Republican factions" in *BCF*, 494.
12. Quoted in David Williams, *I Freed Myself: African American Self-Emancipation in the Civil War* (Cambridge: Cambridge University Press, 2014), 80.
13. McPherson, *BCF*, 497–98.
14. *Semi-Weekly Standard* (Raleigh, NC), July 2, 1862, CA.
15. Douglass, *FDP*, 3:531, 534, 538.
16. Douglass, *FDP*, 3:531, 533; see also 539.
17. Douglass, *FDP*, 3:541.
18. Quoted in Guelzo, *Fateful Lightning*, 168.
19. Halleck quoted in McPherson, *BCF*, 502; D. H. Dilbeck, *A More Civil War: How the Union Waged a Just War* (Chapel Hill: University of North Carolina Press, 2016), 5.
20. Dilbeck, *A More Civil War*, 1–2.
21. Francis Lieber, *Instructions for the Government of Armies of the United States in the Field, General Orders, no. 100, War Department, Adjutant General's Office, Washington, April 24, 1863* (Washington, DC, 1863), 4, 6. Articles 15 and 29.
22. "The End of Peaceable Warfare," *New York World*, article picked up by the *Daily Intelligencer* (Wheeling, VA [WV]), July 14, 1862, CA.
23. From an article in the *Richmond Dispatch*, which ran in the *National Republican* (Washington, DC), August 16, 1862, CA.
24. Quoted in McPherson, *BCF*, 502.
25. McPherson, *BCF*, 503.
26. McPherson, *BCF*, 502–4. Lincoln quotations on 503–4; see also Richard Yates, "Governor Yates Addresses Slavery," in *RACW*, 153.
27. Quotations and commentary in McPherson, *BCF*, 502, emphasis added.
28. Henry McNeal Turner, *Freedom's Witness: The Civil War Correspondence of Henry McNeal Turner*, ed. Jean Lee Cole (Morgantown: West Virginia University Press, 2013), 51; see also Henry McNeal Turner, *Christian Recorder*, July 19, 1862, http://www.thehenrymcnealturnerproject.org/2017/05/for-christian-recorder-july-19-1862.html.

29. Turner, *Freedom's Witness*, 51; see also Turner, *Christian Recorder*, http://www. thehenrymcnealturnerproject.org/2017/05/for-christian-recorder-july-19-1862.html.

30. Douglass, *FDP*, 3:531.

31. As quoted in McPherson, *BCF*, 500.

32. *Marshall County Republican* (Plymouth, IN), August 7, 1862, CA. The paper credits the *Chicago Tribune* for the story. Note also the author mistakenly cites the text as 1 Samuel 13; it is actually 1 Samuel 30.

33. Sidney Dean, *The War: And the Duty of a Loyal People* (Providence: Pierce & Budlong, 1862), 6, 8–9, 12–13.

34. Dean, *War and the Duty*, 14–16.

35. *Memphis* (TN) *Daily Appeal*, June 3, 1862, CA. For other southern views of the Achan story, see R. H. Lafferty, *A Fast-Day Sermon* (Fayetteville, NC: Printed at the Presbyterian Office, 1862), *passim*; C. H. Wiley, *Scriptural Views of National Trials: How We Got In. How to Get Out*, 2nd ed. (Trenton, NJ: Thomas U. Baker, 1864). I. R. Finley uses this text to point to southern sins that parallel Achan's "accursed thing," arguing that these sins are to blame for southern misfortune. I. R. Finley, *The Lord Reigneth* (Richmond: Soldiers' Tract Association, M. E. Church, South, 1863), 13–15.

36. "God Cares for the Poor and Oppressed," *Daily Green Mountain Freeman* (Montpelier, VT), June 24, 1862, CA. The newspaper credited the article to the *North Western Advocate* (undated).

37. "God Cares for the Poor and Oppressed."

38. McPherson, *The War That Forged*, 119; McPherson, *BCF*, 506.

39. McPherson, *The War That Forged*, 119.

40. Quotations in McPherson, *BCF*, 505.

41. Quotations in McPherson, *BCF*, 506–7.

42. McPherson, *BCF*, 507–8.

43. Douglass document reprinted in Paul David Escott, *Paying Freedom's Price: A History of African Americans in the Civil War* (New York: Rowman & Littlefield, 2017), 128–29; Frederick Douglass, *Selected Writings and Speeches*, ed. Philip S. Foner (Chicago: Lawrence Hill Books, 1999), 480–81.

44. Escott, *Paying Freedom's Price*, 129.

45. W. H. Furness, *A Thanksgiving Discourse* (Philadelphia: T. B. Pugh, 1862), 14.

46. Quotations in McPherson, *The War That Forged*, 120.

47. Oakes and Lincoln as quoted in McPherson, *The War That Forged*, 120.

48. McPherson, *The War That Forged*, 120; James Oakes, *The Radical and the Republican: Frederick Douglass, Abraham Lincoln, and the Triumph of Antislavery Politics*, Kindle ed. (New York: W.W. Norton, 2007), 125, 127.

49. Lincoln as quoted in McPherson, *BCF*, 508; McPherson, *The War That Forged*, 112.

50. McPherson, *BCF*, 508–9; Stone, *Emancipation*, 10.

51. Quoted in McPherson, *BCF*, 510.

52. Turner, *Freedom's Witness*, 44, 47; cf. 44–49.

53. Turner, *Freedom's Witness*, 48. See also Frances E. W. Harper, *Discarded Legacy: Politics and Poetics in the Life of Frances E. W. Harper, 1825–1911* (Detroit: Wayne State University Press, 1994), 51.

54. Turner, *Freedom's Witness*, 48; Abraham Lincoln, "Proclamation by Abraham Lincoln, 19 May 1862," No. 90, Presidential Proclamations, series 23, Record Group 11, National Archives, http://www.freedmen.umd.edu/hunter.htm.

55. Turner, *Freedom's Witness*, 48–49.

56. Turner, *Freedom's Witness*, 44, 46.

57. Stone, *Emancipation*, 4.

58. Payne, *Welcome to the Ransomed*, 7–8.

59. *Belmont Chronicle* (St. Clairsville, OH), June 5, 1862, CA.

60. *Belmont Chronicle* (St. Clairsville, OH), June 5, 1862, CA.

Chapter 9

1. As quoted in McPherson, *For Cause and Comrades*, 62–63.

2. Guyatt, *Providence*, 1–2.

3. Guyatt, *Providence*, 2–3.

4. George F. Pierce, "The Word of God a Nation's Life," in *Sermons of the Confederacy*, ed. William Peters (Chattanooga, TN: C.S. Printing, 2014), 282.

5. Quoted in McPherson, *BCF*, 525.

6. *Goodhue Volunteer* (Red Wing, Goodhue County, MN), August 20, 1862, CA.

7. Guelzo, *Fateful Lightning*, 169–70; McPherson, *BCF*, 532.

8. *New York Tribune* quoted in McPherson, *Tried by War*, 119–20.

9. Barton as quoted in McPherson, *BCF*, 532; *New York Times* quoted in McPherson, *Tried by War*, 120.

10. Lincoln quoted in McPherson, *BCF*, 533; see also McPherson, *Tried by War*, 120–21.

11. McPherson, *BCF*, 534.

12. Joseph M. Atkinson, *God, the Giver of Victory and Peace* (Raleigh, NC: [s.n.], 1862), 7.

13. D. S. Doggett, *A Nation's Ebenezer* (Richmond, VA: Enquirer Book and Job Press, 1862), 7–8.

14. Doggett, *A Nation's Ebenezer*, 13–14.

15. Atkinson, *Giver of Victory*, 9.

16. Elliott, *Our Cause*, 23.

17. The point of *Sinners* was not to terrify people; it was to inspire repentance by making people aware of their vulnerability to God's wrath because of their sins.

18. Elliott, *Our Cause*, 23.

19. Elliott, *Our Cause*, 6.

20. Southerner James Henley Thornwell expressed the mysteries of providence, saying that people could not fully know "the whole end of Providence" without "a special revelation." As quoted in Guyatt, *Providence*, 271. Original source: Thornwell, *Danger and Duty*, 12.

21. Elliott, *Our Cause*, 7–10.

22. Elliott, *Our Cause*, 10–11.

23. Elliott, *Our Cause*, 10–11.

24. Elliott, *Our Cause*, 10–11.

25. Elliott, *Our Cause*, 12, 14–15. I have corrected the spelling of "reliance" and "protection" in this quotation.

26. Elliott, *Our Cause*, 10.

27. Edward Lounsbery, *The Safe Refuge in the Day of Calamity* (Philadelphia: Ringwalt & Brown, 1862), 5 (Exodus 12:29–30).

28. Lounsbery, *Safe Refuge*, 6–7.

29. Lincoln, *Works*, 5:420.

30. W. W. Patton, *President Lincoln and the Chicago Memorial: A Paper read before the Maryland Historical Society, December 12th, 1887* (Baltimore: John Murphy & Co, 1888), 12–13. https://archive.org/details/presidentlincoln5014patt.

31. Lincoln, *Works*, 5:419–20, 422–24.

32. Lincoln, *Works*, 5:420.

33. Lincoln, *Works*, 5:422–25.

34. Patton, *Lincoln and the Chicago Memorial*, 14. https://archive.org/details/presidentlincoln5014patt.

35. James D. Liggett, "Our National Reverses," in *RACW*, 161–62.

36. Liggett, "Our National Reverses," 163.

37. Liggett, "Our National Reverses," 163.

38. Liggett, "Our National Reverses," 163.

39. Liggett, "Our National Reverses," 164.

40. Turner, *Freedom's Witness*, 63–64.

41. A. Hartpence, *Our National Crisis: A Sermon Preached . . . September 14, 1862* (Philadelphia: s.n., 1862), 6.

42. As quoted in McPherson, *For Cause and Comrades*, 65–66.

43. Hartpence, *Our National Crisis*, 2.

44. Hartpence, *Our National Crisis*, 1.

45. Hartpence, *Our National Crisis*, 4.

Chapter 10

1. Brownson, *Works*, 17:214, emphasis added.

2. As quoted in Rable, *God's Almost Chosen Peoples*, 88–89.

3. Faust, *This Republic of Suffering*, 32.

4. Faust, *This Republic of Suffering*, 6.

5. Phoebe Yates Pember as quoted in Rosen, *The Jewish Confederates*, 300. Also in Robert N. Rosen, *Confederate Charleston: An Illustrated History of the City and the People during the Civil War* (Columbia: University of South Carolina Press), 89.

6. Quoted in McPherson, *BCF*, 537. For additional detail, see McPherson, *BCF*, chap. 17.

7. Quoted in Stout, *Altar of the Nation*, 154.

8. McPherson, *BCF*, 544.

9. McPherson, *BCF*, 544–45; McPherson, *Tried by War*, 125–26.

10. Lepore, *These Truths*, 247, 273. Douglass quoted on p. 273.

11. Stout, *Altar of the Nation*, 156.

12. Mark S. Shantz, *Awaiting the Heavenly Country: The Civil War and America's Culture of Death* (Ithaca, NY: Cornell University Press, 2008), 189–92.

13. Faust, *This Republic of Suffering*, xvi–xvii.

14. As quoted in Goldfield, *America Aflame*, 262; McPherson *BCF*, 546–56.

15. Abraham Lincoln, "Preliminary Emancipation Proclamation," *American Originals: National Archives and Records Administration*, https://www.archives.gov/exhibits/american_originals_iv/sections/preliminary_emancipation_proclamation.html#.

16. Turner, *Freedom's Witness*, 70–72, 74, 83–84.

17. McPherson, *The War That Forged*, 115–16. Original citation from *Douglass Monthly* 5 (August 1862): 692–94.

18. Quoted in McPherson, *BCF*, 558.

19. McPherson, *BCF*, 558.

20. McPherson, *BCF*, 558; for an argument that God gave Lincoln all the authority he needed to end slavery, see Beecher, "National Injustice," 359, 378–79.

21. Quoted in McPherson, *BCF*, 558.

22. Israel E. Dwinell, *Hope for Our Country* (Salem: Charles W. Swasey, 1862), 16.

23. Quoted in McPherson, *BCF*, 558–59.

24. Turner, *Freedom's Witness*, 81.

25. As quoted in James M. McPherson, *The Negro's Civil War: How American Negroes Felt and Acted during the War for the Union* (New York: Vintage Books, 1965), 49; *Douglass Monthly* 5 (October 1862): 721–22; Douglass, *Selected Speeches and Writings*, 517.

26. All as quoted in McPherson, *For Cause and Comrades*, 119–20.

27. *Christian Recorder*, October 8, 1864, Accessible Archives; Faust, *This Republic of Suffering*, 33–34.

28. Samuel T. Spear, *Radicalism and the National Crisis* (Brooklyn: William W. Rose, 1862), 11.

29. Spear, *Radicalism*, 11.

30. Spear, *Radicalism*, 16.

31. As quoted in McPherson, *For Cause and Comrades*, 120.

32. As quoted in Goldfield, *America Aflame*, 262.

33. As quoted in McPherson, *For Cause and Comrades*, 69–71.

34. See Duffield, *Courage*, 17–19.

35. "Shall Christians Fight?," *Daily Green Mountain Freeman* (Montpelier, VT), October 15, 1862, CA.

36. "Shall Christians Fight?" For a pacifist argument on this text, see Brenneman, *Christianity and War*, 25. This sermon was previously published in 1863.

37. See, for example: Atwood, *Purse*, main text, also 6; Duffield, *Courage*, main text, also 13–14; Lord, *Country's Crisis, 13*; J. K. Mason, *The Sword* (Bangor: Samuel S. Smith, 1861), main text, 5, 9.

38. Mason, *The Sword*, 5–6.

39. Mason, *The Sword*, 7–9. This was a popular scripture in the Civil War. See also Peter Anstadt, *Loyalty to the Government: A Thanksgiving Sermon* (Selins Grove, PA: Office of the Lutheran Kirchenbote, 1863), 12–14.

40. Mason, *The Sword*, 9–11.

41. Daily, *Great Rebellion*, 2.

42. Daily, *Great Rebellion*, 2–3. Daily quotes from Revelation 19:14 and other passages. The "Lion of the tribe of Judah" reference came from Revelation 5:5.

43. Daily, *Great Rebellion*, 2–3.

44. Alonzo Hill, *In Memoriam* (Boston: John Wilson and Son, 1862), 4, https://archive.org/details/inmemoriamdiscou00hill.Hill.

45. Hill, *In Memoriam*, 26–27.

46. Hill, *In Memoriam*, 16–17.

47. E. W. Bentley, *The Duty of Emancipation* (Ellenville, NY: S. M. Taylor, 1862), 8. For a defense of Garrison's devotion to scripture, see Douglass, *My Bondage*, 355.

48. Beecher, "National Injustice," 365.

49. Beecher, "National Injustice," 364.

50. W. H. Furness, *A Word of Consolation for the Kindred of Those Who Have Fallen in Battle* (Philadelphia: Crissy & Markley, 1862), 10.

51. William L. Gaylord, *The Soldier God's Minister* (Fitchburg: Rollstone Job Printing Office, 1862), 7.

52. Gaylord, *The Soldier God's Minister*, 8.

53. Gaylord, *The Soldier God's Minister*, 8–9.

54. Gaylord, *The Soldier God's Minister*, 9, 16.

55. Gaylord, *The Soldier God's Minister*, 16–17.

56. Gaylord, *The Soldier God's Minister*, 17. For a powerful sermon that makes some of the same arguments during the same month, see Miles Sanford, *Treason, and the Punishment It Deserves* (Boston: J.M. Hewes, 1862).

57. McPherson, *For Cause and Comrades*, 92–93.

58. As McPherson noted, "He did, at Gettysburg." Quotations in McPherson, *For Cause and Comrades*, 92–93.

59. Quoted in McPherson, *For Cause and Comrades*, 93.

60. McPherson, *For Cause and Comrades*, 97–98.

61. As quoted in Jacquelyn S. Nelson, *Indiana Quakers Confront the Civil War* (Indianapolis: Indiana Historical Society, 1991), 38.

62. As quoted in Nelson, *Indiana Quakers*, 20.

63. As quoted in Nelson, *Indiana Quakers*, 30–31.

64. As quoted in William C. Kashatus, *Abraham Lincoln, the Quakers, and the Civil War: "A Trial of Principle and Faith"* (Santa Barbara, CA: Praeger, 2014), 1–2.

65. Lincoln, *Works*, 5:478.

66. Lincoln, *Works*, 7:535.

67. Abraham Lincoln, "Meditation on the Divine Will," in *RACW*, 176.

Chapter 11

1. Morgan, *Civil War Diary*, 330–31, November 9, 1862.

2. Allen C. Guelzo, *Lincoln's Emancipation Proclamation: The End of Slavery in America* (New York: Simon and Schuster, 2006), 1, 6.

3. Quotations in McPherson, *Tried by War*, 135–36.

4. Quotations in McPherson, *Tried by War*, 138–40.

5. McPherson, *Tried by War*, 142.

6. McPherson, *BCF*, 572–74; Barton quotation in Goldfield, *America Aflame*, 272.

7. William L. Barney, *The Oxford Encyclopedia of the Civil War* (New York: Oxford University Press, 2011), "Fredericksburg," 134–36 (henceforth *OECW*); McPherson, *Tried by War*, 145.

8. Quoted in McPherson, *BCF*, 575.

9. Turner, *Freedom's Witness*, 91–92.

10. Sarna and Shapell, *Lincoln and the Jews*, 112–18; Jonathan D. Sarna, *When General Grant Expelled the Jews* (New York: Schocken, 2012), 3–4, 21–22.

11. Robert E. Lee, "The Signal Manifestations of Divine Mercy," in *RACW*, 221.

12. Stacy Fowler, *A Sermon Preached in North Yarmouth* (Portland, ME: Brown Thurston, 1863), 3–4; cf. Job 19:25–27.

13. Fowler, *Sermon Preached*, 6.

14. Note that Lord mistakenly cites this verse as Psalms 87:3. W. W. Lord, *A Discourse, by the Rev. W. W. Lord* (Vicksburg, MS: M. Shannon, 1863), 3.

15. Lord, *Discourse*, 4–5.

16. Lord, *Discourse*, 5.

17. Lord, *Discourse*, 6–7.

18. Lord, *Discourse*, 8–10, 13.

19. McPherson, *Tried by War*, 155.

20. McPherson, *Tried by War*, 156.

21. Douglass, *FDP*, 3:543–44 n. 1; he made this statement in October 1862.

22. Quoted in McPherson, *Tried by War*, 156–57.

23. Quoted in McPherson, *Tried by War*, 157–58.

24. Goldfield, *America Aflame*, 267.

25. Urban C. Brewer, *The Bible and American Slavery: A Discourse Delivered* (New York: Reid Gould, 1863), 5.

26. Turner, *Freedom's Witness*, 92–94.

27. Turner, *Freedom's Witness*, 92–94.

28. Douglass, *FDP*, 3:543–44.

29. Douglass, *FDP*, 3:549–51.

30. Douglass, *FDP*, 3:551. Many supporters of the proclamation drew similar parallels between it and the Revolution. See C. L. Goodell, *Thanksgiving Sermon* (Hartford: Case, Lockwood & Co., 1863), 13.

31. Douglass, *FDP*, 3:558.

32. Douglass, *FDP*, 3:551–52.

33. Douglass, *FDP*, 3:553.

34. Douglass, *FDP*, 3:552–53. Corrected spelling of "villainies."

35. Douglass, *FDP*, 3:561.

36. Douglass, *FDP*, 3:562.

37. Douglass, *FDP*, 3:573. See also Brewer, *Bible* and American Slavery, 10–11; Samuel Aughey, *The Renovation of Politics* (West Chester, PA: E. F. James, 1861), 8; C. H. Austin, *The Soldier's Mission* (Utica, NY: Roberts, 1863), 8; William H. Boole, *Antidote*

to Rev. H. J. Van Dyke's pro-Slavery Discourse (New York: Edmund Jones & Co., 1861), 3; Hugh Brown, *Review of Rev. Dr. Raphael's Disco'rse* (North White Creek, NY: R. K. Crocker, 1861), 1.

38. W. H. Furness, *The Declaration of Independence: A Discourse Delivered in the First Congregational Unitarian Church in Philadelphia June 29, 1862* (Philadelphia: C. Sherman & Son, 1862), 4.

39. Douglass, *FDP*, 3:597; Turner, *Freedom's Witness*, 99.

40. Edmund B. Fairfield, *Christian Patriotism: A Sermon Delivered* (Lansing, MI: John A. Kerr, 1863), 18, 26.

41. Fairfield, *Christian Patriotism*, 18, 26.

42. Fairfield, *Christian Patriotism*, 24–25.

43. See, for example, a sermon from July 1863: Rev. C. A. Van Anda, "The 'Powers that Be,' and Our Subjection to Them," in *Lancaster* (OH) *Gazette*, July 23, 1863, CA.

44. Fairfield, *Christian Patriotism*, 17–18.

45. Fairfield, *Christian Patriotism*, 18–19, 22, 25–26.

46. Fairfield, *Christian Patriotism*, 39.

Chapter 12

1. Henry Wallace, *The Fast That God Hath Chosen* (Davenport, IA: Gazette Steam Book and Job Rooms, 1863), 3–4. See also "National Humiliation and Prayer," *Christian Advocate and Journal*, April 23, 1863, 132.

2. Wallace, *Fast*, 11–13.

3. Turner, *Freedom's Witness*, 88.

4. Harper, *Discarded Legacy*, 53.

5. Douglass, *FDP*, 3:545.

6. Douglass, *FDP*, 3:570–72.

7. Edmund B. Wilson, *The Proclamation of Freedom* (Salem, MA: T.J. Hutchinson, 1863), 13–14.

8. Quoted in Oakes, *Radical and the Republican*, chap. 2, section " 'Debauchment' of Public Sentiment."

9. Brewer, *Bible and American Slavery*, 10.

10. Brewer, *Bible and American Slavery*, 6.

11. Brewer, *Bible and American Slavery*, 11.

12. Brewer, *Bible and American Slavery*, 11.

13. Lepore, *These Truths*, 284.

14. Brewer, *Bible and American Slavery*, 11–13. See also "The Unity of the Race," *Christian Advocate and Journal*, October 8, 1863, 324.

15. C. F. Worrell, *God in Our Country's Calamities. A Thanksgiving Sermon* (Hightstown, NJ: Jacob Stults, 1864), 10–11.

16. N. S. S. Beman, *Thanksgiving in the Times of Civil War* (Troy, NY: A. W. Scribner & Co., 1861), 16. Many sermons connected Acts 17:26 with the Declaration of Independence, including Albert Barnes, *The Conditions of Peace* (Philadelphia: Evans, 1863), 48;

Worrell, *Country's Calamities*, 10–11; George Peck, *Our Country* (New York: Carlton/Porter, 1865), 167.

17. N. S. Dickinson, *Slavery: The Nation's Crime and Danger. A Sermon Preached* (Boston: George Noyes, 1860), 7–8. See also Beecher, "National Injustice," 339.

18. The Constitution of the American Anti-Slavery Society (1835) listed Jefferson's statement, "All men are created equal," on the title page, and then quoted part of Acts 17:26 in the first sentence of the preamble. Constitution of the American Anti-Slavery Society, Library of Congress, Slaves and the Courts, 1740 to 1860, https://lccn.loc.gov/2001615799; William and Ellen Craft, *Running a Thousand Miles for Freedom* (London: William Tweedie, 1860), iii. https://docsouth.unc.edu/neh/craft/craft.html In my review of over two hundred slave narratives, I found that Acts 17:26 was among the most popular biblical texts, along with Matthew 7:12, Job 3:17, and Mark 16:15. I accessed the "North American Slave Narratives" collection at UNC–Chapel Hill. See *Documenting the American South*, UNC–Chapel Hill, https://docsouth.unc.edu/neh/. See also Emerson B. Powery and Rodney S. Sadler Jr., *The Genesis of Liberation: Biblical Interpretation in the Antebellum Narratives of the Enslaved* (Louisville: Westminster John Knox Press, 2016), 92–102.

19. This verse was printed in many *New York Tribune* advertisements in various newspapers. See *Grand Haven* (MI) *News*, December 24, 1862, CA. The verse had a long history of antislavery use. Just to cite a few, see Alexander McLeod, *Negro Slavery Unjustifiable* (1802), 10th ed. (New York: McLeod, 1860), 12; W. G. Hillman, *National Calamities from God* (Mansfield: Herald Book, 1865), 21; N. L. Rice, *The Pulpit: Its Relations to Our National Crisis* (New York: Scribner, 1862), 49; John W. Scott, *The Times, and Signs of the Times* (Washington, PA: Tribune Office, 1862), 18; Joseph G. Symmes, *National Thanksgiving* (Philadelphia: Martien, 1864), 12; A. Witherspoon, *The Hand of God* (Rutland: Tuttle/Gay, 1863), 4; James Marshall, *The Nation's Gratitude* (Philadelphia: King/Baird, 1865), 21, 27; A. J. Gordon, *The Chosen Fast. A Discourse Preached* (Boston: N. P. Kemp, 1865), 5. For a study of this text during the war that relates it to the parable of the Good Samaritan, see "Substance Above Shadow," *Christian Advocate and Journal*, October 16, 1862, 332. For another southern dismissal of Acts 17:26 as a text about slavery, see *Biblical Recorder* (Raleigh, NC), Wednesday, January 9, 1861, http://digital.olivesoftware.com/Olive/APA/Wakeforest/SharedView.Article.aspx?href=BCR%2F1861%2F01%2F09&id=Ar00113&sk=DF85F3E5&viewMode=image.

20. J. C. Mitchell, *A Bible Defense of Slavery and the Unity of Mankind* (Mobile: Thompson, 1861), 16.

21. Peter Doub, "An Essay on Slavery," box 2, folder 9 (undated), in the Peter Doub Papers, Stuart A. Rose Manuscript, Archives, and Rare Book Library, Emory University.

22. See David M. Goldenberg, *The Curse of Ham: Race and Slavery in Early Judaism, Christianity, and Islam* (Princeton, NJ: Princeton University Press, 2003); David M. Goldenberg, *Black and Slave: The Origins and History of the Curse of Ham* (Berlin: de Gruyter, 2017); Colin Kidd, *The Forging of Races: Race and Scripture in the Protestant Atlantic World, 1600–2000* (New York: Cambridge University Press, 2006); David M.

Whitford, *The Curse of Ham in the Early Modern Era: The Bible and the Justification of Slavery* (Burlington, VT: Ashgate, 2009); Haynes, *Noah's Curse*.

23. See Mitchell, *Bible Defense of Slavery*, 5–8, 16.

24. Quoted in Blight, *Prophet of Freedom*, 16.

25. Cornelius H. Edgar, *The Curse of Canaan Rightly Interpreted* (New York: Baker & Godwin, 1862), 18–21. See also Edwin Harwood, *Canaan, Shem and Japheth. Sermon Preached in Trinity Church, New Haven, October 25, 1863* (New Haven: Thomas H. Pease, 1863).

26. Edgar, *Curse of Canaan*, 18–21.

27. Edgar, *Curse of Canaan*, 23.

28. James Warley Miles, *God in History* (Charleston, SC: Steam Power Press of Evans & Cogswell, 1863), 6. Other proslavery ministers made this point. See Renyard, "A Visit to Bishop Soule," *Christian Advocate and Journal*, July 20, 1865, 228.

29. Miles, *God in History*, 15–16; Other southerners saw Paul's text not as any proclamation of unity, but just evidence that "God directs the destinies of nations." Edward Reed, *A People Saved by the Lord* (Charleston, SC: Evans & Cogswell, 1861), 4–5; Wightman, *Glory of God*, 3–4; Thornwell, "Our National Sins," 49–50.

30. Miles, *God in History*, 9–10, 14–16.

31. Miles, *God in History*, 26–27.

32. McPherson, *For Cause and Comrades*, 106.

33. As quoted in McPherson, *Tried by War*, 166.

34. As quoted in McPherson, *Tried by War*, 168.

35. Goldfield, *America Aflame*, 275.

36. Chestnut, *Chesnut's Civil War*, 320–21, March 1862.

37. As quoted in McPherson, *Tried by War*, 171–72.

38. As quoted in McPherson, *Tried by War*, 170–71.

39. As quoted in Adam Bright and Michael Bright, *"Respect to All." Letters of Two Pennsylvania Boys in the War of the Rebellion*, ed. Aida Craig Truxall (Pittsburgh: University of Pittsburgh Press, 1962), 41–42. The letter is dated May 8, 1863.

40. Bright and Bright, *Respects to All*, 93, letter dated July 21, 1863.

41. John Reynolds, "This Quasi Religious War," in *RACW*, 219–20, January 9, 1863.

42. Willard Spaulding, *The Pulpit and the State: A Discourse, Preached on Sunday, Feb. 15, 1863* (Salem, MA: Charles A. Beckford, 1863), 10–11.

43. Spaulding, *Pulpit and the State*, 13–14.

44. Spaulding, *Pulpit and the State*, 19–20.

45. Samuel Keese, "The 'Peace Party,'" *The Liberator*, September 16, 1864), 19th Century US Newspapers. See also "A Scriptural Delineation of the Copperheads," *The Liberator*, October 14, 1864, 19th Century US Newspapers.

46. As quoted in Goldfield, *America Aflame*, 275.

47. Philip English Mackey, "Revered George Barrell Cheever: Yankee Reformer as Champion of the Gallows," *Proceedings of the American Antiquarian Society* 82 (1972): 323–24, http://www.americanantiquarian.org/proceedings/44498047.pdf.

48. George Barrell Cheever, *The Proposed Return into Egypt, and Its Consequences* ([Washington, DC?]: s.n., 1863), 1.

49. Cheever, *Proposed Return into Egypt*, 1.

50. Cheever, *Proposed Return into Egypt*, 2–4.

51. Cheever, *Proposed Return into Egypt*, 5–6.

52. Cheever, *Proposed Return into Egypt*, 6–7.

53. Cheever, *Proposed Return into Egypt*, 16–17, 20.

54. Cheever, *Proposed Return into Egypt*, 17–18, 29. See also Elisha L. Cleaveland, *Our Duty in Regard to the Rebellion* (New Haven: Please, 1863), 9, 11.

55. Turner, *Freedom's Witness*, 111.

56. Turner, *Freedom's Witness*, 111, 117.

57. Horace C. Hovey, *Loyalty. A Sermon* (Northampton, MA: Metcalf & Co., 1863), 3, 8–9, 15.

58. J. C. Lord, *A Sermon: On the Character and Influence of Washington* (Buffalo: A. M. Clapp & Co.'s Morning Express Steam Printing House, 1863), 17–18.

Chapter 13

1. See Goldfield, *America Aflame*, 293.

2. Abraham Lincoln, "Gettysburg Address," in *RACW*, 297.

3. Daniel W. Stowell, "Stonewall Jackson and the Providence of God," in Miller, Stout, and Wilson, *Religion and the American Civil War*, 188.

4. Stowell, "Stonewall," 188.

5. Stowell, "Stonewall," 188–89; Buck, *Shadows on My Heart*, 200.

6. Stowell, "Stonewall," 187.

7. Stowell, "Stonewall," 187.

8. James B. Ramsey, *True Eminence Founded on Holiness. A Discourse Occasioned by the Death of Lieut. Gen. T. J. Jackson* (Lynchburg: Water-power Presses, 1863), 3–4.

9. Ramsey, *True Eminence*, 11, 13.

10. Joseph Cross, *Camp and Field* (Macon, GA: Boykin & Co., 1864), 120. https://archive. org/details/06078292.4425.emory.edu/page/n119.

11. Quoted in Stowell, "Stonewall," 189–90.

12. McPherson, *BCF*, 661.

13. Barney, "Gettysburg," in *OECW*, 144–47; McPherson, *BCF*, 662.

14. McPherson, *For Cause and Comrades*, 3, 11; see also chap. 5.

15. McPherson, *For Cause and Comrades*, 75, 79.

16. McPherson, *For Cause and Comrades*, 83–85.

17. William Corby and Lawrence Frederick Kohl, *Memoirs of Chaplain Life: Three Years with the Irish Brigade in the Army of the Potomac* (New York: Oxford University Press, 1992), 185–86. Also cited in *RACW*, 279.

18. Corby and Kohl, *Memoirs of Chaplain Life*, 181–82; Faust, *This Republic of Suffering*, 7–8.

19. Quoted in McPherson, *For Cause and Comrades*, 43.

20. "Morals of the War," *Portage County Democrat* (Ravenna, OH), July 8, 1863, CA. Cited from the *Springfield Republican*.

21. Abraham Lincoln, "It has Pleased Almighty God," in *RACW*, 283–84.

22. Rable, *God's Almost Chosen Peoples*, 265–66; Kurtz, *Excommunicated from the Union*, 31.

23. David Spalding, ed., "Miscellany: Martin John Spalding's 'Dissertation on the American Civil War,'" *The Catholic Historical Review* 52, no. 1 (April 1966): 78–85.

24. Rable, *God's Almost Chosen Peoples*, 265.

25. Rable, *God's Almost Chosen Peoples*, 265–66.

26. David Einhorn, *Sermon, Delivered on Thanksgiving Day* (Philadelphia: Stein/Jones, 1863), 7–8.

27. *New York Herald*, July 20, 1863, CA.

28. Joseph Fransioli, *Patriotism, a Christian Virtue. A Sermon Preached by the Rev. Joseph Fransioli, at St. Peter's (Catholic) Church, Brooklyn, July 26th, 1863* (New York: Loyal Publication Society, 1863), 1–5.

29. John Walker Jackson, *The Union —The Constitution—Peace. A Thanksgiving Sermon* (Harrisburg: "Telegraph" Steam Book and Job Office, 1863), 10–11.

30. Jackson, *Union*, 9–10.

31. *Daily Intelligencer* (Wheeling, VA [WV]), July 25, 1863, CA.

32. *The Spirit of Democracy* (Woodsfield, OH), July 22, 1863, CA.

33. *Daily Ohio Statesman* (Columbus), August 29, 1863, CA.

34. *The Dollar Weekly Bulletin* (Maysville, KY), August 6, 1863, CA. See also Steele, *Thanksgiving by Faith for Our Country's Future; a National Thanksgiving Sermon* (Rochester: Heughes' Book and Job Power Press, 1863), 6.

35. John C. Gregg, *A Patriotic Sermon, Preached before the Congregation in the M. E. Church at Montgomery Square, Pa., July 5, 1863* (Philadelphia: C. Sherman, Son & Co., 1863), 22–23.

36. Tubman quote in James Oliver Horton and Lois E. Horton, *Slavery and the Making of America* (New York: Oxford University Press, 2005), 197; James M. McPherson, *This Mighty Scourge: Perspectives on the Civil War* (New York: Oxford University Press, 2007), Kindle ed., 28.

37. P. K. Rose, "The Civil War: Black American Contributions to Union Intelligence," Central Intelligence Agency website, https://www.cia.gov/library/center-for-the-study-of-intelligence/csi-publications/books-and-monographs/black-dispatches/index.html; see also McPherson, *This Mighty Scourge*, 28.

38. Steele, *Thanksgiving by Faith*, 10–11. For information on Steele, see "Daniel Steele Papers," Syracuse University Archives, https://library.syr.edu/digital/guides_sua/html/sua_steele_d.htm. See also James White, *God in the Crisis. Infidelity, False Prophecy, and Slavery Coming down* (Springfield [Ill.]: Baker & Phillips, 1863), 14–16.

39. Faust, *This Republic of Suffering*, 49–51.

40. "The Funeral of Captain Andre Cailloux," *Harper's Weekly*, August 29, 1863, 551; Faust, *This Republic of Suffering*, 49–51.

41. Lincoln quoted in McPherson, *The War That Forged*, 113.

42. Quoted in McPherson, *The War That Forged*, 113–14.

43. I. N. Sprague, *God's Purposes in the War* (Newark, NJ: Daily Advertiser Office, 1863), 26–27.

44. Sprague, *God's Purposes*, 25.

45. Sprague, *God's Purposes*, 20–21.

46. Barrows, *Honor to the Brave*, 5–7.

47. P. D. Gurley, *Man's Projects and God's Results. A Sermon: Preached on Thursday, August 6, 1863* (Washington, D.C.: William Ballantyne, 1863), 5, 7–13, 15; Rable, *God's Almost Chosen Peoples*, 268.

48. As quoted in Sylvanus Landrum, *The Battle Is God's* (Savannah: Purse, 1863), 3.

49. Stephen Elliott, *Ezra's Dilemna* [sic]. *A Sermon Preached in Christ Church, Savannah, on Friday, August 21st, 1863* (Savannah: Power Press, 1863), 6. For a similar sermon on Nehemiah, see Leroy M. Lee, *Our Country—Our Dangers—Our Duty. A Discourse Preached in Centenary Church, Lynchburg, Va., on the National Fast Day, August 21, 1863* (Richmond: Soldiers' Tract Association, M. E. Church, South, 1863).

50. Elliott, *Ezra's Dilemna*, 6.

51. Elliott, *Ezra's Dilemna*, 7.

52. Elliott, *Ezra's Dilemna*, 12.

53. Elliott, *Ezra's Dilemna*, 13.

54. Elliott, *Ezra's Dilemna*, 14.

55. Elliott, *Ezra's Dilemna*, 22–23, 25.

56. Lee, *Our Country*, 13; the *Biblical Recorder* article reprinted in *Semi-Weekly Standard* (Raleigh, NC), October 23, 1863, CA.

57. *Richmond (VA) Enquirer*, August 25, 1863, CA; Phillips Brooks, *Our Mercies of Re-Occupation* (Philadelphia: Martien, 1863), 11–12.

58. Brooks, *Mercies*, 9.

59. Brooks, *Mercies*, 11.

60. Gabor Boritt, *The Gettysburg Gospel: The Lincoln Speech That Nobody Knows* (New York: Simon & Schuster, 2008), 99–100.

61. Edward Everett, *An Oration Delivered on the Battlefield of Gettysburg* (New York: Baker & Godwin, 1863), 14, 17; Boritt, *Gettysburg Gospel*, 101–5.

62. Everett, *Oration*, 20–21, 24, 26.

63. Everett, *Oration*, 30–31.

64. Boritt, *Gettysburg Gospel*, 112–13.

65. Boritt, *Gettysburg Gospel*, 113.

66. Robert Alter, *Pen of Iron: American Prose and the King James Bible* (Princeton, NJ: Princeton University Press, 2010), 13–14. Alter notes that the biblical phrase "three score and ten" appeared "111 times" in the King James Bible.

67. A. E. Elmore, *Lincoln's Gettysburg Address: Echoes of the Bible and Book of Common Prayer*, Kindle ed. (Carbondale: Southern Illinois University Press, 2009), 41, chap, 3, "Birth and Rebirth"; Allen C. Guelzo, *Abraham Lincoln: Redeemer President*, Kindle ed. (Grand Rapids, MI: W.B. Eerdmans, 1999), chap. 9, "Whig Jupiter"; Fornieri, *Abraham Lincoln's Political Faith*, 46–47; Goldfield, *America Aflame*, 293.

68. Delbanco, *War before the War*, 1–2.

69. Lincoln, "Gettysburg Address," in *RACW*, 297.

70. Lincoln, "Gettysburg Address," 297; Guelzo, *Fateful Lightning*, 407–8; Boritt, *Gettysburg Gospel*, 120–22.
71. See Fornieri, *Abraham Lincoln's Political Faith*, 47.
72. Alter, *Pen of Iron*, 14.
73. Boritt, *Gettysburg Gospel*, 120.
74. Masur, *Civil War Concise History*, 60.

Chapter 14

1. Frederick Douglass, "Mission of the War," in *FDP*, 4:5–7.
2. Benjamin M. Palmer, *Life and Letters of Benjamin Morgan Palmer*, ed. Thomas Cary Johnson (Richmond, VA: Presbyterian Committee of Publication, 1906), 280; also quoted in Guyatt, *Providence*, 274.
3. Masur, *Civil War Concise History*, 62.
4. Quoted in Masur, *Civil War Concise History*, 61–63.
5. Quoted in William C. Davis, *Look Away! A History of the Confederate States of America* (New York: Free Press, 2002), 246; Masur, *Civil War Concise History*, 62.
6. Masur, *Civil War Concise History*, 61; McPherson, *BCF*, 694–95.
7. McPherson, *BCF*, 695.
8. McPherson, *BCF*, 695–96.
9. Masur, *Civil War Concise History*, 62.
10. Masur, *Civil War Concise History*, 62.
11. McPherson, *BCF*, 695.
12. Faust, *This Republic of Suffering*, 27.
13. John Paris, *A Sermon: Preached before Brig.-Gen. Hoke's Brigade, at Kingston, N.C., on the 28th of February, 1864 upon the Death of Twenty-Two Men, Who Had Been Executed in the Presence of the Brigade for the Crime of Desertion* (Greensborough, NC: Ingold, 1864), 5–6, *passim*.
14. Paris, *Sermon*, 4.
15. Paris, *Sermon*, 4.
16. Paris, *Sermon*, 5–6.
17. Paris, *Sermon*, 6–7.
18. Paris, *Sermon*, 7.
19. Paris, *Sermon*, 8–9.
20. Paris, *Sermon*, 9–10.
21. Paris, *Sermon*, 10–11.
22. Paris, *Sermon*, 9–11.
23. Paris, *Sermon*, 11–12, 13–14.
24. Paris, *Sermon*, 11, 15.
25. Abraham Lincoln, *Abraham Lincoln Papers: Series 1. General Correspondence. 1833 to 1916: Abraham Lincoln, Tuesday, Proclamation of Amnesty and Reconstruction*, December 8, 1863, Manuscript/Mixed Material. https://www.loc.gov/item/mal2849300/. This offer did not extend to the government officials and high-ranking military officers.

26. Lincoln, *Proclamation of Amnesty and Reconstruction.*
27. McPherson, *BCF*, 698.
28. Biographical information on Ruffner in Marianne E. Julienne and the *Dictionary of Virginia Biography*, "William Henry Ruffner (1824–1908)," April 29, 2016, in *Encyclopedia Virginia*, retrieved from http://www.EncyclopediaVirginia.org/ Ruffner_William_H_1824–1908. W. H. Ruffner, *The Oath. A Sermon on the Nature and Obligation of the Oath, with Special Reference to the Oath of Allegiance* (Lexington: Gazette Office, 1864), 3.
29. Ruffner, *Oath*, 3–5, 9–11.
30. Ruffner, *Oath*, 11.
31. Ruffner, *Oath*, 13.
32. Ruffner, *Oath*, 14, 16.
33. Masur, *Civil War Concise History*, 63.
34. Jefferson Davis, "Confederate Proclamation of Humiliation and Prayer," in *RACW*, 335. See also "Another Fast Day. Proclamation by Jeff. Davis," *New York Times*, March 18, 1864, sec, Southern News, https://www.nytimes.com/1864/03/18/archives/ southern-news-the-fast-day-retaliation-retaliation.html.
35. Stephen Elliott, *Gideon's Water-Lappers* (Macon, GA: Burke, Boykin, 1864), 8–9.
36. Elliott, *Gideon's Water-Lappers*, 14.
37. Elliott, *Gideon's Water-Lappers*, 12.
38. Elliott, *Gideon's Water-Lappers*, 20–21.
39. Elliott, *Gideon's Water-Lappers*, 7, 16–17.
40. Elliott, *Gideon's Water-Lappers*, 18.
41. Elliott, *Gideon's Water-Lappers*, 21–22.
42. Quoted in Goldfield, *America Aflame*, 326.
43. Quoted in McPherson, *For Cause and Comrades*, 73–74.
44. "History of 'In God We Trust,'" US Department of the Treasury, https://www. treasury.gov/about/education/Pages/in-god-we-trust.aspx; Masur, *Civil War Concise History*, 62.
45. Morton Borden, "The Christian Amendment," *Civil War History* 25, no. 2 (June 1979): 156–67.
46. David Einhorn, "War with Amalek!," in *RACW*, 335–38.
47. Einhorn, "War with Amelek!," 335–38.
48. Borden, "Christian Amendment," 162–63.
49. Quoted in Goldfield, *America Aflame*, 327.
50. Quoted in Gary W. Gallagher, ed., *The Spotsylvania Campaign* (Chapel Hill: University of North Carolina Press, 1998), 107–8; Masur, *Civil War Concise History*, 64–65.
51. Faust, *This Republic of Suffering*, 6, 9–10.
52. Faust, *This Republic of Suffering*, 10–11.
53. *Gallipolis* (OH) *Journal*, August 21, 1862, CA.
54. *Spirit of the Age* (Raleigh, NC), February 2, 1863, CA.
55. *Staunton* (VA) *Spectator*, July 21, 1863, CA. See also *American Citizen* (Canton, MS), December 7, 1861, CA.
56. *Weekly Standard* (Raleigh, NC), June 3, 1863, CA.

57. John D. Sweet, *The Speaking Dead. A Discourse Occasioned by the Death of Serg't. Edward Amos Adams* (Boston: Commercial Printing House, 1864), 16.

58. In addition to Isaac, Clark cites others: God called Jacob to lose his son, Benjamin, to save the family. God required David to see his son, Absalom, killed "for the suppression of rebellion." Perkins K. Clark, *Sacrifices for Our Country* (Greenfield, MA: Printed by S. S. Eastman, 1864), 10–12.

59. Clark, *Sacrifices for Our Country*, 11–12, 21.

60. Clark, *Sacrifices for Our Country*, 12; Sweet, *Speaking Dead*, 17.

61. Masur, *Civil War Concise History*, 65; Goldfield, *America Aflame*, 328; Delaware soldier as quoted in McPherson, *For Cause and Comrades*, 61–62.

62. Quotation in Faust, *This Republic of Suffering*, 34.

63. As quoted in Faust, *This Republic of Suffering*, 35–36.

64. A. W. Wild, *A Sermon Preached at Greensboro, Vt., July 10, 1864* (Montpelier: Freeman Printing Establishment, 1864), 4.

65. Wild, *Sermon*, 4–5. See also 10–11, 16–17.

66. Masur, *Civil War Concise History*, 65.

67. Turner, *Freedom's Witness*, 120.

68. Goldfield, *America Aflame*, 320, 329.

69. Frederic Henry Hedge, *The National Entail* (Boston: Wright & Potter, 1864), 3, 16.

70. Douglass, "Mission," 7.

71. Douglass, "Mission," 7–8, 11.

72. Douglass, "Mission," 12–13.

73. Douglass, "Mission," 13–16.

74. Douglass, "Mission," 21–23.

75. Blight, *Prophet of Freedom*, 420–21, 745 n. 11; Douglass, "Mission," 24.

76. Oakes, *Radical and the Republican*, chap. 6, section "The Election of 1864."

Chapter 15

1. Goldfield, *America Aflame*, 335–36.

2. Quotations in Oakes, *Radical and the Republican*, chap. 6, section: "The Second Meeting, August 25, 1864."

3. Quotations in Oakes, *Radical and the Republican*, chap. 6, section: "The Second Meeting, August 25, 1864."

4. Masur, *Civil War Concise History*, 68.

5. Turner, *Freedom*, 144.

6. Masur, *Civil War Concise History*, 68; Oakes, *Radical and the Republican*, chap. 6, section "The Election of 1864."

7. *Lincoln Catechism*, 12.

8. *Lincoln Catechism*, 13–15.

9. *Lincoln Catechism*, 15–16.

10. Goldfield, *America Aflame*, 338.

11. "Atlanta Campaign," in Barney, *OECW*, 20–22.

12. Quotations in "Atlanta Campaign," 20–22.

13. Quoted in "Sherman, William Tecumseh," in Barney, *OECW*, 284–85; J. T. Headley, ed., *Grant and Sherman: Their Campaigns and Generals* (New York: E.B. Treat, 1865), 591.

14. Sherman's letter quoted in Goldfield, *America Aflame*, 320. Also quoted in Benjamin Schwarz, "Lee and Sherman," *The Atlantic*, April 1, 2006.

15. Herrick Johnson, *The Shaking of the Nations* (Pittsburgh: W.S. Haven, 1864), 17–18.

16. Nadal, *Christian Nation's Ordeal*, 5–6, 8, 14.

17. J. W. Hough, *Our Country's Mission, or The Present Suffering of the Nation justified by its Future Glory* (Burlington, VT: Free Press, 1864), 19. Many sermons connected the "All men are created equal" statement from the Declaration with Acts 17:26. For another sermon that made this connection in the fall of 1864, see Lavalette Perrin, *Our Part in the World's Struggle* (Hartford, CT: Case, Lockwood & Co., 1864), 10.

18. R. B. Stratton, *A Sermon, Delivered on Thanksgiving Day, November 24th, 1864* (Lee, MA: Josiah A. Royce, 1865), 7; see also H. M. Johnson, "Unity of the Race," *Christian Advocate and Journal*, June 23, 1864, 193.

19. J. L. Burrows, *Nationality Insured! Notes of a Sermon* (Augusta, GA: James Nathan Ells, 1864), 3–4.

20. Stephen Elliott, *"Vain Is the Help of Man." A Sermon* (Macon, GA: Burke, Boykin & Co., 1864), 10.

21. Elliott, *Vain*, 4–5.

22. Elliott, *Vain*, 6.

23. Elliott, *Vain*, 3–4.

24. Exodus 14.

25. Elliott, *Vain*, 7–8.

26. Elliott, *Vain*, 8–9.

27. Elliott, *Vain*, 10.

28. Elliott, *Vain*, 10.

29. Elliott, *Vain*, 12.

30. Elliott, *Vain*, 12.

31. As quoted in Guyatt, *Providence*, 274.

32. White, "Lincoln's Sermon," 209–10.

33. Quoted in Barney, "Forrest, Nathan Bedford," in *OECW*, 128–29; "Sherman, William Tecumseh," 284–85.

34. Quotations in Goldfield, *America Aflame*, 280; Masur, *Civil War Concise History*, 64.

35. Bruce Tap, *The Fort Pillow Massacre: North, South, and the Status of African Americans in the Civil War Era* (New York: Routledge, 2013), 1–2; Masur, *Civil War Concise History*, 64.

36. Goldfield, *America Aflame*, 280.

37. Elliott, *Gideon's Water-Lappers*, 14.

38. Masur, *Civil War Concise History*, 64.

39. Turner, *Freedom's Witness*, 132.

40. Masur, *Civil War Concise History*, 64; McPherson, *BCF*, 796; Goldfield, *America Aflame*, 322.

41. Goldfield, *America Aflame*, 321; Masur, *Civil War Concise History*, 64; McPherson, *BCF*, 796.

42. Quoted in Goldfield, *America Aflame*, 321–22.

43. The verse is Philippians 4:11. Harvey, "Bible in the Civil War," 360; quotations in Lesley J. Gordon, *A Broken Regiment: The 16th Connecticut's Civil War* (Baton Rouge: LSU Press, 2014), 151.

44. As quoted in Goldfield, *America Aflame*, 323.

45. McPherson, *BCF*, 798–99.

46. As quoted in Goldfield, *America Aflame*, 321.

47. Faust, *This Republic of Suffering*, 62–63.

48. Bacon, *Plea for Sacredness*, 3.

49. Bacon, *Plea for Sacredness*, 4–5.

50. Bacon, *Plea for Sacredness*, 7, 10. Bacon paraphrases these verses, which I've quoted from the KJV.

51. Bacon, *Plea for Sacredness*, 11.

52. Bacon, *Plea for Sacredness*, 11.

53. Lincoln, *Works*, 7:543.

54. Lincoln, *Works*, 7:542.

55. Fornieri, *Abraham Lincoln's Political Faith*, 35.

56. "Don't let Johnson speak" quote is from Guelzo, *Redeemer President*, chap. 10, "Malice toward None," ; *Saturday Review of Politics, Science, and Art* 22 (December 15, 1866): 733; "Slobbered" quote is from Gary Wills, "Lincoln's Greatest Speech," *The Atlantic*, September 1999, https://www.theatlantic.com/magazine/archive/1999/09/lincolns-greatest-speech/306551/.

57. White, "Lincoln's Sermon," 211; Guelzo, *Redeemer President*, chap. 10, "Malice Toward None."

58. Noll, *America's God*, 426–38.

59. Abraham Lincoln, "Second Inaugural Address," The Avalon Project, Lillian Goldman Law Library, Yale University, https://avalon.law.yale.edu/19th_century/lincoln2.asp. Quotations from the "Second Inaugural Address" in this section are from this version. See also Lincoln, *Works*, 8:332–33.

60. Lincoln, "Second Inaugural Address."

61. Lincoln, "Second Inaugural Address."

62. Douglass as quoted in White, "Lincoln's Sermon," 223; Blight, *Prophet of Freedom*, 458. See also Alter, *Pen of Iron*, 16–17.

63. Lincoln, "Second Inaugural Address."

64. Lincoln, "Second Inaugural Address."

65. Lincoln, "Second Inaugural Address."

66. Lincoln, "Second Inaugural Address."

67. Lincoln, "Second Inaugural Address."

68. Lincoln, "Second Inaugural Address."

69. Lincoln, "Second Inaugural Address."

70. Stauffer and Trodd, *Tribunal*, 73; Guelzo, *Fateful Lightning*, 472.

71. Guelzo, *Redeemer President*, 420, chap. 10, "Malice toward None."

72. Noll, *America's God*, 431.

73. Noll, *America's God*, 431–34.

74. Lincoln, *Works* 8:356. On this point, see the insightful analysis of John Burt, "Collective Guilt in Lincoln's Second Inaugural Address," *American Political Thought* 4 (Summer 2015): 467–68.

Chapter 16

1. My description of the assassination depends mainly on Martha Hodes, *Mourning Lincoln*, Kindle ed. (New Haven: Yale University Press, 2015), "Good Friday, 1865."

2. "The Assassination Plot," *Boston Daily Advertiser*, May 2, 1865, 19th Century US Newspapers. Originally printed in the *Washington Star* on April 29. Also reprinted in "THE ASSASSINS: The Plot to Assassinate President Lincoln," *New York Times*, May 1, 1865.

3. As quoted in Hodes, *Mourning Lincoln*, 120.

4. Hodes, *Mourning Lincoln*, 11.

5. Hiram Sears, *The People's Keepsake; or, Funeral Address on the Death of Abraham Lincoln* (Cincinnati: Poe & Hitchcock, 1865), 15–16.

6. S. C. Baldridge, *The Martyr Prince: A Sermon on the Occasion of the Assassination of President Lincoln* (N.p.: s.n., n.d.). No page numbers listed, but the quotation is from the fourth page, including the title page. See also John W. McCarty, *Lessons from the Life and Death of a Good Ruler* (Cincinnati: Boyd, 1865), 14.

7. A. B. Dascomb, *A Discourse Preached to His People at Waitsfield, Vt.* (Montpelier, VT: Walton's Steam, 1865), 16.

8. Jacob Thomas, "Sermon Preached in the African Methodist Episcopal Church," in *A Tribute of Respect by the Citizens of Troy* (Troy, NY: Young & Benson, 1865), 44.

9. S. Reed, *A Discourse Delivered on the Occasion of the Funeral Obsequies of President Lincoln* (Boston: Rand & Avery, 1865), 10.

10. As reported by John A. Bingham, congressman from Ohio. As quoted in Thomas Reed Turner, *Beware the People Weeping: Public Opinion and the Assassination of Abraham Lincoln* (Baton Rouge: Louisiana State University Press, 1982), 71.

11. A. G. Hibbard, *In Memory of Abraham Lincoln* (Detroit: Gulley's Steam Printing, 1865), 3.

12. Hodes, *Mourning Lincoln*, 98.

13. See "The Nation's Grief," *Boston Daily Advertiser*, April 17, 1865, 19th Century US Newspapers; "Local Matters," *Daily Evening Bulletin* (San Francisco, CA), April 17, 1865, 19th Century US Newspapers.

14. A. N. Littlejohn, "Sermon VIII," in William R. Williams et al., *Our Martyr President, Abraham Lincoln. Voices from the Pulpit of New York and Brooklyn* (New York: Tibbals & Whiting, 1865), 145–46, https://archive.org/details/ourmartyrpreside00will.

15. "Nation's Grief," *Boston Daily*; "Local Matters," *Daily Evening Bulletin*; "The Churches," *Daily Cleveland* (OH) *Herald*, April 17, 1865, 19th Century US Newspapers; Rev. C. A. Staples, "The Great Crime," *Milwaukee* (WI) *Daily Sentinel*, April 18, 1865, 19th

Century US Newspapers; "Multiple Classified Advertisements," *North American and United States Gazette* (Philadelphia), April 18, 1865, 19th Century US Newspapers; "Henry Ward Beecher on the Death of President Lincoln," *Boston Daily Advertiser*, April 25, 1865, 19th Century US Newspapers.

16. Sarna and Shapell, *Lincoln and the Jews*, xii–xiii.

17. Rolla H. Chubb, *A Discourse, upon the Death of President Lincoln* (Mansfield, OH: Herald Book and Job Printing, 1865), 7. See also Samuel Gorman, *Abraham Lincoln, Late President of the United States, Fallen in the Defence of His Country* (New York: C. A. Alvord, 1865), 18. Other biblical comparisons served as well, including Solomon and David; see L. M. Glover, *The Character of Abraham Lincoln* (Jacksonville, IL: Journal Book, 1865), 14. On Moses as biblical figure most often compared to Lincoln, see Rable, *God's Alr 1st Chosen Peoples*, 382.

18. N. L. Brakeman, *A Great Man Fallen. A Sermon Preached in the Methodist Church, Baton Rouge, La.* (New Orleans: New Orleans Times, 1865), 26–27. See also Gorman, *Abraham Lincoln, Late President*, 19; William Irvin, *A Sermon, Preached on Sabbath Morning, April 16, 1865. The Day after the Death of President Lincoln* (New York: John A. Gray & Green, 1865), 11–13.

19. Glover, *Character of Abraham Lincoln*, 11–12.

20. Wilbur F. Paddock, *A Great Man Fallen! A Discourse on the Death of Abraham Lincoln* (Philadelphia: Sherman, 1865), 8–9.

21. Irvin, *Sermon Preached*, 11–13.

22. Brakeman, *Great Man Fallen*, 24. See also Glover, *Character of Abraham Lincoln*, 11–12; A. D. Mayo, *The Nation's Sacrifice. Abraham Lincoln* (Cincinnati: Robert Clarke & Co., 1865), 10–11. Others drew similar comparisons to show Lincoln's superiority to Washington. See Charles Hammond, *A Sermon on the Life and Character of Abraham Lincoln* (Springfield, MA: Samuel Bowles, 1865), 17–20; Irvin, *Sermon Preached*, 11–12.

23. Chubb, *Discourse*, 6.

24. Brakeman, *Great Man Fallen*, 26–27.

25. "Lincoln's Belief in the Bible," *Arkansas Democrat* (Little Rock), February 13, 1899, 19th Century US Newspapers.

26. Daniel Rice, *The President's Death—Its Import* (Lafayette, IN: s.n., 1865), 3. Methodist minister N. L. Brakeman also cites this quote, but with different wording. Brakeman, *Great Man Fallen*, 9. See also Marvin R. Vincent, *A Sermon on the Assassination of Abraham Lincoln* (Troy, NY: Scribner, 1865), 24–25; Thomas Swaim, J. L. Janeway, and J. P. Dailey, *Discourses Memorial of Abraham Lincoln* (Lambertville, NJ: Pierson, 1865), 7. For three published versions of this address, see Lincoln, *Works*, 4: 190–91. N. L. Brakeman also cited Lincoln's comparisons to himself and Washington on religious matters. Brakeman, *Great Man Fallen*, 10.

27. Brakeman, *Great Man Fallen*, 11. Brakeman cited Lincoln's conversion at Gettysburg as an argument for the importance of politics to Christianity. See also Rice, *President's Death*, 3. Others who cited this story of Lincoln's conversion at Gettysburg include H. H. Northrop, *A Sermon Commemoration of the Assassination of President Abraham Lincoln* (Carthage, IL: Carthage Republican Print, 1865), 7; Sears, *People's Keepsake*,

14. William Sterling, *The Martyr President. A Sermon* ([Williamsport, PA]: "Bulletin" print, 1865), 3; Dascomb, *Discourse*, 17–18; Swaim, Janeway, and Dailey, *Discourses Memorial*, 17; Denis Wortman, *A Discourse on the Death of President Lincoln* (Albany: Weed, Parsons, 1865), 10–11; George W. Colman, *Assassination of the President* (Boston: S. Chism, 1865), 11; William M. Johnson, *Our Martyred President. A Discourse on the Death of President Lincoln* (Troy, NY: Daily and Weekly Times, 1865), 12.

28. F. M. Dimmick, *Funeral Sermon on the Death of the Late President Lincoln* ([Omaha?]: s.n., 1865), 13; See also Brakeman, *Great Man Fallen*, 9.

29. According to Sean Conant, who doubts the story's authenticity, "Lincoln supposedly told" this story to "an unnamed Illinois clergyman." It was later printed "in the *Oshkosh Northwestern* on April 21, 1865." Sean Conant, *The Gettysburg Address: Perspectives on Lincoln's Greatest Speech* (New York: Oxford University Press, 2015), 154.

30. Seiss, *The Assassinated President*, 14–16.

31. Seiss, *The Assassinated President*, 19.

32. Seiss, *The Assassinated President*, 19–20. See also Thomas, "Sermon Preached in the African Methodist Episcopal Church," 45.

33. Seiss, *The Assassinated President*, 23–24.

34. Matthew Simpson, *Funeral Address Delivered at the Burial of President Lincoln* (New York: Carlton & Porter, 1865), 14, https://archive.org/details/funeraladdressde00simp.

35. Beecher, "Abraham Lincoln," in *Patriotic Addresses*, 701–2. See also Chubb, *Discourse*, 9.

36. Beecher, "Abraham Lincoln," 701–2.

37. Harper, *Discarded Legacy*, 55.

38. Gorman, *Abraham Lincoln, Late President*, 4–5. See also Hammond, *Life and Character*, 5.

39. Warren Hathaway, *A Discourse Occasioned by the Death of Abraham Lincoln* (Albany, NY: J. Munsell, 1865), 10.

40. Hathaway, *Discourse*, 10.

41. Thomas, "Sermon Preached in the African Methodist Episcopal Church," 45.

42. Hammond, *Life and Character*, 5–6; Gorman, *Abraham Lincoln, Late President*, 4–5. For similar interpretations, see Sterling, *Martyr President*, 1.

43. William Stewart, *The President's Death: And the Lessons It Teaches: A Sermon Preached in the Baptist Chapel, Brantford, C.W., on the Evening of Sabbath, April 23rd, 1865* (Brantford: Office of the Brantford "Courier," 1865), 10. https://archive.org/details/cihm_63595.

44. Frederick Starr Jr., *Martyr President: A Discourse* (St. Louis: Sherman Spencer, 1865), 12–13.

45. C. B. Crane, *Sermon on the Occasion of the Death of President Lincoln* (Hartford: Case, Lockwood and Co., 1865), 7.

46. Wortman, *Discourse on the Death*, 10.

47. Faust, *This Republic of Suffering*, 6–7.

48. Faust, *This Republic of Suffering*, 8–9.

49. Starr, *Martyr President*, 15; Baldridge, *Martyr Prince*, 14–15.

50. W. H. Hornblower, *Sermon Occasioned by the Assassination of President Lincoln* (Paterson, NJ: Chiswell & Wurts, 1865), 10–11.

51. Thomas, "Sermon Preached in the African Methodist Episcopal," 44.

52. B. F. Bradford, *The Cause of Rebellion: Or, What Killed Mr. Lincoln* (Buffalo: A. M. Clapp & Co., 1865), 13.

53. John H. Drumm, *Assassination of Abraham Lincoln* (Bristol: William Bache, 1865), 11–12.

54. Rice, *President's Death*, 4; Likewise, see Drumm, *Assassination of Abraham Lincoln*, 12.

55. Drumm, *Assassination of Abraham Lincoln*, 11–12.

56. Vincent, *Sermon on the Assassination*, 8.

57. Vincent, *Sermon on the Assassination*, 14.

58. Chubb, *Discourse*, 11.

59. Chubb, *Discourse*, 11–12; see also Paddock, *Great Man Fallen*, 18–20.

60. S. Morais, *An Address on the Death of Abraham Lincoln* (Philadelphia: Collins, 1865), 5.

61. John Chester, *The Lesson of the Hour. Justice as Well as Mercy* ([Washington, DC]: Washington Chronicle Print, 1865), 15. See also Glover, *Character of Abraham Lincoln*, 13; James Cooper, *The Death of President Lincoln* (Philadelphia: James B. Rodgers, 1865), 17; Charles F. Mussey, *The Mighty Fallen. A Discourse Occasioned by the Assassination of President Lincoln* (Batavia: Daniel D. Waite, 1865), 10–11.

62. Hathaway, *Discourse*, 10.

63. D. L. Hughes, "President Lincoln's Death," in *Lincolniana* (Boston: William V. Spencer, 1865), 101.

64. Chester, *Lesson of the Hour*, 15; Hathaway, *Discourse*, 10–11.

65. Dascomb, *Discourse*, 4. Cf. S. D. Burchard, "Sermon XIV," in Williams et al., *Our Martyr President*, 269.

66. Dimmick, *Funeral Sermon*, 11.

67. Baldridge, *Martyr Prince*, 9–10.

68. Sterling, *Martyr President*, 6.

69. Chester, *Lesson of the Hour*, 13.

70. Vincent, *Sermon on the Assassination*, 36; see also 42–43.

71. Robert Russell Booth, *Personal Forgiveness and Public Justice. A Sermon Preached in the Mercer Street Presbyterian Church, New York, April 23, 1865* (New York: Anson D. F. Randolph, 1865), 10, emphasis added.

72. Booth, *Personal Forgiveness*, 11.

73. Booth, *Personal Forgiveness*, 11. For another sermon that combines Romans 12 and 13 in this way earlier in the war, see D. D. Buck, *The Civil Ruler as God's Minister* (Rochester, NY: E. Darrow & Brother, 1863).

74. Booth, *Personal Forgiveness*, 11–13.

75. Booth, *Personal Forgiveness*, 14–16.

76. Booth, *Personal Forgiveness*, 18–19.

77. Booth, *Personal Forgiveness*, 7–8.

78. Isaiah 28:15, 18–19.

79. Alonzo H. Quint, "Southern Chivalry, and What the Nation Ought to Do with It," in *Three Sermons Preached in the North Congregational Church . . . April 13, and . . . April 16, 1865* (New Bedford, MA: Mercury Job Press, 1865), 31–34, 40.

80. Quint, "Southern Chivalry," 31–34, 40.

81. Quint, "Southern Chivalry," 37, 42.

82. Quint, "Southern Chivalry," 42.

83. Quint, "Southern Chivalry," 45. Jeremiah 18.21.

84. Hornblower, *Sermon Occasioned by Assassination*, 15; See also Burchard, "Sermon XIV," 269.

85. J. B. Wentworth, *A Discourse on the Death of President Lincoln* (Buffalo: Matthews & Warren, 1865), 26–32.

86. Wentworth, *Discourse on the Death*, 31–32.

87. Mussey, *The Mighty Fallen*, 12–13. See also Sterling, *Martyr President*, 5.

88. Crane, *Sermon on the Occasion*, 28–29; See also J. E. Rankin, *Moses and Joshua. A Discourse* (Boston: Dakin and Metcalf, 1865), https://archive.org/details/mosesjoshuadisco00rank.

89. Bradford, *Cause of Rebellion*, 18–19. For this same point, see Brakeman, *Great Man Fallen*, 21. See also J. L. Robertson, *A Sermon, Commemorative of Our National Bereavement* (Geneva: William Johnson, 1865), 14–15; Sears, *People's Keepsake*, 17; Sterling, *Martyr President*, 6; Seth Sweetser, *A Commemorative Discourse on the Death of Abraham Lincoln* (Worcester, MA: Press of J. Wilson and Son, 1865), 26–27; Vincent, *Sermon on the Assassination*, 35; Crane, *Sermon on the Occasion*, 27–28; William A. Snively and William Preston, *Memorial Sermon and Address on the Death of President Lincoln* (Pittsburgh: Printed by W. S. Haven, 1865), 20; Edwin J. Hart, *A Sermon Preached in Merrimack . . . on the Occasion of the Assassination of Abraham Lincoln* (Manchester, NH: Henry A. Gage, 1865), 10; Chubb, *Discourse*, 12; Glover, *Character of Abraham Lincoln*, 15; Rankin, *Moses and Joshua*.

90. Booth as quoted in Harold Holzer, *President Lincoln Assassinated!!: The Firsthand Story of the Murder, Manhunt, Trial, and Mourning*, Kindle ed. (New York: Library of America, 2014), section "John Wilkes Booth, Friday the Ides, April 13th," loc. 1522.

91. As quoted in Holzer, *President Lincoln Assassinated*, section "John Wilkes Booth, Diary, April 22, 1865," loc. 16401654.

92. Hughes, "President Lincoln's Death," 115. See also Glover, *Character of Abraham Lincoln*, 13; Swaim, Janeway, and Dailey, *Discourses Memorial*, 22.

93. "The drama of J. Wilkes Booth's life, on this stage, is over," *Daily National Intelligencer* (Washington, DC), April 28, 1865, 19th Century US Newspapers; "The Remorse and Vagrancy of Booth," *New Haven* (CT) *Daily Palladium*, April 29, 1865, 19th Century US Newspapers; "Assassination Plot," *Boston Daily Advertiser*, May 2, 1865, 19th Century US Newspapers; "Booth's Flight," *Congregationalist* (Boston), May 5, 1865: 71, 19th Century US Newspapers.

94. Chester, *Lesson of the Hour*, 13.

95. Faust, *This Republic of Suffering*, 156–59. The digital exhibit entitled *Remembering Lincoln* on the Ford's Theatre website says that "possibly one-third of the United States' population turned out to see the slain President's funeral train." "Timeline:

Assassination's Aftermath," Remembering Lincoln, Ford's Theatre, http://rememberinglincoln.fords.org/exhibit/events.

96. Beecher, "Abraham Lincoln," 711–12.

97. John H. Egar, *The Martyr-President* (Leavenworth, KS: Bulletin Job Printing Establishment, 1865), 14.

98. Isaac E. Carey, *Abraham Lincoln. The Value to the Nation of His Exalted Character* (Freeport, IL: publisher not identified, 1865), 3.

99. Carey, *Abraham Lincoln*, 8. See also Samuel B. Willis, *Voices from the Dead* (New York: Thomas Daniels & Son, 1865), 2–3. J. F. Garrison said that the "Martyred President, though 'being dead, yet speaketh,' and to the end of time will speak." J. F. Garrison, *The Teachings of the Crisis. Address Delivered in St. Paul's Church, Camden, N.J.* (Camden, NJ: S. Chew, 1865), 17–18.

100. Crane, *Sermon on the Occasion*, 16.

101. Crane, *Sermon on the Occasion*, 18. See also Hathaway, *Discourse*, 20–22; Mussey, *The Mighty Fallen*, 13–14; Crane, *Sermon on the Occasion*, 6–7. In an unpublished sermon, Samuel Johnson preached: "Not in vain shall the Martyr of a Nation fall. Martyrdom is one of God's great reserved powers on earth. The grand days of judgment always point to some uplifted cross, some priceless sacrifice. . . . It is God's power on earth to destroy intolerable evils." Samuel Johnson, *A Discourse Preached on the Day of the National Funeral of President Lincoln, Wednesday, April 19, 1865* ([Salem, MA?]: [s.n.], 1865), 10; Paddock, *Great Man Fallen*, 6.

102. Numerous scriptures warned against idolatry, including several in Psalms (146:3–5, 93:1, 97:2). See, for example, Vincent, *Sermon on the Assassination*, 39.

103. Johnson, *Martyred President*, 13.

104. Adam Reid, *A Discourse on the Death of Abraham Lincoln, President of the United States* (Hartford: Case, Lockwood, & Co., 1865), 13–15.

105. Reid, *Discourse on the Death*, 16.

106. Reid, *Discourse on the Death*, 17–19. See also Mussey, *The Mighty Fallen*, 11. Charles Ray, *A Sermon Preached before the United Congregations of Wyoming, N.Y.* (Buffalo: A. M. Clapp & Co., 1865), 4.

107. For these details and more, see the groundbreaking book by Chesebrough, *No Sorrow Like Our Sorrow*, xviii. Chesebrough's painstaking research is the starting point for any study of sermons on the Lincoln assassination. See also Turner, *Beware the People Weeping*, 51.

108. As quoted in Chesebrough, *No Sorrow*, xix. The study cited by Chesebrough here is Charles J. Stewart, "Lincoln's Assassination and the Protestant Clergy of the North," PhD diss., University of Illinois, 1963.

109. Mark A. Noll, "Presidential Deaths and the Bible: 1799, 1865, 1881, 1901," presented to the American Society of Church History, January 2016. See also Noll, "Image of the United States."

110. Booth, *Personal Forgiveness*, 7–8; Chesebrough, *No Sorrow*, xviii.

111. S. Salisbury, *Sermon; Preached at West Alexandria, Ohio, April 30th, 1865* (Eaton, OH: Eaton Weekly Register, 1865), 11.

112. Sarah Lyall and Matt Flegenheimer, "Sorry, Abe Lincoln Is Not on the Ballot," *New York Times*, May 16, 2020; Richard Wightman Fox, *Lincoln's Body: A Cultural History* (New York: W. W. Norton, 2015), preface.

Epilogue

1. William Adams, "Thanksgiving Sermons"; Discourses by Rev. William Adams, D. D., of the Madison-Avenue Presbyterian Church, Rev. Samuel Adler, of the Jewish Temple, East Twelfth Street, and Others. American Nationality, "Sermon by the Rev. Dr. William Adams, of the Madison-Square Presbyterian Church," *New York Times*, December 10, 1865, sec. News, http://www.nytimes.com/1865/12/10/news/thanksgiving-sermons-discourses-rev-william-adams-d-d-madison-avenue.html.
2. Lincoln, "Gettysburg Address," 297.
3. Elliott, *Our Cause*, 21–22.
4. McPherson, *For Cause and Comrades*, 11–13; see also chapter 5, "Religion Is What Makes Brave Soldiers."
5. J. E. Rankin, *Battle not Man's, but God's. A Discourse* (Lowell, MA: Stone & Huse, 1863), 5.
6. McPherson, "Afterword," 409.
7. Doggett, *A Nation's Ebenezer*, 7–8; Rankin, *Battle Not Man's*, 8, 10.
8. Barrows, *Our War*, 5.
9. Ezra H. Gillett, *Thanksgiving Sermon, Preached in the Presbyterian Church at Harlem, November 27, 1862* (New York: A. J. Brady, 1863), 12, https://archive.org/details/thanksgivingserm00gill.
10. Pierce, "Word of God," 282.
11. George F. Pierce and B. M. Palmer, *Sermons of Bishop Pierce and Rev. B. M. Palmer, D.D., Delivered before the General Assembly at Milledgeville, Ga., on Fast Day, March 27, 1863* (Milledgeville, GA: Boughten, Nisbet & Barnes, 1863), 30, https://archive.org/details/sermonsofbishopp00pier.
12. Sherman, "War is hell," as quoted in McPherson, *The War That Forged*, 32; Woodworth, *God Is Marching On*, 216; Brownson, *Works*, 17:214; see also Faust, *This Republic of Suffering*, 32.
13. Paine, *Political Lessons*, 5–6. See also Stone, *Emancipation*, 4; Barrows, *Our War*, 5.
14. Shalev, *American Zion*, 151, also chap. 5, *passim*.
15. Buck, *Civil Ruler*, 4–5. See also Booth, *Personal Forgiveness*, 10–11.
16. Buck, *Civil Ruler*, 4.
17. Wild, *Sermon*, 5–6.
18. Barrows, *Our War*, 11, 18.
19. The denial that revenge was a major factor as quoted in Mark E. Neely, *The Civil War and the Limits of Destruction* (Cambridge, MA: Harvard University Press, 2009), 34–35. All other quotations as quoted in McPherson, *The War That Forged*, 49–50.
20. Edwin H. Fay, "May God Protect and Bless You," in *RACW*, 284. Sherman quoted in Kurtz, *Excommunicated from the Union*, 50.

21. Landrum, *Battle Is God's*, 4; General Orders, No. 83; "Hatred of our Enemies," *Biblical Recorder* (Raleigh, NC) 28, no. 19 (May 13, 1863).

22. Faust, *This Republic of Suffering*, chap. 2, "Killing."

23. Frederick Douglass, "The Pro-slavery Mob and the Pro-slavery Ministry," *Douglass Monthly*, March 1861.

24. See *Daily State Sentinel* (Indianapolis), January 30, 1864, CA. References to Paul's "one blood" statement appeared frequently, not only in sermons but in religious newspapers as well. See "Religious Sympathy," *Christian Advocate and Journal*, October 26, 1865, 340, http://login.proxy.library.vanderbilt.edu/login?url=https://search-proquest-com.proxy.library.vanderbilt.edu/docview/125981080?accountid=14816; G. Havin, "Letter to Rev, Dr. Lee, of Richmond, Va," *Christian Advocate and Journal*, November 23, 1865, 369, http://login.proxy.library.vanderbilt.edu/login?url=https://search-proquest-com.proxy.library.vanderbilt.edu/docview/125974425?accountid=14816.

25. Douglass, *Great Speeches*, 35–36.

26. Harper, "Bible Defense of Slavery," 8–9.

27. Boyd, *Discarded Legacy*, 51.

28. Lepore, *Name of War*, x.

29. James Lynch, *The Mission of the United States Republic: An Oration. Delivered by Rev. James Lynch, at the Parade Ground, Augusta, Ga., July 4, 1865* (Augusta, GA: Chronicle & Sentinel Office, 1865), 5, 7, 8–9. Lynch traced "the colored man's original right to freedom" to Genesis chapter 1, where God listed "an inventory of whatever should be property, but the colored man does not happen to be an item in the inventory" (p. 10). Lynch slightly misquoted the Declaration of Independence, writing, "All men are created free and equal" (p. 7).

30. Lynch, *Mission*, 10–11.

31. Lynch, *Mission*, 14.

32. J. W. Nevin, "The Nation's Second Birth," *German Reformed Messenger (1851–1867)* (Philadelphia), July 26, 1865. See also Noll, *CWTC*, 76–77. For an excellent assessment of Mercersburg theology, see Holifield, *Theology in America*, chap. 23.

33. Nevin, "Nation's Second Birth." See also Noll, *CWTC*, 76–77, 83; McIlvaine, *Pastoral Letter*, 4–5; Hodge, *President Lincoln*, 435–36.

34. Schantz, *Awaiting the Heavenly Country*, 1–4, 31.

35. For example, E. S. Atwood, *In Memorium. Discourse in Commemoration of Abraham Lincoln, President of the United States* (Salem, MA: Office of Salem Gazette, 1865), 6.

36. Horace Bushnell, "Our Obligations to the Dead," in *Building Eras in Religion* (New York: C. Scribner's Sons, 1881), 319–20, 325–26.

37. Bushnell, "Our Obligations," 327–29.

38. Bushnell, "Our Obligations," 331–32.

39. Bushnell, "Our Obligations," 333, 341–42.

40. James T. Robinson, *National Anniversary Address Delivered at the Baptist Church, North Adams, Mass., July 4th, 1865* (North Adams, MA: W.H. Phillips, 1865), 4–5, 11.

41. Robinson, *National Anniversary Address*, 12, 21. For a similar interpretation see Denis Wortman, "Welcome Home to the Soldiers! Sermon of Rev. D. Wortman, to the Returned Veterans, Sunday Evening, July 9, in the 1st Ref. Dutch Church," *Evening*

Star, July 15, 1865, Samuel J. May Anti-Slavery Collection, http://ebooks.library. cornell.edu/cgi/t/text/text-idx?c=mayantislavery;idno=38922016.

42. Lepore, *Name of War*, x; John Adger, "Northern and Southern Views of the Province of the Church," *Southern Presbyterian Review* 16 (March 1866): 390, 392–93.

43. Adger, "Northern and Southern Views," 398–99, 410. Cf. Noll, *CWTC*, 77–78.

44. Adger, "Northern and Southern Views," 398–99, 410. Cf. Noll, *CWTC*, 77–78. See Charles Reagan Wilson, *Baptized in Blood: The Religion of the Lost Cause, 1865–1920* (Athens: University of Georgia Press, 2009).

45. C. H. Wiley, *Scriptural Views of National Trials: Or the True Road to the Independence and Peace of the Confederate States of America* (Greensboro, NC: Sterling, Campbell & Albright, 1863); Calvin H. Wiley, *Life in the South: A Companion to Uncle Tom's Cabin* (Philadelphia: Peterson, 1852). See Guyatt, *Providence*, 268–69.

46. Wiley, *Scriptural Views*, 7, 17, 25.

47. Wiley, *Scriptural Views*, 115, 169–70, 172–73; see also 178.

48. F. R. Abbe, *"Wisdom Better Than Weapons of War" a Discourse, Delivered on the Day of National Thanksgiving at Abington, Mass. December 7, 1865* (Boston: Press of T.R. Marvin & Son, 1865), 3, 10–12, 15.

49. Lincoln, "Second Inaugural Address," 202.

50. As quoted in Noll, *CWTC*, 20. Original source: Palmer, "Witness of the Spirit," 137.

51. Brooks Holifield makes this case well. Holifield, *Theology in America*, 494–95. See also Molly Oshantz, *Slavery and Sin: The Fight against Slavery and the Rise of Liberal Protestantism* (New York: Oxford University Press, 2012). See also Pietsch, "Reference Bibles and Interpretive Authority," in Goff, Farnsley, and Thuesen, *Bible in American Life*, 122.

52. Rable, *God's Almost Chosen Peoples*, 397.

Appendix

1. Byrd, *Sacred Scripture, Sacred War*.

2. Lincoln Mullen, *America's Public Bible: Biblical Quotations in U.S. Newspapers*, http:// americaspublicbible.org/ Mullen's project covers newspapers throughout the nineteenth century, but I have limited my selection to newspapers published during the years of the secession crisis, the war, and its aftermath (1860–1865). For information on the machine learning methodology, see Mullen's explanation, https://americaspublicbible. org/methods.html. Note that this methodology, while extremely accurate, is not flawless. The figures I have cited in these tables are based on the data available from Mullen's newspaper project and my collection of other sources (sermons, diaries, etc.), and may be subject to revision with additional information. That said, this is the most extensive study to date of the Bible and the American Civil War.

3. Some of these provided details of tragic deaths, as when a two-year-old was scalded when his mother was distracted after pouring boiling water into a tub. *Delaware Gazette*. (Delaware, Ohio), December 29, 1865, CA. Another example of a verse that was often cited in newspapers but rarely with reference to the war was: "Give us this day our daily bread" (Matthew 6:11).

Index

For the benefit of digital users, indexed terms that span two pages (e.g., 52–53) may, on occasion, appear on only one of those pages.

Tables are indicated by *t* following the page number